California's Changing Majority

Historic and Contemporary Dynamics

Revised Printing

Steven M. Millner, Ph.D.

Louis M. Holscher, Ph.D., J.D.

Iris M. Jerke, M.A.

San Jose State University

KENDALL/HUNT PUBLISHING COMPANY
4050 Westmark Drive P.O. Box 1840 Dubuque, Iowa 52004-1840

Contents

Part III
From 1900 to 1949

Part IV
From 1950 to Present

Introduction

As California entered the twenty-first century it is the Nation's most populated and economically powerful state. It sends more representatives and tax revenue to Washington, D.C. than any other location by a considerable margin. California's massive agricultural production continues to help keep the world's multitudes fed while employing thousands. The state's entertainment complex creates film and television images, sound bites and media stars in products that penetrates all the globe's villages while causing millions to engage in "California dreaming." If those dreams are accurate they must be of a still growing region. Immigrants and newborns have continued to add hundreds of thousands of new residents to the state in each of the first four years of the new century. The promise of jobs in this "Golden State" continues to lure newcomers from Ireland, India, Italy, Indonesia, and Southeast Asia as well as traditional world spots such as Mexico, Korea, Russia, and the Philippines. While many of the newcomers housed themselves inside California's rapidly growing metropolitan centers, thousands of "old timers" quietly slipped into the state's sprawling suburbia. All who entered or stayed found themselves in a California that had become profoundly different in a remarkable way. As the new century dawned, there was not a single racial or ethnic group that could accurately lay claim to being the state's numerical "majority."

The implications of this new California reality are profound. Does it not suggest that this is probably America's future? Clearly it does, as California has often been a barometer of future change for this nation. If so, how will the state and nation's future work? Will the citizens of this new California be able to find solutions to problems that threaten the very viability of the state? Will the recall of an unpopular governor and his replacement by a charismatic former actor, known as Arnold Schwarzenegger, produce real solutions or will we simply have now a tabloid face dealing with lingering budget stalemates and political gridlock? Will our health care system be able to process California's now aging baby boomers and uninsured children? Will the once thriving public system of higher education be supported enough to allow the children of the "New Majorities" to become degreed? Or will the children of this emerging California find their hopes for affordable public college education sacrificed so that the state's wealthy can continue to enjoy low automobile tax rates? Will women in this state become fully liberated from the lingering effects of sexism and racism or will females in today's California be allowed to lead the nation toward a more fulfilling future. As critically, will sufficient economic growth be sustained to employ the youth looming in the state's education pipelines and those global citizens who continue to "rush" to California?

Other questions about this "New California" must be addressed. Will we find politicians who can find means to convince citizens to get out of their gas guzzling Hummers and oversized SUVs or will the state's voters continue to emulate those privileged elected officials who drive such vehicles? Such patterns have potentially disastrous consequences for all who are going to live in this locale. As importantly, will we find enough water and clean air to keep the state's environment viable? These issues of the environment have as much relevance to inner-city Californians as they do to suburban youth. As do matters dealing with the state's justice system.

Has California's "Three Strikes" and "You're Out" law produced a more secure state or have we simply developed a prison industrial complex that rewards prison guards with high pay while warehousing residents who eventually reenter our state seething with anger? Is this really a new trend or have we often done this in the past to "Indians," Chinese-Americans, Mexican-Americans and African-Americans? Can we now produce means to convince young Californians to ponder why there is so much wanton killing of those who look, speak, and "style" so much alike? In what ways can such "gangsterism" be reduced? Shouldn't we study gangs in hopes of learning why they continue to have appeal to inner-city youth? If knowledge about gangs might provide some means to eventually reduce such violence, how can young Californians learn to better tolerate and reduce their disdain for those who happen to be different such as Gays? If we fail to do this can any of us be safe on our streets, in our parks or in the corridors of our schools?

Even with these contemporary problems there is much that remains wonderful about California. But how will we be able to preserve what is civil, friendly, just and hopeful among the state's residents? Will racial tensions, ethnic conflicts and generalized ill will destroy what's left of California communities and send too many into gated enclaves or behind prison walls? Will this new, non-majority, multi-ethnic California prosper and thrive or will our children and elderly have to flee to spots such as Idaho, villages in Jalisco, or cities as far away as Seoul, Berlin, or Atlanta to find viable futures? If we are to avoid too much White **and** Black flight, can we do it by carefully analyzing the solutions that some of today's groups are creating in spots such as the San Gabriel Valley as they successfully grapple with sometimes troubling aspects of California's present? If there are today, hopeful patterns might it be because some of those involved in such promising trends learned from solutions used during this state's past? Awareness of California's previous changes suggests that what we are currently going through as a state is not really unique in terms of shifting "majorities."

The question becomes how often have there been time periods when the state productively or disastrously changed "majorities"? That being so, what important knowledge can we gain by looking at those consequences and how might we learn from such episodes? Might readers grasp that more residents should pursue lives of civic engagement if California's current wrongs are to be made right so that residents' collective futures will be better secured? By reading these pages will one learn that when "minorities" have become "the majority" in California's past, without corresponding efforts to bring about newer forms of equality, that previous generations simply handed down festering problems that eroded the state's future? Given California's significance to the Nation and the world, can we afford to figuratively flee from studying these serious matters or should we examine them carefully so that we might keep this Golden State vibrant and thriving?

In the articles and primary sources that follow, portions of California's varied legacy are examined. Readers of these materials will detect few direct solutions to the issues we now collectively face. Those who turn these pages will find that racial hatred, violence, injustice, homophobia, and indifference have often marked this state's past. These realities were not selected because the editors dwell only in negatives. "Sheroes" and heroes have emerged to battle against these tendencies. There have been and will continue to be community battles around these issues. Some will be won by the "good guys," while other racial and ethnic squabbles might leave stagnation, ill will and bleak sentiments. The future, like California's past will not involve any straight line of easy progress. It will take work, intelligence, and faith in humanity if a better California is to be achieved. Hopefully readers will get ideas about the courage, honesty, and perseverance needed in the future by reading about this state's previous residents who tackled and sometimes solved their generation's issues. The editors hope that learning about such qualities can help the women and men of today's California to acquire such attributes. They will be sorely needed if California's future is to be viable. The editors of this publication remain convinced that this can happen. *(SMM, LH, IJ)*

About the Editors

Steven Michael Millner, Professor and Chair of African-American Studies at San Jose State University was born in Columbus, Ohio and came of age there and in Duarte, California. He holds a B.A. from San Jose State University and the M.A. and Ph.D. from the University of California at Berkeley. All of his Degrees are in Sociology.

As a teenager in the 1960s Professor Millner became a political activist after serving as the president of a youth chapter of a NAACP branch. He has combined social activism with objective scholarship throughout his career. In the early 1980s he joined a handful of Black scholars in the arduous chore of integrating the faculty at the University of Mississippi where he specialized in Southern Studies. After several academic years as well as twelve summers in that state he returned to California and San Jose State University. Soon after his return to the West, he spent five years teaching part-time in the maximum-security prison at Soledad, California.

Professor Millner has written extensively about the Civil Rights Movement and the American West. *(SMM)*

Louis Martin Holscher, Professor and Chair of Mexican American Studies at San Jose State University. "Lou" Holscher was raised in Spokane, Washington where he attended Catholic schools, including Gonzaga Preparatory, and graduated in 1968 from Washington State University. After spending two years in the U.S. Army, Lou went to graduate school on the G.I. Bill. He received a M.A. and Ph.D. in Sociology from Washington State University, a M.A. in Education Management and Development from New Mexico State University, and graduated with honors from the Arizona State University College of Law. He has worked as a staff attorney for both the Arizona Court of Appeals and Federal Court of Appeals in San Francisco.

As professor Dr. Holscher taught a wide variety of courses in sociology, criminal justice and Chicano Studies at a number of universities, including New Mexico State University, University of Arizona, Arizona State University, and San Jose State University, including guest lectures in Canada and Mexico. Professor Holscher has published numerous articles on Chicano music and popular culture, race and ethnic relations, crime, and criminal justice.

Outside academia, he has worked for the United Farm Workers Union as a boycott coordinator, and is a major collector of Chicano, soul, and blues music. *(LH)*

Iris Margareta Jerke, history professor at San Jose State University and San Jose City College. Ms. Jerke was born and raised in Germany. During her twenty year stay in the multi-ethnic city of Berlin (West, Germany) she gained a well-founded diverse cultural background. Extensive travel throughout Europe and the United States added to her understanding of different race relations inside and outside of the United States. Before pursuing a career in academics, Ms. Jerke owned a business in Germany.

Between the years 1998 and 2003 Ms. Jerke received an A.A. in Intercultural Studies at DeAnza Community College, Cupertino, a B.A. in African American Studies, a B.A. in Social Science with emphasis in Race, Class, Gender, and Ethnicity and a M.A. in U.S. History with a concentration in African American History from San Jose State University.

Ms. Jerke received honors as a President's Scholar and Dean's Scholar; she is the recipient of several scholarships and a First Year Fellowship from the University of California, Department of History, Davis, California.

Her academic interests are African American History, 19th century American History, and History of the West. *(IJ)*

Part I

From 1769 to 1847

Introduction

The arrival of the Spanish as missionaries, explorers, and soldiers started a process of changing Alta California's Native American "majority." Though small in numbers the Spanish newcomers were determined, organized, and self-confident about their God and seeking gold. That the overwhelming bulk of these first arriving Spanish were men, who were not priests, had especially important consequences for the female inhabitants of early California. That these newcomers had horses, guns, ships, and prior experience subduing "Indians" while in Mexico was also decisive. As these first California Spanish imposed their will on the "Indians" they became a new "majority" in power though not numbers. Thus began a process that would have a long-term impact still observable in what was to become a golden spot. Those early "changing majority" dynamics remain visible in a variety of areas.

Most of California's physical locations still carry Spanish names. Looking at "traditional" buildings in this state has one glancing at an adobe style pioneered by the newcomers during this period. Echoes of this first era, when newcomers claiming to be "settlers" arrived, are heard and seen more than just faintly. The language and culture of those who conquered remain a vital part of the state's mode of operation. Those Spaniards who came north from Mexico forged both a "new majority" and a tradition of migratory processes that has been repeated many times. Sometimes the "new majorities" have come from the east, other times from the south and west. At other times the majority would change because those who controlled the government changed. This happened to the Spanish in just a few decades, as they were replaced in 1822 as the "majority" when Mexico's people won their independence. Members of this young Mexican nation quickly secularized a Spanish Mission system that

1

had been created at such a heavy human cost. While Mexicans claimed they were reforming a system that brutalized "Indians" their replacement system was hardly a step forward for Native Californians. Mexico's new "majority" who were "ricos" [rich] introduced rancheros and exhibited a very liberal attitude toward allowing English speaking "merchants" and traders to join them in Alta California and to even marry their daughters. As those dynamics played out after the Spanish had been forced to relinquish social control, the long-term consequences for both Native Americans and Mexicans would be profound. Exploring the legacy of this early era and why it left such an impact on today's California is examined in the section that follows. (SMM)

Michael J. González

The Child of the Wilderness Weeps for the Father of Our Country: The Indian and the Politics of Church and State in Provincial California

The complex and often tragic circumstance of first contacts between Spanish missionaries and Native Californians is the subject Michael J. González explores in the artical that follows. That author describes how California became another location for the continuation of disputes that had come to characterize relations between Catholic Church officials and secular Spanish forces in a "New World." Though struggles over control of valuable resources sometime split the Spanish "newcomers" in early California, it is clear that both factions asserted power over this region's "Indians." In this way members of both groups imposed their wills on Indians as if they were a new and entitled "majority." Yet the "natives" produced forms of resistance to Spanish ways that were still evolving when California territory would become first Mexico in 1821 and later part of an expanding United States of America in 1848. Decades of those early patterns are reviewed by González so that readers can come to understanding why the "children" of early California had reason to "weep."(SMM)

From the Spanish era (1769–1821) into the Mexican period (1822–1846), Franciscan missionaries vied with provincial governors and their subordinates to rule Indians. The Spanish Crown, and later independent Mexico, expected each group to help convert the Native Californians into tax-paying Catholics, but the rivals debated who would supervise the transformation. The clamor attracted many participants. Priests from other orders, foreign visitors, American

From California History, 1997, 76(2-3) by Michael González. Copyright © 1997 by California Historical Society. Reprinted by permission.

emigres, and military men—indeed military men often doubled as governors—likewise wondered what kind of regimen to impose on the Indians. These outsiders, however, rarely contributed new ideas and left the conflict to the devices of the Franciscans and provincial executives.

At one remove, California's dispute resembles the church-state conflicts that convulsed Latin America and Europe into the nineteenth century. In Mexico, France, and Spain, the members of each institution argued that only one side cared for the people while the other threatened religious fanaticism or anarchy. California's contest follows similar logic. From the beginning of settlement, the Franciscans insisted that the province and its native inhabitants prospered from the clergy's guidance. The priests filled mission lands with cattle or orchards. Amid the plenty appeared Indians, who, by yielding to the lure of gifts, or even to the occasional display of force, abandoned their pagan ways and accepted instruction in the Catholic religion. Initially, the civil administrators had few means to challenge the priests' economic and spiritual influence. Undaunted, the governors and some settlers protested that the mission routine stifled initiative and left the neophytes (Indian converts) helpless before their Franciscan tutors. The critics, many envious of Franciscan lands and Indian subjects, argued that a better existence awaited the natives if they dwelled in farming settlements alongside gente de razón (Mexican and Spanish settlers).[1] The conflict ended in 1834, when the provincial government secularized the missions and planned to distribute church property to converts. Bereft of their estates, the

Franciscans soon lost power, and those who did not return to Mexico remained in California to minister their Indian and gente de razón congregations. The governors and their constituents, meanwhile, heady from the sight of land freed from church control, forgot concerns for the neophytes' welfare and divided up territory intended for Indians.[2] By the American invasion in 1846, gente de razón in and out of government had fattened themselves on the land's wealth, with a few citizens enjoying prosperity beyond any standard reached by the priests.

Yet, the province's disputes differed from troubles in other parts of the globe. Elsewhere, the poor and destitute, individuals whose status paralleled that of the Indians, had little sway over the religious and civil leadership. If the downtrodden participated in conflicts, it was to fight for, or suffer from, crusades that mostly served their betters. California's Indians, though never articulating arguments that could impress Franciscans and governors, wielded influence unusual for a subjugated people. Of course, it is hard to measure how the native Californians perceived their grasp on the clerical or civil imagination. Some court testimonies or written remembrances convey the Indians' ideas, but because Spanish, Mexican, and Anglo-American amanuenses recorded these thoughts, the indigenous voice often passed through hostile or indifferent transcribers.[3] To complicate matters, the Indians did not comprise one group. Instead, they belonged to an ethnically diverse people whose tribelets, languages, and customs possessed great variety.[4]

Though muted or lacking a single mind, the Indians participated in church-state controversies. In a province where they numbered the large majority, the Indian presence initiated a dialogue words could not deliver. The Native Californians, at once servants, warriors, or prospective citizens, declared by virtue of their multitudinous tasks that they, and not priests and civil officials, could dictate the province's fate. In response, the authorities pursued policies, sometimes with compassion, other times with malice, that addressed the Indians' circumstances. As we will see, whoever could master the Indians, or in other cases win their cooperation, settled the question of who ran California best, Franciscans or governors

Historiography

Contradictions menace neat theories, however. Scholars such as Sherburne Cook note that priests and governors needed each other to survive in a remote province, and no subject, even Indians, stopped one rival from helping the other.[5] Franciscans administered the sacraments to their civil counterparts and occasionally supplied them with food. For their part, governors ordered troops to hunt down fugitive neophytes or help priests convert Indians.[6] To be sure, most times the topic of Indians provided for little harmony, but, if provincial business did not involve Native Californians, the prospects for cooperation improved. Money matters, for instance, often angered clerics and administrators before circumstance cooled tempers and granted the wisdom that one group needed the other to prosper. Historian Hubert H. Bancroft illustrated how financial questions initially sparked

resentment. He reported that at the beginning of colonization priests resented commands to help impoverished *gente de razón*. In the 1780s, governors Felipe de Neve, and later Pedro Fages, annoyed the clergy when they set low prices for the goods settlers bought from mission warehouses.[7] Rosaura Sânchez explains that bad feelings accumulated in later years when Franciscans bowed to the governors' request to lend money and they begrudged pueblo officials and settlers some loans. She notes that by the 1830s the priests had lent nearly seven hundred thousand pesos to their civil counterparts.[8] To the friars' chagrin, the loan recipients proved to be unreliable risks when their businesses sputtered or they refused to repay their debt. The *gente de razón*, meanwhile, imagined that the priests presided over swelling treasuries and did not deserve quick compensation. Even after secularization, when priests fell into poverty and cried out for help, few settlers believed that the friars needed money. Historian David Weber explained that the Reverend Diego García, the first bishop of California, lamented that the *gente de razón* donated so little to the church that he lacked cash to build his residence or a seminary.[9]

Other sources imply, however, that both sides learned to share their wealth. Woodrow Hansen shows that through the early nineteenth century the clergy relied on civil officials to collect mandatory tithes from settlers. The friars returned the favor and let administrators take a 5 percent cut of the proceeds.[10] When Mexico City made tithing voluntary in 1833, national leaders asked citizens to heed their conscience when the collection plate passed on Sunday,[11] While many people in this poor country could not afford charity, in places like Los Angeles, the *ayuntamiento* (city council) records show that residents often reached into their purses to help the church. To celebrate Mexican independence with a Mass, the *ayuntamiento* asked citizens in 1837 to donate money so that a priest could perform the ceremony.[12] There is no record that locals responded, but apparently such appeals worked other times. A year later, the council announced that the parish priest needed funds for a Mass "to honor the *Virgin del Refugio*," and it circulated a list of thirty-four men who gave pesos and *reales.*[13]

Like conflicts over money, legal and political arguments obscured any hint of concord between the two sides. Indeed, so many disagreements crowd the record it is no surprise that historians emphasize religious and civil discord. In some instances, Franciscan arrogance embittered their civil rivals. Manuel Servín explains that throughout the late eighteenth century provincial executives ordered the priests to organize elections in which the Indian converts elected their own *alcaldes.*[14] The missionaries ignored the command and appointed trusted neophytes to office. Other times, if the Franciscans failed to thwart civil authorities they sought help from Mexico City. After Comandante Pedro Fages (California did not receive its first governors until 1777) questioned the wisdom of sending troops to defend the future mission at San Buenaventura, an irate Father Junípero Serra convinced the viceroy to replace Fages with Fernando Rivera y Moncada.[15]

The new official, however, challenged the Franciscans, demonstrating that the provincial administrators could share the blame for church-state rancor. Soon after assuming office, Rivera y Moncada violated sanctuary and burst into Mission San Diego hunting for wanted Indians.[16] Serra excommunicated the comandante to restore church dignity, but it is doubtful the priests could intimidate their rivals. Daniel Garr notes that when civil officials founded settlements at San José and Villa Branciforte they ignored Franciscans who complained that the settlements sat dangerously close to the missions.[17]

Despite all these disputes, documents from Los Angeles show that the two sides often asked the other to help fulfilll political or legal responsibilities. Sometimes provincial executives took the oath of office in the city and invited priests to bless the ceremony.[18] When Carlos Carrillo assumed the governor's seat in 1837, he cut short his inauguration so "his excellency, together with the *ayuntamiento* and the people, could attend a solemn *Te Deum Mass.*"[19] On other occasions, city leaders welcomed the friars' attempts to regulate the public's morality. The same year that Carrillo took office, Father Narcíso Duran discovered that Manuel Arzaga, a retired army officer, lived with a woman who was not his wife. After the priest complained to the *alcalde*, city officials sent the woman to live at Mission San Gabriel and banished Arzaga to San Diego.[20]

Education, though, featured the best displays of cooperation. Municipal records and other sources from Los Angeles reveal that after lay teachers resigned to pursue other interests, priests accepted city council offers to work in the classroom. Military men sometimes tried instructing, but apparently most parents and civic leaders preferred clerics over officers or enlisted men.[21] When in 1836 the teaching position fell vacant (during the Mexican period, only one teacher, sometimes two, worked in Los Angeles), the *ayuntamiento* prevailed upon Father Alejo Bachelot, an experienced teacher in the Sandwich Islands, to take the job.[22] Three years later, the school once more lacked a teacher, and the city council asked the local curate to teach "forty to forty-five boys in the rectory."[23] The clerics' frequent turns in the classroom gave some priests the confidence to judge the city council's approach to education. After the American conquest, a Mexican priest urged the *ayuntamiento* to build a college and pull students away from "these examples of stupidity and immorality who congregated in Los Angeles' streets."[24] If lay teachers presided in the classroom, the religious presence remained in the primers children used for reading and writing. One primer warned children "that the fear of God is the beginning of wisdom."[25] Another cautioned youth to heed the law "because God sees all roads to iniquity"[26] The residents appreciated clerics who taught, and when priests departed for other assignments, disappointment spread. After Father Bachelot received orders from the bishop to return to the Sandwich Islands, the *ayuntamiento* and members of the populace appealed the decision. No new directives arrived, and Bachelot sailed out of San Pedro Bay with sad citizens in his wake.[27]

Indian Policy

Compromise, however, usually vanished when the friars and civil officials regarded Indians. Such interest in the natives suggests that each side only wished to control the cheap labor they represented. Certainly, a glance at California's demography and the disciplines each side used to motivate native workers supports this contention. At the height of the mission period in 1830, the neophytes and gentile Indians totaled 98,000 souls and outnumbered the priests, soldiers, and settlers nearly ten to one.[28] The multitude invited priests and settlers to consider how Indian workers could exploit California's resources. For the Franciscans, neophyte laborers made the missions self-sufficient, and, as we willl see, they also produced various items for trade. If converts lost interest in work, the priests revived enthusiasm by whipping neophytes who stole livestock or tried escaping into the interior.[29]

The civil authorities and their *gente de razón* constituents proved to be more demanding masters. Initially, the settlers rented Indian laborers from the missions and convinced gentiles to mind crops and cattle in exchange for coins or alcohol. By the 1830s, when neophytes gained their freedom from the secularized missions, the *gente de razón* grew bolder in dragooning native workers. In Los Angeles, municipal leaders ordered the night constable to arrest Indian drunks and make them work off their sentences fixing roads and public buildings.[30] After the American conquest in 1847, the city council instructed the "watchmen of the week" to collect Indian vagrants and assign them to "a master they will serve."[31] Around the same time, a judge noted that ex-neophytes often loitered at Mission San Gabriel. He promised to sweep up the loafers and "compel [them] to work hard."[32]

The exploitation of Indians, while horrific, does not contradict the clerics' and civil officials' claims that they were the Native Californians' protectors. Indeed, it can be said that many Indians who suffered whipping, forced labor, or other outrages faced punishment for displaying rebellious streaks.[33] For those who accepted their subservience, they flattered the pretensions of priests and civil administrators who played the parental sage to the Indian's obliging and willing child.[34] This arrangement suggests that authority figures wished their native wards to forever languish in an immature state. Others, however, found no delight in infantalized vassals and welcomed the chance to shepherd their Indian "children" to adulthood. But whatever the guise friars and governors imagined for their native subjects, it made little difference what the Indians wanted or needed. Only their patrons knew how to provide for the Indians' happiness.

The Franciscan fathers certainly relished their parental obligations. At the beginning of the mission era, Father Junípero Serra claimed that the "the spiritual fathers," the priests, "should be able to punish their sons, the Indians, with blows."[35] Later, Father Fermín Lasuén said that the priest, "like any good father . . . of a civilized nation . . . should forbid his children to go out with bad companions."[36] During the Chumash rebellion in 1824, Padre Ripoll of Santa Barbara saw troops muster to punish the rebels and

rushed out to stop them. The priest threw himself at the commander's feet and begged, "My God, don't kill my children."[37]

The civil authorities likewise favored parental images. After Governor Felipe de Neve heard in 1780 that soldiers harassed neophytes, he ordered the offending troopers whipped and invited Indians to witness the punishment.[38] Years later, when Juan Bautista Alvarado penned José Figueroa's eulogy to honor the governor who secularized the missions, he celebrated the dead man as "the Father of our country," whose passing caused the Indian, "the child of the wilderness," to mourn.[39] Sometime later in 1841, Santiago Argüello, the prefect of southern California, looked out his office window in Los Angeles and saw a local resident "beat an Indian with the flat of his sword." Argüello ordered a criminal investigation to bring the man up on charges.[40]

To be sure, talk of hapless Indians basking in parental love would have soothed anyone troubled by the natives' suffering. But the talk of nurturing Native Californians was not always cant. In the American South, a place whose form of servitude might resemble the treatment accorded Indians, apologists spoke of slaves reclining in the bosom of the master's family. The rhetoric rang hollow, however, for it is difficult to imagine slave owners pleading with executioners to spare rebellious chattel, much less calling an assembly to watch brutal overseers receive the lash.[41]

In California, parental imagery usually prompted more sincere conduct, as priests and governors wanted their native subjects to mature in a world fashioned by religious or secular hands. The Franciscans wished to fill California with Indian consverts who practiced Christian virtue in a world maddened by political and scientific revolution. Meanwhile, some civil authorities wanted to test liberal ideas in the province. Associating mission life with the excesses of the ancien régime, they proposed to free the neophytes from Franciscan control and award them portions of church property. Neither group succeeded, but measuring the triumph and failure of either side is not our intent. Instead, it is important to see how the men of church and state used the Native Californians to fulfill their designs for the province. And when the Indians reacted slowly to the schemes sketched by their saviors, priests and governors feared the defeat of their ambitions and blamed the natives for failures whose real authors sat in the missions or in the provincial capital.

Church

Let us first examine Franciscan thinking. The Franciscan arrival in California coincided with the Enlightenment and the Age of Revolution, and the missionaries, fearful of the era's assaults on Catholic dogma, needed Indians to convert California into a redoubt impervious to change. During the period's excitement, the divine right of kings and church authority crumbled, revealing the idea of the individual, the new cult to which European and American savants directed their oblations.[42] The lineaments of the individual first appeared during the scientific revolution of the seventeenth century,

when Newton published *De Principia,* his masterpiece on the theory of gravity. Newton theorized that natural laws governed the cosmos, and any educated observer could understand nature's workings by studying the forces that regulated the movement of the heavens. More radical minds extended Newton's logic and postulated that, if one person could understand how the universe functioned, then perhaps there was no reason to believe that God controlled nature. And if divine authority lost its majesty, then other institutions, from the aristocracy to the papacy, likewise would lose their mystique. Newton's reasoning culminated in the belief that the only valid experience was that of the individual who had the intelligence to govern himself without the intervention of monarchs or priests.[43]

By the late eighteenth century, the time when Franciscans began building California's missions, political documents such as the United States Constitution or the French Declaration of the Rights of Man crowned the individual, or the ideal of what an individual should be, with inalienable rights. No longer subject to the whims of church or state authorities, the individual now loomed as a viable being who responded to incentives other than the fear the powerful had once used to exert their will. Private property, whether it took the shape of a farm or business, rewarded the individual with profit if he worked hard. Initiative, ambition, indeed cupidity, the very attributes that the ancien régime decreed as evil, now emerged not as sins, but as sacrosanct principles that only needed the seasoning of education or morality to control.[44]

To the Franciscans the individual was anathema.[45] Ambition and self-interest, attributes that shined forth from the individual's character, were but glosses for the more fiendish appetites of greed, lust, and gluttony. For the priests, covetous habits followed the logic of the eighteenth century, when revolution and scientific skepticism seemed the handiwork of people consumed by self-interest. To escape these depredations, the Franciscans rejected modern thought and possibly found solace in the teachings of Erasmus, a sixteenth-century Dutch theologian who wanted to purge pomp from Catholic belief and return to the simple practices of the Apostolic Age.[46] Erasmus, and those who later followed him, celebrated the "primitive church," the first Christian communities that renounced wealth or ambition and prayed to restore the purity of Eden.[47] While the connection between, Erastian thought and the Franciscans requires more elaboration, the ideas of Serra and his brother priests suggest that the Dutchman's teachings had acquired great currency in the New World.

Erastian ideas worked their way into Mexico in the eighteenth century and prompted a clerical debate over whether Catholicism had lost its spirit. Needless to say, few critics dared question church dogma unless they cherished a trip before the Inquisition.[48] Nevertheless, Erastianism inspired brave churchmen to complain that incense, elaborate vestments, and holy relics deadened the upper classes and manipulated the Indians' ignorance. Francisco Antonio de Lorenzana, archbishop of Mexico, feared in 1766 that religious processions and the veneration of sacred objects led the people, especially the Indians, away from piety. Lorenzana's friend and bishop of Puebla, Francisco Fabián y Fuero, added soon after that "religious spectacles," grand pageants staged on holy days, persuaded destitute Indians to donate money so the church could throw up "fabulous temples."[49] God, the bishops believed, required reverence, and, in Mexican cities and towns, ostentation and ritual superseded faith.[50] Though many Mexicans seemed committed to religious pomp, in the mid-eighteenth century the natives of precolonial California stood free of excess and tantalized clerics to believe that they could learn more sincere forms of Christianity.

When the Franciscans first entered the province, Erastianism and images of Eden intertwined. The priests observed Indians living off the land's plenty, and rather than hoard the bounty nature granted them, the natives shared with the visitors. At last! The conduct of the first Christians and the innocence of paradise materialized in the form of California Indians who practiced the pieties Mexican believers had lost. Images of Eden abound in the priests' letters. After the Franciscans established the first mission at San Diego and set out to scout California's interior in 1769, they arrived in the midst of summer, when the sun pounds California's greenery into brown scrub. Junípero Serra, who admitted in his first letters that the Spaniards arrived in July, "the driest part of the year," did not let the arid expanses intrude on his sightings of Eden. He noted that around San Diego, "Land is plentiful and good. . . . Besides there are so many vines grown by nature and without help, that all it would require [is little work] to cultivate." He exulted that "there are roses of Castile [here] and trees in abundance." Generous Indians walked amongst the blooms. "On many occasions," reported Serra, "we were regaled by the *gentiles* and they gave us food."[51]

At the same time Serra penned his letters, Fray Juan Crespi, then attached to the Portolá expedition seeking Monterey Bay, observed the same wonders flowering in the August heat farther north. When the party reached what is now Los Angeles, he saw a "large vineyard of wild grapes and an infinity of rosebushes in full bloom." The land teemed with happy Indians who, to today's eyes seem to have been eager to wave the strangers on to other places. To Crespi, however, they wanted to share the land's plenty with the visitors. At one place in the present-day San Fernando Valley, "friendly and docile Indians came to see us, bringing presents of sage and seeds." When Crespi and the expedition left the Los Angeles basin, more delegations appeared and bestowed "gifts of raisins, seeds, and honeycomb, very sweet and filling."[52]

The Indians, already inclined to perform Christian habits, only required the ministrations of the priests to complete their evolution into baptized believers. The natives' generous and sincere conduct, which so impressed the first Franciscans, would now, after conversion, become the template for the return of the primitive church. To be fair, the Franciscans grew less enchanted with their charges and later claimed that Indian innocence only disguised the influence of the "Evil One."[53] But initially, the plan to lure native converts into a mission indulged the priestly wish to banish individual selfishness and re-experience the

sense of community enjoyed by ancient Christians.[54]

While few accounts describe the missions' daily activities, the spare portraits illustrate the communal ideal favored by the priests. At dawn, the priests rang a bell to summon the neophytes from mission dormitories or quarters just beyond the compound's walls; all gathered in or just outside the church for morning prayers, then received their chores before retiring to eat breakfast. At noon, the bell sounded again to call the community, and unless absorbed in tasks far from the mission, all stopped their chores to pray the Angelus before sitting down to lunch. When finished, they returned to work until the bell, tolled at sunset to end the workday. One more prayer or Mass again turned the neophytes' thoughts heavenward, and the assembly prepared for dinner.[55]

During the day, the neophytes performed tasks that ensured the community's survival or produced goods that would bring cash to the mission treasury. At the outset of the mission era, most neophytes worked to make the mission self-sufficient. Inside the mission, women wove shirts, pants, blouses, and other items for Indian apparel. Nearby in surrounding fields, the men cultivated rows of wheat, corn, or fruit trees for the mission mess. Further out, other men watched cattle and sheep that would eventually meet the butcher's ax and soon bubble in cauldrons of *pozole* (stew).[56]

In later years, the priests directed neophytes to make products for trade. By the beginning of the nineteenth century, the priests sold mission food or clothes to the inhabitants of nearby settlements and presidios (forts). The missionaries also smuggled hides and tallow to Yankee ships that docked off the coast and awaited carts piled high with illicit products. All these activities did not enrich individual neophyte workers or accrue to the personal accounts of the Franciscans. Instead, all money from neophyte enterprise went into the mission's fund, and the priests determined how the money would best benefit the community.[57]

The chance to restore the primitive church may account for the priests' desires to separate the neophytes from the gente de razón. Throughout the mission period, priests forbade neophytes from consorting with the soldiers and settlers who lived in nearby presidios or pueblos. The missionaries complained that the gente de razón schooled the Indians in bad habits. But to the Franciscans' dismay, Indian corruption went beyond the pleasures of gambling or the bottle. The priests worried that Indian women often suffered the unwanted advances of gente de razón men. Sometimes the attackers only wished to steal a kiss or apply a furtive hand across the breasts, but often they forced themselves on the women and raped them. Even after the gente de razón assailant had scampered off, his ravages continued. Many times, the soldiers and settlers infected Indian women with venereal disease, which they spread to their lovers, husbands, and children.[58]

Apparently, the neophytes' contact with the gente de razón left them physical wrecks: A survey of the missions in 1813 asked the rector of each mission to describe neophyte misconduct. Some priests lamented that the Indians continued to practice sorcery, but others reported that the neophytes practiced evils that reflected gente de razón corruption. Venereal disease, an ailment that first festered in California's presidios and towns, now infected mission inhabitants. At San Gabriel the rector pitied children "permeated to the very marrow with venereal disease [which is] the only heritage their parents give them."[59] Drinking and gambling, another set of afflictions spawned amongst the gente de razón, also assaulted neophyte virtue. According to the priest at San Fernando Mission, "drunkenness" loomed as one of the neophytes' most notorious vices.[60] Up north at Mission San Antonio, the pastor mourned that "games of chance . . . absorbed" the Indians.[61]

These moral concerns, while sincere, revealed deeper, more hidden worries. By complaining about the pestilence unleashed on the indigenous population, the priests expressed another fear that the settlers infected Indians with notions of individualism and private property.[62] From the first expeditions that settled California in the late 1700s to the Híjar-Padres expedition of the nineteenth century, the few settlers who made the trip received grants of land and seed so they could make the province productive.[63] Priests cringed at the thought of settlers using the bequests to turn a profit and disrupt the Franciscan sense of community. Therefore, when the Franciscans lamented that the gente de razón exposed the Indians to pestilence, one of the contagions no doubt was self-interest. Although few settlers could cite, much less read, the philosophical tracts extolling enlightened thought, their receipt of land and association with governors hostile to the church suggested that they had indeed embraced individualism. When the Franciscans complained to the first governors that the *gente de razón* threatened the neophytes, these appeals usually mentioned little about physical ailments and dwelled on the dangers of settler independence. At the outset of the mission era, for example, Serra worried that "pueblos without priests" threatened the neophytes.[64] The head of Santa Clara Mission complained in 1780 that law or religion seemed wasted on the *gente de razón*, a sad prospect that would cause "much annoyance . . . to our poor, converted Christians."[65] Years later, Father José Señan, father-president of the missions in the early nineteenth century, wrote to the governor that if *gente de razón* continued to receive land grants, "they would have no king to rule them nor Pope to excommunicate them."[66]

State

Missionary complaints, however, failed to impress religious or civil superiors in Mexico, who favored new ideas about converting Indians.[67] The work of David Brading and C. Alan Hutchinson suggests that by the late eighteenth century, the Franciscan practice of herding Indians into a mission drew fewer and fewer advocates in Mexico City, or at the provincial capital of Monterey.[68] In Mexico, many priests and civil administrators admired enlightened thought, but lamented that the Mexican Indians' poverty belied any claim that the Franciscans could carry reason or progress to the northern colony.[69] The leaders of church and state argued that Mexico would sit in the world's first

rank only when the status of the native populace improved. By the wars of Mexican independence from Spain, the various measures promoted by the Indians' champions fired rebel hearts and evolved into Mexican liberalism. Admittedly, the new leaders promising change focused on the Mexican interior, but their activities created the environment that inspired the secularization of California's frontier missions. But before we see how the Native Californians fared under secular rule, it is best to understand why intellectual developments in Mexico would worry or impress provincial priests and governors.

Throughout the eighteenth century many members of Mexico's upper echelons lavished attention on the Indians.[70] Some Mexican *criollos* (people of European ancestry, born in America) tired of the prestige attached to the Old World and embraced the Indian, not the Spaniard, as their hero. The native they imagined, however, little resembled the ignorant, degraded mass crowding the countryside or streets. Rather, they invoked the Aztec warrior who had once defied the Spaniard and possessed qualities the *criollos* wanted to see in themselves. The exiled Jesuit Francisco Clavijero claimed in 1781 that the Aztecs' triumphs eclipsed the glories of Greece and Rome.[71] At the beginning of the Mexican fight for independence, the clamor for Aztec idols increased. Fray Servando Teresa de Mier, a Dominican exiled to London, urged his compatriots to summon the shade of Cuauhtémoc and restore the tranquility that prevailed in Mexico before the conquest.[72] Around the same time, Carlos Maria Bustamante, one of the rebellion's ideologues, exhorted the insurgents "to re-establish the Mexican [i.e., Aztec] empire."[73]

The Aztec revival coincided with plans to improve the lives of the current Indian populace. Observers had long commiserated that Mexico abounded in poor, destitute Indians whose privation could lead to revolt.[74] The condition of native Mexicans varied from region to region, but a few generalities can describe their existence under colonial rule.[75] In rural areas, Indians scratched out a living from communal plots (ejidos), while their brethren in cities performed menial tasks. From such humble circumstances sprang an intrepid few who entered the priesthood or gained wealth as merchants. The ability of so few to prosper testified not to Indian sloth but to the suffocating force of a caste system that condemned the Mexican natives to inferiority. Under colonial law and custom, Indians could not bear arms, sit in the viceregal government, or occupy church office higher than curate. As caste shackled the Indians, the supposed purity of Spanish and criollo blood allowed Mexico's whites every legal advantage.[76]

Many critics, most of them Spaniards or criollos who recognized how their privilege pained the Indians, deliberated how to correct the colony's economic and political injustice. While every wrong, from poor schools to excessive Indian taxation, earned criticism, most commentators traced Mexico's troubles to the "collective," the group, racial, or social identity that subsumed the Indians to the fate their caste, assigned them.[77] In the late 1700s pamphleteers fired off proposals to extend political and economic equality to the native Mexicans, but the viceroy considered few reforms. When the colony gained independence in 1821, however, the triumphant rebels revived measures from years before and unveiled Mexican liberalism. The 1824 Constitution, for example, abolished racial categories and offered full citizenship rights to all Mexican males. Many liberals argued, however, that the Indians would remain legal and social outcasts until they had a chance to escape their squalor.

To help the impoverished natives, José Luis Mora, Vicente Gómez Farias, and other liberals planned to break up church estates and distribute territory to the male heads of Indian households. They insisted that land ownership would flip the recipient slough off inertia. As the freeholder swung a hoe or rake, he would cultivate good character alongside the fruits and vegetables sprouting on his property. The liberals presumed that when the Indian peasant received his grant, he would understand that merit, rather than caste, fixed one's place in society. Each individual would rise or fall according to how well he worked his property. If one labored hard, profit would come; yet if one loafed, poverty, destitution, or worse, would be the proper reward.

The liberals welcomed the discipline promised by a work ethic, but they also desired the riches diligent Indians would grant Mexico. In time, the Indians would produce food for market and learn the joys of making a profit. The money they earned would fill pockets and invite them to purchase other items. Eventually, argued Mora and friends, Indian farmers would help drive the Mexican economy by producing and consuming the goods the nation needed to find prosperity.

In California, many settlers shared the liberal conviction that the Indian wanted to be a yeoman farmer. The *gente de razon* erred, however, when they assumed that the distribution of land would transform Indians into happy cultivators eager to wring money from their plots. In fairness, the mistake seemed inevitable, since the Californios were trying to imitate their liberal contemporaries in Mexico. Sometimes, the provincials echoed the liberal refrains that had sounded first in Mexico's salons and coffeehouses. The *gente de razón,* for example, invoked the Aztec past to claim kinship with ancient Mexicans. In 1827, the California *diputacíon,* the body of citizens elected by the municipalities to advise the governor, proposed to rename California "Montezuma." The members also suggested a new coat of arms for California, in which an Indian with a plume, a bow, and a quiver would stand inside an oval bordered by an olive branch and an oak.[78] Neither idea came to pass, but the Indian romance continued. Governor José Figueroa told the *diputacíon,* three years later that in "California you will recognize the country of our ancestors. You will see the original homes where the Aztecs lived before they moved onto Tenochtitlán and founded the empire of Montezuma."[79] Other times, prominent Californios did not drape themselves in Aztec regalia, but they sympathized with their Indian neighbors.[80] Mariano Vallejo and Pío Pico, among many distinguished locals, lamented the neophytes' servitude under Franciscan "fanaticism" and said that California's natives had a right to be free.[81]

These outpourings of sentiment implied that, at least in the abstract, a significant number of Californio leaders and settlers considered the Indians their equals. While some *gente de razón* wanted to embrace the Indians as brothers, by the early nineteenth century, warfare, horse-stealing, and other outrages turned most provincials against the Native Californians. Indeed, if we may digress, other evidence suggests that hostility toward the Indians may explain the Californio penchant for staging bloodless coups. For some *gente de razón,* affording Indians the privilege to tote firearms was a measure of equality that would have made California politics more tumultuous. Throughout the Mexican period, the residents of Monterey, Los Angeles, and occasionally San Diego, debated which settlement should seat California's governor. The site chosen by the provincial executive earned the rank of "capital" and received the customs house, a treasure that pleased dishonest locals who eyed the duties paid by passing ships. The men who reigned as governor either came from competing settlements or they held rank in the Mexican army. Peace, however, rarely graced the tenure of any governor. A volatile populace greeted the head of the province, and if one part of the public used force to topple the provincial executive, another group arrived to defend the embattled leader. At least five times between 1832 and 1846, rival parties mustered troops to ensure that their favorites donned the governor's sash.[82]

Nevertheless, no matter how impassioned the struggle for provincial power, the bickering *gente de razón* never staged epic battles in which one side slaughtered the other. Most times, the opposing forces met on a battlefield and slew an unlucky few before the force with the most men called on its enemy to surrender. These peculiar war tactics have elicited wry comments from historians, who often compare the confrontations to scenes from comic opera.[83] The battles certainly involved blustering, but the *gente de razón* avoided violent contests because the carnage would decimate the military and leave thinned ranks to defend settlements from restive Indians. Historians H. H. Bancroft and, later, George Harwood Phillips, report that by 1835, native marauders rustled horses from ranchos throughout the province and sometimes carried settlers into slavery.[84] More alarmingly for southern California, the residents of Los Angeles and San Diego often trembled at reports that raiders threatened to march on the settlements.

The Californio strategy to limit political violence and prepare for Indian attacks probably emerged in 1832, when José María Echeandía battled Agustín Zamorano for the governor's seat. Claiming California from Los Angeles to the Mexican border, Echeandía pondered how to combat troops Zamorano led down from Monterey. Apparently, few *gente de razón* flocked to his standard, and to increase his meager force, Echeandía promised freedom to the mission Indians in his jurisdiction if they fought for his side. Chaos erupted. If Zephyrin Engelhardt and Gerald Geary are accurate, the Indians rushed out of the missions, shouting "Soy libre"—I am free. They showed little interest in Echeandía's cause and devoted themselves to drinking, fighting, and gambling. The sight of unruly Indians no doubt worried the *gente de razón* that the mob would swoop down on settlements and ranchos. A chagrined Echeandía rescinded his emancipation decree and ordered the neophytes home to the missions.[85] Echeandia's experiment with Indian auxiliaries taught the lesson that Californios should not enlist native allies for political fights. In subsequent battles for the governor's seat, the disputants refused to arm Indians and risk the outbursts that had so alarmed Echeandía.[86]

To return to the discussion of brotherhood, the contradiction of honoring, even while fearing, the Indians is a puzzle easily reconciled. Before secularization, many observers noted that the church commanded the province's best lands, and the *gente de razón,* deprived of wealth, access to prosperity, and political influence, seemed as helpless as the Indians.[87] And, as suggested by the declarations of respect for Aztecs or neophytes, liberal minds could claim the natives as equals because all groups witnessed Franciscan might. When prominent Californios called for the break up of mission territory, many wanted the Indians to receive portions of church land. Yet, because the provincials endured the Franciscan yoke along with their native compatriots, a few *gente de razón* demanded part of the mission estates. If the poorest and most abject Indians could receive parcels, then the Californios, the natives' supposed brethren, certainly deserved their share.

Secularization had long intrigued California's administrators as the best way to satisfy the needs of their *gente de razón* and Indian constituents. At least four different provincial executives issued orders to seize mission land.[88] Felipe De Neve issued the first order in 1777. The priests protested and succeeded in overturning the command. Pedro de Solá issued another order in 1821, but the Franciscans once more prevailed. A decade later, José María Echeandía made one more attempt to secularize the missions, only to fail like his predecessors. José Figueroa finally succeeded in 1834, and decreed that administrators would supervise the missions' secularization over a three-year period.

Despite the differences that altered one plan from the other, they all shared the idea of distributing land and other items to emancipated neophytes. Like reformers in independent Mexico, provincial executives believed that farming plots would free individuals from the mission collective and encourage them to think for themselves rather than submit to priests. The secularization plans involved the distribution of church land to adult males. (In some cases Indians who did not feel comfortable leaving the mission could stay; but instead of obeying a priest they looked to a civil overseer.) The land parcels measured 200 square *varas* (a vara roughly measured more than a yard) and came with grants of seed, tools, and sometimes a passel of farm animals, such as mares, cattle, and sheep.[89] To discourage *gente de razón* from wheedling land titles away from the Indians, each plan forbade the native proprietors from leasing, selling, or renting their plots.[90]

The Indians did not thrive under secularization, and many eventually lost their property despite legal protections. When land fell free from church control, those Californios who once sympathized with the Indians now had little cause to remember any bond with their native counterparts. Even if a few *gente de razón* sincerely supported justice for the Indians, by the late 1830s the prospect of developing church territory obscured all other emotions. Affection withered for the ex-neophyte, and where some Californios once hailed the natives as fellow citizens before secularizetion, after 1834 they only saw laborers who could be controlled to reap the land's riches.

The native demise may seem self-inflicted, but the circumstances always betrayed the subtle or explicit work of the *gente de razón*. Although Indians had learned how to farm or tend cattle in the missions, they apparently acquired little preparation in how to offer their goods for trade or conduct business with merchants. Once free, some natives fell into arrears, and sold their property to *gente de razón* creditors. Californio guile also ruined the freed natives. By enticing the Indians with alcohol or drawing them into gambling debts, enterprising *gente de razón* soon relieved the ex-neophytes of their land titles.[91] By the beginning of the 1840s, many Indian grantees had lost their stakes and now worked for *gente de razón* landowners who prescribed routines harsher than any toil at the missions. As we saw earlier, if Indians landed in jail, judges in many Californio communities condemned the convicts to work off their sentences in labor gangs.[92] For those who avoided prison, hunger and their desire for alcohol made them easy game for clever landowners. Farmers and rancheros throughout California offered impoverished ex-neophytes food and alcohol if they agreed to work.[93] In one case, the offer went unfulfilled; Tiburcio Tapia of San Bernadino refused to compensate his Indian workers and drove them off his property when they finished their task.[94]

The *gente de razón's* activities may invite charges of hypocrisy and fraud. Certainly the Californios, who had cited liberal doctrine to promote Indian emancipation, benefited greatly from secularization. Mariano Vallejo claimed the land around Mission San Francisco Solano, north of San Francisco Bay, and hired ex-neophytes to work on his estate. In southern California, his contemporary, Pío Pico, helped himself to territory that once belonged to Mission San Luis Rey, and he retained the resident Indians as employees.

The Californios hardly merit a defense for taking advantage of the Indians. Yet the *gente de razón,* although cruel and insensitive, had little incentive to respect the Native Californians after secularization. Their standard of liberal conduct allowed them the luxury to excuse any abuse they heaped on Indians. In one sense, liberalism assumed progress. In a world free from the influences of church, caste, or any other impediment, all individuals had a chance to rise according to their own talents. Also, as reformers had argued in Mexico, in a liberal society the individual regulated his own behavior. Therefore, when the ex-neophytes reputedly squandered their liberty on a round of cards or drinks, they faced the contempt of many *gente de razón* who could claim that by rejecting the progress the Indians deserved to sink into misery.

Matters grow complicated, however, as liberal ideas intersected with the acknowledgment that the people ruining the Indians were none other than *gente de razón.* In many cases, the men who sat on city government, as was the case in Los Angeles, owned the establishments where Indians bought alcohol.[95] The local leaders also doubled as farmers and grew the grapes they distilled into the Indians' favorite intoxicating beverage, *aguardiente.*[96] The reports of Indian "orgies," spectacles that included a few *gente de razón,* frequently agitated city council meetings.[97] It did not behoove city leaders to say that their own number and their constituents, some of whom claimed to be liberals, prevented the advance of Indians. Liberals would then stand accused of illiberal conduct. To resolve the paradox and justify the discipline of the Indians, city leaders re-interpreted liberalism not to mean political or, economic progress, but improvements in health and hygiene. In communities like Los Angeles, local leaders transposed political and economic concerns onto the body and said the Indian deserved discipline because he was unclean.[98] City leaders also complained about Indians fighting or gambling, but a review of the city council, minutes from Los Angeles shows that many lamentations about indigenous behavior centered on dirty bodies. In the late 1840s, two citizens complained at an ayuntamiento meeting that "the aborigines become intoxicated [and spread] venereal disease."[99] During another session, the council worried that disease would float off the bodies of drunks and ordered the arrest of any inebriate who failed "to bathe regularly." Because most complaints about public intoxication often concerned Indians, it is not a stretch to imagine that the infected drunks were Native Californians.[100] Around the same time, the council heard complaints that Indians bathed in the *zanjas,* the city's, irrigation canals. Concerned that they could infect society, the *ayuntamiento* ordered the Indians to perform their ablutions elsewhere.[101] Soon after, more *gente de razón* worried about pestilence wafting off Indian bodies. The *alcalde* ordered Indians to stand in the back of church during Mass because they were a "filthy and dirty people."[102]

The End

Reports of unclean Indians overlooked the fact that in arid communities like Los Angeles, all inhabitants, from established merchant to humble field hand, had little water to wash off the landscape's dust. Nevertheless, emphasizing the Indian's filth accorded neatly with the *gente de razón's* proclivity to see the native Californian any way they wished. If provincial authorities could imagine grimy Indians, they could conjure up natives who would embody the visions of their religious and civil patrons. In the late eighteenth and early nineteenth centuries, the priests wanted Indians to forsake their traditional ways and make the missions a prosperous, pious community. During the same time, provincial administrators hoped the Indians would learn self-interest and find success as farmers and craftsmen. Yet, Franciscan and civil dreams for the Indians did not materialize. Instead, the only role each side allowed the native was the work detail. Throughout the Spanish and Mexican periods, the Indians labored in mission fields, tended *gente de razón* properties, or performed various chores in provincial settlements. Occasionally, some Indians

unhappy with their lot rebelled, while others found solace in alcohol. Whatever the form of native misconduct, the provincial powers found one more pretext to condemn the natives, and what they really debated was who had the authority to impose discipline. Sometimes disputes over money, land, and political power started arguments, but the Indian, always the Indian, caused the most enduring conflict between religious and civil leaders. Without the native Californians, any history of provincial politics is incomplete, and their story requires more research still.

Notes

1. Ramón Gutiérrez says the term *gente de razón,* meaning literally "people of reason," is confusing and vague. He explains that "there is a great deal of confusion among contemporary scholars over precisely what this label meant and to whom it applied." See *When Jesus Came the Corn Mothers Went Away* (Stanford: Stanford University Press, 1991), 195.

2. Hubert Howe Bancroft, *The History of California,* 7 vols. (San Francisco: The History Company, 1888), 3:346–47.

3. Rosaura Sánchez speaks of the difficulty of recovering the Indian's voice. See *Telling Identities, Californio Testimonies* (Minneapolis: University of Minnesota Press, 1995).

4. A good introduction to the life and ways of the native Californians is Robert Heizer and M. A. Whipple, eds., *The California Indians: A*

Source Book (Berkeley: University of California Press, 1951).

5. Sherburne Cook, "The Indian Versus the Spanish Mission," in *The Conflict between the California Indian and White Civilization* (Berkeley: University of California Press, 1976), 76–84.

6. Douglas Monroy, *Thrown among Strangers* (Berkeley: University of California Press, 1990), 80. For another good study of church-state strategies to convert the Indian, see Lisbeth Haas, *Conquests and Historical Identities in California* (Berkeley: University of California Press, 1995).

7. Bancroft, *History*, 2:406, 517–18.

8. Sánchez, *Telling Identities,* 90. David Weber, in *The Mexican Frontier; 1821–1846* (Albuquerque: University of New Mexico Press, 1982), 400, says that the figure is closer to 500,000 pesos.

9. See Weber, *The Mexican Frontier,* 72–76.

10. Woodrow Hansen, *The Search for Authority in California* (Oakland: Biobooks, 1960), 2–3.

11. Weber, *The Mexican Frontier,* 75–76.

12. Los Angeles City Archives, v. 2, September 12, 1837, 197. There are several sets of the *ayuntamiento* records. The Spanish originals, called the Los Angeles City Archives, sit in the city clerk's office in Los Angeles. They are accompanied by English translations. Spanish transcriptions of the originals, called the Los Angeles Ayuntamiento Archives, sit at U.C. Berkeley's Bancroft Library. I use all three versions, and each set will be identified. Unless stated otherwise, the Spanish versions of the *ayuntamiento* records are used.

13. Ibid., v. 3, September 1, 1838, 309–10, trans. Before 1850, a peso equaled one American dollar. A *real* was worth at least twelve cents. See Michael P. Costeloe, *The Central Republic in Mexico, 1835–1846. Hombres de Bien in the Age of Santa Ana* (Cambridge, England: Cambridge University Press, 1993), 18.

14. Manuel Servín, "The Secularization of the California Missions," *Southern California Quarterly* 47:4 (1965):136–38.

15. Monroy, *Thrown among Strangers,* 42–43

16. Ibid.

17. Daniel Garr, "Church-State Boundary Disputes," in Dora Crouch, Daniel Garr, Axel Mundingo, *Spanish City Planning* (Cambridge, Mass: MIT Press, 1987), 248-49.

18. Los Angeles became the capital of California in 1835 and earned the rank of city. Within a year, Mexico City once more made Monterey the capital, but it allowed Los Angeles to retain the designation of city. Daniel Garr, "Los Angeles and the Challenge of Growth," *Southern California Quarterly* 61 (Summer 1979):147–55. A casual reading of the ayuntamiento Archives shows that, after 1835, citizens continued to call Los Angeles a city.

19. Los Angeles City Archives, v. 3, October 6, 1837, 179, city clerk's office of Los Angeles.

20. Bancroft, *History,* 3:638.

21. Mariano Vallejo, a prominent ranchero in northern California, said that soldiers assigned to the classroom sometimes beat their charges. Vallejo, "Historia de California," 5 vols., Earl Hewitt, trans., 4:135, Bancroft Library The page numbers in the translation are inconsistent and unreliable.

22. Bancroft, *History,* 3:638.

23. Narciso Botello, "Anales de Sur, ms., 178-79, Bancroft Library.

24. Los Angeles Ayuntamiento Archives, May 6,1850, v. 5,303, Bancroft Library.

25. Del Valle Collection, Seaver Center for Western History, Natural History Museum for Los Angeles Country. Grammar book in Spanish with six pages, and each page with a different style of writing, p. 1, Box 13, Item #679.

26. Antonio Coronel Collection, Seaver Center for Western History Natural History, Museum for Los Angeles County Grammar book in Spanish, n.p., Item. #714.

27. Bancroft, *History,* 3:317-18. Also see Los Angeles City Archives, v. 4, April 12 (?), 1837, p. 296, city clerk's office. Bachelor died en route to the Sandwich Islands.

28. Population estimates come from two sources. For the *gente de razón* see Leonard Pitt, *Decline of the Californios* (Berkeley University of California Press, 1971), 4-5. By 1830, the *gente de razón* totaled more than ten thousand people. The figures for the Indians are more exact. See Sherburne Cook, "The Indian Versus the Spanish Mission," 4, table 1.

29. For more on mission discipline see Cook, "The Indian versus the Spanish Mission," 91-134.

30. Pio Pico, *Historical Narrative,* trans., Arthur Botello, edited by Martin Cole and Henry Welcome (Glendale Calif.: Arthur H. Clark, 1973), 89; also see William Wilcox Robinson, *The Indians of Los Angeles: The Story of a Liquidation of a People* (Los Angeles: Glen Dawson Press, 1952 for a more current interpretation of the servitude endured by the Indians, see Tomás Almaguer, *Racial Fault Lines in California: The Historical Origins of White Supremacy in California* (Berkeley: University of California Press, 1994), 45-51.

31. Los Angeles Ayuntamiento Archives, July 3, 1847 p. 440, Bancroft Library.

32. Ibid, n.d., v. 3,1847, p.139.

33. My argument fails to consider the problem of Mexican Californians' impressing Indian children. By the end of the 1830s, the residents of Los Angeles regularly met Ute war parties at Tehachapi Pass and exchanged guns and horses for Paiute children. See Gerald Smith and Clifford Walker, *The Indian Slave Trade Along the Mojave Trail* (San Bernadino: San Bernadino County Museum, 1965). As late as 1857, Vicente Gómez, a resident of southern California, claimed that slave traders "brought children . . . from Baja California . . . with the object of selling them in Los Angeles"; Gomez, "Lo Que Sabe Sobre Cosas de California," ms., v.3, 759, Bancroft Library.

34. See Erik Erikson *Childhood and Society* (New York: W.W. Norton and Company, 1964), 275-358 for more on child development and the formation of society.

35. Quotation in James Sandos, "Junipero Serra's Canonization and the Historical Record," *American Historical Review* 93:5 (1988): 1254.

36. Quotation in Dora Crouch, Daniel Garr, and Axel Mundingo, *Spanish City Planning in North America,* 240.

37. Quotation in Angustias de la Ord, *Occurrences in Hispanic California,* trans. Francis Price and William Ellison (Washington D.C.: American Academy of Franciscan History 1956),7.

38. Edwin Beilharz, *Felipe de Neve: First Governor of California* (San Francisco, 1971), 9-10.

39. José Figueroa, *Manifesto to the Mexican Republic,* trans. C. Alan Hutchinson (Berkeley: University of California Press, 1978), 96.

40. Archives of the Prefecture, v. 1, June 4, 1841, 370, part B, in English, city clerk's office of Los Angeles. There is no indication if the attacker ever faced trial.

41. A good overview of paternalism in the antebellum South can be found in George Frederickson, *Black Image in the White Mind* (New York: Harper Torchbooks, 1972), and Kenneth S. Greenberg, *Honor and Slavery* (Princeton: Princeton University Press, 1996).

42. For excellent reviews of enlightened thought's impact on philosophy, art, and religion in Europe and North and South America, see Hugh Honour, *Neo-Classicism* (London: Penguin Books, 1968), and George Kubler, *Mexican Architecture in the Sixteenth Century,* 2 vols., (New Haven: Yale University Press, 1948); also see his *The Shape of Time: Remarks on the History of Things* (New Haven: Yale University Press, 1970).

43. D. A. Brading has written extensively and wonderfully on the Enlightenment's impact on Mexican society. See *The First America: The Spanish Monarchy, Creole Patriots, and the Liberal State, 1492-1867* (Cambridge, England: Cambridge University Press, 1991), especially, 561-602 Also see *Prophecy and Myth in Mexican History* (Cambridge, England: Cambridge University Press, 1980) and *The Origins of Mexican Nationalism* (Cambridge, England: Cambridge University Press, 1985).

44. For more on instilling a sense of civic duty in Latin America, consult Brading, *Origins of Mexican Nationalism;* also see Charles Hale, *Mexican Liberalism in the Age of Mora, 1821-1853* (New Haven: Yale University Press, 1968); Jaime Rodriguez, ed., *The Evolution of the Mexican Political System* (Wilmington, Delaware: SR Books, 1984); and Jean Franco, *Plotting Women: Gender and Representation in Mexico* (New York: Columbian University Press, 1989). The political tract prepared by José Luis Mora, *Catecismo politico de la federacion mexicana* (Mexico, 1831), Nettie Lee Benson Rare Book Collection, University of Texas at Austin, is an

example of how Mexican liberals wanted to transform the nation.

45. For more insights about those who attacked, and supported, the Enlightenment, see Isaiah Berlin, *The Crooked Timber of Humanity* (New York: Alfred Knopf, 1991).

46. See Arthur Quinn, *Broken Shore* (Inverness, Calif.: Redwood Press, 1981), 34–35, for the best intellectual study of the Franciscans in California. For other studies on the Franciscan mentality, see John Leddy Phelan, *The Millennial Kingdom of the Franciscans in the New World* (Berkeley: University of California Press, 1970); Jacques LaFaye, *From Quetzalcóatl to Guadalupe* (Chicago: University of Chicago Press, 1974), and Antonine Tibesar, O.F.M., ed., *The Writings of Junípero Serra,* 2 vols. (Washington D.C.: Academy of American Franciscan History, 1955), I:xxiii–xxx.

47. All information on the Erastian and primitive church comes from Brading, *The First America*, 492–513.

48. For more on the Inquisition in Mexico, see Fernando Cervantes, *The Devil in the New World* (New Haven: Yale University Press, 1994).

49. For Lorenzana and Fabian y Fuero quotations, see Brading, *The First America*, 495–97.

50. Ibid, 490–97

51. Junípero Serra to Father Francisco Palou, July 3, 1769, in Tibesar, *Writings of Junípero Serra,* I:144–45. For ideas on Eden in America, see Silvio Zavala, *Sir Thomas More in New Spain* (Mexico City: Colegio de Mexico, 1955).

52. *Fray Juan Crespi, Missionary Explorer on the Pacific Coast, 1769-1774,* Herbert Bolton, ed. (Berkeley: University of Californian Press, 1927), 146–55.

53. For more on the charge of Satanic influence in Indian communities, see Governor José María Echeandía's report on neophytes charged with sorcery, in Cook, "The Indian versus the California Mission," 149; also see Father Gerónimo Boscana, *Chinigchinich,* in Alfred Robinson, *Life in California* (Pasadena: Grabhorn Press, 1950).

54. An eloquent defense of the mission system can be found in Francis Guest, O.F.M., "Cultural Perspectives, on California Mission Life," *Southern California Quarterly* 65(1983).

55. Description of the Indians' activities from Cook, *The Conflict between the California Indian and White Civilization,* 97–99. For more perspectives on mission life, see *Columbian Consequences: Archaeological and Historical Perspectives on the Spanish Borderlands West,* 2 vols., ed., David Hurst Thomas (Washington D.C.: Smithsonian Institution Press, 1989).

56. Robert H. Jackson and Edward Castillo, *Indians, Franciscans, and Spanish Colonization: The Impact of the Mission System on California Indians* (Albuquerque: University, New Mexico Press 1995), 11–30.

57. Ibid. For a neo-Marxist view of the mission economy, see Daniel Fogel, *Junípero Serra, the Vatican, and Enslavement Theology* (San Francisco: ism Press, 1988), 41–81.

58. Examples come from Antonia Castañeda, "Sexual Violence in the Politics and Policies of Conquest," in *Building with Our Hands,* eds., Adela de la Torre and Beatríz Pesquera (Berkeley: University of California Press, 1992).

59. *As the Padres Saw Them,* Maynard Geiger, O.F.M., and Clement Meighan, eds., (Santa Barbara: Santa Barbara Mission Archive Library, 1976), 105.

60. Ibid.

61. Ibid., 105-106.

62. For ideas about the body as political symbol, see Caroline W. Bynum, *Fragmentation and Redemption* (New York: Zone Books, 1991), and Mary Douglas, *Natural Symbols* (New York Pantheon Books, 1982).

63. For more on plans to settle the province see Crouch, et al., *Spanish City Planning,* esp. 5-61.

64. Serra complaint is in ibid., 240.

65. Ibid., 241.

66. Señan comment is in Servín's "The Secularization of the California Missions," 137.

67. For the sake of simplicity when we discuss the colonial period, we will refer to New Spain as Mexico.

68. See Brading, *Prophecy and Myth in Mexican History,* 37-44. Hutchinson, *Frontier Settlement in Mexican California,* 110-80. Michael Costeloe, *Church and State in Independent Mexico: A Study of the Patronage Debate,* 1821-1811 (London: Royal Historical Society, 1978), provides a good review of the liberal critiques of the church.

69. Admittedly, it is difficult to piece together the social and personal world of Mexico's liberals. My ideas come from Costeloe, *The Central Republic in Mexico, 1836-1846.* Also see Hugh Hamill, *The Hidalgo Revolt* (Gainesville: University of Florida Press, 1968).

70. Brading, *The First America.* The status of the Indian in New Spain had concerned the colonial intelligentsia since the conquest. During some periods, the feeling was more intense than at other times.

71. Ibid., 450-53.

72. Brading, *Myth and Prophecy in the Mexican Nation,* 41.

73. Ibid., 42

74. For more on the fear of social upheavals and suspicions of the *léperos,* the lower classes of Mexico, see Torcuato S. Di Tella, "The Dangerous Classes in Early Nineteenth Century Mexico," *Journal of Latin American Studies* 5 (1973), and Donald Stevens, "Riot, Rebellion and Instability in Nineteenth-Century Mexico," *Five Centuries of Mexican History,* Virginia Guedea and Jaime Rodriguez, eds. (Mexico, 1992).

75. One study that examines the diversity of the Indian experience is John K. Chance, *Race and Class in Colonial Oaxaca* (Stanford: Stanford University Press, 1978).

76. All ideas on society in colonial Mexico come from Jaime Rodriguez, *Down From Colonialism* (Los Angeles: Chicano Studies Research Center, UCLA, 1983). Also see Rodriguez and Colin M. MacLachlan, *The Forging of the Cosmic Race:*

Reinterpretation of Colonial Mexico (Berkeley: University of California Press, 1980).

77. The best, and most entertaining, study on the dangers of the collective is Michael P. Rogin's *Ronald Reagan: The Movie, and Other Episodes in Political Demonology* (Berkeley: University of California Press, 1987); for the evolution of Mexican liberalism see D. A. Brading, *The First America*, 583–602.

78. See Bancroft, *History*, 3:38, for the campaign to change the province's name and seal.

79. Quotation in C. Alan Hutchison, "The Secularization of California's Missions," *The Americas 21* (1965): 248–49.

80. Pitt, *Decline of the Californios*, 2–3.

81. See, for example, Vallejo, "Historia de California," v. 3, n. p.. Vallejo opens the third volume by saying that the Californios battled against "superstition" and "tyranny," references to the priests' power.

82. Admittedly, the Californio penchant for coups or counter-coups may defy easy enumeration, as one battle overlapped with the other. For the best description of power struggles in California, see Bancroft, *History*, 2:3

83. Pitt, The *Decline of the Californios*, 5. Pitt has written the best study of Mexican California to date. The only weakness of his excellent book is his first chapter, in which he discusses the political culture of Mexican California. Otherwise, his work endures and remains unparalleled.

84. Bancroft, *History*, 3:608–49; George Harwood Phillips, *Chiefs and Challengers: Indian Resistance and Cooperation in Southern California* (Berkeley: University of California Press, 1975). For more on the abduction of Californio captives, see Bancroft, *History*, 4:68, and Smith and Walker, *The Slave Trade Along the Mojave Trail*, 8–10.

85. The entire story of Echeandía's use of Indian allies is in Zephyrin Engelhardt, O.F.M., *The Missions and Missionaries of California*, 4 vols. (San Francisco: James Barry and Company, 1913), 3:416–17, and Gerald Geary, A.M., The *Secularization of the California Missions* (Washington D.C.: The Catholic University of America, 1934),124–25.

86. The Californios and Mexican troopers, however, used Indian auxiliaries when they hunted runaway neophytes. Sherburne Cook, *Expeditions to the Interior of California Central Valley, 1820–1840* (Berkeley: University of California Press, 1961), 152–58.

87. Many Spanish and Mexican civil administrators, along with French naval officers and American trappers, commented on the missions' prosperity. One of the best and most vivid accounts is the diary left by Jedediah Smith, the American trader and trapper. See *The Southwest Expedition of Jedediah Smith: His Personal Account of the Journey to California, 1826–1827*, ed., George Brooks (Glendale: Arthur H. Clark Company, 1977), 96–105.

88. The best description of secularization remains Bancroft, *History*, vol. 3. Hutchinson's *Frontier Settlement in*

Mexican California is the most thorough, modern study. For a good, abbreviated account, see Servin, "The Secularization of the California Missions: A Reappraisal," 133-40. All information on the plans to secularize the missions comes from Bancroft and Servin.

89. For example, see Figueroa's first secularization decree in 1833, a measure that did not take effect until a year later. Bancroft, *History*, 3:328, n. 50.

90. Ibid.

91. David Weber provides a good review of the Indians' troubles after secularization. See *The Mexican Frontier*, 60-64.

92. San Diego Ayuntamiento Archives, 2 vols., compiled by Benjamin Hayes, v. I, p. 142, Bancroft Library.

93. Robert Heizer and Alan Almquist, *The Other Californians* (Berkeley: University of California Press, 1976), 48-50; for a more poetic view describing the "grimy bond" between landowner and Indian, see Monroy, *Thrown among Strangers*, 153-54.

94. Smith and Walker, *The Indian Slave Trade along the Mojave Trail*, 5-10.

95. Los Angeles City Archives, v. 3, "Fondo Municipal de 1836," pp. 75-83, city clerk's office of Los Angeles. See the entry for Manuel Requena, *alcalde* of Los Angeles in 1836. Requena applied for a liquor license. I am grateful to my colleague, Helen Lara-Cea, who informed me that the storekeepers and bar owners also served in municipal offices throughout Mexican California.

96. In many Mexican Californian communities, the residents grew grapes, citrus, and other fruit in surrounding fields. Grapes seemed to be the most profitable crop, as proprietors either sold the fruit to vintners or distilled it themselves. See the Los Angeles City Archives, v.3, "Fondo Municipal," for the years between 1830 and 1845 to see how many landowners and shopkeepers paid a license to market *aguardiente*, city clerk's office of Los Angeles.

97. Report of Rafael Gallardo of the Police Commission, Los Angeles City Archives, March 13, 1847, v. I, 361, city clerk's office of Los Angeles. For information on segregating *gente de razórs* from Indians, see Los Angeles Ayuntamiento Archives, July 3, 1847, v. 5, 431-42, Bancroft Library.

98. See Jean Franco, *Plotting Women*, 95-97; also see, Peter Stallybrass and Allon White, *The Politics and Poetics of Transgression* (Ithaca: Cornell University Press, 1986), 145-47.

99. Petition of Francisco Figueroa and Luis Vignes, Los Angeles City Archives, v. I, February 19-21, May 2, 1846, trans., 412-17, city clerk's office of Los Angeles.

100. See Sherburne Cook, "Small Pox in Mexican California," *Bulletin of the History of Medicine* 7:2 (1939); also see Los Angeles Ayuntamiento Archives, v.3, n.d., 1844-1850, 7-11, Bancroft Library.

101. Information from William Wilcox Robinson's, "The Indians of Los Angeles," *The Historical Society of Southern California Quarterly* 20:4 (1938):156-57.

102. Los Angeles Ayuntamiento Archives, v. 5, November 17, 1845, 271, Bancroft Library.

Zephyrin Engelhardt

Secularization of the California Missions

At the time of the War of Independence from Spain, California's twenty-one missions possessed nearly all of the best land in California and had thirty thousand converted Indians under the control of sixty padres and three hundred soldiers. The liberal Mexican government demanded the liberation of the Indians from the missions after secularization. This was supported by a number of revolts instigated by the Natives.

By 1834, the newly independent missions operated with less governmental support and faced a difficult time. The Franciscan missionaries, who controlled the missions even after 1834, feared that the citizenship rights and landowner rights of Indians would not be protected after secularization—and they were right—in short time the Indians were left with nothing. White colonists struggled to get their hands on at least half of the good mission lands. However, half of the mission land was also supposed to be appropriated for the Native people after secularization. Thus, the Indians were not the only ones that lost under the Mexican rule, in time many of the mission buildings were dismantled and others left to the elements as the church lost control over the lands. Restoration of the missions would not occur till much later. (LH)

When Spain came to the New World, members of the several monastic orders of the Church, notably the Franciscans and the Dominicans, came along to found missions among the Indians. As part of its colonial policy, Spain decreed that these missions, once well established, would be secularized: that is, the care of them would be turned over to the secular priests. This policy was not always routinely followed, however, for a variety of reasons. In some cases, there was a scarcity of secular priests, but frequently it happened that the missions founded by

Source: *The Missions and Missionaries of California* by Zephyrin Engelhardt, 1913.

the orders developed into powerful economic and religious interests, which the orders were not willing to give up. This situation prevailed in Mexican California, which had, after all, been founded entirely as a mission colony under the aegis of the Franciscans. By the time of the Mexican Revolution, the missions had obtained possession of nearly all the best land in California and had thousands of Indians under their control. They had made the province prosperous and virtually self-sufficient. Secularization was eventually accomplished there in 1834, but only after a protracted struggle lasting many years, during which there was no lack of intrigue, scheming, wrangling, and name-calling by partisans of both sides of the question. The issue was complicated by the mixed motives of all concerned. Government officials pressed for secularization, ostensibly to free the Indians for land ownership and the exercise of the rights of citizenship. But there was also much pressure upon these officials from colonists who wanted some of the mission lands confiscated. Then, too, the loyalty of the Franciscans was called into question, for they had not always bothered to hide their antipathy toward the government at Mexico City and their devotion to the Spanish monarchy. The Franciscans had their own good reasons for wanting to hold the missions. They eventually became reconciled to turning them over to secular clergy, but were understandably hesi-

tant, fearing that Indian rights would be violated and the land confiscated. A law of 1813, passed under Spanish rule, had set the conditions for secularization, but it had never been put into effect in California. But the accession in 1832 of a liberal Mexican regime bent on reform finally gave the needed impetus. Governor José Figueroa of California at first tried the gradualist measure of "emancipating" Indians, but met with little success. In August, 1832, Figueroa asked the advice of the two leading officials, Fathers Garcia Diego and Narciso Durán. Father Durán replied in a letter of October 3, reprinted below, spelling out his reasons for being reluctant to go along with immediate secularization. But the policy did go into effect the following year, and, in general, the Franciscans' fears concerning the rights of the Indians and the confiscation of the land were realized.

I shall divide this reply in the following manner:—1. The missions which can be secularized in conformity with the law of September 13th, 1813.—2. The obstacles, difficulties, and dangers which will be encountered.—3. The ways and means which seem to me more adequate to accomplish a general secularization happily.

With regard to the first point it may forthwith be set down as a matter of fact that all the missions of Upper California exceed the ten years of existence demanded by the law, some by twenty, thirty, and forty years, so that, if ten years is to be the rule, all may be secularized. However, Your Honor must be convinced of the defect in this rule. It is clear that, owing to the distance of the place where the law was framed, no consideration was taken of even the topographical and geographical peculiarities of this country. It appears to me that another principle of maturity ought to be adopted, one that is less exposed to irreparable and sad mistakes, and which would not involve the loss of what has been achieved in half a century. This principle, according to which we should judge a mission ripe for secularization, should be gathered from the neophytes. It should regard the shorter or longer period since which the last pagans were received into the mission, and the greater or less aptitude noticed in them for living by themselves in a civilized manner; for it is evident that the less connection these Christian missions have with the pagan, the more must they be considered to have abandoned the vicious habits of the latter, and to have advanced in civilization; and from the greater or less inclination observed in them for work, the greater or less must their fitness to live by themselves be judged.

Following this principle, I am of the opinion that a trial secularization could be made at the missions of San Juan Capistrano, San Buenaventura, Santa Barbara, Purisima, San Antonio, San Carlos, Santa Cruz, and San Francisco; for in all these missions it is many years since a pagan Indian was admitted. On the other hand one sees in these neophytes some interest to cultivate their little gardens, which they care for moderately well and raise some produce when conditions are favorable, as when they are given the aid of implements, animals, and other conveniences, though not without the pain of seeing them lose those articles through the vice of drink, which has spread among them horribly. These might be secularized along with the missions if a certain amount of property which they might enjoy as their own were allotted to them. The rest of the property could be reserved in order that there might always be a fund or capital belonging to the community, and administered by themselves through mayordomos of their own choice and race, for expenses of Divine Worship, spiritual administration and others that might occur. In the beginning it would be well that the missionary have some kind of authority over said fund, but without any coercion of the mayordomos and alcaldes, because these are to bear all the responsibility before the government for the losses that may result for not appreciating the fatherly advice of the missionary. All this should be carried out with the warning to the neophytes that they will be put back to the old conditions under the missionaries, whenever it should be discovered that through sloth, preference for wild fruits, or an inclination to vagrancy or other vices, they neglect their property and frustrate the advance of civilization and agriculture which the government expects of them. At the same time, the government should see that similar results are observed in the white people, so that the natives may receive practical lessons through the eyes, which is the shortest road to progress. With these precautions the difficulties and drawbacks following the secularization of the missions may partly be overcome.

However, as soon as the experimental secularization of the said eight missions has been decreed, two difficulties will present themselves to the government. The one is the indifferent and slothful disposition of the neophytes, the other is the necessity of supporting a hundred burdens which circumstances have rendered inevitable, namely, the maintenance of the troops who for twenty-three years have been subsisting upon the toil of the unfortunate Indians to the not little hardship and worry of the missionaries; for the latter are compelled to regard themselves as executioners, as it were, of these poor neophytes, inasmuch as they are forced to increase the amount of work to satisfy the demands of the soldiery, and also owing to the lack of consideration on the part of the military storekeepers (habilitados) in their demands and sometimes in the manner in which they make their requests. The indolent and slothful disposition of the neophytes is surely notorious and evident, since any one can observe with what little eagerness they do all that pertains to the community, notwithstanding that they know they are working for themselves. Nor is their activity much more lively and steady when working at some private task, or when they cultivate a piece of land allotted to themselves, inasmuch as for the sake of a diversion or some festivity in a neighboring mission they will abandon everything to damage from animals, and in one day with indifference allow the hopes of a whole year to be destroyed. It was only by means of the hard work and care of the missionaries that, under God, the great miracle of supporting these communities has been accomplished. It is true that their indifference and indolence is not quite so remarkable in keeping their own fields and gardens; but when they shall have to supply their own implements and tools, as will have to be the case when they become emancipated proprietors, it is much to be feared that they will not plant nor achieve much. If they evince some interest in having a garden, it is because some exemptions from community work are allowed them, and some liberty to roam about, which they would not have if they did no private planting.

As yet the missionaries have not the pleasure of seeing their neophytes devote themselves to agriculture for love of work; for this is against their naturally wild disposition and habits, which they inherited from their pagan state, so that it costs them much to lay aside the freedom natural to wild beasts, in which condition rude nature in a manner provided the necessaries without personal labor. This is the liberty they still crave. They are barely able to appreciate that which is proper to human beings, except for the faint hope, founded or unfounded, of being able to enjoy in some degree their former liberty of roving about. The truth is, that the labor of the missionaries to make men of them is the most laborious in the world, because what has been said about the character of these California Indians is so common to all that there is scarcely known a single exception. For this I appeal to the testimony of all, Your Honor's included, as well as to that of all those who have come into close contact with them. Inasmuch, however, as it would not be strange that any one should think that I or the missionaries have an interest in undervaluing the Indians, and emphasizing their inaptitude and immaturity for emancipation for the reason that we find ourselves well fixed in the management of their affairs, in my name as well as in the name of all the missionaries of San Fernando College I protest against such a supposition. I moreover sincerely and urgently beseech the Supreme Government and Your Honor to grant us the favor of relieving us from the burden and to place other persons in charge. We shall be satisfied to zealously attend to spiritual matters for only the necessary subsistence until other missionaries arrive to take our places. I assure you, and I protest to Your Honor, that though the bando of José Maria de Echeandía of the 6th of January, 1831, provided it had been feasible and issued in good faith, was for us incomparably more advantageous than the system proposed, we nevertheless would have reason to deplore it.

The other obstacle to secularization is the necessity for these communities to support the troops whom the government does not pay in such a manner that with their pay they can procure subsistence wherever they find it. It is now twenty-three years that these poor soldiers know nothing about their salaries. Had it not been for the communities of Indians under the management of the missionaries, there would not have been any soldiers for the internal peace and the external defense, because they would have perished from hunger. Consequently, after the missions have been secularized, we can no more rely on them for anything; for, if the Indians notice that they must pay taxes on their private property, they will soon manage to have nothing, will abandon everything, and go off to the wilderness and tulares in order to live on the products of nature, and there will be no possibility of forcing them from their haunts. In their opinion they will thus gain, inasmuch as they will find themselves free from necessities whose absence in their savage state they never felt. It is the place of the governor to know his resources, and whether they can support the troops independently of these communities.

The third and last point which I have proposed to answer is to treat of the means for carrying out a universal secularization of the missions without destroying what has been planted and reared with so much labor. To arrive at this goal I find two royal roads which both lead to it. The one is simple and insures quick and happy results, but it is expensive to the government, because for some years it requires aid from the treasury. The other is a little more complicated, and its results cannot be so quick, but it involves no expense. It needs no more than to open a gate which has no bolts nor locks, and it is in the power of the governor to open it with facility.

The first way consists in founding a new chain of missions and presidios to the east of the old missions, and leaving it to the neophytes to join the new establishments or to organize civilized pueblos on the sites of the old missions. The natives near the new missions, as is likely, will attach themselves to them, and those neophytes who remain at the old missions will form civilized pueblos. In this manner the opportunity of scattering in the wilderness and the tulares is shut off, and they would lose the hope of returning to their nomadic life, as they would either have to join the new missions or lead a rational life in the pueblos, so that insensibly, as it were, they would be bound to lead a life of virtue. This seems to me the surest way of securing happy results from a general secularization. Unless these exits are shut off, some think a dispersion is much to be feared without any hope of ever recovering the runaways. There would then be imminent danger for the safety of the country, especially if, some day when allied to the savages of the frontier, they should acquire firearms from foreigners in return for skins. In this there is real danger for Upper California; but as neither the treasury nor the missionaries are in condition to take this road, I desist from enlarging on the proposition, and am satisfied to have pointed it out, until God grants us more favorable times.

The other less rapid road to the end, though safe and inexpensive for the government, is to found a bishopric in Upper California alone and leaving the tithes absolutely to the administration of the bishop. With this help alone he would establish a seminary for the ecclesiastical education of the sufficiently numerous sons of decent and honorable families, who have no goal or suitable career in this limited society. There is hope that many of these might have a vocation for the sacred ministry. These alone would furnish a native and select clergy to serve the Church with honor. From this same nursery in a short time would emerge a surplus of priests for the founding of a second missionary college, of either the secular or regular clergy, and in this way alone provisions could be made for new missions and old pueblos. One man can effect this, a bishop, as long as he does not come to

rest, but to work, and by means of the tithes alone, provided they are controlled by the Church alone. Ecclesiastical property allowed to operate freely works wonders for the benefit of all. This is a fact which is evident, of daily experience, and proved by all nations. The Church in her organization is economical, and her hands seem to be those that multiplied the bread in the deserts. Let the governor but protect her, when it may be taken for certain that in a few years she will have her seminary for ecclesiastical education, the college for missionaries, a cathedral, the rest of the ministry in running order, and the old pueblos supplied with select laborers. Then a general secularization of all the missions can be effected without the risk of scattering the newly-made Christians; then with giant strides will the natives advance in civilization; and among the white people will also be banished vagrancy which is the real pest of California society.

These ideas which I have the honor of explaining to Your Honor in obedience to your orders have come to me during the twenty-seven years which I have spent in the service of these missions, and they are almost as old as my office of missionary. I express myself thus in proof of my impartiality, and I protest that I only aim to help as well as I can, in order that the government may be enlightened to choose with understanding among so many projects and plans which are offered to benefit California those that seem more suitable to this end, and in order that in a moment may not be destroyed what has been reared during more than half a century at the cost of so much expense and toil.

Part II

From 1848 to 1899

Introduction

California's American era formally began with the conclusion of the "U.S.A. War on Mexico" that was ended with the signing of the Treaty of Guadalupe Hidalgo (1848). The process of transforming California started even before the discovering of gold near Sacramento in 1849. Mineral riches accelerated a process of change that had long-term consequences for Spanish speakers [Californios] whose ancestors had previously changed the "majority" [in terms of power] in the state. Many of those who rushed in as '49ers pushed aside Mexicanos or treated them as a defeated people.

While '49ers came from throughout the globe, many were from Texas and other parts of the American South. This had profound consequences for California's African American pioneers. In the selection that follows, these complex dynamics are analyzed. While much more occurred during this era, these articles describe how much more complex California became as the new "majority" and the Golden State became Americanized. (SMM)

Leonard Pitt

"Greasers" in the Diggings

The stereotypes and discrimination that Chicanos continue to experience in contemporary California have their roots in the mid-nineteenth century. After the American conquest of the West in the 1850s Anglos (Americans of European ancestry) came quickly to dominate California, both demographically and politically. Not accepting the citizenship rights given to the Californios (Spanish-speaking Californians) by the Peace Treaty of Guadalupe Hidalgo, Yankees pushed the Native Californian miners aside. Thus, the Californios not only lost control of the land, they lost out economically and culturally.

Leonard Pitt details the harassment and violence faced by Spanish-speaking miners during the Gold Rush in his essay. The events of the nineteenth century in California's history contributed to the creation of barrios in the twentieth century throughout California. The legacy of this period is still a force in California today; widespread discrimination against Chicanos is found in employment, education, and politics. (LH)

In his book, The Decline of the Californios: A Social History of Spanish-Speaking Californians, 1846–1890 (1966), Leonard Pitt examines the painful process by which native Californians born of Spanish-speaking parents lost their numerical supremacy, land, political influence, and cultural dominance.

In an important chapter entitled "'Greasers' in the Diggings: Californians and Sonorans Under Attack," reprinted here in its entirety, Pitt treats the gold rush as the first real conquest of California and establishes a link between the misfortunes of nineteenth-century Californios and the disadvantaged social status of *contemporary Mexican Americans. "The modern predicament of the Mexican American jelled a century ago, from 1849-1885," Pitt asserts, "and not after the turn of the century, as some suppose."*

Why did the Spaniards and Mexicans fail to discover gold before 1848? What would have happened to them had they done so? These are two of the "iffiest" questions in all of California history.

The Mexicans had, in fact, discovered minor deposits of gold in southern California more than a decade prior to the historic Coloma discovery, but they did miss the big find in the Sierra. The causes of their oversight include a fear of Indian attack in the interior and a decision to hug the coast for protection; no population pressure ever drove them inward. The Spanish tradition of looking for signs of *oro* among the Indians, as in Hernán Cortés' conquest of the Aztecs, also played a role, although a negative one, for the California Indians did not manipulate gold. Another cause may have been that the contentment of rancho life after 1834 had sapped the rancheros' energy necessary to explore new territory. Or perhaps the trouble was, simply, bad luck: Captain Gabriel Moraga's forty-six expeditions before 1820 had brought him near, if not directly atop, the Mother Lode, yet no gleam caught his eye. The Spanish Americans generally did not want for daring as explorers or for skill as miners; centuries of experience in both had equipped them ideally for the fateful discovery they somehow failed to make.

As to what might have been their history had they chanced upon the Sierra gold, the possibilities are numerous. They range from the attainment of genuine cultural maturity and political independence to an even more crushing defeat than the one they received after 1849. Perhaps California would have become one of the most populous and heavily defended places in the Spanish Empire or in the Mexican Republic. The Californios might have had genuine Mexican military support in a war with the Yankees, and thus also a better treaty settlement. Conquest by a European power would not have been entirely out of the question either. The answer, of course, depends upon *when* one supposes the gold to have been discovered: the earlier the better for the Californios, from the standpoint of the growth of Yankee expansionism in the 1840s. One suspects, however, that Manifest Destiny somehow was bound to triumph along the Pacific Coast and eventually convert California into a Yankee province.

The Californios themselves scarcely ever engaged in such ruminations, for they were not a people to pine over lost opportunities and were faced with realities that gave them enough food for thought. The discovery of gold in 1848 made an enormous impact on them—the greatest in their brief experience: it brought them riches, for one thing; it threw them together with other Latin Americans, for another; and, most important, it opened them to full-scale Yankee penetration and conquest.

As news of the discovery spread in 1848, Californios speedily converged on the Sierra from all directions and, in a sense, made up for lost time. The experience of the Angeleños was typical. With Don Antonio Coronel taking on the function of patrón, the thirty Californios, Sonorans, and Indian servants had good luck from the outset. They immediately enticed some mountain tribesmen to accept baubles in exchange for gold nuggets and, after spying out the Indians' trove and plying them with more trinkets, they obtained their digging labor into the bargain. In one day, Antonio himself ended up with 45 ounces of gold; Dolores Sepúlveda found a 12-ounce nugget; and Señor Valdez discovered a boulder buried only 3 feet down which had once blocked the flow of an ancient alluvial stream and produced a towelful of nuggets in a short time. He sold his claim to Lorenzo Soto, who took out a whopping 52 pounds of gold in eight days and then sold it to Señor Machado, who also became rich. Even a Sonoran servant became fabulously wealthy overnight.

In all, about 1,300 native Californians mined gold in 1848, the year of the bonanzas. If they had missed the opportunity to discover Sierra gold in the past, they did not do so now; nearness to the placers gave them the head start on the thousands of prospectors still getting their wits together for the voyage halfway around the world. The Californios had additional advantages in knowing precisely where and how to find gold and in gladly pooling their resources and dividing their labor. As a result, the organized Californians, though less numerous than the 4,000 individualistic Yankees in the mines that year, probably extracted as much gold as they. Coronel, a struggling Mexican schoolteacher, had pocketed enough gold to become a prominent landowner, viticulturist, and community leader. He and many other Californios resolved to make a second expedition the next year. They dismissed the news that a few Californios had been harried from their claims by fist-swinging Oregon Yankees, who refused to acknowledge that the Treaty of Guadalupe Hidalgo granted some Mexicans full citizenship: in 1848 "everything ended peacefully."

In the year that followed, the story changed drastically. Coronel's return trip to the mines began badly, with a near-fatal brawl in a Sonoma saloon. One day he and *compadre* Juan Pedilla were waiting for the wet January weather to clear, when a former Bear Flagger began to bully Pedilla for having served as Bernardo Garcia's henchman in the wartime atrocity against Cowie and Fowler. Pedilla insisted that the charge was a lie, and the American replied with an assault. After a severe beating, Pedilla lay in an upstairs room, hovering near death for several weeks, while below his accuser continued to threaten his life. Only Coronel's good reputation and the intercession of friendly Americans restrained the former Bear Flagger.

After nursing his friend back to life, Coronel returned to the Sierra. He fell in among Chileans, Mexicans, and Germans doing well at dry diggings until confronted with posters declaring that foreigners had no right to be there and must leave the mines at once; resistance would be met by force. Although his threat never materialized, excitement mounted. In a nearby camp, a Mexican gambler's tent had been raided, and some Yankees accused five foreigners of stealing 5 pounds of gold. Coronel's associates doubted the accusation against at least one apparently honorable man and raised 5 pounds of gold to offer as ransom. Coronel conferred with a Yankee delegation and gave them the gold. The delegates then retired to consider the offer but never re-emerged from the drunken and agitated crowd, which by then numbered into the hundreds. The money did no good; all five prisoners were convicted and flogged at once, and two of them, a Frenchman and a Chilean, were charged with a previous murder and robbery. Guilty or not, the pair scarcely understood enough of the proceedings to reply to the accusations. When Coronel next saw them they were standing in a cart, lashed together back to back and pinned with a note warning away defenders such as might come from Coronel's camp. A horse then jolted the cart from under the men, and California had witnessed its first lynching. The incident resulted, Coronel thought, from a declining gold supply and the Yankees' increasing jealousy of successful Spanish Americans.

As quickly as possible Don Antonio led his group away from the newly named "Hangtown," and resettled in the remote northern mines. But even there a hundred gringos appeared with the gruff announcement that the entire riverbed belonged exclusively to Americans who would tolerate no foreigners. Furious, some of Coronel's people who had reached the limit of their endurance planned armed resistance, even at the cost of their lives, but Coronel held back and sadly announced, "For me gold mining is finished."

By July many other Californios had cause to echo Coronel's words. As the only true native-born citizens they did have a legitimate place in the mines, yet they knew no way to convince 100,000 hostile strangers of this truth. Fisticuffs or hand combat simply was not the Californians' style. Consequently, one of them carried into the field of combat a safe-conduct pass, signed by the army's secretary of state, which certified him as a bona fide citizen deserving of every right and privilege, of every lawful aid and protection. What good the pass did is not recorded, but the attacks mounted. For most Californios, the best answer was to go home and stay there: "Don't go to the mines on any account," one *paisano* advised another. Out of pride, which prevented them from being converted into aliens by Yankee rogues and upstarts, few Californians ventured back into the maelstrom after 1849.

Musing over the gold rush from a safe distance, the Californians once more concluded that outsiders were, by and large, despicable. Mariano Vallejo said of the forty-niners without sparing any nationality, "The good ones were few and the wicked many." Hugo Reid ticked off the list of troublemakers:

vagabonds from every quarter of the globe. Scoundrels from nowhere, rascals from Oregon, pickpockets from New York, accomplished gentlemen from Europe, interlopers from Lima and Chile, Mexican thieves, gamblers of no particular spot, and assassins manufactured in Hell for the expressed purpose of converting highways and biways into theatres of blood;

then, last but not least, Judge Lynch with his thousand arms, thousand sightless eyes, and five-hundred lying tongues.

The Californians now simply reverted to their customary circular logic, which held that evil came from outsiders, that outsiders were mostly evil, and that evil mothered evil. In no other way could they explain the ugly behavior of so many people, especially Americanos.

After a century of slow population growth, during which the arrival of twenty-five cholos or fifty Americans seemed a momentous occasion, suddenly and without warning, California faced one of the swiftest, largest, and most varied folk migrations of all time. More newcomers now arrived each day in California than had formerly come in a decade. Briefly told, the story of the Californians in the gold rush is their encounter with 100,000 newcomers in the single year of 1849—80,000 Yankees, 8,000 Mexicans, 5,000 South Americans, and several thousand miscellaneous Europeans—and with numbers that swelled to a quarter million by 1852. Even assuming the goodwill of every last one of these strangers, they outnumbered the Californians ten and fifteen times over and reduced them to feelings of insignificance.

It is the destiny of ethnic groups in the United States to be thrown together with people of "their own kind" whom they neither know nor particularly like—perhaps even despise. This was the lot of the Californios in 1849, with the massive migration of Latin Americans. It was bad enough that by 1850 the Mexican cholos outnumbered the 15,000 Californios;

even worse, angry Yankees simply refused to recognize any real distinctions between Latin Americans. Whether from California, Chile, Peru, or Mexico, whether resident of twenty years' standing or immigrants of one week, all the Spanish-speaking were lumped together as "interlopers" and "greasers." In this molding, the Californians, who had always kept aloof from cholos and earlier had won some grudging respect from the Yankees, lost most heavily. Their reputation as a people more heroic, handsome, and civilized than other "Spaniards" now dissolved. Their proximity to the greasers between 1849 and 1852 put them in actual jeopardy of their lives. In essence then, the Latin-American immigrants were a sort of catalyst whose presence caused the sudden and permanent dissolution of the social elements.

The biggest waves of Latin Americans came from Chile and northern Mexico. The Chileans excelled in baking and bricklaying and other skins and thus found themselves in especially great demand in California. They settled down at the foot of San Francisco's Telegraph Hill, in a place called "Little Chile," or went into the mines to dig, until expelled by the Yankees.

Even more prominent and numerous were the northern Mexicans. Distinguishable from other Latin Americans by their billowy white pantaloons, broad sandals, and sombreros, the "Sonoranians" or "Sonorans," as the Yankees called them, first entered the Sierra late in 1848, after either trudging across the Colorado deserts or sailing via Mazatlán. Some had sojourned in California earlier; in 1842, well before the advent of James Marshall, a Sonoran had discovered gold near San Fernando Mission. More visibly mestizo, less consciously Spanish than the Californians, they seemed "primitive" by local standards. Apache raiders kept them from their own mines and pastures, so that the Sonorans pounced on the California discovery as a panacea. The northern Mexican patróns themselves encouraged the migration of the peons by sponsoring expeditions of twenty or thirty underlings at a time, giving them full upkeep in return for half of their gold findings in California. The migration included so broad a spectrum of the population of Sonora and Sinaloa and was so large and continuous throughout 1850, that it compelled the governors of northern Mexico to admonish repeatedly about the dangers of life on gringo soil.

The Sonorans came on swiftly, heedless of any warnings, knowing that they had vital services to offer California—as prospectors and hired hands, as supply merchants and mule skinners, also as monte gamblers and prostitutes. The leading merchants of Altar and Horcasitas, Sonoran towns near the international boundary, stripped their shelves in the spring of 1849, loaded up every available pack animal, and scurried for the mines. There they sold everything they had brought, dug some gold, and shortly left their followers to return to Sonora for new stock or for quick investment in Mexican securities—much of this accomplished before most of the Yankee Argonauts had even arrived.

Sonorans gravitated mainly toward the San Joaquin River tributaries, called the "southern mines" or "dry diggings," especially near a spot named in their honor, Sonora. Here they introduced Yankees to many of the rudimentary mining techniques that typified the early gold rush era. Sonorans somehow could probe the topsoil with knives and bring up nuggets, or work the *batea* (pan) to great advantage. Where water was scarce and quartz plentiful, as in the southern mines, they had the endurance to sit for hours and winnow dirt in their serapes, sometimes using their own gargantuan breath if the wind died down. They could also improvise the *arastra* (mill), consisting of a mule harnessed to a long spoke treading in a circle and grinding ore under a heavy, flat boulder. Others eventually caught on to those techniques and machines and later surpassed them, but the Sonorans' sixth sense for finding gold and their willingness to endure physical hardship gave them great advantages. Talent made them conspicuously "lucky" and, therefore, subject to attack by jealous Yankees.

Although the Californios quietly withdrew from the Sierra and left the field to the Mexicans and the Yankees, the scene in the mines deserved their closest attention. For the mines became the staging ground for widespread attacks on their ranchos and pueblos, the rehearsal place for broad-scale assaults on the Spanish-speaking.

The problem of precisely how to react to the remaining "Spaniards" made the Yankees squirm. They shifted from violence to legislation, from legislation to litigation, and back again to violence. Some wished to exploit, others to expel, and still others to control the Latin Americans. On occasion, some Yankees even proposed allowing them completely free access to the mines.

It would have given small comfort to Coronel, Vallejo, Reid, and other Californios to learn that good and decent men had inspired the purge trials of the winter and spring of 1849. Yet, in truth, a great deal of antiforeigner agitation originated from the most reputable new citizens—army officers, lawyers, merchants, clergy, and public officials. It is a fact that the first organized and officially sanctioned outburst against Spanish Americans came from three hundred "white-collar" Yankees. While stranded in Panama in January 1849, on their way to San Francisco, they heard distressing rumors that "foreign plunderers" from all over the Pacific littoral had already siphoned off $4 million worth of gold in California; how much remained for "true citizens" thus was problematic. On a slight provocation, the Yankees called a public meeting to deal sternly with the interlopers. No less a dignitary than the justice of the Oregon Territory presided over the gathering, and in the background hovered General Persifor F. Smith, traveling to Monterey to take charge of the army. Smith drafted a circular declaring that, in California, he would "consider everyone who is not a citizen of the United States, who enters upon public land and digs for gold as a trespasser." This declaration won him three hundred vows of support.

The miners, who twice confronted Coronel with the charge that "foreigners" had "no right" to dig gold, were simply enforcing Smith's hastily improvised "doctine of trespass." In April, vigilantes at Sutter's Mill drove away masses of Chileans, Mexicans, and Peruvians; and

during a similar purge along the Sacramento River on the Fourth of July lives were lost, property was destroyed, and foreigners' goods were sold at auction. More than a thousand victims, mainly Chileans, came pouring down into San Francisco shortly afterward, many of them embarking for home. "General Smith is blamed by everyone as the sole cause of the outrage."

Smith beat a hasty retreat when he discovered that the consequences of the plunderers' activities had been grossly overrated: gold was still plentiful, and most of the dust already exported from California had found its way into the hands of American supply merchants. His successor, Brigadier General Bennet Riley, rode through the mines trying to undo some of the damage caused by the doctrine of trespass by telling Americans that technically all diggers were guests on government land and that thereafter none should be denied access to its bounty.

Resentment against the "greasers" mounted, however, a product of deep and abiding feelings of nationalism, racism, and despair over the debasement of free labor. The nationalism was partly a hangover from the war. Some men imagined seeing "whole battalions, armed to the teeth . . . moving through the heart of Mexico . . . gotten up by the great capitalists and friends of Santa Anna . . . rising in one solid mass whose cry is 'California's recovery or death!'" Yankee veterans unhappy in the diggings and nostalgic for army comradery saw in the coming of the "greasers" the pretext for a "muss," whether for mayhem or for merriment. Northern Europeans—the Irish in particular—and Australians became implacable foes of the Spanish Americans, more so perhaps than many native-born citizens of the United States. The notorious San Francisco gang, the "Hounds," for example, which was staffed by former New York Volunteers and Australians, took particular delight in attacking the Chileans who came to San Francisco after fleeing enemies in the mountains.

The forty-niner's xenophobia also stemmed from fear of unfair economic competition. Back home, one could normally see who became rich, how rich, and by what means; a community could use institutional means to regulate the process and keep it fair. But on the periphery of civilization, controls broke down: men sometimes prospered by unfair means; the population upsurge, the ceaseless shuffling of men from camp to camp, and their scrambling for the top of the social ladder defied control by ordinary methods. Thus the forty-niner improvised new devices, even vigilante justice.

Fear of economic competition had some basis in reality. Sonoran peddlers marched into the mines and sold 10,000 pack mules in three years, thereby depressing the prices of mules (from $500 to $150 a head in a matter of weeks) and of freight rates (from $75 to $7 per hundredweight in two months). This reversal of fortunes evoked no complaint from the Yankee miners, who could buy onions, potatoes, and other supplies all the more cheaply and had come to associate Mexican mule bells with savory cooking odors and a few cheap comforts of life; but it brought, in 1850, a pained outcry from Stockton entrepreneurs, who sought mass expulsion of their business rivals. Moreover, when the Mexicans set to work

as peons in the employ of their patróns, they did make themselves the target of the prospectors. Miners who began muttering against the Mexicans and plotting violence felt keenly conscious that the Spanish Americans were cheapening the value of labor.

The treatment of immigrant Spanish Americans in the mines hinged also on the slavery question. They came into California precisely when the Yankees felt most irritated on this score and could see most clearly the parallels between Negroes and their masters, on the one hand, and peons and patróns, on the other. Yankee prospectors ejected from the mines with equal vigor any combination of bondsmen and masters. In July a prominent Texan, Thomas Jefferson Green, and his slaves were unceremoniously tossed out of Rose Bar on the Yuba River. The prospectors put into effect a local code prohibiting the mining operations of all master-servant teams, whatever their relationship. Three months later this provision cost the life of a Chilean and led to the ear cropping and whipping of Chileans and Mexicans who tried to oppose it.

With California's entry into the Union as a free state, the plight of the Spanish Americans in the mines worsened momentarily. Their protagonists proclaimed that, if slaves were prohibited from the mines, then so should be the "refuse population from Chile, Peru and Mexico and other parts of the world [who are] . . . as bad as any of the free negroes of the North, or the worst slaves of the South." The apparent inconsistency in immigration policy annoyed both the friends and the enemies of slavery. In the first California legislature, nativists freely categorized the Pacific immigrants as a race whose morality and intelligence stood "but one degree above the beasts of the field." The State Assembly, in no uncertain terms (by a vote of twenty-two to two), asked Congress to bar from the mines all persons of foreign birth, *even* naturalized citizens.

This extreme nativism soon brought about its own backlash. A fraction of the entrepreneurs in the mines began to worry less about the alleged dangers of unlimited immigration or of competition from "foreign capitalists" and more about the "disaggregated, fractioned, broken up" techniques of mining; more about the possibilities of investing capital and hiring Mexican laborers, and less about expelling the interlopers. Usually outshouted at public meetings and outvoted in the legislature, this Yankee faction nonetheless had on its side the logic of economy and the ear of a few outspoken politicians who began a campaign to exploit, rather than exclude, aliens.

Advocates of this new position were most numerous and effective in the southern mines. There, the Sonorans evicted from the northern placers late in 1849 found relative safety, hiring themselves out to Yankees who maintained loaded pistols, "cool eyes . . . [and] steady nerves" against possible opposition by other Yankees. The Yankee patróns especially appreciated the Sonorans' skill and willingness to work for a daily wage of a dollar in food and a fraction of gold. "Greasers" worked speedily, when prompted, although work itself—and riches or savings—bored them, and gambling, drinking, dancing, and indolence cut down their work time. The argument ran as fol-

lows: The American, "with all his impatience of control, his impetuous temperament, his ambitions and yearning will . . . [never] be content to deny himself the pleasure of civilized life in the states for the sake of $4.00 to $3.00 per day, to develop the resources of the dry diggings"; the Mexican, on the other hand, is "milder in spirit, more contented to endure, more willing to suffer, more weak spirited, if you please," but for those very reasons he is the man for the job. Although a mere "hewer of wood and drawer of water," he would unlock California's wealth much as the Negro had done in the South. American freight shippers at the same time learned that the Mexican *arrieros* (mule skinners) were the most reliable of hired hands—skillful, proud of their work, and sure to get the pack train through the worst blizzard, over the toughest mountain trail. A genuine paternal fondness sometimes linked the arriero and his new Yankee patrón.

Yankee tradesmen of the southern mines came to see the Spanish Americans as particularly good customers. It occurred to them that, in contrast with the stingy Yankee who saved his money and sent it home, the Latin American invariably wanted to take home goods, not money; he spent all he had. Just as the Spaniard's eccentric work habits could be turned to the operator's profit, so could his spendthrift tendencies be turned to the advantage of the merchant. General Riley discovered that "Americans, by their superior intelligence and shrewdness in business, generally contrived to turn to their own benefit the earnings of Mexicans, Chileans and Peruvians."

The tension between Yankee and Latin American miners climaxed in the Foreign Miners' Tax Law of 1850, one of the most original if benighted laws ever passed in a California legislature.

Thomas Jefferson Green, its author, boasted that he personally could "maintain a better stomach at the killing of a Mexican" than at the crushing of a body louse. A Texan, he had come to this opinion in a Mexican prison while brooding over the failure of a filibustering expedition. After a harrowing escape from the prison, Green published an account of his exploits, together with a tirade against all things Mexican (and Negro) and a proposal that the United States swallow up all of Mexico. He had come to California in the hope of using slaves to plant cotton, although the episode at the Yuba River smashed that idea completely. Because he had served in three Southern legislatures, however, and had a good reputation among Southerners, he easily won election as state senator from Sacramento.

Green had legendary powers of persuasion, even over men who disliked his social ideals. It was he who always gained adjournment of the California Senate to "more comfortable surroundings"—namely, his own bar—and thus earned his colleagues the sobriquet, "Legislature of the Thousand Drinks." In his tax bill—a kind of personal rejoinder to the men who had expelled him from Rose Bar for attempting to use Negro bondsmen—he proposed to issue mining permits to foreigners at a cost of $20 monthly (he later reduced it to $16). The tax, he thought, would bolster the bankrupt state treasury by $200,000 each month and would also encourage Yankee operators to buy licenses for their operatives, and to employ them "at a fair rate . . . until the labor is performed according to contract." The law would delight Americans no end and discourage mob action, or what Green grandly called "the interruption of the stronger power which is in the people." This possibility so neatly wrapped up all the nagging problems of labor competition, foreign monopolies, taxation, bondage, immigration, and mob violence that the Assembly passed it nineteen to four and the Senate seven to four; the latter house, by a vote of eleven to two, also gave Green a special commendation for originating so "splendid" a plan.

Although later condemned as an intemperate and malicious act, "conceived in drink and brought forth in jollity," the Foreign Miners' Tax Law actually had quite sober intentions. Its main difficulty was that instead of flatly trying to either exploit, expel, or give free rein to the foreign-born, it tried to straddle the issue. It promised something for everybody: the prospector would be able to evict all "unprotected" aliens, the operator would be able to undercut the "agents of foreign bankers" who sponsored immigration, the government would receive money to pay its bills (among them, the expense vouchers of the legislature), the collectors would make a commission of $3 on each permit sold, and the immigrants themselves could claim the protection of the law if they paid their tax. On the face of it, one could hardly have asked for a more equitable solution.

Yet the Foreign Miners' Tax Law hardly worked that way at all. In Tuolumne County, where most of the potential taxpayers were entrenched, the impost caused outright defiance. Printed posters immediately denounced the tax and implored its intended victims to "put a bridle in the mouths of that horde who call themselves citizens of the United States, thereby profaning that country." Two French radicals, schooled in the Revolution of 1848, engineered a rebellion and for its success needed the cooperation of the Mexicans. Although the Mexicans were gun-shy, they nevertheless went to tell the Yankees what was on the mind of all non-Yankees. An impressive array of 4,000 "aliens"—mostly Mexicans—congregated on the outskirts of Sonora on Sunday, May 19, to consider proper action against the law, which was to take effect the next day. To the collector's face the delegation flatly declared that the foreign-born might pay $3 or even $5 monthly, but not $20—a token sum for protection against rowdies, but not an entire monthly fortune. When the collector held his ground and demanded the full amount, most foreigners fled the town. One remaining Mexican threatened the sheriff, or so it seemed to the bystander who killed him with a bowie knife. Local officials prohibited merchants from selling supplies to any foreign miners and spread an alarm to nearby camps to call up reinforcements for the forthcoming "war" at the county seat.

One hundred and fifty war veterans promptly stopped work at Mormon Gulch, selected a captain, put on the remains of their uniforms, and, with regimental colors high, marched to Sonora for action. Sonora received them warmly with fulsome speeches, food, and free liquor. By nightfall the town seethed with inevitable rumors of Mexican incendi-arism, assassination, and massacre. Officers posted pickets, stored weapons, and briefed the men for the next day's action. Sonora was under martial law.

Next morning, into the diggings marched four hundred Americans—a moving "engine of terror"—heading for Columbia Camp, the foreigners' headquarters. They collected tax money from a few affluent aliens and chased the rest away, with a warning to vacate the mines. One trooper recalls seeing "men, women and children—all packed up and moving, bag and baggage. Tents were being pulled down, houses and hovels gutted of their contents; mules, horses and jackasses were being hastily packed, while crowds were already in full retreat." The posse finally arrested the two "hot-headed Frenchmen . . . of the red republican order," who started everything, fined them $5 for "treason," and dismissed them. Thus ended the "muss." The men liquored up for the road, hoisted the Stars and Stripes to the top of a pine tree, fired off a salute, and headed for home. Next day, about five hundred French and German forty-eighters stormed into Sonora shouting revolutionary slogans and vowing to liberate the Frenchmen. Upon hearing that the pair had been freed, the would-be liberators dispersed sheepishly.

Sonora had just about recovered from the excitement of this "French Revolution" when a new attack broke over the heads of the Spanish speaking. A series of robberies and violent deaths came to light near town in which the victims were Yankees and the murder weapons *riatas;* this made it easy to blame "foreigners of Spanish American origin." Next, a Sonoran and his three Yaqui

Indian retainers were caught burying two bodies and would have been lynched, but for the timely intervention of the justice of the peace and the sheriff, who remanded the prisoners to the district court. On the morning of the court trial (July 15), the Mormon Gulch veterans again descended on Sonora in military order and spoiling for action. Informed that the prisoners might be hirelings of a "notorious Mexican chief" at Green Flat, they marched there, rounded up practically every male in sight, herded them back to Sonora, and literally corralled them for safekeeping overnight. In the morning, the justice of the peace investigated the "caze of murther against 110 Greasers . . . captured by 80 brave Americans," but, having determined that the Mexicans were innocent newcomers, he let them go. After a momentary riot scene in the courtroom, the Sonoran, on bended knees, convinced the jury that he and his Indians had killed no one but had accidentally discovered the bodies and were trying to dispose of them according to Yaqui burial custom. The crowd dispersed grudingly.

Unhappily, another gruesome death, uncovered the very next day, again made Sonora the prey of every rumor incriminating Latin Americans. Since all previous measures had failed to stop the atrocities, it was proposed to cleanse the hillsides thoroughly of every Spanish American with the least tinge of "evil." The present emergency demanded that "all Mexicans should suffer for a few." The "better element" of Yankees in the southern mines, who normally recoiled from drastic measures, now feared that their territory was fast acquiring the reputation of a bandit refuge, which was bad for business, and

felt impelled to join the broadside attack. Outshouting one dissenting voice, a large public meeting in Sonora voted to force all foreigners to deposit their arms with Americans and apply for permits of good conduct. All Latin Americans, except "respectable characters," were given fifteen days in which to depart. The Mormon Gulch veterans set to work enforcing these dicta with gusto.

The screening plan to expel the "obnoxious" Spanish Americans worked well. It reduced the danger of *bandido* attack and frightened off economic rivals. Between May and August, from five to fifteen thousand foreign-born diggers scattered from the southern mines. Mexicans went elsewhere looking for surcease of trouble but were dogged everywhere; eventually, they came streaming out of the Sierra, some showing signs of "pinching want." Even those who paid the extortionate $20 found that it bought very little protection, for if the collector neglected his monthly rounds their certificates lapsed, and if the Americans of one county refused to honor permits bought in another, the Spanish-speaking had little recourse but to leave. They knew that they alone of all foreign miners were being subjected to the tax: when they taunted the collectors to tax Irishmen, Frenchmen, and other Europeans they received no satisfactory reply. Masqueraders posing as collectors came into Mexican camps, solemnly tore up valid permits, and demanded money for new ones; when rebuffed, they auctioned off the victim's dirt and installed in his claim a "loyal citizen." One imposter carried off his charade so well at Don Pedro's Bar that he convinced a posse to help him chase away forty peons and their patron and killed two Mexicans in the action, before his identity was uncovered.

Even when seeking an escape from California, Mexicans found the Americans lying in wait for them. On the Colorado River, a United States Army lieutenant had express orders "to make all Sonorans passing out of California with gold, pay a duty . . . and for my trouble, to put the whole of it in my pocket." A troop of California militiamen blandly confiscated from homebound Sonorans more than a hundred "stolen" mules and horses, ignoring the brand marks proving ownership and compelling the Mexicans to walk 300 miles, including 100 miles across desert.

In the preceding year misunderstanding, fear, and hatred had created an atmosphere so hostile to "Sonorans" as to sanction fraud and murder. Nonetheless, the argument for both protecting and exploiting the foreign miners once more gathered strength. The earliest and most effective counterattack against prejudice was made by the San Francisco Vigilance Committee of 1849, which summarily expelled the "Hounds" from town and made amends to the Chileans who had been tormented by them. Thereafter many individuals took up the cause, speaking in behalf of civil law or laissez-faire competition or on grounds of simple revulsion against mob violence. Among those spokesmen were judges, editors, lawyers, a sheriff, a brigadier general, merchants, mine operators, and the French consul. Several sympathetic collectors ceased selling permits. Even the state attorney general disliked the tax so thoroughly that he refused to defend the collector prosecuted in the California Supreme Court and

ignored the governor's threat to prosecute him for dereliction of duty.

Xenophobia had injured its perpetrators as well as its victims. As Mexicans fled the southern mines in 1850, the profits of Yankee merchants plunged alarmingly. Eight-dollar crowbars in one afternoon dropped to fifty cents—a plot of land worth several thousand dollars went begging "for a few bits." Out of sheer dollars-and-cents self-interest, if nothing else, businessmen collected money, hired a lawyer to sue the local collector, and circulated a mass petition asking the governor to lower the impost to $5; all but one merchant signed the document. In July and August, after the second wave of expulsions caused retail losses as high as $10,000 a day in three southern counties, merchants who had helped expel the "evil characters" during the bandit scare became aware that all Mexicans were fleeing, not merely the undesirables. A crowd gathered at Georgetown, down the road from Sonora, and went on record as denouncing antiforeigner vigilantes and as supporting civil law. As a result the Stockton *Times* reported that the screening plan enforced at Mormon Gulch and elsewhere was "speedily held in contempt."

These forces had planned to persuade the governor to reduce the tax, the legislature to repeal it, or, best of all, the courts to nullify it. In the state Supreme Court they pleaded that it infringed the exclusive right of the federal government to govern federal lands and abridged the protection granted to aliens by the state constitution and by two treaties with Mexico. Neither of these arguments, however, swayed the high tribunal, which advanced a philosophy of states' rights in all matters relating to the federal government. Two Southern attorneys convinced the court that a state (1) could rightfully tax federal lands, unless specifically prohibited from doing so, and (2) had police powers to defend itself against undesirables. The court, in effect, agreed with the author of the tax act, Green, who had grandly declared that congressional inaction on the California mines had thrown the state back onto "universal laws . . . higher, greater, and stronger than the written constitution." Gratuitously, the court added that even had the law violated a treaty—which had not been demonstrated—it might still be valid, for state laws could take precedence over treaties. Thus, the Spanish Americans had unknowingly become the victims of the imponderable and pervasive sectional controversies of the day.

Notwithstanding its new judicial seal of approval, the tax was a practical failure, as even its original supporters admitted. The Mexican was not the Negro slave; California was not Texas. The governor, aware that the tax was reaping more resentment than revenue, cut the rate to $20 for four months. Even after this corrective, however, the state obtained only $30,000 instead of an expected $2,400,000. The collector in a county that had 15,000 potential taxpayers, sold only 525 permits and was so harassed on his job that he resigned. By 1851 Stockton's leading citizens had developed such loathing for the tax—"a law for the killing of children to get their fat"—that they decided to rally the entire county and lobby in the state capital to obtain its repeal. This they accomplished early in 1851.

The tax had failed to make the state wealthy, to prevent mob action, and to convert immigrants into hirelings as promised. It had eliminated the Latin Americans already in California and curtailed new immigration, a result that did not altogether fill the original bill. Now, having pushed the tax aside, the boosters of the foreign miners hoped to summon them back and make amends. The Yankees had a sudden vision that with the law gone, tens of thousands of Latin Americans would come flooding out of Mexico and Chile and the California towns and wash up into the southern mines, thus opening a new era in gold mining.

That dream failed to materialize, however, since the Spanish Americans by now mistrusted the Yankees and suspected that gold was giving out. They withdrew to Los Angeles and other villages or returned home, informing their countrymen of the dangers of venturing forth into California. Of course, small parties of Spanish Americans continued to enter the diggings, rummaging about on their own hook and staying alert to the possibility of trouble. The one lone Mexican patrón who dared bring in peons in 1852 stood out so conspicuously that he became the center of an international incident. His case made the complete circuit to Mexico City, Washington, and back to California. The district attorney investigated it for the United States Secretary of War, who determined that, although the crowd of Americans who stopped the Mexican was "wholly unprincipled and deserving of punishment," Mexican nationals should seek reparations in the state courts, since the federal government took no responsibility for riots. Thereafter, no Patrón was courageous or indiscreet enough to enter the mines, and the Yankee triumph over "foreign capitalists" and "slaves" was complete.

In the long view of California history, the Mexican miners represent merely a link in a long chain of migrants who reach across the "Spanish borderland." They unwittingly followed the trail blazed by the Spanish soldier Juan Bautista Anza and used later by Mexican cholos and colonists. They foreshadowed the coming of the "wetbacks" and the braceros in the twentieth century. As ever, the Mexicans met with mixed success in California, often defeat. They did find some gold, but had to fight for every ounce. That they escaped Yankee bondage was perhaps the most fortunate thing that happened to them.

The migration of the Mexican forty-niners affected the Californios in two ways: for one thing, it put the Yankees in an ugly frame of mind toward all the Spanish-speaking, including the native-born; for another, it sent the newcomers into the established old communities of California, where they fused imperceptibly with those born there. This tended to break down the old and somewhat artificial distinction between "native Californians" and "Mexicans." The fusion went on continuously there after.

The Mexican newcomers had, however, one major advantage over their California-born brethren; whereas they could ultimately evade the gringo enemy by returning home, the Californios, attacked on their own soil, could not.

John S. Hittell

Mexican Land Claims in California

The Treaty of Guadalupe Hidalgo and its Statement of Protocol gave the Mexican owners of land in California specific guarantees (land grants). The Land Law of 1851 was supposed to recognize and document the land grants held by Mexicans. The Anglos, however, placed the burden of legal proof of the land grants on the Mexican landowners. Written documents were hard to come by and landowners had to rely on verbal evidence of testimonies in their behalf. As a result, the Land Commission rejected thirty-two out of eight hundred twelve titles. Yet, the original Mexican owners lost most of their land.

The imposition of a new system of taxation and the payment of exorbitant legal fees to White lawyers in order to defend the titles to their lands in front of the land commission ran the Mexicans into debt. They needed to be represented by White lawyers because the court processes were conducted in English.

By the 1880s, Mexicans were relatively landless, and Anglo squatters, ranchers, and farmers owned most of the lands that had been Mexican owned only thirty years before. *(LH)*

The issue of land ownership in California after the Mexican War was dominated by two factors: the enormous amount of acreage claimed under Spanish and Mexican grants, and the insatiable hunger for land on the part of thousands of "Anglos" arriving every year from the East. Something had to give, and, in the end, it was the land grants of the older California residents, the Treaty of Guadalupe Hidalgo notwithstanding. During 1849 and 1850, two entirely contradictory reports on the validity of the old land grants were made for the federal government.

Source: Hutchings' *California Magazine*, 1857.

One, under the auspices of the Department of the Interior, generally confirmed the grants, but the other, made by Captain Henry W. Halleck for the territory of California, called virtually all of them into question. To resolve the land problem, Congress created a Land Commission in 1851 to pass upon the validity of all titles. The commission was heavily weighted in favor of American land seekers, but it must be said in fairness that some of the grants were enormous and of a thoroughly unmanageable size. The following article by John S. Hittell, rather favorable to the original claimants, sums up the work of the Land Commission.

The establishment of the American dominion in California made it necessary that the titles to land, owned in the State, under grants from Mexico, should be recognized and protected in accordance with the principles of American law. Protection was due to the land owners under the general principles of equity and the laws of nations, and had been expressly provided in the treaty of Guadalupe Hidalgo. It was necessary that the protection should be in accordance with the principles of American law, because the vast majority of the population soon came to be composed of Americans, who naturally introduced their own system of law—the only system suited to their method of conducting business.

But there was a question of much difficulty as to how this protection should be furnished. The Mexican titles were lacking in many of the conditions necessary to a perfect title under the American laws. The land systems of the two countries were constructed on entirely different principles and with different objects. The Mexican system was a good one for the purposes to be attained by it; it was suited to the wants of the natives of California. They were stockgrowers—their only occupation—and wealth and staple food were furnished by their herds. They owned immense numbers of horses and horned cattle, and to furnish them with pasture, each ranchero required a large tract of land, which might be used by his own stock, exclusively. The public land in California was very extensive; it was worth nothing; there was little demand for it; no evils had been experienced, none were feared from the accumulation of great tracts, in the hands of a few owners; every grant was supposed to be a benefit to the State, by furnishing a home to a new citizen; and so, large grants were made without stint, on nearly every application. If the applicant could show that the land was public property, and unoccupied, he could obtain from 10,000 to 50,000 acres without expense, on condition that he would make the ranch his home, build a house on it, and place several hundred head of horned cattle upon it. These grants were usually made without any accurate description of the land; there never had been any government survey of any portion of the territory; there were no surveyors in the country to locate the boundaries; neither would the applicants have been willing in most cases to pay for surveys; nor was there any apparent need for them, land being very cheap and quarrels about boundaries very rare.

Sometimes the land granted was described with certain fixed natural boundaries. In other cases, the grant might be described as lying in a narrow valley, between two ranges of mountains, and extending from a tree, rock, or clump of willows, up or down the valley far enough to include three, six, or ten square leagues. The most common form of grant was for a certain number of square leagues, lying in a much larger district, bounded by well known landmarks. Thus the famous Mariposa grant of Fremont is for ten square leagues—44,386 acres, equivalent to a tract about nine miles square—in the district bounded by the San Joaquin river on the west, the Sierra Nevada mountains on the east, the Merced river on the north, and the Chowchillas on the south; which district includes nearly 100 square leagues. Under such a grant, the Mexican law allowed the grantee to select any place within the larger limits, and make it his home.

The grants made were not carefully registered. The law prescribed that the petitions for land should all be preserved, and a record of them kept, and that a registry should be made of all the lands granted; but the affairs of the Governor's office were loosely conducted; and in many cases where the claimants have been in possession for twenty years, and have an undoubted title, there is nothing in the archives or records of the former government to show for it. In many respects the California governor had been very careless about granting lands. Sometimes they would grant the same lands to several persons; and there was one instance wherein Gov. Micheltorena ordered that every person in the Northern District of California, who had petitioned for land before a certain date, and whose petition had not been acted upon, should be the owner of the land asked for; provided the nearest Alcalde should certify that it belonged to the public domain. In these cases no title to the grantees was ever made by the Governor.

I have thus briefly mentioned the main peculiarities of the Mexican system of disposing of the public land in California, as distinguished from the American system. The Mexican government made no survey of the land; granted it away in immense tracts, without any fixed boundaries, leaving the grantee a wide discretion in regard to location, and keeping no careful registry of the grants.

When the great immigration of '49 filled the land with Americans, it became necessary to provide for the recognition and protection of the good Mexican titles by the American Courts. But how was this to be done? By the ordinary State Courts? The judges would not be sufficiently able, and would be ignorant of the laws under which the grants had been made; and the juries would be composed of Americans whose interests would lead them to do injustice to the large land-owners. Besides, the lawmakers and judges elected by a deeply interested populace could not be depended upon to do justice under such circumstances.

Or should the protection be rendered by the appointment of a commission, instructed to make a summary examination of all claims, declare all those valid which had been in possession previous to the conquest, and of which some record might be found in the archives; leaving the other claims to be tried in the U. S.

Courts? This was the policy which should have been pursued.

But that plan was not to prevail. Mr. Gwin's bill "to ascertain and settle the private land claims in the State of California," became a law, on the 30th of March, 1851. This act provides for the appointment of a special Judicial Committee (to be composed of three judges), before which all claimants to land, in the State, under Mexican titles, should bring suit against the Federal Government, within two years after the date of the act, under penalty of forfeiting their land. It provided further, that a law agent should be appointed, who should "superintend the interests of the United States in every case." It provided further, that appeals might be taken in these land cases, from the judgments of the Commission to the U. S. District Court, and from the latter, to the Supreme Court of the United States. It provided further, that in the trial of these cases, the Commission and the courts should "be governed by the treaty of Guadalupe Hidalgo, the law of nations, the laws, usages and customs of the country from which the claim is derived, the principles of equity, and the decisions of the Supreme Court of the United States."

This act provided that the owners of land should sue the Government or lose their land. But why be subjected to so severe a condition? The land owners had committed no offence, that they should be threatened with spoliation. It was not their fault that the Mexican land system differed from the American. The introduction of a new system by the Government did not justify the invalidation of titles, which had been good before,

and the subjection of the owners to tedious and expensive litigation. When the American Government took California, it was in honor bound to leave the titles to property as secure as they were at the time of the transfer, and express provision to this effect was made in the treaty. Let us imagine that California were to be again transferred to some other power, whose land system is far more complex and strict than our own, and that all our present titles should be declared incomplete and insecure, and that every land owner should be taxed to one-fourth of the value of his land to pay for defending his title before a foreign and hostile Court, and, if successful, should not get his title until six or eight years after the commencement of the litigation—would we not exclaim against it as extremely unjust? But what is the difference between that supposed case and the actual one under consideration? There is no difference between the principles involved in the two cases; each supposes a great wrong—such a wrong as has been committed by the Federal Government of the United States upon holders of land in California under Mexican grants.

The Land Commission was opened in this city, January 1st, 1852, and in the ensuing fourteen months, 812 suits were brought, and these were all decided previous to the 3d of March, 1855, at which time the Commission dissolved.

It was severe hardship for owners of land under grants from Mexico, that they should be required to sue the government of the United States (which ought to have protected-not persecuted them), or lose their land; but this hardship was rendered much more severe by the peculiar circumstances under which the suits had to be tried. The trials were to be had in San Francisco at a time when the expenses of traveling and of living in San Francisco were very great, and the fees of lawyers enormous. The prosecution of the suits required a study of the laws of Mexico, in regard to the disposition of the public lands, and this study had, of course, to be paid for by the clients. In many cases the claimants had to come to San Francisco from remote parts of the State; having three hundred miles to travel, bringing their witnesses with them at their own expense. The witnesses were nearly all native Californians, and it was necessary to employ interpreters at high prices.

Meanwhile the claimant could not dispose of his land, on account of the cloud there was on his title: neither could he have it surveyed by the U. S. Surveyor so as to give notice to the public where his land really lay. As he could not give a secure title, nor, in most cases, tell where his boundaries were, the Americans were not disposed to buy the land. Many squatters were, no doubt, glad of a pretext under which they might take other people's land and use it without paying rent; but the circumstances were often such that they were justified in refusing to buy. The number of settlers or squatters became large; they formed a decided majority of the voters in several of the counties; their political influence was great; politicians bowed down before them; all political parties courted them; and most of the U. S. Land Agents, and District Attorneys, appointed under the influence of the California Congressmen, became the representatives of the settler interest, and failed to represent the true interest of the United States. Every device known to the law was resorted to to defeat the claimant, or delay the confirmation of his grant, as though it were the interest of the Federal Government to defeat every claimant, or to postpone his success as long as possible.

Eight hundred and twelve important suits, to be tried according to the principles of strange laws, and on evidence given in a strange tongue, and where the testimony, in many of the cases, covered hundreds of pages of manuscript, were not to be disposed of in any brief period. In fact, the Commission did not clear its docket until more than three years after its organization. This delay, which would have been disastrous in any country, was doubly so in California. During the greater portion of this time, the titles to most of the good farming land in the settled districts of the State, were declared to be unsettled. The delay was an encouragement to dishonesty and often a justification of honest squatters. They wanted to cultivate the ground; they could not learn whether the land they wished to occupy was public or private property; they knew the question would not be decided soon, and therefore they might know, if dishonest, that they might make a profit by seizing land which they were morally certain would be, and should be, confirmed to the claimant; and if honest, they could not be expected to pay for property, to which, in many cases, the title was one in which they could place no confidence. The consequence of the system was, that a large portion of the most valuable farming land in the State was occupied by squatters. This occupation contributed greatly to injure the value of the property. The land owner could not sell his land, nor use it, and yet he was compelled to pay taxes. His ranch brought serious evils upon him. It was the seat of a multitude of squatters, who—as a necessary consequence of antagonistic pecuniary interest—were his bitter enemies. Cases we know, where they fenced in his best land; laid their claims between his house and his garden; threatened to shoot him if he should trespass on their inclosure; killed his cattle if they broke through the sham fences; cut down his valuable shade and fruit trees, and sold them for fire-wood; made no permanent improvements, and acted generally as tho' they were determined to make all the immediate profit possible, out of the ranch. Such things were not rare: they are familiar to every person who knows the general course of events during the last five years in Sonoma, Napa, Solano, Contra Costa, Santa Clara, Santa Cruz and Monterey Counties. Blood was not unfrequently spilled in consequence of the feuds between the land holders and the squatters; the victims in nearly every case, belonging to the former class.

After the Federal Government had committed the error of compelling every Californian land owner to bring suit for his own land, which he had held in indisputable ownership under the Mexican dominion, and even before the independence of Mexico and Spain—and after the Government stubbornly contested every case before a tribunal whose learning, ability, and honesty, was and is, universally admitted—after all this, it is strange that those persons, whose claims were confirmed, and who had been in possession of their land before the American conquest, and in cases where there was no sus-

picion of fraud, were not allowed to take their own property once for all. But no; Uncle Sam told all the Californians who had gained their suits, that they should not take their land till they had sued him again; he would appeal every case; the claimant must make another fight for his property, or be despoiled.

Here, then, was the whole work to be gone over again in the Federal District Courts, of which there are two in the State; and in each district there are about four hundred claims, to be tried by a judge, much of whose time is occupied with the trial of admiralty cases. The land suits must all be defended, or attended to, by the United States District Attorney, much of whose time is occupied with criminal cases, and civil business in which the Federal Government is interested. The result is delay upon delay. . . .

Only two pleas have been made to extenuate or justify the stubborn opposition made by the agents of the Government to the recognition of the Californian land holders. These pleas are, *first,* that many of the claims are fraudulent; and, *secondly,* that the Californians claim too much land.

It is not true that *many* of the claims are fraudulent. The Land Commission did not reject one claim, and the District Courts have rejected only two, on the ground of fraud. There may be twenty-five fraudulent claims in all; I believe not more. There may be many claims which would not have been valid under the Mexican law; but these are not fraudulent, and have been, or will be, rejected. But even if there were a hundred, that would be no reason why the Government should attempt to rob the holders of land under titles undoubtedly good in equity and under the Mexican law. A distinction might be made between the two classes, of the suspicious and the undoubtedly good claims. But the Federal Government made no distinction. The Peralta grant, which was made in the last century, and has been in constant possession ever since, under a perfect title according to the Mexican law, was subjected to the same litigation and vexatious delay, and was given over to the tender mercies of the squatters in the same manner with the most questionable title in all the land.

The other plea is still worse. It may be that the welfare of the people requires the land to be equally divided among them; but shall that justify the Government in robbing—directly by violence, or indirectly by litigation—the owners of large tracts? If it be wrong for me to rob my neighbor of his dollars, is it right for Uncle Sam to rob Peralta, or any other Californian, of his land? And let it be remembered that temporary dispossession is morally as wrong as entire and final spoliation. I admit that it were far better for the country that the Mexican grant-holders should not own so much land; I admit that it were better, looking at the question abstractly, that the settlers should own all the land they claim; I admit that the settlers are more active and industrious, and contribute vastly more, in proportion to their means, to the development and wealth of the State, than do the native holders of the large grants; but all this has nothing to do with the main question. . . .

Not only has the system adopted by the Federal Government, in regard to Mexican grants, been most injurious and unjust to the claimants, but it has also been very injurious to the country at large. It has deprived the people in the most populous agricultural districts, of permanent titles; has prevented the erection of fine houses, valuable improvements, permanent homes; has contributed to make the population unsettled; to keep families from coming to the country; and, in fine, has been one of the chief causes of the present unsound condition of the social and business relations of California.

Iris M. Jerke and Steven M. Millner

African Americans in California Schools from 1850 to 1890: San Francisco and Sacramento

With the westward movement numerous African Americans settled in Northern California, especially the thriving towns of San Francisco and Sacramento. Though California granted non-Whites freedom, it was of a limited type. Laws mandating racial segregation were passed and usually enforced, although lynching for racial transgressions was rare. The evolving system of practices that denied Blacks full rights was mainly built on case law. This refers to a system that is erected by judicial decisions that become the precedent for later behavior.

California's African Americans struggled in the nineteenths century to achieve the right to testify against White people in courts, to achieve voting rights for the men of their community, and to be able to send their children to the public schools. All these rights were seemingly theirs based on being "free," but they were forced to struggle to make those rights realities.

African American women were in the forefront of these efforts in the early era. The women were most adamant about chances for their children to go to school. They sensed that only with education would their offspring, especially the girls, have any hope of escaping the crippling aftereffects of slavery. The women from the Black community knew that if educated, their daughters and sons might avoid becoming mere low-level domestic servants and laborers. This especially was a role to avoid as it left one open to a variety of potential abuses. Joining these efforts to make California a "promised land" for African Americans were journalists writing in the state's emerging Black newspapers. These writers often became crusaders who worked with church officials and others to address the needs of their readers. The struggles of those pioneers produced an end to separate schools for "colored" students eighty years before that became the law of the land in 1954 via *Brown v. Board of Education Topeka, Kansas.* (IJ)

In 1850, when California entered the Union as a free state, section eighteen of its Constitution of 1849 stated "[n] either slavery, nor involuntary servitude, unless for the punishment of crimes, shall ever be tolerated in this State."[1] Those who opposed slavery may have been hopeful as no exclusionary laws for non-White citizens of the state were provided for in that initial document. More hope might have been justified as, for purposes of taxation, African Americans were to be treated as citizens. Viewing these developments at the time, the legal status of African Americans during this crucial phase of state building might have seemed remarkably open. Nonetheless, by the mid 1850s, African American residents in California had been excluded from voting, barred from offering testimony against any White person in any of the state's courts, and proscribed from using the few forms of public transportation. Moreover, when California opened public schools in 1852, African American children would be excluded from attending facilities their parents paid taxes to support. These were developments that were in marked contrast to what had been.

With the United States conquest of the West completed in 1848, what had been a general Mexican tolerance of diverse ethnicities was replaced by discrimination that came close to institutionalized racism. Before 1848, Blacks in California were integrated into the general community. After practicing miscegenation for generations, the distinction between "regular" Mexicans and "Afro-Spanish Mexicans" had become difficult to make, but with the influx of White settlers and especially Southerners, skin color took on the importance attached to it in other regions of the United States. This would become the case in all public behaviors.

Early Trends in the Education of California's African Americans

As early as 1847, San Francisco citizens recognized the importance of education. For the want of a public school, a committee was established. Worth mentioning is the fact that one of the three members was William Alexander Leidesdorff, a well-respected and economically successful man whose background included a mother who was a woman of color from the West Indies.[2] The public school committee's members were successful in opening a facility on Portsmouth Square that became the first public school of California after the American occupation. Enrollment was open to both genders and all ethnicities. In March 1848, the elected San Francisco Board of School Trustees counted sixty school-age children between four and eighteen in the city. A graduate of Yale University, Thomas Douglass, was hired as teacher and paid a yearly salary of $1,000.[3] The school lasted only one year. With the discovery of gold, many San Franciscans moved to the mining area, taking their children with them. Thomas Douglass was left with only eight students by the end of the first school term. While the initial phase of the gold rush depopulated many California cities and schools, plans for the state were being rapidly established during this period.

During the California Constitutional Convention of 1849-1850, provisions for the establishment of a free common school system were made. Article IX, Education, Sec. Three ". . . provide[d] for a system of common schools, by which a school be kept up and supported in each district at least three months in every year, and any district neglecting to keep and support such a school, may be deprived of its proportion of the interest of the public fund during such neglect."[4] However, the delegates could not agree on how to pay for the operation and maintenance of the common schools. More school laws for California were passed in May of 1851 and in 1852 that provided additional ideas of how school systems were to be structured. These laws provided for appropriation of public school funds to districts based on a census count of children between the ages of five and eighteen living in the district. Public school laws were changed in 1855 in a manner that would become a source of tremendous controversy. The content of section eighteen was adjusted so that "public" education money could only be used for the schooling of the state's White children. While principally targeting Black and Chinese children, these new statutes also had implications for Mexican Americans who might have been suspected of being "colored."

As more Whites came to California during the 1850s racial discrimination and segregation continued to increase. The newcomers saw all non-Whites as competition for the various riches of the West. These hostile attitudes were especially directed at African Americans and Chinese. While racism against the Chinese has been carefully documented, California's Blacks also had their rights violated, were harassed, and often forced out of the mining regions. Partly as a response to these mid-1850s trends, California's Blacks came to reside in cities where they mainly worked as cooks, maids, barbers, commercial sailors, seamstresses, coachmen, but also as carpenters, blacksmiths and even as newspapermen. A few became businessman, community leaders, ministers, and educators, with some also acting as civil rights activists. Concentration afforded some protection.

During the 1850s one third of California's African American population settled in either San Francisco or Sacramento. Since these were the first two towns with organized African American communities, they instigated struggles to force the admittance of Black children into established schools funded by public monies. These struggles had begun even before the crisis years of the mid 1850s.

Exclusion and Segregation Emerge as Patterns in San Francisco

In 1849, a free private school had been opened in San Francisco and operated by a Mr. Pelton. It appears that Pelton's school was initially supported by donations. Pressured by eager parents who were demanding educational instruction for their children, the city council of San Francisco organized the first free public school in California outside of the state law. On April 1, 1850, the city changed the status of Pelton's private school to a public one and began paying him the lucrative salary of five hundred dollars per month. The Pelton school was to be open and free to all students wishing to obtain an education. This openness, though, came with a cruel twist, as evidence strongly suggests that Pelton's "public" school would not enroll Black students. Importantly, the Pelton school pattern of exclusion of Blacks was established even before the passage of the 1855 school law that legally excluded African American children from all the state's public schools.[5]

The African American community of San Francisco in the mid 1850s became the largest in the West, with sixteen hundred people. Within those numbers were parents who had been regularly appealing to the city's board of education to admit their children to the established public schools. When not successful in gaining entrance for their children to what were becoming all-White schools, parents from the Black community started a separate, privately financed school. Established on May 22, 1854, the school for Blacks would be located in the basement of the St. Cyprian Methodist Episcopalian Church, then on the corner of Jackson and Virginia Streets. The Black parents arranged for the hiring of a Black teacher, the Reverend John J. Moore. On opening day twelve students enrolled in what was to become San Francisco's school for "colored children." Though unwilling to admit African American students to what were now considered "White" schools, members of the school board did decide to pay the rent (fifty dollars a year) and for the salary of a Black teacher. Thus was opened San Francisco's "colored school." After only a short time, twenty-three stu-

dents were enrolled in the "colored school" and when by 1859 the African American community in San Francisco numbered about 2,200 citizens, one hundred students were crammed into the "colored school." Importantly, the City by the Bay had become the first municipality in the state to establish a separate, publicly supported "colored school." This action would be followed rather quickly in other locations.

Economic Privation of Black Education Becomes the Norm in Sacramento

The Sacramento African American community opened its first school in May 1854. During its first months the school was privately funded as the Sacramento Common Council [school board] declined to pay for either rent or a teacher's salary. For several months a Miss Elizabeth Thorn-Scott operated Sacramento's "colored school" in her home. While Thorn-Scott instructed fourteen students, a Black school committee kept pressure on the city's common council to begin supporting the new "colored school." In October 1854, members of that body voted to establish a state sanctioned "colored school" for the area's students. When in February of 1855 fifty dollars for the support of the school was appropriated, accommodations were found in the Siloam African Baptist Church in Sacramento. The school opened in its new location on April 18, 1855. Fifty dollars was insufficient pay for Miss Thorn-Scott's teacher salary so parents took over that responsibility. Members of the African American community, under the leadership of a J. B. Sanderson[6] requested more money for the support of the "colored school" and in January of 1856, the common council allocated an additional one hundred fifty dollars for Sacramento's "colored school." Thirty students were enrolled at that time. In anticipation of getting married Miss Scott left Sacramento in 1856 to establish a family in Oakland. Her departure may have had something to do with the poor circumstances of her teaching post. In May of 1856, Sacramento's White officials started adjusting their level of support for the "colored school." Deciding that Sacramento's Blacks were paying very little in taxes, members of the governing board lowered public support of the school to twenty-five dollars per month. Faced with these changed circumstances the African American community's members took action. They held fundraisers, circulated, and presented petitions to the Common Council, and pressed for changes in the state legislative bodies. By 1861, Sacramento's "colored school" situation had improved. By then the African American community owned its own school-house and had hired a teacher to instruct the forty-one students in what was labeled *Ungraded School No. 2, Colored.* The school suffered a major loss in 1859 when its chief benefactor, Mr. Sanderson, left for San Francisco.[7] Sanderson's choice of San Francisco as a spot to relocate was a strange selection if he sought a tranquil location. He was headed for a community that had long wrestled with issues surrounding the educational status of its African American children.

Repression of African Americans' Rights in the 1850s: The Moore and Lester Cases

Throughout the 1850s the number of San Francisco's African American students increased, as did community pressure to accommodate their needs. There was also an escalation of tendencies of White control. In 1855, elements of San Francisco's White community became disgruntled when rumors spread that Reverend John. J. Moore, the teacher of the "colored school," had participated in an educational convention. The convention was organized for White educators and Moore's mere attendance angered important elements of San Francisco's Whites. Convention attendees accused of allowing Moore to intrude where he did not belong stated "the Negro was there as a listener but was not allowed to vote."[8] Nevertheless, discussions concerning his conference attendance heightened awareness of the "colored school" among San Francisco's White citizens. Some were convinced that even having "colored schools" would ultimately lead to race mixing. The existence of such a climate prompted growing resistance against the enrollment of any non-White children in citizen-supported schools. As San Francisco's Whites' hostile attitudes became expressed, the state legislation got involved. The *Sacramento Daily Union* published on January 30, 1855, the following pronouncement from California's State Superintendent Paul K. Hubbs: "Our public school system permits of no mixture of the races . . . Whilst I will foster by all proper means the education of the races, I should deem it a death blow to our system to permit the mixture of races in the same school."[9] Fears triggered by this "incident" led to an amending of the California School Law in 1855. To the sections that provided for the funding and distribution of public monies, a clause was added that denied Negro, Chinese, and Indian children any right to attend publicly funded schools. This new clause meant that public funds would be appropriated to school districts based only on their number of White students.[10] This act was designed to keep Black children from receiving public funds for their education. Many of California's Black parents refused to accept either the new legislation or segregated schooling. Many Whites from that era did what they could to insure that these policies were enforced.

An anonymous letter was sent in 1857 to the *San Francisco Herald* regarding the attendance of an African American student in San Francisco's only high school. Peter Lester, a politically active African American businessman had enrolled Sarah Lester, his fifteen-year-old daughter in the city's previously all-White high school. Circumstances indicate that by "passing" [as White] Sarah had previously graduated from the San Francisco's Spring Valley School. She was intelligent, light-skinned, and behaved inconspicuously; factors that played a role in her initial high school admittance. Her academic performance at the high school was exceptional; she ranked second in her class. Sarah's attendance at the high school sparked a debate between members of the Black and White communities. Blacks argued for Sarah Lester's right to stay in the school while many Whites called for her immediate expulsion. The editors of the *San Francisco Herald,* known to be a pro-slavery newspaper, pressured the members of the board of education to keep all non-White students out of the public schools. They argued this must be done no matter how light-skinned a child was. Several Whites protested in support of Sarah's right to stay and even threatened to organize a school boycott but the majority of the board voted for her removal. As the controversy swirled, the board's decision was surely influenced by the fact that additional African American families applied to have their children admitted to the high school. The board's decision to expel Sarah was not imposed as Peter Lester had previously decided to move his family to Victoria, Canada. As the civic battle simmered, the pattern of excluding Black students from the city's few opportunities for advanced education remained a focus from which Blacks would not retreat.[11]

Mobilized by the Sarah Lester case, members of San Francisco's Black community became activated and began fighting on several fronts. Foremost among their immediate goals though was the right of their children to a public education. They were not shy about public expressions. In the year of the Sarah Lester controversy, an angry black parent wrote to the *Mirror of the Times:*

> *The necessity of establishing schools for the education of our youth, would seem too evident to need urging. And yet there is scarcely a village or town in California that possesses a common school for the education of Colored children. It is true that we are com-*

pelled to pay taxes for the support of those already established, and from which our children are excluded; but that is of course, only just and right. It is also true that we are denied our portion of the public school-fund, but as we are not possessed of any rights which the white man is bound to respect, it is perhaps only right and proper that we should continually give and never receive. Without schools for the education of those who are to compose the next generation of actors on this great stage, we cannot expect our condition to be permanently improved—for it is upon the present youth of the country that we must make impressions that will perfect what we can only hope to commence.

. . .

Thomas Duff, Mariposa, December 8, 1857[12]

While expressing a collective sentiment is an important phase of a protest movement's development, Blacks in the state were getting ready to go to a different level.

California's African Americans Mobilize to Achieve Civil Status

To better organize their pleas for civil rights, African American residents of California came together in a first *State Convention of the Colored Citizens of the State of California* in 1855, held in Sacramento. On their agenda was the

achievement of all civil rights for African Americans in the State with priority given to the right to vote and the right to testify in court cases involving White persons. "Taxation without representation," a grievance heard from British colonial subjects several decades earlier, was used as a slogan by California's Blacks to justify extending rights to their community. Members of the African American community declared that they paid taxes that supported public schools, but few public monies were appropriated to support instruction of their children. They further argued, since African American men had no right to vote, they had no power to change the direction of the legislative bodies. A third grievance African Americans faced was the prohibition of testifying against any White person in legal matters.[13] This was especially troubling to delegates of the convention since they declared that it left them open to many possible abuses. African Americans would not gain full testimony privileges in California before 1863, when an amendment to the state constitution was passed. Black men would lack the elective franchise in California until the passage of a National Constitutional Amendment, the Fifteenth, in 1870.

Education, though, was a theme for delegates at the 1855 *Colored Citizens of the State of California Convention*. Those assembled acknowledged that education served as a means of change, as "a quality, a means to dignify men, to enable them to command respect of their fellows and increase their intelligence and wealth."[14] At a second convention in December of 1856, an education committee was established with a goal to insure the proper education of California's African American children. The committee's hope was for an overhaul of the 1852 and 1855 revised California School Laws that strictly prohibited African American children from attending public schools.[15] Such desires would not be easily achieved as African American students would be forced to wait twenty years before being granted admittance to California's "White" schools. The Southern backgrounds of those who opposed Blacks in California may have played a central role in these developments.

California's third Superintendent of Education, Andrew Jackson Moulder, was born in Virginia and consistently favored the exclusion of non-White students from public schools. In 1859, he made a statement against California's non-White citizens that led to the amended Common School Laws in 1860. The statement follows in its entirety.

Negroes in the Public Schools.—I regret to announce that the odious tastes of the Negrophilist school of mock philanthropists have found their way, to some extent, into California. In several of the counties, attempts have been made to introduce the children of Negroes into the Public Schools on an equality with Whites.

Whenever consulted on the point, the Superintendent has resolutely resisted such attempts, and employed all the power conferred upon him by law, to defeat them.

In his communications on the subject, he has instructed our school officers that our public schools were clearly intended for white children alone.

The law provides that in the month of October, the School Marshals shall take the census of the white children between the ages of four and eighteen years.

Upon this census, the apportionment of the State and County School Funds is based. It matters not how many Negro children there may be in a School District, it receives no funds for their education.

Had it been intended by the framers of the law that the children of the inferior races should be educated side by side with the whites, it is manifest the [school] census would have included children of all colors.

If this attempt to force Africans, Chinese, and Diggers [Indians], into our white School is persisted in, it must result in the ruin of the Schools. The great mass of our citizens will not associate on terms of equality with these inferior races; nor will they consent that their children should do so. Grant, for the purpose of the argument, and only for that purpose, that this antipathy is unreasonable—that it is but a prejudice—the fact is patent that it is deeply rooted, and widespread. Until our people are prepared for practical amalgamation, which will probably not be before the millennium, they will rather forego the benefits of our Schools than permit their daughters—fifteen, sixteen, and seventeen years of age—to affiliate with the sons of Negroes. It is practically reduced to this then, that our Schools must be maintained exclusively for whites, or they soon will become tenanted by blacks alone.

This intermingling of Negroes with Caucasians is, moreover, a positive cruelty to the former. They are, when by association when children, brought up in the belief that the intimacy can continue in after years. It can only bring mortification and chagrin—and that, the more their sensibilities are cultivated—when time disabuses them of this idea. For these reasons, the State Superintendent has emphatically prohibited their admission into our white Schools. At the same time, it is not desirable, neither does our School Law render it necessary, that they should be brought up in ignorance and heathenism. Any District may establish a separate School for the benefit of the inferior races, and apply a certain portion of the public funds to its support, provided the citizens do not object, which it is presumed they will not do, unless for cogent reasons.

The question involved in these remarks is not a mere abstraction. It is practical—now pressing upon us for solution. The purpose of this introduction, is to ask further legislation on the subject. Under the existing law, the State Superintendent could do nothing more than employ the influence of his official position to discourage the attempts referred to. He has no authority to punish for disobedience of his instructions. It is recommended, therefore, that power be conferred upon him to withhold public moneys from any District that permits the admission of the children of inferior races—African, Mongolian, or Indian— into the Common Schools.

The State Superintendent disclaims any prejudice against a respectable Negro—in his place; but that place is not, in his opinion, an association, on terms of equality, with the white race.[16]

Moved by these sentiments, the state legislature in 1860 gave acting State Superintendent Moulder full authority to deny public funds to school districts if they did not comply with the 1852 school law that prohibited the admission of non-White children. The Common School Law of 1860 was approved on April 28 and the new Section eight read:

Negroes, Mongolians and Indians shall not be admitted into the public schools; and whenever satisfactory evidence is furnished to the superintendent of public instruction to show that said prohibited parties are attending such schools, he may withdraw from the district in which such schools are situated all shares of the State school funds; and that the superintendent of common schools for the county in which such district is situated shall not draw his warrant in favor of such district for any expense incurred while the prohibited parties aforesaid were attending the public schools therein; provided, that the trustees of any district may establish a separate school for the education of Negroes, Mongolians and Indians and use the public school funds for the purpose of the same.[17]

This amended law stayed in effect until 1866, when it was modified to allow non-White children to be admitted to White schools if White parents did not object.

California's African American Women and Churches Take the Offense

California's school boards provided meager support to "colored schools" even after they were established, leaving African American citizens to perform roles as fundraisers and frequently virtual sole supporters of the segregated African American schools in the decades of the 1850s–1860s. There was nothing new about this pattern. It should not be a shock that it was Black women who often took the initiative. For instance, African American women in Sacramento had been the ones who acquired the property on which the initial Black school facility was located.[18] In 1854, Black women, who included Emily Allen, Priscilla Yantis, Rebecca Gibbs, and Jane Ware, did what Dermas described as the "impossible": getting a deed to land from a White benefactor that ultimately provided the location for a building that became Sacramento's first "colored school."[19] Getting land was only a start, as afterwards Sacramento's Black women [and men] labored for several years raising money for building repair materials and school supplies, and thus made a mere vision an actual facility. Black women, though, often remained in the lead. It was they who held a Street Fair in April of 1858 for the benefit of their Sacramento "colored school." This was a production that took months of planning, weeks of labor, and long hours of physical execution. Whether they raised a large amount of money is not as crucial as what this suggests about the desire of Sacramento's Black female community. It

should be no surprise that Black women played a special educational support role in that era. In this early period seventy-four percent of the African American females in California were able to read and write and these women fervently believed in virtue being derived through education. They assumed that education led to a more prosperous lifestyle and would enhance the overall status of their community. Not surprisingly, a higher attendance of girls than boys were registered in the "colored schools."[20] This pattern affirms trends that others have noted about Black women who migrated to the West. Black women in California were convinced that their children had to be educated to be good Bible-reading Christians. They also may have sensed that their daughters might also become schoolteachers if given any chance. They would have known that being a teacher meant that their daughters could avoid being domestic servants. Avoiding that role allowed one more security from a variety of potentially abusive circumstances. Black women so close to slavery were well aware of what could happen to daughters who worked "in house." Many of those California Black women may have had the blood markings of "house service" backgrounds. Most Blacks in that era knew of the existence of these exploitative patterns. Perhaps this too motivated these women to labor, so that their daughters might become educated and that their services might be provided in schoolhouses as opposed to private White houses. Driven by such awareness, Sacramento's Black women might have been even more focused than Black men to make schools available to their offspring. Their actions suggest this might have been the case.

African American churches were also instrumental in the establishment of "colored schools." Phil Montesano in *The Black Churches in Urban San Francisco, 1860–1865: Their Educational, Civic, and Civil Rights Activities*[21] noted that Bethel A.M.E. Scott Street Church rented out a room to a "colored school" for $800 a year. However, the interest of the A.M.E. Churches in education went further than that. A report from the 1863 A.M.E Conference was issued, stating

> . . . we pledge ourselves to devote a larger share of our efforts in the future to the moral and religious improvement of the rising generation . . . Let our Sunday School officers supply each school with a good library from the A.M.E. Book Concern, of the S. S. Union. Encourage our children to cultivate the habit of reading.[22]

While Black churches acted in concert in both San Francisco and Sacramento to support education, individual Black men and women steeped in those institutions would also be instrumental in the early processes that produced educational chances for Blacks. One minister would be especially crucial.

Reverend J. B. Sanderson and the Development of San Francisco's "Colored Schools"

Similar to the A.M.E. Church's action to support education was the establish-

ment of a Sunday School by the Zion Church. Their school contained a library with over three hundred books.[23] Yet, it was Bethel A.M.E. Church that stayed in the forefront of education for Black children in San Francisco. In 1859, Reverend J. B. Sanderson came to San Francisco and was placed in charge of that city's first public "colored school." He would hold this position throughout the years of the Civil War. The "colored school" would be housed in the A.M.E. Church until their building was sold. With this sale difficulties escalated for the city's school minded African Americans. J. B. Sanderson wrote in a personal letter,

> [w]hen the synagogue was purchased the removal of the colored school was decided upon. That school for years was kept in the basement of the St. Cyprian Church. It was the last school removed from a basement. The Board had tried, the colored people had tried for months to purchase a lot on which to erect a school-house for us. Who would sell a lot for a colored school?— Property holders usually object to a school upon, or contiguous to their property or homes. They dislike the crowds and noise of children. Added to this was the old prejudice against the Negro. They said, "What! A nigger school in our neighborhood! No, No!"—There was no lack of lots for sale; but when it came out that the lot was wanted for a colored school, either it was said, "No lot for sale." or an exhorbitant [sic] price was demanded.[24]

Sanderson's wishes got through to some in high White places. In 1861, the Superintendent of Education for San Francisco, Mr. George Tait, pleaded to the city's board for better school conditions for his "colored charges."

> *The room occupied by this school for the past few years is disgraceful to any civilized community. A decent respect for the wants and feelings of a common humanity demands that the colored pupils be supplied with better and more ample accommodations for the children. I would suggest that a small building be erected in some central location, so that the children may have access to it, as, having but one school, they must come from all parts of the city.[25]*

Superintendent Tait's campaign for a new location for the "colored school" was successful and in 1864 a new schoolhouse was erected on Broadway near Powell Street. Tait remarked, "[t]he colored children richly deserve their present comfortable and neat school house after having endured unmurmuringly for many years their squalid, dark and unhealthy quarters."[26] In 1869 the school would be moved again, this time to the corner of Broadway and Taylor Street.[27] No matter its location, the duties of those charged with educating Black youth could be onerous.

Until 1864, Rev. Sanderson alone taught all 192 students enrolled in San Francisco's "colored school." As the Civil War moved toward its conclusion, another Black teacher was hired and Sanderson was promoted to a role of being a teaching-"principal" of the school. Superintendent Tait remained the sympathetic White behind the tepid movement that gave San Francisco's "colored school" some improvement. He told his board of education,

> *[a]s but one school is open to all the children of our colored people, among whom are found not a few heavy taxpayers, it would seem but just that this school, of all others, should have the services of teachers thoroughly educated, and chosen with special reference to the requirements of the school.[28]*

Having established a reputation in both Sacramento and San Francisco, Sanderson was called on to devote part of his scarce free time assisting numerous groups, including the Young Men's Union Beneficial Society, which was devoted to self-education.[29] Constantly on the go Sanderson found the time to help in the recruitment and hiring process of teachers to get other "colored schools" established. His reputation as a tireless teacher became known with Blacks throughout California. Parents with means from this still repressed population would dispatch their children from distant communities to become boarders and thus enroll in schools connected to Reverend Sanderson. While esteemed in his own group, Sanderson was not immune to the racial patterns of the day. In 1865, barely two months after the end of the Civil War, Reverend Sanderson lost his job as principal of San Francisco's primary "colored school" when his African American assistant left the district. When an African American replacement teacher could not be recruited, a White female teacher quickly stepped forward. California's racial etiquette of that era prevented White women from working with or under the supervision of an African American man. Adhering to the social mores of the time, Reverend J. B. Sanderson found himself discharged as the teaching-"principal" of San Francisco's first "colored school." He was demoted to the status of being a regular "teacher," then reassigned to a less esteemed "colored school" that had been opened in a more remote locale. A White male principal was hired to replace Sanderson and San Francisco's first public "colored school" was taught and regulated by an all-White staff.[30] Undaunted by these developments, Sanderson remained in service to San Francisco's African American community and in 1867 assumed a position teaching in the "colored evening school" in that rapidly growing metropolis.[31] Black communities in other parts of the state were also experiencing trials and tribulation in the 1860s.

Sacramento's Blacks Struggle to Maintain an Educational Foothold

Floods, fires, and epidemics wreaked havoc in Sacramento's African American community in the late 1850s and early 1860s. The desire members of that community retained for education remained strong. In 1860, members of the common council [school board] hired Mrs. Juliana Folger to teach the forty-one African American students. The council's mone-

tary provision was so meager that it forced members of the Black community to contribute furniture, materials, books, slates, and even the physical building for "their school." This took months to accomplish as the facility was literally built piece by piece by members of the community. Months after completion, the "colored school" would be severely damaged by a raging flood. That disaster was minimal compared to the damage an arsonist inflicted in 1863 when the "colored school" building was gutted by fire. Even White officials suspected this was a racial hate crime directed at keeping Blacks in "their place." These dire conditions led in 1864 to members of the African American community approaching the common council's members, asking for funding for their "colored school" that would make it equal to what local Whites enjoyed. While not being granted the full measure of their request, Sacramento's Blacks were allocated ten dollars a month so that the "colored school" could be moved to the basement facilities of the African Baptist Church. In 1865, the "colored school" was moved to a second church, Sacramento's African Methodist Episcopal Church, until re-building could be completed at the school's initial location. By the time this was accomplished, Mrs. Folger had been named principal of the "colored school" with Annie Yantis acting as her assistant. While these women remain constants for Sacramento's African American pupils, much in the state and nation was beginning to change. The victory of the Union in the Civil War and the formal end of slavery marked the future as perhaps being very positive.[32]

California's Adaptation to National Reconstruction

While the policies of Reconstruction were felt most prominently in the defeated South, the passage of Constitutional Amendments and Federal Legislation had implications for the Golden State's residents. With the adoption of the Fourteenth Amendment and the Federal Civil Rights Act of 1866 forms of integration were seemingly becoming part of the national law. Neither San Francisco nor Sacramento complied with the Civil Rights Law of 1866 that provided Blacks equal access to public facilities in terms of schools. Like localities throughout the nation, both cities kept their educational facilities strictly racially separate. There was a major step taken that some read as "progress." California's school law was amended once again in 1866 to now require the provision of public money for "colored schools." This forward step included specific language that did mandate segregated schools would be necessary to house non-White children. The provision could be activated by the submission of a petition to a school council by ten non-White families. If that number of non-White families petitioned they were expected to receive support from local school officials. Once petitioned, a school council could assist in the establishment of a separate facility. By establishing this petition process California's legislators were effectively creating a kind of local option in how a community could respond to the racial conditions of the new era. This meant, children of color might be admitted to a public school if a White parent did not file an objection. If objections were lodged, children of color were to be banned. The possibility of expulsion did not apply whenever a non-White student lived with White guardians or a White parent.[33] This legislation had potentially far-reaching implications for California's cities.

Despite the narrow possibility of change available, both San Francisco's Board of Education and the Sacramento Common Council continued to apply their previously established policies of rigid racial segregation. Adherence to these local customs often made life extremely difficult for Black parents who wanted convenience for their children. The "colored schools" were often located so far away from Blacks' homes that school attendance became virtually impossible. Long distances, horrible travel conditions for minors, and inclement weather often made Black school attendance appear bleak.[34] Despite segregated schools that were often inadequate, some three hundred African American children still attended San Francisco's segregated "colored schools" in the late 1860s. Sacramento's Black pupils made similar sacrifices as they too maintained their attendance patterns in that location's still separate school.

Philip A. Bell of the Black Press Leads a Crusade for Educational Justice

By the early 1870s, the established Black press of San Francisco had become a forceful voice of the African American community and its member publications were deeply involved in all issues related to education. In the opening years of that decade the *Pacific Appeal's* editors wrote, "[t]he proper education of our children is paramount to all other considerations."[35] The Black journalists of that era voiced ongoing concerns about the conditions of the city's segregated colored schools. By 1874, writing in the *San Francisco Elevator,* a different observer noted that only two-thirds of the money due for each pupil was being appropriated to 'colored schools,' though White schools received one hundred percent of what their pupil numbers entitled them to receive. Continuing to reveal important discrepancies in treatment, members of the Black press further reported that, "in twenty counties funds designated for "colored schools" had been diverted to whites."[36] This was an era when a single voice in print could make a profound impact. A Black man's career demonstrates this to have been the case.

Philip Alexander Bell, editor of the *Pacific Appeal* often sparked constructive action by constantly using his paper to report on and criticize San Francisco School Board actions in the late 1860s. Bell was so militant about school issues that he even prematurely tried to arouse the African American community to engage in a school boycott. While such an action seemed unthinkable to those so recently denied any schooling chances, Bell did continue to rail against the appalling conditions of the locally segregated schools. He did want to see the existence of the main Black school maintained. This was not always a given. The San Francisco "colored school" had a

prime, central location that was coveted by those from outside the Black community. There was no guarantee its existence could be sustained.

In 1867, General Henry A. Cobb, the Chairman of the Visiting Committee of the Industrial School complained about the "colored school" being located on Broadway Street near downtown San Francisco. Chairman Cobb called this location a "nuisance." Bell quickly used the pages of his paper to counterattack Cobb and those members of this visiting group who agreed with their chairman's sentiments. Bell also lambasted members of the local board of education in his newspaper. He revealed his belief about what he thought was Cobb's barely hidden motive, asserting that Cobb considered the "colored school" a "nuisance" because it was located directly adjacent to a newer White school. Showing bias that was endemic during the era, San Francisco's school board members agreed with White parents who were protesting and with Cobb. They forced the removal of the "colored school" in 1867. The still segregated Black students were relocated to Jackson Street near Taylor. This was not the end of the controversy, as in 1868 members of the board of education closed the recently relocated "colored school" altogether and this without warning. Though members of the African American community and Bell were outraged, it was the journalist who used his publication's pages as a vigorous forum to condemn the actions of the White officials. Those officials only reluctantly responded to pressures from Bell and others by making provisions for the "colored school" to be temporarily moved into the basement of an A.M.E. Church on Powell Street. These new premises would prove to be barely adequate. This basement school had no toilet, was not equipped with school furniture or material and had hardly any ventilation. The city's African Americans seemed to have sensed some other darker [or in this case whiter] motives were in play.

As the dispute simmered, Bell published a long, blistering editorial that included the assertion "that the black people of San Francisco know their rights, and knowing, dare maintain them, and will not allow an ex-slave dealer (General Cobb) to trample on them with impunity."[37] After this publication Bell and other members of the African American community leaders met for a strategy meeting. While some Blacks wanted to pressure officials of A.M.E. Church to reject the school district's intention to use their basement, this did not go far enough for Bell. He staked out a bolder and more visionary position for his community and its children. Using his paper he called for the immediate admittance of the African American children to all the district's schools. Anything less than this should require that district officials be made to strictly adhere to the provision of separate but equal "colored schools" according to state law. To Bell this implied real equality. If the board's members failed to do this, Bell wrote that parents and leaders of the African American community should take the board's leaders into the state's courts. While Bell was boldly assertive, the majority of his paper's readers seemed to favor moderate actions. They did desire some response.

Pressured by the African American community to respond, members of the board of education established a facility on Greenwich Street to be the location of another temporary "colored school." This site was the location of a dilapidated, former White schoolhouse. Besides being worn out, the location's physical environment was not agreeable. This was especially so during the rainy season when the area would be "[s]urrounded by a quagmire of slush." Observers, such as Bell, believed the facility did not even deserve the title of "inferior." He was not alone as on this occasion most parents of the Black children stood with their community leaders in boycotting this "new" "colored school." They based their boycott on an 1869 California Statute (p. 839), which stated that if at least ten Black families petitioned, a school board would have to create a separate school for the education of their children. During January of 1869, the San Francisco school board had not established a location for another "colored school" and there was the real chance the board was in technical noncompliance. Equipped with this knowledge Bell and others called for more community meetings. By July of 1869 San Francisco's "colored school" was moved to a more suitable location at the corner of Taylor and Vallejo streets.[38] Philip A. Bell's use of both the press and direct action clearly helped San Francisco's Black community weather some of the more threatening days of the post Civil War era. These turned out to be methods used repeatedly by African American community activists in future fights.

Ward v. Flood: a Watershed Legal Case

As the decade of the 1870s unfolded, a Black family, emboldened by the community's success in previous battles, took the San Francisco Board of Education to court. They alleged that their daughter was deprived of her equal protection under federal law by being rejected by an all-White school closest to her residence. The decision to pursue such a lawsuit had been agreed to at an African American convention held in Stockton, California, in 1871. In that gathering it was decided that members of San Francisco's Black community would hire a White lawyer to argue a test case.[39] John W. Dwinelle was the prominent White lawyer hired to represent the Mary Ward family. This would turn out to be one of the most important cases of that century for California's Blacks' rights.

In 1872, Mrs. Harriet Ward had Dwinelle file a lawsuit on behalf of her daughter Mary Frances Ward. In the case that came to be listed as *Ward v. Flood* 48 Cal 36 (1874), the family challenged the legality of segregation in California's public school system. In lower court hearings, Harriet Ward testified on behalf of her daughter and indirectly for the entire Black community of San Francisco when she declared

> [w]e are all of African descent . . . residents of San Francisco, . . . [and] have a right to be received . . . at the school nearest their residence.[40]

Though they lost in the lower courts, Dwinelle proceeded with the case to the level of California's Supreme Court. Arguing in 1874, Dwinelle alleged that there existed de facto segregation throughout California's public schools and that this was illegal. He asserted that his client was being denied her right to the "equal protection of law" based on the Fourteenth Amendment and was thus being denied her full citizenship rights. Disagreeing with Dwinelle's legal position, members of the California Supreme Court affirmed the decision of the lower courts with Chief Justice C. J. Wallace firmly establishing the notion that in this state "separate schools for colored children" would prevail. The leaders of San Francisco's African American community recognized that they might have lost a decision, but sensed that an end to segregation was on the horizon. They returned to their City by the Bay determined that African American children would get much more "equality" or that the school board would be taken back to court again and again. They had identified lawyers willing to argue for them and had found families willing to step forward. Pooled resources had also become a strategy that could be counted on in the future. The school child, Mary Frances Ward, may have lost a Supreme Court case, but by 1875 she was quietly enrolled in one of San Francisco, first integrated schools. This, after members of the board of education publicly stated that the district could no longer adequately fund racially separated schools.[41] This was the beginning of a new day for that city and the state.

Ward v. Flood (1874) had another crucial and positive element in that it now made education for California's African

American children mandatory. Deliberations of the court and language from *Ward v. Flood* made it clear that school districts were to abide by *California Political Code,* Sec. 1669, which required that even non-White children were to be educated. Separate schools were the legal ideal, but if such "separateness" was not practical, such children were to be admitted to White schools.[42] Educational rights for Black children that had been described with words such as "may" or "shall" were now deleted from the school laws and replaced by the crucial term "must." Things for California's Black children would never be the same.

The Momentum of Black Educational Progress Is Sustained

Using direct actions, the continuing powers of a crusading Black press and other sources of pressure, those who fought for the educational rights of the African American children won more victories in the years before 1880. The word "White" would be deleted from the state's school codes and public schools were gradually required to be just that: open for *all* public students. These processes remained gradual, as it would not be until the end of the 1880s that provisions were made, first in San Francisco and later in Sacramento, to finally close the separate schools for African Americans that each locality had started in the 1850s. Both of those locations were progressive compared to some other California spots. Before 1873, the central California town of

Visalia fought even against the establishment of a "colored school." Nor would they admit Black students to the local White school. It was only after being sued and faced with a court order in 1890 that the Visalia school district desegregated their schools and admitted Black students (see *Wysinger v. Crookshank* 82 Cal 588, 720). That Visalia case would form another basis for African American parents throughout California fighting forms of mandated segregation. While de jure segregation in California's public school systems was ended for Blacks by 1890, de facto segregation based on local residence was emerging. This pattern would become the basis for many more battles in the decades to come and remains a part of today's California system.

Notes

1. California Constitution of 1849. California State Archives, Sacramento.
2. William Alexander Leidesdorff came in 1841 to San Francisco. Born and raised in the West Indies, the son of a mulatto woman and a White man came in 1834 to Louisiana. He gained his citizenship and sailed in 1841 to California. In San Francisco, Leidesdorff was very active and successful as a merchant. In 1844, Leidesdorff became a Mexican citizen. This citizenship granted him land in the Sacramento Valley. By 1847, Leidesdorff served on several committees in San Francisco. From 1845 to July 1846, Thomas A. Larkin for the Port of San Francisco appointed Leidesdorff vice-consul. W. S.

Savage. "The Influence of William Alexander Leidesdorff on the History of California." *Journal of Negro History* 38, No. 3 (1953): 322–332.

3. Soulé, Frank, John H. Gihon and James Nisbet. *The Annales of San Francisco.* Palo Alto: Lewis Osborne, 1966, 197–200.

4. Quoted in Broussard, Albert. *Black San Francisco: The Struggle for Racial Equality in the West 1900–1954.* Lawrence, Kansas: University Press of Kansas, 1993.

5. Swett, John. *History of the Public School System of California.* San Francisco: A.L. Bancroft and Company, 1876, 14.

6. J. B. Sanderson was born in New Bedford, Massachusetts, in 1821. Sanderson was born to free parents, light colored, and educated. In 1854 he arrived in California to uplift his financial situation. Sanderson was involved in the schools in Sacramento and San Francisco. Rudolph M. Lapp. "Jeremiah B. Sanderson: Early California Negro Leader." *Journal of Negro History* 53, No. 4 (1968): 321–333.

7. Demas, Marilyn. *Ungraded School No. 2 Colored: The African American Struggle for Education in Victorian Sacramento.* Sacramento: Sacramento Historical Society, 1999.

8. Quoted in Bell, Howard H. "Negroes in California 1849–1859." *Phylon* 28, No. 2 (1967), 152.

9. *Sacramento Daily Union,* 30 January 1855.

10. Statutes of California, 6th Session, 1855, Section Eighteen.

11. In Lawrence B. De Graaf, Kevin Mulroy, Quintard Taylor, eds. *Seeking El Dorado: African Americans in California.* Los Angeles: Autry Museum of Western Heritage, 2001; *Mirror of the Times,* 12 December 1857.

12. In William Loren Katz. *The Black West: A Commentary and Pictorial History of African American Role in the Westward Expansion of the United States.* New York: Simon & Schuster, 1986.

13. Proceedings of the First State Convention of the Colored Citizens of the State of California. Sacramento: Democratic State Journal Print, 1855.

14. Colored Citizens of the State of California State Convention. "Proceedings of the First State Convention of the Colored Citizens of the State of California. Held at Sacramento: 11/20–22, 1855 in the Colored Methodist Church." Sacramento: Democratic State Journal, 1865.

15. The 1852 legislation provided the common public schools to be financed from state funds and directed by a board of trustees, quoted in Office of Historic Preservation. *Five Views: An Ethnic Historic Site Survey for California.* Office of Historic Preservation, 1988, 61–63.

16. Quoted in William Warren Ferrier. *Ninety years of Education in California, 1846–1936.* Berkeley: Sather Gate Book Shop, 1937, 98.

17. Quoted in William Warren Ferrier. *Ninety years of Education in*

California, 1846–1936. Berkeley: Sather Gate Book Shop, 1937, 98.

18. Demas, Marilyn. *Ungraded School No. 2 Colored: The African American Struggle for Education in Victorian Sacramento.* Sacramento: Sacramento Historical Society, 1999, 20

19. Demas, Marilyn. *Ungraded School No. 2 Colored: The African American Struggle for Education in Victorian Sacramento.* Sacramento: Sacramento Historical Society, 1999.

20. In William Loren Katz. *The Black West: A Commentary and Pictorial History of the African American Role in the Westward Expansion of the United States.* New York: Simon & Schuster, 1986, 292–294. In Lawrence B. De Graaf, Kevin Mulroy, Quintard Taylor, eds. *Seeking El Dorado: African Americans in California.* Los Angeles: Autry Museum of Western Heritage, 2001.

21. Philip M. Montesano. "The Black Churches in Urban San Francisco 1860–1865: Their Educational, Civic, and Civil Rights Activities." Bancroft Library, University of California, Berkeley.

22. Journal of Proceedings of the Third Annual Convention of the Ministers and Lay Delegates of the African Methodist Episcopal Church held in Bethel Church San Francisco [from September 4th to September 10th, 1863, p. 22] San Francisco: B.F. Sterrett, Printer, 1863.

23. *San Francisco Bulletin*, 13 September 1862, p. 3; *Pacific Appeal*, 17 May 1862, p. 2, for some examples of church activities.

24. Sanderson, Jeremiah Burke. "Jeremiah Sanderson Papers 1821–1912." Bancroft Library, University of California, Berkeley.

25. Quoted in William Warren Ferrier. *Ninety Years of Education in California, 1846–1936.* Berkeley: Sather Gate Book Shop, 1937, 100.

26. Quoted in William Warren Ferrier. *Ninety Years of Education in California, 1846–1936.* Berkeley: Sather Gate Book Shop, 1937, 100.

27. In Lawrence B. De Graaf, Kevin Mulroy, Quintard Taylor, eds. *Seeking El Dorado: African Americans in California.* Los Angeles: Autry Museum of Western Heritage, 2001.

28. Quoted in Lee Stephen Dolson, Jr. *The Administration of the San Francisco Public Schools, 1847 to 1947,* Unpublished Ph.D. Dissertation, University of California, Berkeley, 1964.

29. *San Francisco Municipal Report 1863-4* (San Francisco, 1864), 204.

30. In Lawrence B. De Graaf, Kevin Mulroy, Quintard Taylor, eds. *Seeking El Dorado: African Americans in California.* Los Angeles: Autry Museum of Western Heritage, 2001; *Elevator,* 23 June and 28 July 1865.

31. Letter of Notification, Sept 11, 1867, from Office of Superintendent in Sanderson, Jeremiah Burke. "Jeremiah Sanderson Papers 1821–1912." Bancroft Library, University of California, Berkeley; *Pacific Appeal,* 7 Sept. 1867.

32. Demas, Marilyn. *Ungraded School No. 2 Colored: The African American Struggle for Education in*

Victorian Sacramento. Sacramento: Sacramento Historical Society, 1999.

33. *California Revised School Law 1866,* Sections 57 and 59; *California Statutes 1865–1866,* p. 383; "An Act, to Provide for a System of Common Schools," (approved March 24, 1866), Section 57 excludes those minority children "not living under the care of white persons."

34. *San Francisco Municipal Reports,* 1861–1862, pp. 202, 204; *Pacific Appeal,* 12 June and 19 June 1875, 27 May 1870.

35. *Pacific Appeal,* 25 November 1871, 15 March, 17 May, 30 August, 15 November and 22 November 1873.

36. *Pacific Appeal,* 25 November 1871; *San Francisco Elevator,* 21 February 1874.

37. *Elevator,* 17 July 1868, p. 2.

38. *Elevator,* 7 May 1869, p. 3; 14 May 1869, p. 3; 29 May 1869, p. 2 and 16 July 1869, p. 2; Roy Walter Cloud. *Education in California: Leaders, Organizations, and Accomplishments of the First Hundred Years.* Stanford: Stanford University Press, 1952, p. 45. For information on Denman, see John Swett, "Public Education in California: Its Origin and Development with Personal Reminiscences of Half a Century." New York: American Book Company, 1911, 198–200.

39. In William Loren Katz. *The Black West: A Commentary and Pictorial History of African American Role in the Westward Expansion of the United States.* New York: Simon & Schuster, 1986.

40. Quoted in Helen T. Catterall, ed. *Judicial Cases Concerning American Slavery,* vol. 5. Carnegie Institute of Washington, 1937; reprint, New York: Octagon Books, 1968, 338. For background on the court case and the challenge to segregated education, see Charles Wollenberg. *All Deliberate Speed: Segregation and Exclusion in California Schools, 1855–1975.* Berkeley: University of California Press, 1976, chapter 1. See also Rudolph M. Lapp. *Afro-Americans in California.* San Francisco: Boyd and Fraser Publishing Company, 1979, 20.

41. Quoted in: Helen T. Catterall, ed. *Judicial Cases Concerning American Slavery,* vol. 5. Carnegie Institute of Washington, 1937; reprint, New York: Octagon Books, 1968, 338. For background on the court case and the challenge to segregated education, see Charles Wollenberg. *All Deliberate Speed: Segregation and Exclusion in California Schools, 1855–1975.* Berkeley: University of California Press, 1976, chapter 1. See also Rudolph M. Lapp. *Afro-Americans in California.* San Francisco: Boyd and Fraser Publishing Company, 1979, 20.

42. Delilah L. Beasley. *The Negro Trail Blazers of California.* Los Angeles: Times Mirror Printing and Binding House, 1919.

Vanessa Gunther

Indians and the Criminal Justice System in San Bernardino and San Diego Counties, 1850–1900

California's Native Americans in the nineteenth century faced massive discrimination from virtually every sector of California's society. Their contact with the criminal justice system, as criminal defendants, witnesses, and victims was almost always negative. Prosecutors faced no opposition in obtaining guilty verdicts for even the smallest crime for non-White persons in California's courts; however, they found it very difficult to obtain guilty verdicts against White defendants in rape and murder cases. The skin color of the victims was also important in deciding a case; when the victim was non-White, a guilty verdict against a White was seldom obtained.

This article details how racism and discrimination against Native Americans permeated every aspect of California's culture, including the legal system. It raises fundamental questions about fairness in the American judicial system, and equal protection under the law. *(LH)*

American Indians appearing in the law are too often tribes asserting sovereignty, chiefs caught up in the web of the system, or white men's Indians stereotyped by their race. Yet when we look into the trial court records, we find real people and the operational level of law. When we look beyond these records into the print media of the 19th century, we discover American Indians resisting, changing, and surviving, often despite the criminal justice system.[1]

The limited population—and thus power base—that whites initially worked from is best seen in an 1851 report in the *Los Angeles Star* stating that the anxiety of whites was due to "Indian law *[being]* badly enforced in this county—the reason of many inconveniences we suffer in the City."[2] The author of the report goes on to acknowledge that "some trespasses on the rights of Indians by white men . . ." had occurred, and although investigation was encouraged, the author fell short of demanding punishment for the whites who had abused the Indians. This contradiction appeared in numerous articles where the crimes committed against Indians were denounced for their savagery, but punishment not demanded.

A case in point was an 1852 incident in which several Indian women at the Mission San Gabriel were "cruelly abused, by three white men." One of the victims had been an invalid who was "nearly strangled" in her attempt to ward off her attacker. Eventually the cries of the women brought several Indian men to their defense, and the assailants fled. The response in the press was "shame on the man who will take advantage of the helpless and degraded condition of these Indians and their ineligibility to appear as witnesses. . . ."[3] Yet, other than obtaining the names of the assailants, little more was done by the authorities. However, as the women would have been prevented from testifying against them in court, one wonders what benefit additional investigation would have been to the women. The abused Indians were instructed what to do in case of another attack, and for the whites, the incident was forgotten.

Notably missing from the records are cases in which Indian women were the victims of sexual assault. While women were sadly the victims of more than their share of violent crimes, both as the victim of their Indian brothers or the whites, there are few cases that survive in which a woman pursued her attacker in court. The most prominent reason for this would have been this inability to testify against her attacker and the misconceptions whites held about the sexual nature of non-white people. As Linda Parker has noted, many whites associated people of color with lascivious behavior.[4] Another reason was the inadequate level of prosecution and punishment by the local courts.

Witness the case of Josefa. In 1850, Josefa was approached by Juan de dios de Garcia and propositioned; she declined the proposition and was soundly beaten. The defendant was later found guilty, but only received a fine of one dollar.[5]

News reports attempted to assuage concerns about the Indian character with frequent reports of natives who presented themselves as "good Indian[s]," and warned whites of actions that could provoke hostility between the races.[6] Yet, at the same time, many reports fell back on the racist sentiments that flourished during that era. Most often, Indians who were found within the city limits dead, either by excessive drink or foul play, were mentioned only in passing in the press, by total numbers, the occurrences becoming "so frequent of late, that it causes very little notice or remark."[7] Real concern was reserved for those crimes that were committed inside the world the whites could influence.[8] And frequently the only arbitrators between the Indian and the white worlds were the Justice Courts.

In accordance with the 1849 California Constitution, each township was authorized to have two Justices of the Peace. Initially, Justices were limited to hearing only civil cases. However, the dearth of such cases and the preponderance of criminal cases forced the expansion of the Justice of the Peace duties in 1851 to include cases that involved petty larceny, assault and battery, disturbing the peace, and misdemeanors not exceeding $50 or sentences not exceeding three months in the county jail. However, the Justice Courts' decisions were appealable to the Court of Sessions—a county judge sitting with two Justices of the Peace—which served much the same function as the court of the Justice of the Peace but had the added benefit of the county court judge, who could refer cases to the Grand Jury. In 1863, however, the California Legislature abolished the Court of Sessions.

Intermixed with the local judiciary (the Justice of the Peace courts) were the state courts and the federal District Courts. However, the most accurate reflection of local sentiments toward the Indians would prove to be the lower Justice Courts.

During the 1850–1860s, the predominant charge brought against Indians in San Diego County concerned crimes against persons. This is not necessarily an accurate reflection of the frequency of Indians' appearances in the legal system, because nuisance charges, such as drunk and disorderly, may have been dealt with on a less formal basis. Of those cases that were recorded in the Court of Sessions, assault charges dominate. Sentencing shows an impressive 100 percent conviction rate for those records that were preserved. The Court of Sessions for the 1850s recorded four assaults committed by Indians, two by Indians on other Indians and two against whites. Two murder complaints were heard; again the cases were equally divided between Indian-on-Indian and Indian-on-white crime. Only one petty larceny case was heard, that of the case against "Ursula," who stood accused of stealing some black silk. Ursula admitted to the crime and was sentenced to three months in the county jail.

Those convicted could expect a stiff fine, or to spend the next one to two years in state prison. In *People v. Francisco & Mariano (Indians)*, October 17, 1859, Francisco was sentenced to one year in state prison while Mariano received two years. In *People v. Tomas (Indian)*, September 29, 1857, Tomas assaulted another Indian and received an unspecified state prison sentence. *In People v. Jose (Indian)*, April 1, 1851, Jose assaulted a police officer and received a $500 fine.

Charges of murder were heard and then passed on to the state courts for further consideration. Of the two cases in which Indians stood accused of murder in the Court of Sessions, one involved two Indians, one of whom, Pablo Narcis, stabbed the other, Clemente, in the chest with a pair of spurs. The trial of April 14, 1853, *People v. Pablo Narcis*, resulted in an acquittal.

A second incident in the same year had involved an Indian named Manteca (*People v. Manteca*, January 14, 1853). Surviving documents record the testimony of an unnamed Indian who stated he was approached by a coworker who confessed that he had seen Manteca and his companions kill a white man. Yet, court documents also indicate Manteca voluntarily reported that he had seen two other Indians kill a white man, "with bones and stones." Apparently the victim was a soldier with whom they had earlier quarreled. No further action seems to have been taken in the case, and there is no documentation to indicate that charges were ever brought against the two unnamed Indians who were alleged to have committed the murder.

Several of the Indians examined by the court maintained that they had no idea who Manteca was, or had no information about an alleged crime. The incident proved to be frustrating for the prosecutors, as they were unable to confirm that Manteca had actually murdered an "American," as he also had reportedly boasted to other Indians. The case appears to have been dropped.

In the San Bernardino courts, much the same picture arises as in the San Diego system, for cases that were considered more than nuisance in nature. In a hearing that strongly resembled the San Diego case against Manteca, the Grand Jury in San Bernardino heard the case of *People v. Juan de Dios (an Indian)*. Accused of assault in October 1853, de Dios never had charges filed against him, as no crime could be proved.[9]

Similarities in sentencing for nonviolent offenses between the San Diego and San Bernardino counties can be seen in the case of *People v. Jose* (1864). The charge of burglary was proffered against Jose by the Court of Sessions in San Bernardino. Jose pled guilty and was sentenced to one year in state prison.[10] However, the similarities between sentences diverge when crimes against another person are considered. In the San Bernardino case of *People v. Santiago—An Indian* in March 1864, Santiago pled guilty to assault with intent to commit robbery; he was sentenced to five years in state prison.[11] Far from being an indication of prejudice, however, his sentence was in keeping with other sentences handed down to white defendants. In the first-degree murder trial of the Indian Andreas in 1862, he was found guilty and sentenced to be hanged by San Bernardino District Court Judge Benjamin Hayes.[12] Again, his punishment was not outside the norm for the crime committed.

Ronald Woolsey has examined the apparent reluctance of whites to fully pursue charges against Indians during the early years of American domination, due to the inability to prove a case. While news accounts are replete with demands for justice and filled with lurid stories of crimes that are presumed to have been committed by Indians, records show that the prosecution of Indians for crimes actually declined from 1850–1856.[13] This may be due, in part, to the fact that San Bernardino County (created in 1853) was populated by a large number of Indians. Indian-on-Indian crime went essentially unreported, due to the Indian reluctance to allow white intrusion into their personal affairs. Additional limitations on the system included judges who did not speak English, and a prosecutor who spoke no Spanish. These linguistic limitations were compounded by the lack of a professional police force to help enforce the law.[14] However, while all of these factors may have contributed to the decline in overall prosecutions, the change in venue for many cases was most likely the primary reason for the decline of Indian numbers in the system.

In the Los Angeles County and San Bernardino courts, another trend can be noted: the incarceration of Indians who had not been charged with a crime. In 1850, Joaquin Machado was incarcerated by San Gabriel Judge Michael White. Bail was set at $5,000, but there were no charges pending against the Indian. Machado petitioned for his release from the Los Angeles Court of Sessions, and his release was granted.[15] Similarly, in 1862, a note by the recorder of the Court of Sessions requested the release of an Indian named Manuel from custody. No charges had been filed, and it is uncertain how long Manuel had languished in jail.[16] Such behavior may have been for social control of the Indian population or simply a problem of nonfeasance. Nevertheless, in spite of these negative forces, the legal system worked; the Indians gained their liberty.

While the predominant non-nuisance charge levied against Indians in court was assault, the press during the 1850s–1860s did not report this fact. During this time, considerably more articles accusing Indians of theft appeared than any other crime. Public whipping was the punishment for many of the Indians accused of theft in Los Angeles during the 1850s. When, in 1851, two Indians stood in Justice Court accused of stealing two bullocks at the instigation of a white man named Dunn, each Indian received 25 lashes.[17] Four Indians who had stolen a barrel of alcohol and a cloak, confessed and were each given 25 lashes.[18] An Indian boy, accused of stealing $40, a pistol, and a bottle of whiskey, was given 13 lashes. Whipping was further used to control recalcitrant Indians on the Sebastian Reservation in 1858 when they refused to work. The "ringleaders were taken out and received from twenty to one hundred lashes. . . ."[19]

In contrast, for those whites convicted of theft, punishment usually resulted in a fine or imprisonment of one to two years.

In California of 1849, the death penalty and the costs of incarceration in prison were related issues. The practice of the mining camps was to give the criminally accused a trial by jury and, if found guilty, to sentence the enemy deviant to whipping, banishment, or death. Sentence was carried out immediately. With the creation of towns and jails, the question was whether local taxpayers and later state taxpayers wanted to build prisons or to save the costs of incarceration with the penalties of whipping or death. In 1851 the California Legislature would decide that juries, the sovereign people, should decide the appropriate penalties for crimes against property. The statute gave the jury discretion in robbery cases of setting prison sentences of one to ten years or death. The first appellate case to test this statute found it constitutional.[20]

During this era, Indians and their esteem for property were considerably misunderstood by the general populace, which may be the reason for the courts' more lenient sentencing—if whipping could be considered preferable to prison. Southern California Indians, however, did have sophisticated concepts of property. Individuals claimed land for their use, and leadership within tribes was frequently given to those who had greater material success.[21] In part, property ownership and disbursement would tie an individual more intimately to his tribe. Those outside the tribe were given less consideration, which may account for the Indians' willingness to take items from whites—an attempt to raise their own prestige. According to Diegueño Indian custom, punishment for stealing was a public flogging.[22] And English flogging practices had made whipping acceptable for all races since American colonial times. Thus the propensity of whites to impose corporal punishment on Indians in Los Angeles County became a common practice. In 1853, testimony of Ramon Figuaroa indicated the "sheriff that always goes with a cane after Indians." The whipping issue was still important in the 1878-1879 California Constitutional Convention. The debate was on, and its contours are not unfamiliar a century later.[23]

San Diego court documents indicate that Indians, like whites, were victims of murder or assault. However, the conviction rate of killers of Indians was poor. In 1861, Joseph A. Anderson stood accused of knifing an Indian woman named Ramona to death in May. Despite having the testimony of another white man, the altercation between the two was ruled self-defense.[24] In 1858, a Mr. Heath stood accused of murdering an Indian who had defended his wife in the streets. Heath reportedly went home, made bullets, and then accosted the Indian in his sleep. When the case went for trial, Heath was acquitted. While sensational, the response of the jury was not unusual.[25]

Notable exceptions occurred when the individual admitted to the crime, as in the case of Maria Antonio Ortega, who appeared before the San Diego Court of Sessions in 1857. He stood accused of killing two Indians who had stolen his cattle. Testimony by David Williams against Ortega indicated that Ortega had "surprised" the Indians, "took them prisoner, escorted them to his rancho, and shot them both there."[26] Such self-imposed justice was not always accorded judicial approval.

The charge in which Indians are overwhelmingly represented in both the press and in the Justice Courts, was the charge of drunk and disorderly. The number of cases brought before the San Bernardino courts became so significant that the press eventually resorted to recounting only the numbers of Indians arrested the previous week for drunken behavior. The sentences the Indians received were considerably less than those a similarly disposed white man would receive. However, it became clear that Indians were arrested for the most part for their ability to work. As a group disenfranchised and with limited financial means, the placement of Indians in the labor pool by the court system served the needs of the community. Indians were needed for manual labor, to expand or repair roads, perform agricultural labor, or even laundry, one of the most arduous tasks in the 19th century.[27] Wages in the area for Indians was from eight to ten dollars a month, and predictably attracted limited interest.[28] It was a paltry sum considering the riches that a man could reportedly make mining for gold in the north or in the Amaragosa. With few takers for voluntary labor, involuntary labor became the norm.

The transition of California to American control mid-century resulted in an odd juxtaposition among California

Indians; those in the north were slaughtered in order to obtain access to potential gold areas, while those in the south were pursued as a malleable labor source. There are reports that Indian children were literally stolen from their parents by whites.[29] The paternalistic language whites used to justify the forced labor of Indians shared many of the same traits as that used by Southerners to legitimize slavery. Attempts to indoctrinate the Indian into white society, at least as a worker, were frequently couched in humanistic, albeit racist, language.

In 1852, the *Los Angeles Star* ran a series of articles about the California Indian, in which Indian culture and tradition were discussed. Several weeks later, a follow-up article was directed to those "philanthropists" in the community who wanted to ameliorate the poor condition of the Indians. The article maintained that

> *any person having, or hereafter obtained a minor Indian, male or female, from the parents or relations of such Indian minor, and wishing to keep* it, *such person shall go before the Justice of the Peace, in his township* [who] *shall give such person a certificate, authorizing him or her to have the care, custody, control and earnings of such minor, until he or she obtain the age of majority.*[30]

The philanthropists aside, the services the Indians provided, while limited because of their numbers, undoubtedly assisted in the material success of the communities, and the individuals who exploited their labor.

In order to exploit the labor of Indian adults, a different tactic was used. Throughout the 19th century, those individuals whose presence or behavior was deemed unacceptable to the community, but whose actions were not specifically legislated against, often found themselves the victims of disorderly conduct laws. Because the vagrancy laws specifically excluded Indians, their behavior was overwhelmingly controlled by municipal laws that regulated drunk and disorderly behavior. Between Indian men and women, a reverse discrimination occurred in the sentences that were meted out. Indian women generally received sentences that were half that received by their brothers. In cases involving white women, the opposite was true. White women received fines for drunkenness that were two to four times higher than white men. The exception to this occurred when the woman involved was not a good representation of "Victorian Womanhood." The rationale behind the disparity can be seen in the labor pool that was needed. Even those men who could not put in a full day's work were excused from jail before serving out their entire sentences.[31]

Clearly the fear and racist feelings that characterized white behavior during the middle years of the 19th century were frequently exploited for personal and community gain. As time passed and the white population shifted from one of minority to majority, the conflicts that occurred between Indians and whites took on a new hue. The area was evolving economically from one dependent on cattle to agriculture. The result was a further encroachment onto Indian lands and fewer resources for the tribes to depend upon.

In addition, an outbreak of smallpox in the Indian communities in the 1860s depleted not only the numbers of Indians, but those tribal members able to provide for others. This further compelled interaction between the races and exacerbated conflict.

By the 1870s to 1890s, Indian-white conflict had passed from the stage where whites complained of the loss of a few head of cattle to a more systematic presence of Indians in white courts. During this time, the similarities between San Bernardino and San Diego counties began to diminish. Faced with a depression that decimated these largely agricultural areas in the early 1870s, concerns about financial survival abounded. This was complicated by the further intrusion of whites onto native lands, which forced an increased intimacy between the groups.

During this time, the first reservations were created in the area, and the Indians were safely ensconced on them, at least from a white perspective.[32] However, while this may have removed the Indians from white contact, it exacerbated the problem of securing adequate amounts of food, as the reservations were unable to provide for the needs of the Indians.[33] And the limited resources that the government allowed for their support were magnified by the endemic corruption within the Indian service.[34] As with many appointees during the 19th-century political scene, patronage and conflict of interest seemed to be the norm.[35] Because of the economic conditions of the day, Indian agents were further limited in their ability to supplement their income. For many agents, this meant exploitation of the only resource they controlled, their

Indian charges. Much of the violence that erupted between the Temecula Indians (Cahuilla) and whites during this time resulted from whites stealing Indian land and the inability of the Indians to feed themselves. No small amount of blame was placed on the Indian agent.[36]

Considerably more Indian cases per capita were brought before the lower courts in San Diego during the 30 years between 1870 and 1900 than in the previous two decades. In large part this was due not to an increased Indian population, as federal census reports indicate a relative decline in the Indian population, but to increased contact with whites and changes in federal law. For those cases that were heard in federal courts, the overwhelming majority concerned crimes against another person. However, in the local courts, instead of cases that primarily focused on crimes against another individual, more than half the cases that went to court during this time were crimes against property, most frequently involving the theft of stock animals. Most documentation reports that the Indians who stole the animals also consumed them. The conviction rates surviving in the court documents indicate that more than half of the Indians charged were convicted. In contrast, the Justice Courts in San Bernardino heard cases that were more evenly matched between crimes against another person and those against property. At the same time, cases in which Indians were accused of assaulting another Indian received only modest consideration in the white courts and the white press. In 1888, two Saboba Indians became involved in an altercation in which one was severely cut with a dagger.

The assailant was subdued by bystanders but escaped. And, like most news accounts of altercations involving Indians, there is no indication that charges were pursued in court.[37]

The growing number of courts that heard Indian cases expanded with the formal development of the reservations. Many Indian cases were removed from local courts and were heard in federal District Courts. This engendered some additional hostility by the white press, as Indians were frequently kept in county jails while awaiting trial. Owing to the shrinking world between whites and Indians, the knowledge that individuals were in their jails but outside their jurisdiction could inflame community passions.

Unfortunately for both San Diego and San Bernardino counties, this era demonstrated a higher propensity among whites to assault, rape, or murder Indians with whom they came into contact. This was the time when Sam Temple murdered Juan Diego, the husband of Ramona, a story later immortalized by Helen Hunt Jackson.[38] And of those whites who stood accused by Indians, a new weapon had been unleashed against them, the testimony of the Indians themselves. Prior to 1872 an Indian could not sue in the state courts. Nor was his evidence admissible in courts of justice until 1872.[39] This may have been the reason so many more cases of assault wound up in court than in previous years. This was also a time when Indians were more apt to testify in court in cases that did not directly affect them as well.

While no accounts were found of an Indian testifying against a white man in a San Bernardino court, in which the Indian was neither the victim nor the defendant, several occurred in San Diego. The first, in 1882, was recorded in the trial of Andronico Lopez who stood accused of murdering a man named Aguilar. Lopez apparently had been playing poker with a group of men in a local grocery. When Aguilar left with his poker winnings, Lopez followed him and assassinated him on the road. His departure from the grocery was noted by a ten-year-old Indian boy named Juan Pino. Juan's testimony in part helped secure a change in Lopez's plea from not guilty to guilty. Lopez was later sentenced to ten years in state prison.[40]

News accounts of the 1870s favored articles on the more sensationalistic incidents of murder and assault. In many cases, Indians, as before, were simply presumed to be the perpetrator, as in the murder of Henry Hand and his wife near Rincon in June of 1870. Both were shot to death in their home. Nothing in the home had been stolen, and the article admitted that there was no evidence to indicate who the murderer was, and yet the blame for the crime was squarely placed on the Indians.[41] Four months later, two additional murders were blamed on the "cruel savages" in the area. In each instance, the information related in the newspaper was circumstantial, and no eyewitnesses were identified.[42]

The primary evidence used to link an Indian to a murder was the ever-present "Indian footprints." These ubiquitous bits of evidence were frequently accepted as the sole determination that Indians were the culprits. Fortunately for the Indians, the lack of any hard evidence prevented

witch-hunts for any Indian who would suf-
fice to appease the community outrage.
Most Indians who were brought before
the local courts under suspicion of murder were released because of "no evidence," as in the case of Kossuth and
Philip who were examined in the San
Bernardino Justice Court in 1871, under a
charge of murder. They were later released
for lack of evidence.[43] This is not to indicate that Indians were blameless in several
of the crimes that occurred in the area.
The increasingly adversarial role that
Indians and whites adopted, along with
the anonymity many Indians enjoyed
because of their traditional mobility,
would have made it difficult to prosecute
anyone based on a footprint. Kossuth
reappears in the courts over the years for
violent behavior, for which he was fined
and served jail time.[44]

News accounts continued to reveal the
open hostility that whites often felt toward
Indians for whatever reason, and as a
result reflected the prejudices and concerns of the population. As one report
maintained, "where there is so much
smoke there must be some fire." When
four Indians went on trial in Riverside for
the assault and robbery of a white man, all
were acquitted. The next day, however,
two of the four were arrested again for
shooting at a Mexican—allegations that
were not proven.[45]

The frustration felt by whites, whose
members had been the victims of crime,
coupled with the limited conviction rate
by the courts, caused intense feelings of
hostility. Community sentiment is mirrored in the comments of a news editor in
1873:

*The Indian arrested at Toros a few
weeks ago for mule stealing and sent
from this place [San Bernardino] to
San Diego county was taken out of jail
at Julian city and beaten to death in a
cruel and cowardly manner. The jail at
Julian is a useful institution for securing a prisoner while the necessary pre-
liminaries for "saving the county
expenses" are being arranged.[46]*

From 1870 to 1900, the vast majority of
cases that were heard by the lower courts
of San Bernardino were for drunk and disorderly behavior. These misdemeanor
cases resulted in an almost 100 percent
conviction rate for the accused, as the
Indian defendant almost exclusively pled
guilty. Most paid with their time, usually
five days in jail for men or from one to two
days for women. Of the remaining felony
crimes that Indians were most likely to be
accused of, more than half were for violent offenses. However, of those cases,
only 50 percent resulted in conviction.
Cases that involved a white victim had an
almost guaranteed conviction.

One such case was that of Prospero in
1871. Sometime during the early evening
hours of August 30, Prospero entered the
property of a Mr. Watkins. While there,
he demonstrated some bizarre behavior,
including throwing off the blankets of
Watkins' Indian servant, Julia, and light-
ing matches on his knee. All the while,
Prospero was mumbling to himself.
Concerned that Prospero would set the
hay on fire, Julia ran for assistance. While
she was away, Prospero entered the house
and shot Watkins in the chest. Three days
later Watkins died, and Prospero went on

trial for murder. He was sentenced to 20 years in state prison.[47]

Another murder trial involving an Indian occurred ten years later, in *People v. Francisco* (1881). The defendant stood accused of murder, but after several continuances in the case, the charges were dismissed with the court "unable to determine whether a crime had actually been committed."[48]

As may be expected, the limited conviction rate of the courts when Indians stood before them fostered some concerns about judicial leniency, even when it was apparent no crime had been committed. This can best be demonstrated by the case against Antonio Ales, a Soboba Indian who stood accused of murder in 1888. During his trial in a federal District Court in San Diego, Ales was accused of shooting Petronilla Alvanez "in the back when about 35 steps away and running from Ales. . . ." Ales admitted to the crime, but was acquitted.[49] News accounts of the trial supposed credit for the acquittal belonged to Ales' attorney and the Indian agent, Mr. Preston.[50] It should be noted that the victim in this case came to Ales' house with "immoral intentions toward his daughter," and an altercation ensued. Had the defendant been white, no doubt the press would have lauded his actions as a man protecting those he held dear. For an Indian, stripped of the humanity that would prompt such an action, the editors felt Ales should have been punished.

Additional cases heard in federal courts included cases in which Indians were responsible for violence against their own members—the victims often women. On September 19, 1889, two Indian men were accused of the brutal beating murder of an Indian girl. Their intentions were not recorded in the official record. Each denied the charges, but later one maintained the other had committed the murder. That same individual, while being held in the San Diego County jail, was accused of assaulting two policemen. Despite this, both were later acquitted.[51]

Of the four other possible rape and/or murder cases that went before federal courts during the latter decades of the 19th century, all resulted in verdicts of not guilty or acquittal.[52]

In a bizarre murder, in which an Indian woman was possibly raped, charges were brought against two Indian men who pled not guilty and were exonerated during the trial. The Indian woman died as a result of a skull fracture; her body was then covered by oak brush and the brush ignited. Any possible determination of a crime beyond murder would have been impossible, unless it had been witnessed. One of the witnesses at the trial was then charged three months later; he was also acquitted.

The remaining case that was heard in District Court during this time also involved a murder charge. In *U.S. v. Mo-jan-qua-di-ver and Chu-dul-en-u and Ham-ah-sa-la-nu,* three men stood accused of choking to death a fellow Indian on the Yuma Reservation in 1891.[53] All were found guilty and hanged on January 15, 1892. It is interesting to note that only in the federal trials were Indians referred to by their traditional names. However, the conviction rates do not differ significantly from those experienced in the lower courts.

The progression of Native Americans through the courts of California during the 19th century reflected the changing needs and power bases that each group enjoyed at a particular moment in time. Whites who came to the area, primarily as farmers and cattlemen, eventually established a densely populated region where the traditional ways of the Indians had no place. As custodianship for the land changed from Indian to white hands, the nature of the crimes that were committed and those who became the victims was altered. Fear and prejudice infected many of the altercations between whites and Indians. This behavior was doubly visited on Indian women who suffered the abuses of their own men as well as the advances of whites.

If there is anything to be learned of the previous accounting of the Indian in the Southern California legal system, it is how clearly law reflects the culture of those who impose it. The misogynistic and racist tendencies of 19th-century men are revisited in each complaint.

Notes

1. Clare V. McKanna, Jr.'s *Homicide, Race, and Justice in the American West, 1880-1920* (Tucson: University of Arizona Press, 1997) is one of the few books that deal with American Indians in the trial courts. His focus upon the Apache in Arizona is clearly a breath of fresh air, but is limited to cases of homicide.

2. "The Indian Law," *Los Angeles Star* (Aug. 16, 1851), 1, col. 1. For the best account of the impact of this law, see Clifford E. Trafzer and Joel R. Hyer, eds., *"Exterminate Them": Written Accounts of the Murder, Rape, and Slavery of Native Americans During the California Gold Rush, 1848-1868* (East Lansing: Michigan State University Press, 1999).

3. "Disgraceful," *Los Angeles Star* (June 26, 1852), 2, col. 3.

4. Linda S. Parker, "Statutory Changes and Ethnicity in Sex Crimes in Four California Counties, 1880-1920," *Western Legal History*, 6, 1 (1993).

5. Court of Sessions, Los Angeles, *People v. Juan de dios de Garcia,* Sept. 10, 1850. Testimony of Jesus Parado. This may be the same individual who appeared in a San Bernardino court in October 1853 accused of assault. In that case, charges were dropped against him.

6. "Jose Zapatcro" and "From the Mormon Camp," *Los Angeles Star* (Nov. 8, 1851), 2, col. 2 and 3.

7. "Murder," *Los Angeles Star* (Feb. 8, 1855), 2, col. 1. The article considered there to be two culprits in the numerous Indian murders, those who sold them liquor and the Indians themselves who then murdered each other. No consideration was given to the possibility that whites may have been equally culpable as murderers.

8. "Coroner's Inquest," *Los Angeles Star* (Feb. 21, 1852), 2, col. 1.

9. Grand Jury, San Bernardino, *People v. Juan de Dios,* Oct. 13, 1853.

10. Court of Sessions, San Bernardino, *People v. Jose,* 1864.

11. Court of Sessions, San Bernardino, *People v. Santiago—an Indian,* Mar. 8, 1864.

12. District Court of San Bernardino, *People v. Andreas—an Indian,* June 20, 1862.

13. Ronald C. Woolsey, "Crime and Punishment: Los Angeles County, 1850–1856," *Southern California Quarterly,* 61, 1 (Spring 1979): 84.

14. This shortcoming was rectified in 1854 when the state of California allowed the treasurer of Los Angeles to retain money from the general fund to create a police force named the Los Angeles Rangers. *Statute of California,* Chap. 48, May 15, 1854.

15. Court of Sessions, Los Angeles, "Reprimand of Michael White," Nov. 30, 1850.

16. Court of Sessions, San Bernardino, In re Manuel, Oct. 8, 1862.

17. "Stealing Cattle," *Los Angeles Star* (Nov. 8, 1851), 2, col. 1.

18. "Indians and Aguadiente," *Los Angeles Star* (Feb. 17, 1852), 2, col. 3.

19. "Jurupa," *Los Angeles Star* (Oct. 30, 1852), 2, col. 1.

20. "Grand Indian Outbreak," *Los Angeles Star* (Feb. 20, 1858), 2, col. 2; Gordon Morris Bakken, "Death for Grand Larceny," in John W. Johnson, ed., *Historic U.S. Court Cases, 1690–1990: An Encyclopedia* (New York: Garland Publishing, Inc., 1992), 34–35.

21. A. L. Kroeber and Lucille Hooper, *Studies in Cahuilla Culture* (Banning, CA: Malki Museum Inc., 1978), 65.

22. Lora L. Cline. *The Kwaaymii: Reflections on a Lost Culture* (El Centro, CA: IVC Museum Society, 1979), 67.

23. Court of Sessions, Los Angeles, *People v. Alviron S. Beard,* Nov. 11, 1853.

24. Court of Sessions, San Diego, *People v. Joseph A. Anderson,* Aug. 26, 1861.

25. District Court, San Bernardino, *People v. Heath,* Oct. 23, 1858.

26. Justice Court of San Diego, *People v. Maria Antonio Ortega,* Jan. 8, 1857.

27. *The Guardian,* Mar. 1, 1873, 3, col. 1. Indians were used on the Cajon Pass road, for example. The practice of using Indians as manual labor continued well through the latter part of the century.

28. Woolsey, "Crime and Punishment," 80.

29. "The Tulares," *Los Angeles Star* (Oct. 16, 1852), 2, col. 1. Two of the Tulare chiefs had come into Los Angeles seeking assistance in preventing whites from encroaching on their land and stealing their children. The Indians were "dismissed" with the promise that the matter would be looked into.

30. "California Indians," *Los Angeles Star* (Aug. 14, 1852), 2, col. 3.

31. Justice Court of San Bernardino. In *People v. Juan and Jesus,* 1873, each man was given a fine of $5 or five days in jail. Neither could pay, but Juan was released early due to his "inability to work."

32. Calls for Indian reservations had been heard since 1850, and land was set aside under military control, but the practical aspects of the plan began to show wear, and the idea had been abandoned. As more whites began to claim land that included Indian settlements and forced their expulsion, permanent placement for the Indians was discussed.

33. The *Riverside Press,* Jan. 11, 1879, 4, col. 2, includes a news report that several Indians secured the corpse of a

horse killed because of its age by its owner. They had sought permission to take the body prior to consuming it. "The Indians in the South," *Los Angeles Star* (Oct. 2, 1858), 2, col. 1, complains of the starving conditions being endured by the Indians and the lack of response by the government. The frequency with which Indians were accused of stealing livestock is not merely an indication of a convenient food source for the Indians, although that may have played a part. The *Los Angeles Star,* Sept. 18, 1858, reported rumors about Indians massing on the Mohave (Mojave) River. However, they did "not anticipate any hostilities from those miserable, half-starved creatures who may be found wandering on the banks of the river, in hopes of picking up some morsels of food, or even a stray animal from the wayfarers."

34. *The Riverside Press,* Sept. 13, 1879, 1, col. 3. "The San Bernardino Indians are seriously dissatisfied with Mr. Lawson, Government Agent. They complain that he has collected their wages from Mr. Crafts (and perhaps others) and only paid them a part." Many of the charges that were levied at Lawson in this report were recanted one week later in an article entitled "A Correction."

35. "Mission Indians in Southern California," *The Guardian,* (Feb. 3. 1872), 1, col. 5. The report acknowledges the declining harvest the Indians have endured "since they have come under the control of the United States, those lands have been taken from them, and they are now poor."

36. "The Temecula Indians," *The Weekly Guardian* (Oct. 19, 1875). 1, col. 6.

37. "The Dagger Again," *The San Jacinto Register* (Sept. 13, 1888), 3, col. 4.

38. Sam Temple can only be described as a hothead. He appears with some frequency in court documents during this time, frequently for violent offenses. The best contextualization of the Ramona story is James A. Sandos, "Between Crucifix and Lance: Indian-White Relations in California. 1769–1848," in Ramon A. Gutierrez and Richard Orsi, eds., *Contested Eden: California Before the Gold Rush* (Berkeley: University of California Press. 1998), 196–229.

39. *Report of the Special Agent for California Indians to the Commissioner of Indian Affairs* (San Jose, CA: Cleveland Printing Co., Mar. 21, 1906), 10.

40. Superior Court of San Diego, *People v. Andromico Lopez,* cases 375 and 399, Nov. 1, 1882.

41. "A Man and Wife Murdered," *The Guardian* (June 11, 1870), 3, col. 1.

42. "The Latest Indian Outrage" and "Another Man Murdered by Indians," *The Guardian* (Oct. 22, 1870), 1, col. 4.

43. "In Justice Wagner's Court," *The Guardian* (Apr. 3, 1871), 3, col. 2.

44. "Judge Wagner's Morning Leeve," *The Guardian* (Feb. 7,1874), 3, col. 3.

45. *The Riverside Press,* (Mar. 22, 1879), 4, col. 1.

46. *The Guardian,* (Feb. 18, 1873), 2, col. 1.

47. District Court of San Bernardino, *People v. Prospero,* case 154, and Superior Court of San Bernardino, case 3392, Sept. 14, 1872.

48. Superior Court of San Bernardino, *People v. Francisco,* case 303, Dec. 14, 1881.

49. District Court of the United States, *U.S. v. Antonio Ales—an Indian,* July 1, 1888. RG 21 District Courts of the United States, Criminal Docket and Register, Vol. 1 1888–1908, 385.

50. *"Ales Set Free," The San Jacinto Register* (Nov. 22, 1888), 7, col. 4.

51. District Court of the United States, *U.S. v. Ibah-pour-co-mo-hou, alias Chango Jose and Ah-la-dick-hom, alias Miguel, alias Mike,* Oct. 21, 1889.

52. District Court of the United States, *U.S. v. Francisco Ward,* Jan. 9, 1890; District Court of the United States, *U.S. v. Jim Helm,* Sept. 29, 1899; District Court of the United States, *U.S. v. Mateo Pa & Francisco Pa,* Nov. 28, 1894; and District Court of the United States, *U.S. v. Antonio Ashman,* Jan. 10, 1895.

53. The Yuma Reservation was on the Arizona-San Bernardino border.

Part III

From 1900 to 1949

Introduction

California had become established as a location for the ambitious, greedy, and adventuresome by the early 1900s. Risk takers and those driven by a desire to make a new start had been coming to the state for decades. Those who came, from what Ron Takaki calls a "different shore" [Asia], had often found opportunity, but also racial oppression. Still Asians came and helped change California. They also changed as they adopted local customs and behaviors on the way to becoming "Americanized."

Whether Chinese, Japanese, Korean, Sikh or Filipino, they encountered an atmosphere that included California legislators willing to use the weapons of legal codes to restrict the civil rights of Asian Americans. None of the immigrants from Europe ever encountered the state sanctioned laws that all people of color have had to overcome in the "land of the free." Asians like Blacks, Indians, and Mexicans had to struggle to overcome these legally imposed forms of discrimination. California's lawmakers were among the worst offenders in especially targeting Asian Americans. Materials in this section affirm this sad reality. How these processes unfolded needs to be examined by each generation of the state's residents.

Yet, the California experience for immigrants has been and continues to be a varied process. Early on, Sikhs from India devised alternative strategies as they sought a different future in California. Gonzalez description of their adaptation provides insights about how newcomers try various ways to succeed in California.

This section concludes with a description of those whose stories were most often omitted during this era (1900–1950) from scholarly narratives: women. The stories of women making new lives in California have long been omitted and/or were treated as an afterthought. With the "womenpower" needed during World War II this could no longer be a Californian practice. Black women and their wartime labor contributions to the Nation and California were vital in the 1940s.

How African American women reacted to California's circumstances after leaving the South and finding themselves living amidst a "new majority" of Whites and others is described in the final article in the section that follows. That most of these women contributed and stayed after the war's conclusion suggests a great deal about them and the South they had left. That most embraced California, suggests that the state may have been warming up to those who had given so much to this nation. Since many of the dynamics of modern California were established in the decades covered in this section, those conditions are well worth reviewing. (SMM)

Joel Franks

Mainland Chinese Americans and California Sports: 1880–1950

The process of becoming a resident of California usually means adaptation to and assimilation into new customs. This is especially true for youth who have not completely settled into the cultural patterns of the region or country of their birth. A variety of institutions often spur the process of becoming a Californian. Functioning in educational settings and consuming television and radio programs are among the many ways that today's newcomers learn to fit in.

As Joel Franks' article points out, participation in sports has also been a means for immigrants to blend towards acceptance of *and* into California's mainstream. Involvement in the activities of sports for immigrants and their offspring is a complex process. While Franks' description reveals much about early Chinese patterns, it is also suggestive about how others might be experiencing the dynamics of today's California sporting processes. *(SMM)*

An Overview

The anti-Chinese movement and subsequent anti-Asian movements fostered unintended consequences on the United States' mainland. To be sure, these movements effectively denied Asian immigrants entrance into the most dynamic sector of the American economy by excluding them from the kinds of economic opportunities offered European immigrants. Moreover, the Asian exclusionists made difficult the natural reproduction of Asian people in America during the late 1800s and for too much of the 1900s. Yet they also helped encourage people of Asian descent to form ethnic enclaves on the American mainland and to build economically, socially, and culturally durable communities.

There is little point in presenting these communities as little heavens on earth. They were the creations of people made relatively powerless in American society. Unlike other often exploited and oppressed European immigrants, Asian immigrants were substantially denied the possibility of citizenship for generations because of the Naturalization Act of 1790. They were, moreover, caught in a crossfire of racial chauvinism and class conflict. Yet they were far from just victims. They sought to transplant their cultural and social practices and institutions to America as best they could and adapt these practices and institutions as necessary to the changing, largely hostile environment. In the relative isolation of various ethnic enclaves, they could live, work, and do business with one another. They could also fulfill their own recreational needs.

In the small Chinatowns of the San Joaquin Delta area, Peter C. Y. Leung writes, Chinese farm laborers attained recreation from Chinese support systems. They patronized movie theaters, tea houses, brothels, and opium dens. Much, then, of the Chinatown recreational activities, shortsightedly viewed by outsiders as peculiarly vice ridden, depended heavily upon the demographic and class composition of the American West Coast Chinese population, which consisted largely of men engaged in hard work as laborers or, in some cases, petty proprietors; performing generally poorly paid work that consumed much of their time and taxed much of their energy. Thus the leisure revolution that transformed the culture of many

Euroamericans after the Civil War possessed relatively little meaning to thousands of early Chinese immigrants (Leung: 1988).

These Chinese ethnic enclaves were not, however, impregnable from external cultural forces. In the late nineteenth century, various Chinese immigrants engaged in some of the more popular sporting pastimes of American culture such as baseball, prize fighting, pedestrianism, and bicycling. Euroamerican sports promoters seemingly exploited Chinese immigrants, participating in a sport otherwise dominated by white males, as a novelty to amuse chauvinistic spectators. At the same time, it does a disservice to these people to think of them as gullible victims of their own quest to escape racial, economic, social, and cultural separation from the white dominated mainstream. Perhaps, for various reasons, they enjoyed performing in the sports favored by the dominant culture; that by mastering a game, however trivial, unnecessarily competitive, and even brutal, Chinese immigrants could provide for themselves a liberating self-esteem denied them by Euroamerican society.

What, then, are we to make of this patronizing 1887 San Francisco *Chronicle* description of a baseball game in San Francisco's Chinese community?

Any Sunday afternoon on Stockton street one may see a team of rising Mongolians wrestling with the technicalities of the Great American game, while different pawnbrokers, pork butchers, and influential high binders and their wives beam down approvingly from the rickety balconies.

Certainly, the writer of this description wanted to assure the *Chronicle's* readers that the "rising Mongolians" lacked skill in "the Great American game." In so doing, the reporter articulated a seemingly common theme of incompetent Chinese ludicrously participating in post-Civil War American sports. In 1884, a national sports weekly, the *Sporting Life,* stated that "a California man is trying to teach a lot of Chinamen how to play baseball with a view to organizing a Chinese baseball team." But there was slight cause for concern, because "he has met with little success thus far and will meet with less in the future."

The next year, however, some baseball fans in the San Francisco Bay Area were intrigued by culturally diverse participants playing a game in Alameda. The Alvarado Club of Alameda took the field against a nine consisting, according to the San Francisco *Chronicle,* of "Spaniards, Portuguese, Dutch, Americans, and Chinese." The sight of a so-called "Celestial" playing the national game especially amused the crowd. Such supreme confidence in Chinese ineptitude in baseball was, in part, a product of a popular racial ideology, which burdened people of color, regardless of sex, as lacking in "manliness"—the very thing which presumably created good, freedom-loving, hard working, and mature Americans, as well as fine athletes. Engrained in the ambiguous ideology of American republicanism was a producer's ethic, which argued that the manly, free-labor pursuits of the artisan, mechanic, and farmer had built America in the face of powerful opposition. This antagonistic force consisted of large-scale capitalists, financiers, absentee landlords, and Southern plantation owners who did no useful work on their own and counted upon the unmanly, dependent, servile labor of Black slaves and Chinese coolies to supplant the dignified work of white labor.

Historians such as Warren Goldstein and Elliot Gorn have directed attention to the role of manliness in nineteenth century American sports (Goldstein: 1989; Gorn: 1986). The effort to assign manliness to the world of play was important as a way of distinguishing the mature, skilled, and courageous application of athletic talents from the childlike antics of children, ruffians, and, by extension, people of color, women, and a good number of even European immigrants.

The spectacle of Chinese young men placed in a position of displaying their skills in "the manly art" of late nineteenth century prize fighting might easily arouse ridicule from those who had constructed a preconceived racial, ethnic, gender, and class composite of the proper pugilist. At a San Francisco sporting club called the Wigwam, "the Chinese champion sloggers of the world" were matched against one another in the mid-1880s. In publicizing the event, the San Francisco correspondent to the *Sporting Life* stated that this fight for "the Chinese heavy weight championship" might, in fact, claim some respect from the white sporting public, because the Chinese, unlike many Euroamerican boxers, "haven't learned to hippodrome"; that is, cheat. Two local black boxers, June Dennis and Jim Hall, seconded for Jim Bung and Ah Fat respectively. If these Chinese boxers wanted to show whites their skill and courage, they sadly misunderstood their audience. The

San Francisco *Examiner* summarized the evening's entertainment: "The dark-hued did the talking, whites the laughing, and the copper colored the fighting."

In addition to prize fighting and baseball, Chinese immigrants performed in a pedestrian contest in San Francisco in 1880. Pedestrianism was a colorful and, for awhile, popular urban sport, which could be described as marathon race walking. In the city which had become a mecca for the American anti-Chinese movement, centered on the West Coast, the contest's promoters publicized the fact that two unnamed Chinese racers were among the contestants. Anonymous novelties to the white sporting public, these Chinese athletes prematurely dropped out of the race, leaving white assumptions about the racers' lack of "manliness" generally intact.

Chinese athletes might not always face white exclusion. In the midst of the bicycling craze in Southern California and throughout America during the 1890s, Los Angeles's Fowler Bicycle Racing had a Chinese member named Ah Sam. According to the Los Angeles *Evening Express,* Ah Sam was an ace racer, endeavoring to head north to challenge the Bay Area's champion Chinese rider from Oakland.

Barely perceptible signs of emerging Chinese assimilation in mainland America are somewhat balanced by more traditional cultural practices expressed in Chinese immigrant communities. The powerful nineteenth century anti-Chinese movement on the mainland encouraged not only the formation of Chinese ethnic enclaves, but would set in motion forces that, by and large, effectively guaranteed that Chinese communities would remain largely "bachelor societies" until World War II.

Meanwhile, the sporting practices of first generation Chinese immigrants expressed their cultural roots just as much as their ability to adapt to new surroundings. In the 1880s the San Francisco *Chronicle* depicted a scene in which a group of Chinese men appropriated a block of San Francisco's Powell Street to play a game likened by the reporter to shuttlecock. The participants used their hands and feet to keep a corked object in the air. The object could hit the ground but once. If it fell to the ground again, the player who failed to strike it was declared out.

Yet another way in which Chinese immigrants demonstrated their physical prowess suggests the complex interaction of traditional and emergent cultural practices, ritual, and commercialized amusement. In California's Monterey County, nineteenth century Chinese immigrants established important fishing and farming communities. At Point Alones, along what is now the famed seventeen mile drive, a Chinese village became a tourist attraction in the 1890s for those staying at the nearby Del Monte Hotel. One of the truly luxurious resort hotels on the West Coast, the Del Monte Hotel, in the words of Sandy Lydon, "bussed . . . the rich, famous, and (sometimes) educated visitors from the East Coast" to Point Alones where they "found the Chinese villagers to be curiosities, like the twisted cypress trees and the crashing waves" (Lydon: 1985, 167).

Among the attractions offered by the Point Alones Chinese was the ring game. The ring game practiced in Monterey county and other parts of California was probably related to a Southern Chinese religious ritual involving T'u Ti, a god of Wealth. A giant firecracker exploded a ring of woven bamboo into the air, inciting the participants to struggle for the ring as it reached the ground. The victor displayed skill, strength, and great good fortune, while "receivi(ng) the smile of T'u Ti" (Lydon: 1985, 323).

The Point Alones ring game was held yearly in the late 1890s and early 1900s. Large crowds of whites joined Chinese spectators and participants to watch the event occurring at the end of an annual celebration occurring on the second day of the second lunar month. Chinese immigrants from throughout Monterey County came and organized ring game teams representing various Chinese communities in the region. According to Sandy Lydon, "the man successful in wrestling the ring away from his competition brought luck to himself and honor to his teammates" (Lydon: 1985, 323).

Chinese immigrants on the mainland did develop a second generation in the years before World War II, but often through encouraging the illegal immigration of Chinese females and youths and even then the second generation remained relatively small in number. According to classical literature on American immigration, the low population of second generation immigrants might retard the assimilation process for a particular group. Assimilation in this literature, Eva Morawska writes, is "the progressive weakening and ultimate disappearance of the primordial traits and bonds of ethnicity as succeeding generations adopt the general society's unitary system of cultural values and become absorbed into economic, social, and political networks that are blind to ethnicity" (Morawska: 1989, 189). Thus, in a linear fashion the second generation of pre-World War II Chinese Americans would move from the ring game to baseball and other popular American sports; from cultural practices based on ethnic identity and solidarity to cultural practices more oriented toward individualistic talent and attainment combined, when it came to team sports, with the willingness to submit to some kind of loose, transient group ethos. The problem, as Morawska points out, is that the assimilation process has existed, but the ethnic experience in America has proven far too complex to comprehend in the terms advanced by classical immigration literature. What we find, she argues, is the resiliency of ethnicity and "old world traditions" among immigrants and their descendants interweaving with cultural patterns more in turn with the host society's dominant culture (Morawska: 1990).

Helping to shape both ethnic resiliency and assimilation among Chinese and other Asian Americans is the continued force of institutional racism in twentieth century America. As Sucheng Chan argues, "assimilation does not depend solely on the predilections of the newcomers. It can occur only when members of the host society give immigrants a chance to become equal partners in the world they share and mutually shape" (Chan: 1991, xiv).

The perplexing nature of the assimilation process for Asian immigrants significantly influenced their sporting and recreational practices. Such was the case for

Chinese and other immigrant Asians coming to the mainland late in the nineteenth and early twentieth centuries. Unlike European immigrants who could, in part, empower themselves by substantially shaping the development of an American popular culture, Asian immigrants were very likely too few in number outside of the Pacific Coast, too isolated in their ethnic enclaves, and too well excluded by institutional racism to advance impressively as participants or entrepreneurs in American popular culture. At the same time, Chinese immigrants and their children did not necessarily turn their backs on American sports in the early 1900s. They did participate in such pastimes as boxing, football, basketball, baseball, and other sports.

After the turn-of-the century, a Chinese boxer named Ah Wing gained a measure of prominence and respect from the fickle, frequently bigoted sporting press. A porter living in Sacramento, Ah Wing was described by the San Francisco *Chronicle* as America's only Chinese professional fighter. He was "not only a clever boxer and hard hitter." Drawing upon the stereotype of Asian men as unmanly, the *Chronicle* added that Ah Wing was "possessed of rare gameness, a quality which his race is not generally supposed to exhibit." Apparently, Ah Wing exhibited some effectiveness in the boxing ring. After a 1905 bout in San Francisco, the *Chronicle* exclaimed, "All hail! Ah Wing! . . . He last night sent Manuel Torres to the land of nod, scoring one of the cleanest knockouts ever seen in a San Francisco ring." Nearly twenty years later, Sacramento dispatched another Chinese boxer to even greater fame. George Lee

was a bantamweight, who started professionally in his hometown in 1919. By the early 1920s, his bouts were main attractions in the East and the South. He had even fought, but lost, a championship fight in New Orleans in 1920.

As a second generation surfaced among Chinese on the United States' mainland, so did community athletic teams. In 1919, the Kai Kee Football team out of the San Francisco Bay Area was on the lookout for opponents averaging 145 pounds or less. Coached by Son Kai Kee, who played football at University of California, Berkeley, and starring Earl Owyoung, a Yale graduate, team members usually had jobs which kept them from regularly practicing and finding opponents. But, according to the San Francisco *Chronicle,* they were hopeful of playing an eleven from the Deaf and Dumb school of Berkeley, as well as a Japanese squad of University of California, Berkeley, students.

Individuals of Chinese descent not only performed on integrated elevens, but, in some cases, impressed contemporaries. Son Kai Kee was no star, but he played for a major college football team on the West Coast during the early part of the twentieth century. According to San Francisco *Chronicle* sportswriter, Ed Hughes, Son Kai Kee was motivated to try out for the Cal football team in the fall of 1918 upon hearing of a "Chinese boy" earning an Army commission. Hughes wrote that "Ki-Kee, a Chinese, is trying for an end position. He is rather light, but he is fast and game and he will be given every chance to show what he can do." During the 1920s, a mainland professional team signed a Hawaiian of Chinese descent. Walter Achiu was a drop kicker for the

Dayton Triangles in the youthful National Football League. Achiu apparently described his nationality as "Hawaiian/American/Caucasian" to keep racists at bay.

Reform-minded institutions such as the YMCA and the CYO (Catholic Youth Organization) utilized basketball extensively as an organizing, as well as an Americanizing, tool among urban youth during the early decades of the twentieth century. In San Francisco's Chinatown during the 1920s, the YMCA encouraged athletic competition among its membership. It organized team sports in track and field and soccer, as well as in basketball. Generally, such teams competed against other Asian squads within and outside of San Francisco's Chinatown. All Chinese fives remained recreational fixtures for years among females and males wherever there were major Chinese communities such as the one in San Francisco. To a great extent, the durability of these squads, as well as the durability of other All Asian teams, represented the strength of Asian ethnic enclaves during a time when presumably the assimilation process was integrating people of Asian descent into the mainstream of American life.

In 1918, according to the San Francisco *Chronicle,* the Chinese Athletic Club of San Francisco assembled a baseball team. And in 1919, the San Jose *Mercury* reported on a game between a semi-professional team from San Jose and a nine consisting of Chinese attending the University of California, Berkeley. Called the "Sing Fats," the club was headed by Son Kai Kee. A large crowd watched the game at San Jose's Sodality Park. What they saw was an experienced semi-pro nine crush

the U.C. Berkeley students, 11–0, prompting the *Mercury* to comment that "the Chinese made a poor showing."

Hawaiian Chinese made a bigger impression on mainland baseball people. In December, 1914, the Portland Beavers of the Pacific Coast League signed Lang Akena, who was half-native Hawaiian and half-Chinese. However, Portland's owner, Walter McCreadie, bowed to the threat of player boycott and released Akena. Also in December, 1914, the major league Chicago White Sox reportedly signed Isi Tim, who, according to the San Francisco *Examiner,* was a Hawaiian of full-blooded Chinese ancestry. Nevertheless, when the White Sox opened their training camp for the 1915 season, Tim was not on the roster.

Tennis invited the ardent participation of some Chinese Americans on the mainland. Reflecting the belief that tennis was the possession of middle to upper class Euroamericans, a San Francisco *Examiner* reporter expressed amazement in 1935 that "now we have a Chinese tennis player coming to the fore." This "Chinese tennis player" was Henrietta Yung, an eleven-year-old who was advertised as the "main attraction at a series of exhibitions for the Chinese community" in San Francisco.

In the 1940s, one Chinese American teenager reached amateur greatness in both basketball and tennis. Helen Wong starred on both her church and high school basketball teams in San Francisco. Indeed, she was eventually named to San Francisco High School Sports Hall of Fame, because of her basketball prowess. At the same time, she was also one of the leading junior tennis players in the state.

In order, then, to get a fuller sense of the experiences of Asian American groups in the United States, it is useful to look at their relationship to dominant aspects of American popular culture such as sports. It is important to dismiss simplistic arguments such as the following: (1) second generation Chinese Americans regarding sports like basketball, baseball, football, boxing, and tennis with greater favor suggests the inherent democratic, egalitarian, and American traits of these activities; (2) these people "sold out" their heritage for acceptance among whites. Rather, it is necessary to find, even in the prize fighting ring, a struggle for self esteem and a denial of stereotypes which reduce Chinese and other Asian Americans to cultural practices excluding athletic competence or even interest. It isn't necessary to find glory or role models in a people's participation in sports as long as we find humanity in all of its diversity and complexity.

References

Sucheng Chan, *Asian Americans: An Interpretive History*, Boston: Twayne Publishers, 1990.

Warren Goldstein, *Playing for Keeps: A History of Early Baseball*. Ithaca, NY: Cornell University Press, 1989.

Elliot J. Gorn, *The Manly Art: Bare-Knuckle Prize Fighting in America*, Ithaca, NY: Cornell University Press, 1988.

Peter C. Y. Leung, "Chinese Farming Activities in the Sacramento-San Joaquin Delta, 1910–1941," *Amerasia Journal*, XIV, (no. 2: 1988).

Sandy Lydon, *Chinese Gold: The Chinese in the Monterey Bay Area*, Capitola Calif.: Capitola Book Company, 1985.

Eva Morawska, "The Sociology and Historiography of Immigration," in *Immigration Reconsidered: History, Sociology, and Politics*, edited by Virginia Yans-McLaughlin, New York: Oxford University Press, 1990.

Juan L. Gonzales Jr.

Asian Indian Immigration Patterns: The Origins of the Sikh Community in California

Those who arrive in California from Asia vary in many ways. In that respect thoughtful observers may contend that it is misleading to overuse labels such as "Asian-American." This truism also applies to subgroups from a single nation such as China or India. In the article that follows Juan L. Gonzales Jr. reviews the peculiar circumstances of Sikh immigrants from India as they adjusted to life in early 1900s California. The impact of California's Alien land laws, and other discriminatory practices helped to draw the newly arriving Sikhs into tight knit groups who pooled their resources to acquire agricultural cooperatives. Such economic cooperation often still characterizes California's ethnic newcomers from Asia. But Sikhs did not hesitate to mingle with other Californians. In one of the most important themes Gonzales reports, he reviews the interactions between these immigrants from India and those who were also arriving in California from Mexico. Rarely noted by most of this state's Whites these patterns within groups of people of color began to forge interesting new dynamics that hint at what might also be happening in today's California.

Yet the Sikhs' patterns in other areas have been indicative of how other ethnic group members adapt to difficult circumstances. Denied U.S. citizenship in the 1940s by Federal Court decisions, Sikhs in California's Central Valley created a crusading ethnic-based newspaper that championed their causes as well as shared useful community information. While today's California residents are as likely to get their knowledge about news from the internet, one can find a profusion of new ethnic-orientated weekly newspapers that cater to specific groups. Decades from now scholars might plow through those media to discover what was happening here. Gonzales' article should help readers to better understand today's California by looking back at yesteryear's Sikh experience. (SMM)

This article outlines the immigration and settlement patterns of Asian Indians in the United States from the turn of the century to the present decade. The focus is on the efforts of the Sikh pioneers to succeed in what can only be viewed as a hostile social environment, marked primarily by racial discrimination and legal restrictions on their entry into this country. With modifications in the U.S. immigration laws of 1965 an educated professional class of Asian Indians have monopolized the flow of immigrants from India, with the result that the Sikhs presently constitute a small proportion of the total number of Asian Indians in the U.S. However, the recent political crisis in India has served to galvanize the American Sikh community into political action. This has resulted in a political split between the Sikhs and other Asian Indians in this country. This article concludes with an analysis of the demographic composition of the "third wave" Asian Indian immigrants in the United States and their potential impact on political conditions in India.

The Asian Indians that are the focus of this article are a distinct ethnic group, not only in this country, but in their own country, as they are distinguished by their religious beliefs and practices, their language, their physical characteristics, their customs and culture, and their historical experiences.

While the Sikhs are a small minority group in their own country, as they comprise two percent of the population of India, they nonetheless represented from 85 to 90 percent of the original Asian Indian immigrants, to the U.S. at the turn of the century (Jacoby, 1957:7; Millis, 1911:75). Today the Sikhs constitute from 30 to 40 percent of the Asian Indian population of. California (Jensen, 1980:269). According to the 1980 census the Asian Indian population in the United States is estimated at 361,544. But the majority of Sikhs are found in California, living in both rural and urban locations. However they only represent a small proportion of the total number of Asian Indians living in the Untied States today, as the majority are "Hindus", who constitute approximately 93 percent of the population of India. Of the remaining Indian population, five percent are Muslims, and two percent are Sikhs (Jacoby, 1956:13; Jensen, 1980:296).

The Sikhs that settled in California during the first decade of the twentieth century came from Northwestern India, from the state of Punjab.[1] The Punjab is the original homeland of the Sikhs and is known for its unique geographical, topographical, and climatic conditions. Curiously one of the main attractions of Northern California for the original Sikh settlers was the similarity in weather and geographical conditions found in California and their native Punjab. They also discovered that many of the agricultural products that they were familiar with were also produced in California, which

From *International Migration Review*, Vol. 20, No. 1, Spring 1986 by Juan L. Gonzales, Jr.. Copyright © 1986 by Center for Migration Studies of New York, Inc. Reprinted by permission.

in part accounts for their success in the agricultural industry.[2]

While India is looked upon as a great melting pot of races, religions, and cultures, the Sikhs are nonetheless distinctive in a number of important ways. For example, they are physically different from other Indians in that they are larger in body build and taller than most of their countrymen. In addition they do have a striking personal appearance in that they have traditionally worn beards and turbans. Their religion requires that they observe the "Five K's," which stipulate that they wear their hair and beard unshorn (Kesh), that they carry a comb (Kanga), that they wear a pair of shorts (Kuchha), that they wear a steel braclet on their wrist, and that they always carry a sabre (Kirpan) (Singh, 1964:10). The reason for these religious requirements is that the Guru Gobind Singh, ". . . intended to emphasize the ideal of ascetic saintliness and to raise an army of soldier-saints" (Singh, 1964:10).

Sikhism dates back to the fifteenth century, as its founder Guru Nanek was born in 1469 near Lahore (Wenzel, 1968:247). Guru Nanek's teachings held that there is one God, that this world is an illusion, that all ritual is a distraction, and that idolatry, pilgrimages, and asceticism are to be avoided. However the most distinctive features of Sikh theology are borrowed from Hinduism or Islam. As the Sikh Holy Book, the *Granth Sahib*, ". . . consists of the writings not only of the Sikh Gurus but also of Hindu and Muslim saints of all castes and creeds" (Singh, 1964:xiii).

Sikh Immigration and Settlement in California

Since the 1820s citizens from India were arriving in the United States, but only in small numbers. These immigrants were mainly students sailors, and diplomats (Jacoby, 1979:160). However, between 1902 and 1906 over 800 Asian Indians arrived in the United States.

As was true in Canada, these immigrants were primarily unskilled and uneducated agriculturalists from the rural areas of the Punjab, who arrived as single males or as married men without their wives and children. Similarly they were attracted to the United States as a result of the employment opportunities, the high wages, the investment opportunities, and the possibility of purchasing or leasing agricultural land (Das, 1923:15; Millis, 1911:74).

While more and more Asian Indians were migrating from Canada into California, others arrived directly from India, as word reached the homeland that conditions were harsh in Canada, and that racial hostility was to be expected (Das, 1923:8-9; Hess, 1974:578-579; Millis, 1911:72-73). Consequently the greatest flow of Asian Indians into this country occurred between 1907 and 1911 (*See*, Table 1), with most settling in California (2,742 out of a total of 5,786 in the United States in 1910) (Das, 1923:17). The first Asian Indians arrived in the Sacramento Valley in 1907, and worked in the fruit growing sections of Folsom, Orangeville, Loomis, and Newcastle. Others found the rice growing districts around Marysville and Yuba City most attractive (Das, 1923:19).

Table 1

ASIAN INDIAN IMMIGRATION TO THE UNITED STATES: 1900-1914

Year	Number	Year	Number
1900	9	1908	1,710
1901	20	1909	337
1902	84	1910	1,782
1903	83	1911	517
1904	258	1912	165
1905	145	1913	188
1906	271	1914	172
1907	1,072	1915	82

Source: U.S. Census, 1975:107-108

Initially they hired themselves out as itinerant agricultural laborers, but they quickly formed labor gangs. Like the Japanese immigrants, they selected one of their members, usually the one who demonstrated the greatest command of English, as their leader and representative. They also formed communal living and dining arrangements, which resulted in the development of organized ethnic labor gangs (Das, 1923:29–31, 66–67).

Before long they organized agricultural and economic cooperatives, which allowed them to pool their economic resources for long-term capital investments. Initially their farm holdings were modest, with approximately 40 acres or so typically found in the fruit growing sections of the Sacramento Valley, and an average of 500 to 1000 acres in the rice growing districts (Das, 1923:23–24). Generally all agricultural property and equipment were held in common ownership by five to ten Sikhs, as they worked their farms in common and shared the profits, which they quickly reinvested in more agricultural property and equipment.[3]

Racism and Immigration Restrictions in California

Once they settled in the Sacramento Valley the Sikhs were pleased with the agricultural work available in the area and with the mild climate. Unfortunately, it was not long before the "nativists" in California expressed their feelings and agitated against the further immigration of the "Hindoos."[4]

As was true with the Chinese and Japanese immigrants before them, the Sikhs were also subjected to hostile racial feelings and acts of violence. Once again four groups were at the forefront of the organized efforts to terminate Asian immigration into this country at the turn of the century. The most boisterous of these racist groups was the old revived "Asiatic Exclusion League," who effectively turned public opinion against further immigration from Asia (Hess, 1974:580–582).

Another pressure group that served to promote racial agitation and racist ideologies were the newspapers and magazines of the day, who popularized such phrases as the "Hindu Invasion" and "The Tide of Turbans".[5] For example, *Collier's* alarmed the public with the headline that there were over "10,000 Hindus" living in California in 1910 (Anonymous, 1910:15). In fact, there were fewer than 6,000 Asian Indians living in the entire United States at the time (Das, 1923:17).

Ultimately the efforts of these white supremacists, and the racist propaganda that appeared in local newspapers, served to promote the idea that the Sikhs were "somewhat less than human." Consequently there was little, if any, doubt in the public mind that the Asian Indian could ever become a part of American society.

Perhaps the most important element in this racist conspiracy to prevent further immigration of Asian Indians into California were the local and state politicians. Given the level of public support and media accounts, it is not surprising that the politicians saw this as an opportunity to secure more votes for their election campaigns. Indeed some legislators were able to advance their careers dramatically by making racist statements and speeches against the further immigration of the Asian Indians (Hess, 1969:62–64; Hess, 1974:581–583).

Of particular importance in this analysis is the consideration of the interconnection between the negative public opinion that developed toward the Sikhs in California, the indefatigable efforts of organized groups to prevent further immigration, in particular the Asiatic Exclusion League, the profit motives of the newspapers and magazines, and the political ambitions of legislators that resulted in the passage of anti Asian laws at both the state and federal level.

In this respect the most important document passed in the California legislature was the Alien Land Law of 1913. While the provisions of this law were aimed at Japanese immigrants, it also had a drastic effect on the entrepreneurial ambitions of Asian Indians. This act prohibited aliens, who were not eligible for citizenship, from owning or leasing land in California (Hess, 1969).

The two most important laws passed at the federal level were the Immigration Act of 1917 and the 1923 Supreme Court decision in the "Thind Case". The 1917 Immigration Act created, the so-called "Pacific Barred Zone" which held that immigrants from certain parts of Asia, including India, Burma, Siam, and others, would no longer be allowed to immigrate to the United States (Hess, 1969).

However the most devastating blow was delivered by the U.S. Supreme Court in the "Thind Case" when it ruled that Asian Indians were not "free white persons" and therefore could not become American citizens (Scott, 1923; Singh, 1946; Ireland, 1966). Even more disastrous was the provision that all Asian

Indians naturalized prior to this decision had received their documents "fraudulently" and therefore were not really American citizens after all[6] (Hess, 1969:63-64).

Sikh Political Activities in America

The Sikhs, as a distinct cultural and religious group in their own country, have had a long tradition of active involvement in the political affairs of India (Brown 1948; Hess, 1974:585-588). During the early period of immigration to this country a small number of Asian Indian immigrants were university students. Eventually they became involved in political activities, and some would say the revolutionary activities, of the "Ghadar Party" (literally meaning "revolution" or "mutiny" party). Their objective was to gain the economic and political support of Asian Indian immigrants in the United States and promote the revolution against the British in India (Brown, 1948; Hess, 1974:585).

For this purpose they published a newspaper, the *Ghadar,* in several languages with the intent of promoting Indian nationalism and the revolution in India. The activities of the Ghadar Party caught this nation's attention during World War I when these activists urged the immigrant Sikhs in the United States to return to India and start an armed revolution. While some did heed the call for a revolution in India, and did in fact return to their homeland, most supported these revolutionary efforts by attending local meetings and by making direct contributions to the cause (Hess, 1974:585-587).

But of greater significance, these nationalistic interests, and the dissemination of jingoistic political propaganda, served to draw them closer together and resulted in an even stronger feeling of "consciousness of kind" and group identity. At the same time American citizens were very much aware of these nationalistic feelings and activities among the Sikhs and took, for the most part, the attitude of the British and American governments (Jacoby, 1979:167-169). Consequently the level of prejudice, and the incidents of discrimination against the Sikhs in this country, increased and resulted in even further social isolation.

Over the long term the combined effects of prejudice and discrimination in the social and political arena, at the local and national levels, tended to work to the disadvantage of the Sikhs in this country and became a significant obstacle in the path of their eventual acceptance and assimilation into American society. While these political events were taking place a noticeable level of resentment was developing against the Sikhs in California as a result of their economic success and their failure to serve as the new source of "cheap labor" for the captains of industry. Their general response was to draw away from the day-to-day activities of American society, and seek solace in their religion and adherence to their customs and traditions.

The Social Isolation of the Sikh Pioneers

Thus far we have reviewed the major structural and institutional factors that contributed to the social isolation and alienation of the Sikh pioneers. In this regard they were not allowed to become citizens; they were not allowed to purchase or lease property; they were not allowed to send for their wives or future brides in India; they were not allowed to travel out of this country; their participation in the labor force was severely limited to certain occupational categories; they were not allowed to marry Anglo women; and their participation in a nationalistic movement that originated in India and their devout allegiance to their religious beliefs and cultural traditions further alienated and isolated them from the core of American society. In brief the Sikhs were stigmatized as outsiders and as "undesirables" by the American public.

While it may well be an understatement, it is nonetheless true to point out that their potential, for participation in and eventual absorption into American society was made difficult, if not impossible, by all of these social and economic restrictions on their full participation in the benefits of American society. In retrospect it is a small wonder that they were able to survive their first forty years in this country.

To make matters even more difficult the Sikh pioneers were unable to produce a second generation of American citizens, who would naturally serve to move them, as a new ethnic minority, into the mainstream of American life. For it is well known that the second generation, of any immigrant group, will always serve as a bridge to connect the old culture with the new. Likewise it is always the third generation that adopts the customs and values of the new society and completes the process of acculturation.

Unfortunately the expectation that the Sikhs would gradually integrate themselves into the fabric of American society was not fulfilled. Of particular importance is the consideration that they might have entered the mainstsream of American life if only they could have produced a second generation of Asian Indian Americans. In this regard one researcher suggested the possibility of "circuitous assimilation" as a solution to this problem. According to this idea Dadabhay (1954) predicted that the Sikhs would eventually marry Mexican American women in sufficient numbers to insure their eventual assimilation into American society.

Unfortunately this curious idea of "secondary assimilation" did not come to fruition, as the number of exogamous marriages that did take place between Sikh men and Mexican American women was rather small, i.e., when compared to the overabundance of men to women in the Sikh pioneer population. By his own figures Dadabhay points out that the sex ratio among the Sikhs in California in 1940 was 460 males to 100 females (Dadabhay, 1954:140). The differences are even greater when we consider that this skewed sex ratio does not even take into consideration the fact that a good proportion of these females had not yet reached the age of nubility.[7]

An additional point that is frequently overlooked is the consideration that the second generation Sikh-Mexican American children, that were products of these relationships, were typically "lost" to the Sikh culture, as most adopted the traditions and customs of their Mexican American mothers. For all practical purposes these , children were lost to the Sikh community as potential harbingers of assimilation (LaBrack, 1979:134), In almost every case, "The children were typically given Hispanic first names, were baptized Catholics, and spoke both Spanish and English at home" (Leonard, 1982:73).

The Termination of Asian Indian Immigration: 1915-1944

In addition to all of the obstacles to assimilation and various legal barriers to immigration, was the consideration that between their original influx at the turn of the century and the end of World War II, the flow of immigrants from India was drastically reduced. For example, between 1915 and 1929 only 1,646 Asian Indians were admitted to this country, for a yearly average of 110 immigrants. The situation was even more critical during the depres-

sion and war years, when only 183 Asian Indians entered this country, far an average of 12 immigrants per year (See, Table 2 below).

To make matters even worse, approximately 2,000 Asian Indian immigrants were deported by the Immigration and Naturalization Service between 1900 and 1950, and an additional 4,750 returned to India "voluntarily" during this period (Jacoby, 1979:164). In effect, the numerically strapped Asian Indian population in the United States lost almost 7,000 members during this fifty year period. However, one authority has estimated that approximately 3,000 Sikhs entered this. country illegally, mostly via Mexico, between 1920 and 1930 (Jacoby, 1956:8).

The overall conclusion that can be drawn from the sociohistorical experiences

Table 2

ASIAN INDIAN IMMIGRATION TO THE UNITED STATES: 1900 TO 1981

Period	Years	Total Number	Cummulative Rate	Rate Per Year
The Sojourners	1900-1906	870	0	124
First Wave Immigrants	1907-1914	5,943	6,813	743
WW I and the Recession	1915-1929	1,646	8,459	110
The Depression & WW II	1930-1944	183	8,642	12
Second Wave Immigrants	1945-1965	6,371	15,013	303
Third Wave Immigrants	1966-1981	215,640	230,653	14,376

Source: 1981 Statistical Yearbook of the INS

of the Sikh pioneers is that while they were an economic success, they were unable to assimilate into American society, nor were they able to establish families and produce a second generation. But they were able to establish and maintain a strong cultural and religious tradition in American society during these long years of social isolation and rejection. And, as it turns out, it was these "cultural islands" that developed in the agricultural areas of California that formed the basis for a new Sikh society that began to flourish after World War II when Asian Indians were once again permitted to immigrate to this country.

The Second Wave of Sikh Immigrants 1945-1965

As previously demonstrated, the Asian Indians in the United States gradually experienced a decrease in their population. In 1930 the Asian Indian population in the United States numbered only 3,130 and by 1940 it dropped to 2,405. Of this number 60 percent lived in California in 1940, half were employed as farm laborers, 15 percent were farmers or farm managers, and 20 percent were involved in non-farm labor. Only four percent were classified as "professionals" (Hess, 1974:591).

More than one-third of the pioneers over 25 had never received any formal educational training, as their median level of education was less than four years (LaBrack, 1982:61). By 1940 more than half were over the age of 40, one-third were over 50, and almost one out of ten were over 60 (Hess, 1974:591). Clearly without the appropriate modifications occurring in their social circumstances and without the alterations in

U.S. immigration policies this small and declining population was certainly doomed to extinction.

Partly in response to the role that the Indian government played in assisting the United States in its efforts to defeat Japan during World War II, and the indefatigable efforts of prominent American citizens and concerned Asian Indians, did a change occur in the immigration, policies affecting all Asian Indians in this country (Hess, 1969:71-73).

Therefore as of July 1945, with the passage of the Luce-Celler Bill (Public Law 483), Asian Indians were freed from the "Barred-Zone" immigration restrictions, and were given a quota of 100 immigrants per year. As pointed out, Asian Indians were prohibited from entering this country in 1917 and were denied the right to become American citizens in 1923. However, this bill gave them an immigration quota and granted them naturalization rights. As a result of these modifications in our immigration policies, a total of 6,371 Asian Indian immigrants were admitted between 1945 and 1965 (Table 2). In retrospect the immigration ban of the "Pacific Barred Zone" had been in effect for 25 years, and almost succeeded in bringing about the demise of the Asian Indian community in this country.

Perhaps the second most important provision of the Luce-Celler bill was that it lifted the official ban on the naturalization of Asian Indians as American citizens. As a result a total of 1,772 Asian Indians became American citizens between 1948 and 1965 (Hess, 1974:593). Understandably the two decades following World war II was a period of rapid social change in the Asian Indian Community.

For the first time in almost 30 years, Asian Indians were allowed to send for their wives and children, and others were allowed to make marital arrangements with women from the Punjab. Consequently they were finally allowed to establish families and initiate the process of bringing the second generation of Asian Indians into being.

The Third Wave of Asian Indian Immigrants: 1966-1984

In contrast to the "second wave" Sikh immigrants, the "third wave" Asian Indian immigrants tend to be young, well-educated, and heavily concentrated in the professions. They are also more likely to have lived in the urbanized areas of India; and most arrive with the ability to speak, read, and write English.

For example, a study conducted by the Immigration and Naturalization Service in 1981 of all Asian Indians who became naturalized American citizens that year, reveals that half of them held professional or technical positions prior to their naturalization (Table 3). This high concentration in the professional and technical fields reflects the high proportion of well-educated and highly trained immigrants found among the "'third wave" Asian Indian population.[8]

Table 3

ASIAN INDIANS NATURALIZED U.S. CITIZENS IN 1981
BY MAJOR OCCUPATION GROUPS

Occupation Groups	Number of Immigrants	Percent of Immigrants
Professional, Technical, Kindred Workers	3,568	49.3
Managers and Administrators, except farm	469	6.5
Sales Workers	131	1.8
Clerical and Kindred Workers	458	6.3
Craftsmen and Kindred Workers	167	2.3
Operatives, except transport	243	3.4
Transport Operatives	23	0.3
Laborers, except farm	88	1.2
Farmers and Farm Managers	4	0.06
Farm Laborers and Farm Foremen	32	0.4
Service Workers, except private household	245	3.4
Private Household Workers	7	0.09
Housewives and others with no occupation reported	1,798	24.9
Total All Groups	7,233	100.0

Source: 1981 Statistical Yearbook of the INS

In real numbers this means that approximately half to two-thirds of the Asian Indian immigrants who have settled in this country over the past decade were professionals. For example, during the five year period between 1977 and 1981 a total of 98,748 Asian Indians entered this country, for an average of almost 20,000 immigrants per year. According to this data, and our estimate of the number of professionals in the Asian Indian immigrant population, this means that somewhere between 10,000 to 15,000 professionals arrive in this country per year from India.

From the broader perspective this high proportion of professionals in the "third wave" Asian Indian population reflects a characteristic that is common to most immigrants of color who have entered this country since the liberalization of the immigration laws in 1965. As is true in almost all developing nations of the world, India is experiencing a "brain drain" of its own.

Another noteworthy characteristic in the immigration pattern of "third wave" immigrants is their strong propensity to settle in the highly urbanized sections of this country, and their tendency to select certain states as their permanent residence. By far their greatest concentration has occurred in New York and California, as one-third of the Asian Indians in this country presently reside in these two states (Table 4). Similarly when we add the Asian Indian populations of Illinois and New Jersey to those who live in California and New York, we discover that these four states account for half of the Asian Indian population in this country. Also within these states they tend to, settle in the major metropolitan areas, for example in New York City, in the greater Los Angeles basin, and in the San Francisco Bay area (Saran, 1977:65)

Conclusion

While the vast majority of the original Asian Indian immigrants to this country were members of the Sikh religious-ethnic community, they only represent a small proportion of the total number of Asian Indian immigrants that have arrived and settled in the United States since 1965. However, as is true with all of the recent Asian Indian immigrants, the Sikh immigrants who arrived in this country in the past decade also have more education and tend to be heavily concentrated in the professions. But an important advantage for the recent Sikh immigrants, in addition to their higher levels of education, is that they have established strong social and cultural ties with the established members of the Sikh–American community, particularly in California.

What has occurred in the past decade is a pattern of integration of the old Sikh community with the members of the highly educated/professional Sikh immigrants of recent times. As a result the traditional strength of the Sikh pioneer community, and the professional/educated "third wave" immigrants have merged to produce a stronger Asian Indian community in California. The second and third generation Sikh Americans have nurtured a cohesive traditional community, while the more recent urban Sikh immigrants have brought to the Asian Indian community their education and their skills.

Table 4

GEOGRAPHIC DISTRIBUTION AND CONCENTRATION OF
ASIAN INDIANS IN THE UNITED STATES: 1980

State	Number	Percent
New York	60,511	16.7
California	57,989	16.0
Illinois	35,711	9.9
New Jersey	29,507	8.1
Texas	22,226	6.1
Pennsylvania	15,212	4.2
Michigan	14,680	4.1
Maryland	13,705	3.8
Ohio	13,105	3.6
Florida	9,138	2.5
Virginia	8,483	2.3
Massachusetts	8,387	2.3
Cummulative Total	288,654	79.8
Other Areas	72,890	20.2
Total U.S.	361,544	100.0

Source: U.S. Census 1980

The unity and cohesiveness of the Sikh community in California, in particular, has experienced a revivification during the past year as a direct result of the social and political instability that has plagued the Punjab, particularly following the assassination of Indira Gandhi. Obviously the political crisis in India has served, not only to galvanize and polarize the two parties involved in this political confrontation, but has also served to draw the two most important segments of the Sikh community in this country closer together.

Not surprisingly the political crisis in India has served to raise the political consciousness and increase the political involvment of the Sikhs in this country. As expressed in our previous discussion, active participation in national politics is endemic to the Sikh experience, but more important they are a religious people who will take advantage of both traditional and non-traditional political processes to achieve their goals. This observation is particularly germane since it is their religious beliefs and practices, and indeed their religious freedom that is threatened.

The question that must be answered in the short term is whether the Sikhs in India will be granted their religious freedom and given the opportunity to improve their social and economic conditions in the Punjab, or on the other hand, whether they will find it necessary to determine their own future in India and strive for political autonomy and national independence.

Notes

1. As we have indicated the majority of Asian Indians that migrated to the United States at the turn of the century were from the Punjab, 95 percent of whom were Sikhs, the people of India have had a very long history of overseas migration. As Kondapi points out in his book. *Indians Overseas,* that Ptolemy's geography written around 50 A.D. reports on the rapid growth of Indian migration from Burma and Malaya to Indonesia and Indo-China. (See C. Kondapi, *Indians Overseas,* New Delhi: Indian Council of World Affairs, 1951, page 1.)

2. The particular advantage of the Sikh immigrants was that they were familiar with the intensive agricultural techniques required for the successful production of many of the crops that were indigenous to both the Punjab and California at the time.

3. In his study of the international migration of Sikhs overseas Chan draws the conclusion that, "When Sikh immigrants arrived in predominately 'white' countries, they were seen as representatives of 'inferior races.' As such, they found acceptance only if they were willing to 'stay' in their place" (Chan, 1979:194).

4. This was a popular bastardization of the term "Hindu" that was commonly used as a derogatory term for the Asian Indian immigrants in this country at the turn of the century. As a matter of practice the term "Hindoo" was applied to all Asian Indians in the United States at the time in spite of the fact that 95 percent of the Asian Indian immigrants in this country at the turn of the century were Sikhs and not Hindus.

5. Examples of some of these popular magazine articles of the day are as follows: "Hindu Immigrants in America," *Missionary Review,* December 1907; "Hindu in the Northwest," *World Today,* November 1907; "Hindu Invasion," *Colliers,* March 1910; "Tide of Turbans", *Forum,* June 1910; *The Independent,* October 1922; "The Hindu Invasion," *The Pacific Monthly,* May 1907; "Hindu: The Newest Immigration Problem," *Survey,* October 1910.

6. It has been reported that during the first three years following the "Thind Decision" that the federal government sought and secured the cancellation of some fifty documents of citizenship from Asian Indians as a result of this case (Hess, 1974:589).

7. Further proof of the speciousness of the "circuitous argument" is obtained from the results of a study conducted by Karen Leonard who found that prior to 1924 only 73 marriages were legalized by the Sikh pioneers, and of

this number 79.9 percent were consummated with Mexican American women (Leonard, 1982:71). She also found that between 1924 and 1947 only 180 marriages were recorded among the Sikhs in California, and of these 86.7 percent were consummated with Mexican American women. Given this historical analysis of the data we must conclude that the number of marriages contracted by the Sikh pioneers were rather insignificant when compared to the total proportion of single males among the immigrant Sikhs.

8. We should note that when housewives and those who did not report an occupation are subtracted from this list, approximately two out of three of these new citizens (65.6%) report professional occupations (See Table 3).

References

Anonymous 1910 "Hindu Invasion." *Collier's* Vol. 45. March.

Brown, G.T. (1948). "The Hindu Conspiracy, 1914-1917," *Pacific Historical Review,* 42(3):299-310. August.

Chan, S. (1979). "Overseas Sikhs in the Context of International Migrations." In *Sikh Studies: Comparative Perspectives an Changing Tradition.* Edited by Mark Juergensmeyer and N. Gerald Barrier. Berkeley, CA: Graduate Theological Union, Lancaster-Miller Publishers. Pp. 191-206.

Dadabhay, Y. (1954). "Circuitous Assimilation Among Rural Hindustanis in California," *Social Forces,* 33(2):138-141.

Das, R. (1923) *Hindustani Workers as the Pacific Coast.* Berlin and Leipzig: Walter De Gruyter & Co.

Hess, G.R. 1974 "The Forgotten Asian Americans; The East Indian Community in the United States," *Pracific Historical Review,* 43(4): 576-596. Nov.

____. (1969). "The 'Hindu' in America: Immigration and Naturalization Policies and India," *Pacific Historical Review,* 38:59-79.

Jacoby, H. S. (1979). "Some Demographic and Social Aspects of Early East Indian Life in the United State," In *Sikh Studies:* Edited by Mark Juergensmeyer and N. Gerald Barrier. Berkeley, CA: Graduate Theological Union, Lancaster-Miller Publishers, Pp. 159-171.

____. (1956). "A, Half Century Appraisal of East Indians in the United States." Sixth Annual College of the Pacific Faculty Research Lecture, University of the Pacific, Stockton, CA.

Jensen, J. M. (1980). "East Indians," *Harvard Encyclopedia of American Ethnic Groups.* Edited by Stephan Thernstrom. Cambridge, MA: Harvard University Press. Pp. 296-301.

LaBrack, B. (1982). "Immigration Law and the Revitalization Process: The Case of the California Sikh," In *From India, to America,* Edited by Sripati Chandrasekhar. La Jolla, CA: Population Review Publications. Pp. 59-66.

____. (1979). "Sikhs Real and Ideal: A Discussion of Text and Context in the Description of Overseas Sikh

Communities," In *Sikh Studies,* Edited by Mark Juergensmeyer and N. Gerald Barrier, Berkeley, CA: Graduate Theological Union, Lancaster-Miller Publishers. Pp. 127–142.

Leonard, K. (1982). "Marriage and Family Life Among Early Asian Indian Immigrants." In *From India to America.* Edited by Sripati Chandrasekhar. La Jolla, CA: Population Review Publications. Pp. 67–75.

Millis, H.A. (1911). "East Indian Immigration to British Columbia and the Pacific Coast States," *American Economic Review,* 1:72–76. March.

Sara, P. (1977). "Cosmopolitans from India," *Society,* 14(6):65–69.

Singh, K. (1964). *The Sikhs Today.* Bombay: Orient Longmans.

Wenzel, L.A. (1968). "The Rural Punjabis of California: A Religio-Ethnic Group," *Phylon,* 29(3):245–256. Feb.

Paul R. Spickard

Work and Hope: African American Women in Southern California during World War II

The entrance of the United States into World War II gave many people new hope for prosperity. Shipyards, steel plants, aircraft factories, and other war-related industries offered jobs with high pay. Being confronted by racism African American migrants crossed New Mexico, Texas, and Arizona by car or train and came in large numbers to California. African American women, especially, had high expectations of the job market. However, most found themselves still employed in domestic work places with moderate pay instead of high paying war industry jobs after their arrival. By 1942, pressured by labor shortages and the federal government, California's industrialists began to employ African Americans. As World War II progressed, 85 percent of African American women were working in the industrial sector of Los Angeles, but White discrimination and racism in management and unions still kept African Americans out of the aircraft, steel, and shipbuilding industries. Severe labor shortages in the war industries coupled with political pressures from Black women finally began to open positions for Black men and women, first in the aircraft industry and then in other war-related industries. Because they were paid less than White males for doing the same job, Black women found it easier to secure employment in industrial jobs than did Black men. They were not seen as competitors for these jobs since they were expected to leave their positions after the war to stay home. Dealing with sexism and racism, these women usually worked in segregated work teams and under the supervision of White foremen. As World War II came to an end, Black women lost their good paying jobs, but not for long. Since the Depression did not return, many were ultimately re-hired.

Very critically, California's African American women developed a different outlook on life during the war years. Leaving their domestic work places and moving up into white-collar occupations and industrial jobs, many women gained self-esteem and achieved economic independence. By the end of the 1940s militant activism often fueled by Black women was growing in California's ghettoes.

In housing, African Americans still faced discrimination. They were barred from owning or renting in predominantly White neighborhoods. Public housing for African Americans was practically non-existent. Nonetheless, one third of African Americans in Los Angeles became homeowners. Yet housing segregation, discrimination, and transportation problems remained troublesome. Many women spent hours each day to get to their workplaces. This took precious time away from their families and other responsibilities in the community. With the men away at war, African American women were left with raising their children, supporting their family, and handling "all problems" associated with urban life. Black women did find hope during the war years despite these double duties. (U)

Southern California during World War II was a magnet for hundreds of thousands of people from all over the United States. Drawn by the explosive growth of war industries, migrants from every region, of every class and color, made their way to greater Los Angeles. Among them were more than 100,000 African Americans. More than half of those were women. They transformed the Southern California African American community. They came seeking opportunity; they found hard work and, for a time, they found hope.

Before World War II, African American women and their families lived in an old black neighborhood just southeast of downtown Los Angeles near the corner of Central and Pico within earshot of the tracks of the Southern Pacific Railway. Many of the early African American men worked as porters or laborers on this line. Their wives and children stayed in Los Angeles while the men worked lines all over the Southwest. Around them grew a modest-sized community of tens of thousands of African Americans in the 1920s and 1930s. They were surrounded by a welter of other people: Russians and other European immigrants in Boyle Heights to the east, Mexicans in East Los Angeles a little farther east, Japanese in Little Tokyo to the north, Chinatown just beyond that. There were small clusters of African Americans in other parts of Southern California—in San Diego, Calexico, Long Beach, Pasadena, and elsewhere—but the Los Angeles black community was the largest, and the hub around which the others turned.

By 1940, the Los Angeles African American community had reached 60,000 in number and stretched in all directions from this central zone south along Central Avenue, the main thoroughfare of black culture in the West. It was quite a wonderful place, as any old-time resident is eager to recount. As one drove slowly down Central Avenue in 1941, the decaying southern fringes of downtown were left behind for a black city teeming with street life. The Avenue's many stores, humble and grand, all boasted shoppers. And families with small children as well as the unemployed—the fruit of the Depression—"hung out" and were shooting dice. There were moviegoers at the Lincoln Theater, earnest black dentists, and secretaries from the offices of Golden State Mutual Insurance. And there were also prostitutes and drug pushers, Garveyites and disciples of Father Divine, as well as newcomers, just walking the streets and gawking.

At the corner of 41st Street, about a mile and a half south of Pico, stood the Dunbar Hotel, the jewel of Central Avenue. Built in 1928 as the Somerville, this luxury hotel was where notable African Americans came to stay. Mary White Ovington, W. E. B. DuBois, and Jack Johnson stayed at the Dunbar. Billie Holiday, Lionel Hampton, and Bessie Smith stayed there, too, and played in the Big Apple, the Club Alabam, and the Savoy nearby. Hollywood actresses Louise Beavers and Ethel Waters came down from their swank homes on Sugar Hill to see and be seen. Central Avenue was also the center of West Coast jazz. It was the most exciting street west of Chicago.

Central Avenue was part of the glamour that African Americans in the South associated with Los Angeles, part of what drew them to Southern California. Times were hard for Southern black women in

the 1930s and early 1940s, as they were for many other Americans. Prices for cotton and other crops were low. Lots of families who had owned farms became tenants, and tenants became laborers. Men thrown out of work went looking for jobs and did not always come back. Women were often left to support families in the midst of hard times. Throughout the 1930s, large numbers of black women left the rural South, sometimes with husbands but often without, frequently with children in tow, and headed for nearby towns and cities in search of work. Some went farther. For Mississippians who left the South, the natural place to go by virtue of habit, proximity, and ease of transport, was Chicago. For Carolinians it was New York. For those from the Southwest—Texas and Oklahoma—and the Southeast—Louisiana and Arkansas—the West Coast was a possibility. Nearly half of the African Americans who came to Los Angeles came from those four states. Texas was the largest contributor; there was a regular pipeline of black people from Houston to Los Angeles from the 1920s on.

Yet it was more than proximity that drew them. For blacks as for whites, California was not just a place but an idea. In California, the world was made new every day. It was a place where the living was easy, where people could pick fruit right from the trees, where they could own their own homes, where they could find work and hope to retire someday. Those economic dreams seemed especially promising in the early 1940s when the impending Second World War brought new industries to Los Angeles. Shipyards, steel plants, and aircraft factories meant jobs with relatively high pay and high status. African American women and men left their homes in the South and headed for California.

Tina Hill was typical. Hard times in the 1930s had forced her and her sister to drop out of high school in Prairie View, Texas. She related in 1938,

[W]e finally decided to break up housekeeping and go to the city. I decided I wanted to make more money, and I went to a little small town—Tyler, Texas. . . . [But] the only thing I could do there for a living was domestic work and it didn't pay very much. . . . So I decided I'd better get out of this town. I didn't like Dallas because that was too rough. Then someone told me. "Well, why don't you try California?" So then I got Los Angeles in my mind.

In 1940, she invested her savings in a train ticket and headed for California.

Black women came on their own, or with their children, or sometimes following their husbands. Frequently they already had a relative living in California who offered to help them make a start. Some came via the Southern Pacific Railway, but trains were expensive. More came by bus or by car, across the hot dusty stretches of U.S. Highways 66, 80, and 60. Texas, Arizona, and New Mexico were segregated states in those days, with no hotel rooms for black people, so they camped out along the way or, if they were lucky, stayed in the homes of the few African Americans who lived in Amarillo and Santa Fe, Albuquerque and Flagstaff, Phoenix and Barstow.

The inflow of African Americans during World War II was large and sudden. The state officials who counted migrants at the border noted only about 100 blacks per month bound for Los Angeles in the period 1940 to 1942. But toward the end of 1942, some aircraft plants, as well as the Southern Pacific Railway and other major employers, were driven by labor shortages, black protests, and federal government pressure to begin to employ African American workers. Word spread quickly that there was good money to be made in Southern California. In short order, thousands of blacks poured in—as many as 10,000 to 12,000 per month during the summer of 1943. In those months, blacks constituted two-thirds to three-quarters of the total migration to Los Angeles. Altogether, over 140,000 African Americans were added to the population of Los Angeles County in the decade of the 1940s.

The African American women who came to California found their situation was not so pleasant as they had imagined. They did find work, but more often it was in somebody's kitchen at moderate pay rather than in a war plant at high pay. When World War II began, very few African Americans held jobs in the industrial sector of Los Angeles. Eighty-five percent of the black women before the war (and half of the men) were engaged as domestic servants. Early any morning, one could see them on street corners along Central Avenue, waiting for the buses that would take them to Bel Air and Santa Monica and Glendale to their day's work. Tina Hill described her experience as a domestic:

In less than ten days I had found a job living on the place doing domestic work. I started there from some time in August until Christmas. I was making thirty-five dollars a month. That was so much better than what I was making at home, which was twelve dollars a month. I saved my money and I bought everybody a Christmas present and sent it. Oh, I was the happiest thing in the world!

The family I worked for lived in Westwood. I had to cook breakfast, serve. They had a man and a wife and four kids. The smallest ones was twins and they wasn't too old. They had a nurse that took care of the twins. So I had to wash and iron, clean the house, cook. That was my job. So it was all day or practically, and I had very little time for myself. I had every Thursday off and every other Sunday. That just killed me to have to work on a Sunday, but I told myself I wasn't going to cry because I was coming out to do better and I would do better sooner or later.[2]

She quit that job soon enough and tried several others, but was not able to crack the industrial work force until 1943.

Much of the reason for the small number of black women and men in aircraft, steel, shipbuilding, and the other industrial enterprises can be laid at the door of white discrimination. Both management and labor did their part. For example, the manager of industrial relations at Consolidated-Vultee, an aircraft manufacturer, told representatives of the National Negro Congress, "I regret to say that it is not the policy of this company to employ people other than the Caucasian race, consequently we are not in a position to offer your people employment at this time."[3] The president of North American Aviation (later Rockwell International) echoed those sentiments: "Regardless of their training as aircraft workers we will not employ Negroes in the North American Plant. It is against company policy."[4] But labor, if anything, outdid management in discriminating against African American workers. The AFL-affiliated International Association of Machinists first refused black applicants for membership, then segregated them into a separate unit, the Jim Crow auxiliary local that lacked full voting rights or an independent voice. At the beginning of the war, despite a racially open national policy, Los Angeles CIO union organizers were only marginally more receptive to black membership. African Americans were shut out of the aircraft industry until the spring and summer of 1943, when it became apparent that the war-induced labor shortage would not go away. Then management at Lockheed and North American led the way in hiring and training black industrial workers and bulldozed the unions into accepting them.

Because of the convoluted logic of racism and sexism at that time, it was easier for black women than for black men to get the higher paying industrial jobs. At North American, it was hard for an African American man to get a production line job, because men, black or white, were viewed as permanent employees. To put a black man on the line was, in white eyes, to overturn the prewar racial system; so African American men had a hard time laying down the broom and picking up the rivet gun. But to hire an African

American woman for an industrial job was not seen as such a threat to the prevailing racial hierarchy. Women of whatever race were viewed as only temporary employees, because the prevailing ideology said they would go back to being housewives at the war's end (never mind that most had been wage workers before the war). So, even though factory managers' sexism kept them from regarding women as fully competent workers, they still could see their way clear to hiring black women for industrial jobs. Tina Hill went to a school on Figueroa Street for four weeks. She took psychological tests, then learned to drill and rivet and file pieces of metal, all the while earning 60 cents an hour. Margaret Wright did the same thing and then took her place on the line at Lockheed:

> I worked an eight-hour shift. If they asked me to work overtime I got paid for overtime. . . . It was a bit boring at times, but all in all I was doing the same work that other people were doing. If things didn't work right, I could always go to the union. . . . I could either quit, pack up and leave, or whatever, but I did have some say so and a job in the factory. There was another difference, too. Instead of working alone all the time like they do in domestic work, somewhere in the kitchen or wherever you were at by yourself, I was always with a bunch of other women.[5]

Even when they got jobs, however, African American workers generally were denied positions commensurate with their skill level, and they frequently received lower pay than white workers for the same work. They also found themselves on segregated work teams, often with white foremen. Tina Hill recalled, "They did everything they could to keep you separated. They just did not like for a Negro and a white person to get together and talk."[6] Segregation diminished as the years went by and some blacks did manage to ascend to team leader positions, but usually only supervising other African Americans.

Sometimes racial tensions flared on the job. Lyn Childs, a woman who worked in a San Francisco shop repair yard, described a scene perhaps more vivid than, but not fundamentally unlike, many that occurred in Los Angeles:

> I was working down in the hold of the ship and there were about six Filipino men and over these men was a nineteen-year-old officer of the ship, and this big White guy went over and started to kick this poor Filipino and none of the Black men that was working down there in the hold with him said one word to this guy. And I sat there and was getting madder and madder by the minute. I sprang to my feet, turned on my torch, and I had a flame about six to seven feet out in front of me, and I walked up to him and I said (you want me to say the real language?) I said to him "You so-and-so. If you go lift one more foot, I'll cut your guts out." That was my exact words. I was so mad with him.
>
> Then he started to tell me that he had been trained in boot camp that any national group who was dark-skinned was beneath all White people.

So he started to cry. I felt sorry for him, because he was crying, really crying. He was frightened, and I was frightened. I didn't know what I was doing, so in the end I turned my torch off and I sat down on the steps with him.

About that time the intercom on board the ship started to announce, "Lyn Childs, report to Colonel Hickman immediately." So I said, "I guess this is it." So I went up to Colonel Hickman's office, and behind me came all these men, and they lined up behind me, and I said, "Where are you guys going?" They said, "We're going with you." He said (Colonel Hickman), "I just wanted to see Lyn Childs," and they said, "You'll see all of us, because we were all down there. We all did not have guts enough to do what she did, and we're with her."

Colonel Hickman said, "Come into this office." He had one of the guards take me into the office real fast and close the door real fast and keep them out, and he said, "What kind of communist activity are you carrying on down there?" [I said], "A communist! What is that?" He said, "You know what I am talking about. You're a communist." [I said], "A communist! Forget you!" I said, "The kind of treatment that man was putting on the Filipinos, and to come to their rescue. Then I am the biggest communist you ever seen in your life. That is great. I am a communist." He said, "Don't say that so loud." I said, "Well, you asked me was I a communist. You're saying I am. I'm saying I'm a . . ." [He said], "Shh! Shh! Shh! Hush! Don't say that

so loud." He said, "I think you ought to get out of here and get back to work" [I said], "Well, you called me. Why did you call me?" He said, "Never mind what I called you for. Go back to work."[7]

Those opportunities that did open up for African American women were not simply a product of the forces or the labor market. They were also the result of a series of campaigns for jobs by African American organizations. A black woman, Charlotta Bass, was a central figure in the drive to compel businesses to hire blacks. Bass was the crusading editor of the *California Eagle*, the state's largest African American newspaper. Since the 1910s she had covered strikes, lynchings, the Ku Klux Klan, race riots in Houston, housing discrimination in Los Angeles, the case of the Scottsboro Boys, and other stories both topical and dangerous. The *Eagle* was also the daily monitor of activities and achievements among African Americans in Southern California.

During the war, the *Eagle* kept up a constant barrage of front-page stories and editorials aimed at getting jobs and housing for African Americans and at ending harassment. Teaming with the Reverend Clayton Russell of the Negro Victory Committee and other black leaders, Bass daily hammered on city, state, and federal officials to do something about discrimination against African American workers in war industries. Bass, Russell, and their allies petitioned national and local officials for redress. They marched and picketed. They shamed the War Manpower Commission (WMC) and the U.S. Fair Employment Practices Committee into taking action against local companies that refused to hire African Americans.

An example will illustrate their tactics and general success. In July 1942, an official of the U.S. Employment Service (USES) expressed the opinion that black women were not interested in jobs in war industries, that they were better fitted for domestic work. Russell got into the *Eagle* and on the radio and gathered several hundred followers, together with representatives of the NAACP (National Association for the Advancement of Colored People) and the Urban League. They marched on the USES office. Women filled the lines downstairs applying for jobs, while members of the Victory Committee were upstairs negotiating with USES officials. The government agreed to have the WMC investigate, and after several months of continuing pressure, African American women began to find jobs building aircraft and ships. Charlotta Bass kept her *Eagle*-eye out for cases of discrimination—in the municipal railway system, the boilermaker's union, the post office, and elsewhere—and trumpeted the names and details in the pages of her newspaper. By 1944, the combination of worker shortage and militant activism by this fiery woman and her colleagues had achieved black integration into the work force in all major industrial enterprises.

By the war's end, significant numbers of African Americans, women and men, were working in skilled positions in each of the heavy industries that the war had brought to Southern California. Precisely how many is not clear, because the only figures available are from the U.S. Census. The war ended in 1945, but numbers are available only for 1940 and 1950. As the war-spurred industrial boom wound down in 1945 and collapsed in 1946, black women, even more than black men and white women, lost the jobs they had found in industry. As Lyn Childs described it: "The women were laid off first, and then the less senior Black men were laid off next, and last, but as time went on, finally many of the White workers were laid off. But originally the first number that were laid off were women."[8] Margaret Wright recalled: "I knew how to rivet. I knew how to weld. I knew how to work on assembly lines. I knew how to run a dolly—you know [what] the good jobs are. I thought I had several skills that, you know, [were] very good, and I wouldn't have any problems getting a job anywhere else." But she was laid off by Lockheed, and "I had to fall back on the only other thing that I knew, and that was doing domestic work."[9] Tina Hill also worked cleaning people's homes, then in a garment factory reweaving damaged clothing.

Women's income plummeted, but not their independence and self-esteem. The war had permanently changed the job scene for African American women. As Tina Hill put it: "The war made me live better, it really did. . . . Hitler was the one that got us out of the white folks' kitchen."[10] Contrary to most people's expectations, the Depression did not return at the war's end. Manufacturing picked up again, and the companies started calling back their workers. By 1950, half of the black working women were in domestic service, but the other half were back in the skilled industrial, white collar, or professional positions that they had occupied during the war. In this they were unlike their white sisters; more of the whites remained out of the work force. Tina Hill remembered,

> When North American called me back, was I a happy soul! I dropped that job [in the garment factory] and went back. That was a dollar an hour. So, from sixty cents an hour, when I first hired in there, up to one dollar. That wasn't traveling fast, but it was better than anything else because you had hours to work by and you had benefits and you come home at night with your family. So it was a good deal.[11]

She worked for North American Aviation for almost forty years.

Loss of jobs was not the only problem black women faced. Once the color bar in employment had been broken, the biggest problem for Los Angeles African Americans was housing. Los Angeles was a segregated metropolis. African Americans were not barred by law from white towns and neighborhoods, but white antagonism kept them near the city's core nonetheless. More than one black family felt the necessity to display a shotgun prominently and keep it near at hand when they moved out of the central black district and into a white area. As the African American population increased and inched southward during the war, residents of some all-white, working-class suburbs adopted racially restrictive covenants (some had used such covenants since the 1920s) that made it illegal for anyone to sell a house to a black family. These kept the African American population bottled up in Watts and Willowbrook, for instance, and out of such neighboring communities as Southgate and Huntington Park. One woman described her experience in trying to buy a house just outside the black zone:

> My husband and I, who worked very hard during World War II in order to save enough to buy a decent house for our family, were confronted by hostile White realtors who tried to discourage us from wanting to move into an area recently integrated by Blacks in a surrounding community. They refused to take our deposit on a house. The realtors told us that the house was already sold and that there were no other houses in that area for sale.[12]

Sometimes the resistance in white areas was less subtle. In late 1945, Helen Short, her husband, and two small children bought five acres in Fontana, a working-class suburb east of Los Angeles, and started to build a house. After a string of threats from local whites, the Shorts' burned bodies were found in the ashes of their oil-soaked home. No one was prosecuted. Just after the war, in 1946, Klansmen visited ten African American families who had moved into white neighborhoods and burned crosses on their lawns.

Such opposition from whites left African Americans confined to a central ghetto that expanded only very gradually, never enough to accommodate their growing numbers. Most housing in black areas was substandard and overcrowded even before the war; by the war's end, conditions were far worse. In 1940, Little Tokyo had 30,000 Japanese American residents. Four years later, it had been renamed

Bronzeville and held 80,000 (mostly African American) inhabitants. Dorothy Baruch described Little Tokyo storefronts that had been converted into housing:

In place after place children lived in windowless rooms, amid peeling plaster, rats, and the flies that gathered thick around food that stood on open shelves or kitchen-bedroom tables. Ordinarily there was no bathtub; never more than a single washroom or lavatory. Sometimes as many as forty people shared one toilet. Families were separated only by sheets strung up between beds. Many of the beds were "hot," with people taking turns sleeping in them.[13]

Willowbrook and Watts, along with some previously white working-class suburbs, swelled with African American migrants. They housed their inhabitants somewhat more graciously—typically in one-story, two-bedroom bungalows of cheap construction. Such structures by war's end frequently housed two or three black families, with another put up in a makeshift structure out back. Chicken coops and garages became houses. People showered at work and went next door to use the toilet or outhouse. They cooked on open firepits and wood stoves.

Not all African Americans were poor renters in need of public housing. Over a third were home owners. Most owned the small, cheaply constructed bungalows that filled the corridor around Central Avenue as it made its way south to Watts. But there were middle-class blacks, too. Many old-time residents and a few newcomers who had a little cash moved west after the

war into the Crenshaw and West Adams districts. There they bought or built more substantial single-family homes with wide lawns and gardens along quiet streets. Previously these had been all-white districts, and both white residents and public authorities resisted the black incursion. A series of cases challenging the racially, restricted covenants made their way through state courts. Pauletta Fears and her parents did time in jail for contempt when they refused to vacate their home on 92nd Street in 1945, despite protests from the *Eagle* and a picket line of sympathizers. But in 1948 a Michigan case reached the U.S. Supreme Court, and the restrictive covenants were overturned. African Americans in larger numbers began to move west and south into previously all-white areas, but these did not become completely black neighborhoods. In Crenshaw especially, African Americans mixed with Japanese Americans returning from wartime concentration camps and with others to form a polyethnic, middle-class neighborhood that endures to this day.

Related to the housing problem was the difficulty of transport. Public war housing—flimsy temporary buildings and trailers—was built by the state, county, and federal governments to house war industry workers. But only 1,510 units were built in the Central, Vernon, and Watts black districts. Over 5,800 units were built in Wilmington and San Pedro, where the shipbuilding jobs were: almost all of these were segregated units designated for whites. There was little public housing—and none at all for African Americans—in places like Long Beach, Inglewood, and Fontana, where most steel and aircraft manufacturing took place. The concentration of black housing in south central Los Angeles, combined with the scattering of industrial plants far to the south, west, north, and east, meant that African Americans had to travel long distances to work. Typically, a woman from Watts or Central Avenue would spend an hour and a half each way in a car pool or riding the Los Angeles Railway's Red Car. Pauletta Fears recalls getting up at 4:00 in the morning, walking from Florence down to Watts, catching the Red Car for San Pedro, riding for over an hour, then walking the last mile to her job at California Shipbuilding.

All this commuting together with long hours in the factory kept black women away from their homes and children for long hours, sometimes days. Lyn Childs recalled:

> While I came to . . . work in the shipyard, I had a little child that I had to leave behind. I had to leave her with my mother because up here I didn't think I would have any place for her to stay and I was going into a new community and a new town, and I didn't want to bring my child with me. I left her with my mother, and that's one of the most awful things that I did to anybody, because even today that child hurts because I promised her that, "Give me one year and I will come back for you." That one year stretched into two years and finally into three years, and ended up almost five years before I could go back and get her. That's one of the things that is very sad. If there had been any kind of conditions under which I could have

brought her with me, I certainly would have brought her.[14]

Margaret Wright did not have to leave her children. Her challenge was to manage them and her job at the same time: "My kids were little, and so I worked at nights so I would get home in the morning. I didn't have a washing machine, and so I washed by hand, hung the clothes on the line. Then I would have to clean the house, bathe the babies. Then I would have to go shopping."[15]

These difficulties were compounded by the fact that many men were off in the war. Women were left to handle their jobs, children, finances, housing, and other matters on their own. Even when men were present, they were not always helpful. Margaret Wright complained that "[Y]our husband [would] come home, you know, prop his feet up, get his can of beer while you fixed dinner. Or even if we weren't working the same shift, you fixed dinner and left it where it would be convenient for him to get."[16] There was a lot for a woman to do.

As the war went on and more African Americans secured defense jobs, they managed to integrate some of the housing projects in the Long Beach Harbor industrial area. Mixing black and white, Latino, and Asian in these projects proved inflammatory in several instances. But the conflict was not bad enough to dissuade public housing authorities from continuing the experiment in social engineering after the war. Between 1945 and 1952, most of the wartime "temporary" housing projects were converted to permanent status. A dozen other larger and better constructed housing projects were built, from Little

Tokyo down to Watts, and more were planned. They bore names like Avalon Gardens, Aliso Village, William Mead Homes, and Nickerson Gardens that bespoke their sylvan aspirations. At first these were pretty spartan places, but soon they began to live up to the illusory term "gardens" that was often part of their names. Those that survive do not look much like gardens now. But that was the ideal—to create a cheaper, smaller, but recognizably similar version of the bungalows that were going up for middle-class whites out in Orange County and the San Fernando Valley for poor, inner-city African Americans.

The 1940s were not an easy time for African American women in Southern California, but they were a time of hope, and the number of black women grew. They had to work hard, often at menial tasks. They had difficulty finding good jobs, housing, and transportation, managing families with men absent, making stable lives for themselves and their children. They endured discrimination, both subtle and overt, sometimes extending to violence. But they fought back, worked hard, and won places for themselves. They found good jobs and better pay than they had ever dreamed was possible. Their children received better education than could be had in the South; many were graduating from high school, and some were going on to college. Housing, though crowded, was better—even the slums had plumbing and electricity, and the housing projects seemed like gardens. By the end of World War II, blacks and whites went to the same beaches and sometimes shared the same municipal pools. Social

relations between the races were not close, but there was little of the domination and hostility many had known in the South. This was a hopeful era for most Angeleno African Americans.

Then in the 1950s, the hope began to recede. The destruction of the war-era dreams of Los Angeles African Americans is the subject of another paper, but a few summary comments here will mark the way of the future. In the late 1940s and early 1950s, the Los Angeles African American community was ripped apart by allegations of communist involvement in the NAACP. Charges and countercharges flew around the community and were inflated in the *Los Angeles Times* and other organs of white opinion. Charlotta Bass and other community leaders were called to testify before witch-hunting Congressional committees. The *Times,* realtors' organizations, Chief of Police William H. Parker, and others mounted a campaign to prevent the housing authority from building any more public housing projects, and to cut the funding for maintenance at existing ones. With black leadership immobilized, with the dream of good housing gone bust, and with other looming disasters in jobs, education, and relations with the police, Los Angeles blacks began to lose the faith in their future that the war years had created. For Southern California African Americans, women and men, hard work continued, but hope had begun to ebb. By the mid-1960s, the tide was out, and the African American community exploded in the Watts riot of 1965. The story of black women in that disaster has yet to be told.

Notes

1. Sherna Berger Gluck, *Rosie the Riveter Revisited* (New York, New American Library. 1988), 31–32.
2. Ibid., 33.
3. National Negro Congress, *Jim Crow in National Defense* (Los Angeles, CA: National Negro Congress, 1940).
4. James R. Wilburn, "Social and Economic Aspects of the Aircraft Industry in Metropolitan Los Angeles During World War II," Ph.D. diss., University of California at Los Angeles, 1971, 165–166.
5. Connie Field, "The Life and Times of Rosie the Riveter" (Emeryville, CA: Rosie the Riveter Film Project. 1980).
6. Gluck, *Rosie the Riveter Revisited*, 43.
7. Field, "The Life and Times of Rosie the Riveter."
8. Ibid.
9. Ibid.
10. Gluck, *Rosie the Riveter Revisited*, 23.
11. Ibid., 41–42.
12. Keith E. Collins, *Black Los Angeles: The Maturing of the Ghetto, 1940–1950* (Saratoga, CA: Century Twenty One Publishing, 1980), 72–74.
13. Dorothy W. Baruch, "Sleep Comes Hard," *Nation,* 160 (Jan. 27, 1945): 95–96.
14. Field, "The Life and Times of Rosie the Riveter."
15. Ibid.
16. Ibid.

References

Adler, Patricia R. "Watts: From Suburb to Black Ghetto," Ph.D. diss., University of Southern California, Los Angeles, 1977.

Anderson, E. Frederick. *The Development of Leadership and Organization Building in the Black Community of Los Angeles from 1900 through World War II* (Saratoga, CA: Century Twenty One Publishing, 1980).

Bass, Charlotta, *Forty Years* (Los Angeles, CA: *California Eagle*, 1960).

Collins, Keith E. *Black Los Angeles: The Maturing of the Ghetto, 1940–1950* (Saratoga, CA: Century Twenty One Publishing, 1980).

DeGraaf, Lawrence B. "Negro Migration to Los Angeles, 1930 to 1950," Ph.D. diss., University of California at Los Angeles, 1962.

Field, Connie. *The Life and Times of Rosie the Riveter* (Emeryville, CA: Rosie the Riveter Film Project, 1980).

Gluck, Sherna Berger. *Rosie the Riveter Revisited: Women, the War and Social Change* (New York: New American Library, 1988).

Himes, Chester. *If He Hollers Let Him Go* (New York: New American Library, 1971).

Kraus, Henry. *In the City Was a Garden* (New York: Renaissance Press, 1951).

Sandoval, Sally J. "Ghetto Growing Pains: The Impact of Negro Migration on the City of Los Angeles, 1940–1960." M.A. thesis, California State University. Fullerton, 1973.

Smith, Alonzo N. "Black Employment in the Los Angeles Area, 1938-1948." Ph.D. diss., University of California at Los Angeles, 1978.

Wilburn, James R. "Social and Economic Aspects of the Aircraft Industry in Metropolitan Los Angeles During World War II," Ph.D. diss., University of California at Los Angeles, 1971.

Williams, Dorothy S. "Ecology of Negro Communities in Los Angeles: 1940-1959." Ph.D. diss., University of Southern California, Los Angeles, 1961.

Part IV
From 1950 to Present

Introduction

Resisting the dynamics of treatment that singles one out for unfair treatment based on color, ethnicity, language, or sexual orientation is an important way that one can affirm one's "Americaness." Various quests to make Californians more accepting and just have characterized this state's modern era. Whether actions of resistance to police abuse in the streets or the efforts of those seeking to organize the laboring masses, such efforts affirm this country's long journey toward more democracy. Those who were once ignored or unjustly silenced have collectively become California's new numerical majority. Translations of the new numbers into real power and more representative control remains to be achieved. The articles in this section clearly demonstrate that California continues to evolve in ways that remain difficult to predict. One forecast can be made with confidence: change of many sorts will continue.

The final section's materials also provide evidence that most of the new majority dynamics are taking place in California's urban locations, and often via various media. Whether using film or new forms of songs, the state's "new majority" continues to make California a setting that the original residents and the early Spanish would find astounding. Yet, the materials in this section demonstrate that today's Californians continue to take their rights, cultures, and communities with the utmost seriousness. Few in this state remain silent for long when they feel their dignity or rights are infringed. This has become a collective approach shared by most groups of modern residents. Some newcomers are learning this quickly. This is a very American and California way of doing things. The dynamics of changing majorities, that began with a relative handful of Spanish newcomers in the late 1700s, proved complex, not simple. As modern California changes under the pressures of millions of residents, these final selections demonstrate that complexity with ever more change will be a major part of California's future. (SMM)

Watts 1965

A rebellious explosion occurred in the Black sections of Los Angeles County in August of 1965 that forever changed California and this nation. African Americans expressed a rage that had simmered for years as they unleashed a furious anger at the Los Angeles police. Those who viewed themselves as the "Watts rebels" also targeted the symbols of White business domination of their community. This was no minor episode of localized street violence. Youth from the cities of Compton and Long Beach in the east to the community of Santa Monica in the west got involved. The main actions though, took place inside the area of Los Angeles that has come to be known as "South Central." There "rebels" looted and burned stores, threw rocks at the cars of innocent Whites and a very few shot at the police, firemen and national guard members attempting to suppress their actions.

In the articles that follow, Paul Bullock and Bayard Rustin describe the significance of the Watts events. The authors present an assessment the McCone Report lacked. They avoid any moralistic condemning of the rebels as they present an examination of root causes of that era's Black anger. By reading their assessments one can better come to understand the McCone Report document that we choose to exclude. Thoughtful readers may also get a sense of the mood of those early Watts rebels. Theirs was a ghetto "revolt" whose importance should not be underestimated. Their widely televised acts and the grievances they expressed in live interviews helped inspire similarly mistreated Black youth in Oakland just one year later to create a Black Panther Party for Self-Defense.

In the same year, 1966, that the Panthers were emerging in Oakland, a former grade B-movie actor named Ronald Reagan was elected to become California's governor. Ronald Reagan achieved this statue despite publicly opposing the Federal Civil Rights Act of 1964 while also suggesting that Dr. Martin Luther King, Jr. might have been a communist. Despite such extreme views . . . Reagan was swept into the governorship largely by a "Watts backlash." A massive number of Los Angeles area White suburbanites responded with their votes to his calls for "restoring law and order." Few then actually read the McCone Report. Fewer still, read these articles by Bullock and Rustin. If more citizens and officials had done so, tragic events that later came to characterize the arrest aftermath of the Rodney King case in 1991-1992 might not have "burned" Los Angeles and the nation a second time. These closely related articles follow. (SMM)

Paul Bullock

Watts: Before the Riots

This selection is drawn from a research project on the Watts community directed by Paul Bullock, a white economist from the Institute of Industrial Relations at UCLA. The report, composed largely of the views of the black residents of Watts, is a useful antidote to the McCone Commission's official version. Here Bullock traces the origins of Watts and describes the increasing ghettoization of that community prior to the insurrection of 1965.

Whatever may be the stereotypes created by national magazines and the other mass media, Watts is in no sense a completely unified and homogeneous community. The hostile delinquent, the aggressive nationalist, the "middle-class" homeowner, the college-bound youngster, the hustler, the conventional politician, the welfare recipient, the hard-core unemployed, and the hard-working employed are all represented, and only a journalist with a superficial view and a pressing deadline would dare to suggest that any one group symbolizes the "community." The one common bond is skin color, but even here we must recognize the presence of Mexican Americans, now dwindling in number but still noticeable in some neighborhoods.

In the early days of Los Angeles, the area now known as Watts was part of a large ranch, El Rancho Tajuata. When the original owner died, his estate was divided into many parcels to accommodate his heirs. In those days, land in California was easily acquired—legally and illegally—from its Mexican owners, and a number of Americans benefited.

Two subsequent building booms, the first in 1885–88 and the second in 1900–1910, hastened the growth of Tajuata, still an unincorporated area in the county of Los Angeles. Twenty-five-foot lots sold at a dollar down and a dollar a week. Land speculation, largely associated with the building of railroads and of Henry Huntington's Pacific Electric transportation system, eventually led to further settlement of the area, close to the city but not in it. A major spur of the Pacific Electric tracks ran north and south through Tajuata, which was a junction for tracks running to Long Beach and San Pedro.

With the construction of the Pacific Electric railroad came the immigration of poor Mexican laborers, most of them employed by the railroad. By this time the heirs of the original owner had sold the land to subdividers. The PE decided to build a station on the old ranchland and acquired the necessary property from several Anglo subdividers, among whom was Julia A. Watts. The railroad men called it the Watts Station, and the growing settlement became known, unofficially, as Watts. Even then the cheap land and the corruption gave Watts something of a local reputation. One resident, a white American who had lived in Watts for many years, commented:

> A dollar down and a dollar a week became a by-word. This, with the politics and vice which abounded among the white inhabitants, caused Watts to be used as a joke in the theaters and on the streets. A spite deal sold the first land to the Negroes in the southern part of Watts. . . .

Whatever the nature of this "spite deal" may have been, it is certain that some time before the first World War the southern edge of Watts became a Negro ghetto. Locally known as "Mudtown," this rustic community served as a port of entry for Negroes immigrating from the South. In his 1931 novel, *God Sends Sunday,* the distinguished author Arna Bontemps described the early black settlements in Los Angeles:

> In those days, fifteen or twenty years ago, Negroes were not plentiful in the far West. Least of all were they to be seen in rural parts. A few of them, to be sure, had come as early as the historical gold rush with the forty-niners, working in personal service. Others had followed the conquest of the frontier. But the number had remained small until the great transcontinental railway lines established important terminals in Los Angeles and in San Francisco. Then the real immigration began. First, the railroad men, Pullman porters and dining car waiters, brought their families; hearing the rumors of attractive working conditions, their friends followed. Still the tendency was for them to remain in the larger centers and particularly in the location of the train yard.
>
> The small group in Mudtown was exceptional. Here, removed from the influence of white folks, they did not acquire the inhibitions of their city brothers. Mudtown was like a tiny section of the deep south literally transplanted. . . .
>
> The streets of Mudtown were three or four dusty wagon paths. In the moist grass along the edges cows were staked. . . . Ducks were sleeping in the weeds, and there was on the air a suggestion of pigs and slime holes. Tiny hoot-owls were sitting bravely on fence posts while bats hovered overhead like shadows. . . .

If early Mudtown was like a section of the South transplanted, it would not remain so for long. Mudtown was a part of Watts, both geographically and commercially. As the population grew, and as the Anglo and

Mexican inhabitants of Watts moved toward political self-determination, the Negro community became less isolated. Incorporated as a separate city in 1907, Watts was the scene of unending political turmoil as the Anglos sought to maintain their control of community affairs. When industrial development associated with World War I encouraged further immigration from the South, mainly from Texas, Louisiana, and Mississippi, the black newcomers settled either in Watts or in the Central Avenue ghetto to the north, closer to downtown. The expanding Watts ghetto, however, remained surrounded by Anglo communities, existing as a Negro island in an otherwise "lily white" and often hostile sea. Indeed, until World War II, Watts itself retained its racially heterogeneous character, its population divided about equally among Anglos, Mexicans, and Negroes.

The internal politics of Watts became more troubled in the twenties. The Ku Klux Klan, already a force in the Compton area just to the south, schemed to gain control of city government through the use of recall petitions and devices to split the Negro community. Its plans were thwarted by unwelcome publicity, but it remained active. The political difficulties in the small town, coupled with water shortages which could only be overcome through the Owens Valley Aqueduct project, led, in 1926, to the abandonment of cityhood and annexation to the city of Los Angeles.

Its absorption into Los Angeles, however, did not destroy Watts' identity as a community. Anyone familiar with Los Angeles knows that it is not one city but, rather, a series of distinct communities: one lives in Pacific Palisades, or San Pedro, or Eagle Rock, or Highland Park, or Bel Air, each

technically a "neighborhood" within Los Angeles. Watts, of course, had a further claim to distinction: it contained a high proportion, though still a minority, of Negroes. Except for the Central Avenue area and a small middle-class Negro community along West Jefferson Boulevard to the north and west, Negroes in Los Angeles were to be found only in Watts, and, even then, mainly in the southern part of the community below 103rd Street. Northern Watts remained dominated by Anglos and Mexicans. Before World War II, the Mexican and Negro inhabitants were of lower economic status; in 1938, a writer commissioned by the Works Progress Administration (WPA) noted, somewhat snobbishly, that a low grade of labor was demanded by the manufacturing plants which had located on the eastern edge of Watts, and that this fact, plus the impact of the depression, had changed the character of the community. He also noted the mixture of good and poor dwellings in the area, a characteristic which remains in evidence today.

During World War II, the population of Los Angeles boomed and Watts was no exception. Many of the immigrants were Negroes drawn by the lure of jobs in the war industries, and they encountered a critical housing problem when they entered this thoroughly segregated city. Tens of thousands moved into "Little Tokyo," vacated by the Japanese, but other thousands had to find accommodations in the traditionally segregated Central Avenue and Watts ghettos. Some of those who had decent jobs bought or built pleasant homes, many of which are still visible in the western part of Watts below 103rd Street and just east of Central Avenue.

But many others moved into deteriorating or substandard housing, absentee owned, and several hundred more located in public housing projects built by the federal government in the Watts area.

The construction of the public housing projects, which became all-Negro though they were supposedly interracial, accelerated the ghettoization of the community. Three projects were built during the war, and a fourth, William Nickerson Jr. Gardens, was finished in 1955. The earliest—Hacienda Village (1942)—is the most attractive, with trees shading its single-story units. It was constructed as a permanent project, and its designers (Richard Neutra, Paul Williams, and Welton Becket) are now among the most prominent architects in California. Jordan Downs (September, 1944) and Imperial Courts (May, 1944) were semi-permanent projects for war workers, which were later converted into permanent units. Like Nickerson Gardens, they are massive and conventional two-story structures.

By 1946, Negroes represented almost two-thirds of the population of Watts, twice their proportion in 1940. Writing during the war, sociologist Lloyd H. Fisher noted the increasing tension in the community. Watts elementary schools were interracial both in teaching staff and student bodies, but the only high school (actually a combined junior and senior high), David Starr Jordan, was predominantly Negro because Anglo youngsters were encouraged to go elsewhere for their high school education. The nearby junior college in the all-white city of Compton discouraged Jordan High graduates from attending it. Fisher observed a lack of confidence in the police force, the absence of an interracial church, and a lack of leadership and organization within the community. In short, he detected all the major elements which were to explode into violence twenty years later.

Nor was Fisher alone in his observations. In a book on the Los Angeles Youth Project, published in 1949, Duane Robinson described the Watts area in terms which, in essence, were equally applicable fifteen years hence:

> This area is surrounded by strong Anglo-American communities which in the past have manifested discriminatory practices—even physical aggression The Latin American residents are disturbed by the rapidly growing Negro majority. The native Negroes are disturbed by the incoming "southern" Negroes, many of whom have imported and are supporting the approximately eighty churches in the area, ranging from magnificent edifices to tattered tents. Recreational and other facilities are hopelessly overwhelmed. There is no sizable building facility for recreation in the entire area.

Even some bureaucrats and public officials seemed aware that something was amiss in Watts. In a report on conditions of blight in the central area of the city of Los Angeles, the City Planning Commission, in 1947, concluded that Watts was

> an obsolescent area in which all the social and physical weaknesses of urban living are to be found. Some streets are unpaved, others have fine concrete roadways and ornaments;

some structures seem about to fall apart, while next to them exist new, standard buildings. In some areas, a great number of twenty-five-foot lots stand vacant, while in others six or more dwellings are crowded into a similar parcel. Recreational facilities in certain sections are few in number and limited in area. Schools are located in places where the maximum walking distance, rather than the minimum, is required of a great number of children. The shopping district on 103rd Street has little provision for off-street parking, and during busy hours the street is cluttered with double parked vehicles and is almost closed to traffic movement. Some of the worst interracial conflicts occurring in the past decade were in this area. The low rental pattern, the low assessed value of property, the high disease and delinquency rates, all reflect the blighted character of this district.

Clearly, every evidence of social pathology in Watts was a matter of public knowledge as early as 1947. But no action was forthcoming, or even suggested. After its incisive analysis of the problems in the area, the City Planning Commission offered no concrete plan for their alleviation. The conditions which breed riots had already emerged, conservatively speaking, a generation ago. In the light of such public indifference to deprivation and deterioration, the wonder is not that a riot eventually exploded in the area but, rather, that the residents were patient for so long.

The 1950s saw a few changes in Watts, but the movement of the community remained primarily the same, and was per-haps accelerated. In the first half of the decade, the Nickerson Gardens project was completed and both Jordan Downs and Imperial Courts were converted to permanent units, and by the decade's end over a third of the total population lived in public housing. Inevitably, the actual population density in the projects far exceeded the earlier projections, and the streets and yards swarmed with children. Large families were often crammed into relatively small quarters. The percentage of young people under the age of twenty-five rose to a little more than sixty per cent in 1960, and the proportion of homeowners dropped markedly as the projects expanded. The construction of a modern junior high school—Edwin Markham—improved the school system in a physical sense, but the dropout (or pushout) rate at Jordan High School was depressingly high. Anglos virtually disappeared, though a very few remain even today, and the Mexican American percentage of total population dropped to less than eleven per cent, concentrated mostly in the eastern section.

As the community entered the 1960s, the forces of social and economic disorganization became stronger and more pervasive than ever. In a 1959 study, the Welfare Planning Council had noted that there was still no master plan for the Watts area, nor was there any current program of planning or activity even in regard to parks and schools. Its analysis has a familiar ring:

Preoccupation with earning a living for many persons in this area reduces their interest in preparation for or acceptance of leadership of youth groups. This condition, however, does not mean that there is no leadership; rather, it means that it is harder to locate and recruit. The continual immigration of persons from different sections of the country makes it difficult to stabilize and stimulate interests in long range projects or even in the immediate social problems as related to youth. Compounded upon these factors is that most of the residents in this area are employed outside the area which poses a transportation problem of taxing even more the inadequate public transportation system of the area. This hinders the chance of developing a strong feeling of community responsibility with so much of the residents' time spent outside the area.

As the summer of 1965 approached, the character of the Watts community had been fixed inexorably by the events of the previous two decades. The previously separated ghettos—Watts, Central Avenue, and West Jefferson—had now been amalgamated by the vast increase in black population and outflow of Anglos during the 1940s and 1950s, creating a massive, segregated area in the heart of the county which stretches from the western part of the city of Compton on the south to the lower part of downtown Los Angeles; and from Alameda Street on the east to the pleasant, middle-class (and occasionally integrated) Crenshaw-La Brea district on the west. Alameda Street, still the site of the railroad tracks, remains an impenetrable "Berlin Wall," which has always separated the Negro ghetto from the lily-white and decidedly unfriendly communities of South Gate, Huntington Park, Lynwood,

and Bell. Thus, the direction of the ghetto's expansion is predominantly westward, and it is now merging into, and possibly transforming, an area which has been largely Jewish in population.

In the postwar years, the development of Los Angeles' complex freeway system further compounded the isolation of those Negroes who remained in the poorest section of the ghetto. The Harbor Freeway, linking downtown Los Angeles with the coastal communities of Wilmington and San Pedro, bisects the huge central ghetto, leaving what are, in effect, two distinct Negro settlements. The area to the east of the freeway, which includes Watts, is predominantly poor, with a few middle-class enclaves, while the area to the west is predominantly middle-class, with a few low-income enclaves. In the hills above Crenshaw Boulevard, on the western edge of what was later defined as the riot "curfew zone," an integrated high-income community contains impressive homes, often with swimming pools, inhabited by Negro professionals and businessmen. In the West Adams area, an extension of the early West Jefferson middle-class ghetto, the neighborhoods differ from those in the Anglo areas only in the darkness of the residents' complexions.

Even the area east of the Harbor Freeway would not be adjudged a "slum" by those accustomed to the rat-infested tenements of Eastern cities. Single-family dwellings still predominate, though probably a third of the population of Watts itself (narrowly defined as the area between 92nd Street on the north and Imperial Highway on the south, Central Avenue on the west and Alameda Street on the east) still lives in public housing. At the corner of Central

Avenue and 103rd Street, on the western edge of Watts, Will Rogers Park gives the visitor a favorable first impression, with its spacious lawns, baseball diamonds, tennis courts, swimming pool, and large gymnasium. However, programs at the park are limited, partly because its administrators are fearful of "incidents." About a mile farther to the southeast, the famous Watts Towers, fashioned by Italian immigrant Simon Rodia out of steel, cement, and fragments of bottles, shells, and glassware, rise majestically on a small plot of land at the end of a street which leads into the abandoned PE right-of-way.

Then, as now, as the observer moves from one neighborhood to another, he is invariably impressed by the diversity in the physical appearance of Watts. The neat, attractive, and well-maintained houses on Zamora or Pace Avenue south of 103rd—many of them owned by residents who came to Los Angeles during the 1940s—would do credit to the most status-conscious suburb. Nearby are two of the imposing public housing projects, Hacienda Village to the north, and Nickerson Gardens, to the south. The other two projects provide living space for about 5,000 persons in other sections of Watts. Elsewhere, shabby absentee-owned houses contrast sharply with better-maintained residences on the same block or around the corner, the latter attesting to the earnest but probably futile efforts of the inhabitants to preserve some semblance of pride in their aging homes. Just across Central Avenue, on 94th and 95th Streets, a neighborhood of handsome homes attracts thousands of visitors every December to its imaginative display of outdoor Christmas decorations.

As one ventures into still other neighborhoods, new and more mixed impressions come to the fore. Small and usually dilapidated churches, of religious denominations, are everywhere, challenged in number only by the many liquor stores. The main business center is along 103rd Street, with dozens of dingy stores offering their wares at prices and terms well in excess of those charged in Anglo neighborhoods. On the eve of the riot, the only new construction in sight was the still-unfinished Doctors' Building, the iron framework being raised by an all-white crew of building craftsmen. At the other end of 103rd, near Alameda, marijuana and pills of all varieties are readily available on and off the campus of David Starr Jordan High School. In a corner lot adjoining Jordan Downs project, the dropouts and delinquents of the "parking lot gang" terrify the rest of the community.

Watts is characterized by one-parent households. It is a community of young people, the yards and streets filled with children, the classrooms overflowing. The observer is impressed by their apparent health and handsomeness: the boys are muscular and lively, the girls well-developed and neatly dressed. The older teenagers search desperately for "kicks," a respite from the boredom and frustration of a ghetto in which there is nothing to do. Many of the youngsters carry their most prized possession—a "box" (radio)—from which "soul" sounds blare incessantly. Thousands of them will rarely see the world outside the ghetto, except perhaps in jail. The whites they know are policemen, probation officers, merchants, and teachers, and the relationship is often uneasy or hostile.

Bayard Rustin

The Watts "Manifesto" and The McCone Report

Among the many trenchant criticisms of the McCone Commission Report, none had more moment or impact than this one by Bayard Rustin, a veteran strategist, tactician, and gadfly of the civil rights movement. Director of the A. Philip Randolph Foundation—the AFL-CIO's token contribution to the civil rights movement—he helped develop the $100 billion freedom budget or black "Marshall Plan," which has stirred liberal hopes but found negligible congressional support.

The riots in the Watts section of Los Angeles last August continued for six days, during which 34 persons were killed, 1,032 were injured, and some 3,952 were arrested. Viewed by many of the rioters themselves as their "manifesto," the uprising of the Watts Negroes brought out in the open, as no other aspect of the Negro protest has done, the despair and hatred that continue to brew in the Northern ghettoes despite the civil-rights legislation of recent years and the advent of "the war on poverty." With national attention focused on Los Angeles, Governor Edmund G. Brown created a commission of prominent local citizens, headed by John A. McCone, to investigate the causes of the riots and to prescribe remedies against any such outbreaks in the future. Just as the violent confrontation on the burning streets of Watts told us much about the underlying realities of race and class relations in America—summed up best, perhaps, by the words of Los Angeles Police Chief William Parker, "We're on top and they're on the bottom"—so does the McCone Report, published under the title *Violence in the City—An End or a Beginning?*, tell us much about the

---

response of our political and economic institutions to the Watts "manifesto."

Like the much-discussed Moynihan Report, the McCone Report is a bold departure from the standard government paper on social problems. It goes beyond the mere recital of statistics to discuss, somewhat sympathetically, the real problems of the Watts community—problems like unemployment, inadequate schools, dilapidated housing—and it seems at first glance to be leading toward constructive programs. It never reaches them, however, for, again like the Moynihan Report, it is ambivalent about the basic reforms that are needed to solve these problems and therefore shies away from spelling them out too explicitly. Thus, while it calls for the creation of 50,000 new jobs to compensate for the "spiral of failure" that it finds among the Watts Negroes, the McCone Report does not tell us how these jobs are to be created or obtained and instead recommends existing programs which have already shown themselves to be inadequate. The Moynihan Report, similarly, by emphasizing the breakdown of the Negro family, also steers clear of confronting the thorny issues of Negro unemployment as such.

By appearing to provide new viewpoints and fresh initiatives while at the same time repeating, if in more sophisticated and compassionate terms, the standard white stereotypes and shibboleths about Negroes, the two reports have become controversial on both sides of the Negro question. On the one hand, civil-rights leaders can point to the recognition in these reports of the need for jobs and training, and for other economic and social programs to aid the Negro family, while conservatives can find confirmed in their pages the Negro penchant for violence, the excessive agitation against law and order by the civil-rights movement, or the high rates of crime and illegitimacy in the Negro community; on the other hand, both sides have criticized the reports for feeding ammunition to the opposition. Unfortunately, but inevitably, the emphasis on *Negro* behavior in both reports has stirred up an abstract debate over the interpretation of data rather than suggesting programs for dealing with the existing and very concrete situation in which American Negroes find themselves. For example, neither report is concerned about segregation and both tacitly assume that the Civil Rights Acts of 1964 and 1965 are already destroying this system. In the case of the McCone Report, this leaves the writers free to discuss the problems of Negro housing, education, and unemployment in great detail without attacking the conditions of de facto segregation that underly them.

The errors and misconceptions of the McCone Report are particularly revealing because it purports to deal with the realities of the Watts riots rather than with the abstractions of the Negro family. The first distortion of these realities occurs in the opening chapter—"The Crisis: An Overview"—where, after briefly discussing the looting and beatings, the writers conclude that "The rioters seem to have been caught up in an insensate rage of destruction." Such an image may reflect the fear of the white community that Watts had run amok during six days in August, but it does not accurately describe the major motive and mood of the riots, as subsequent data in the report itself indicate.

While it is true that Negroes in the past have often turned the violence inflicted on them by society in upon themselves—"insensate rage" would perhaps have been an appropriate phrase for the third day of the 1964 Harlem riots—the whole point of the outbreak in Watts was that it marked the first major rebellion of Negroes against their own masochism and was carried on with the express purpose of asserting that they would no longer quietly submit to the deprivation of slum life.

This message came home to me over and over again when I talked with the young people in Watts during and after the riots, as it will have come home to those who watched the various television documentaries in which the Negroes of the community were permitted to speak for themselves. At a street-corner meeting in Watts when the riots were over, an unemployed youth of about twenty said to me, "We won." I asked him: "How have you won? Homes have been destroyed, Negroes are lying dead in the streets, the stores from which you buy food and clothes are destroyed, and people are bringing you relief." His reply was significant: "We won because we made the whole world pay attention to us. The police chief never came here before; the mayor always stayed uptown. We made them come." Clearly it was no accident that the riots proceeded along an almost direct path to City Hall.

Nor was the violence along the way random and "insenate." Wherever a store-owner identified himself as a "poor working Negro trying to make a business" or as a "Blood Brother," the mob passed the store by. It even spared a few white businesses that allowed credit or time purchas-es, and it made a point of looting and destroying stores that were notorious for their high prices and hostile manners. The McCone Report itself observes that "the rioters concentrated on food markets, liquor stores, clothing stores, department stores, and pawn shops." The authors "note with interest that no residences were deliberately burned, that damage to schools, libraries, public buildings was minimal and that certain types of business establishments, notably service stations and automobile dealers, were for the most part unharmed." It is also worth noting that the rioters were much more inclined to destroy the stock of the liquor stores they broke into than to steal it, and that according to the McCone Report, "there is no evidence that the rioters made any attempt to steal narcotics from pharmacies . . . which were looted and burned."

This is hardly a description of a Negro community that has run amok. The largest number of arrests were for looting—not for arson or shooting. Most of the people involved were not habitual thieves; they were members of a deprived group who seized a chance to possess things that all the dinning affluence of Los Angeles had never given them. There were innumerable touching examples of this behavior. One married couple in their sixties was seen carrying a couch to their home, and when its weight became too much for them, they sat down and rested on it until they could pick it up again. Langston Hughes tells of another woman who was dragging a sofa through the streets and who stopped at each intersection and waited for the traffic light to turn green. A third women went out with her children to get a kitchen set, and after bringing it home, she discovered they needed one more chair in order to feed the whole family together; they went back to get the chair and all of them were arrested.

If the McCone Report misses the point of the Watts riots, it shows even less understanding of their causes. To place these in perspective, the authors begin by reviewing the various outbursts in the Negro ghettoes since the summer of 1964 and quickly come up with the following explanations: "Not enough jobs to go around, and within this scarcity not enough by a wide margin of a character which the untrained Negro could fill. . . . Not enough schooling to meet the special needs of the disadvantaged Negro child whose environment from infancy onward places him under a serious handicap." Finally, "a resentment, even hatred, of the police as a symbol of authority."

For the members of the special commission these are the fundamental causes of the current Negro plight and protest, which are glibly summed up in the ensuing paragraph by the statement that "Many Negroes moved to the city in the last generation and are totally unprepared to meet the conditions of city life." I shall be discussing these "causes" in detail as we go along, but it should be noted here that the burden of responsibility has already been placed on these hapless migrants to the cities. There is not one word about the conditions, economic as well as social, that have pushed Negroes out of the rural areas; nor is there one word about whether the cities have been willing and able to meet the demand for jobs, adequate housing, proper schools. After all, one could as well say that it is the *cities*

which have been "totally unprepared" to meet the "conditions of *Negro* life," but the moralistic bias of the McCone Report, involving as it does an emphasis on the decisions of men rather than the pressure of social forces, continually operates in the other direction.

The same failure of awareness is evident in the report's description of the Los Angeles situation (the Negro areas of Los Angeles "are not urban gems, neither are they slums," the Negro population "has exploded," etc.). The authors do concede that the Los Angeles transportation system is the "least adequate of any major city," but even here they fail to draw the full consequences of their findings. Good, cheap transportation is essential to a segregated working-class population in a big city. In Los Angeles a domestic worker, for example, must spend about $1.50 and 1 1/2 to 2 hours to get to a job that pays $6 or $7 a day. This both discourages efforts to find work and exacerbates the feeling of isolation.

A neighborhood such as Watts may seem beautiful when compared to much of Harlem (which, in turn, is an improvement over the Negro section of Mobile, Alabama)—but it is still a ghetto. The housing is run-down, public services are inferior, the listless penned-in atmosphere of segregation is oppressive. Absentee landlords are the rule, and most of the businesses are owned by whites: neglect and exploitation reign by day, and at night, as one Watts Negro tersely put it, "There's just the cops and us."

The McCone Report, significantly, also ignores the political atmosphere of Los Angeles. It refers, for example, to the repeal in 1964 of the Rumford Act—the

California fair-housing law—in these words: "In addition, many Negroes here felt and were encouraged to feel that they had been affronted by the passage of Proposition 14." Affronted, indeed! The largest state in the Union, by a three-to-one majority, abolishes one of its own laws against discrimination and Negroes are described as regarding this as they might the failure of a friend to keep an engagement. What they did feel—and without any need of encouragement—was that while the rest of the North was passing civil-rights laws and improving opportunities for Negroes, their own state and city were rushing to reinforce the barriers against them.

The McCone Report goes on to mention two other "aggravating events in the twelve months prior to the riot." One was the failure of the poverty program to "live up to [its] press notices," combined with reports of "controversy and bickering" in Los Angeles over administering the program. The second "aggravating event" is summed up by the report in these words:

> Throughout the nation unpunished violence and disobedience to law were widely reported, and almost daily there were exhortations here and elsewhere, to take the most extreme and illegal remedies to right a wide variety of wrongs, real and supposed.

It would be hard to frame a more insidiously equivocal statement of the Negro grievance concerning law enforcement during a period that included the release of the suspects in the murder of the three civil-rights workers in Mississippi, the failure to obtain convictions against the suspected murderers of Medgar Evers and Mrs. Violet Liuzzo, the Gilligan incident in New York, the murder of Reverend James Reeb, and the police violence in Selma, Alabama—to mention only a few of the more notorious cases. And surely it would have been more to the point to mention that throughout the nation Negro demonstrations have almost invariably been nonviolent, and that the major influence on the Negro community of the civil-rights movement has been the strategy of discipline and dignity. Obsessed by the few prophets of violent resistance, the McCone Commission ignores the fact that never before has an American group sent so many people to jail or been so severely punished for trying to uphold the law of the land.

It is not stretching things too far to find a connection between these matters and the treatment of the controversy concerning the role of the Los Angeles police. The report goes into this question at great length, finally giving no credence to the charge that the police may have contributed to the spread of the riots through the use of excessive force. Yet this conclusion is arrived at not from the point of view of the Watts Negroes, but from that of the city officials and the police. Thus, the report informs us, in judicial hearings that were held on 32 of the 35 deaths which occurred, 26 were ruled justifiable homicides, but the report—which includes such details as the precise time Mayor Yorty called Police Chief Parker and when exactly the National Guard was summoned—never tells us what a "justifiable homicide" is considered to be. It tells us that "of the 35 killed, one was a fireman, one was a deputy sheriff, and one was a

Long Beach policeman," but it does not tell us how many Negroes were killed or injured by police or National Guardsmen. (Harry Fleischman of the American Jewish Committee reports that the fireman was killed by a falling wall; the deputy sheriff, by another sheriff's bullet; and the policeman, by another policeman's bullet.) We learn that of the 1,032 people reported injured, 90 were police officers, 36 were firemen, 10 were National Guardsmen, 23 were from government agencies. To find out that about 85 per cent of the injured were Negroes, we have to do our own arithmetic. The report contains no information as to how many of these were victims of police force, but one can surmise from the general pattern of the riots that few could have been victims of Negro violence.

The report gives credence to Chief Parker's assertion that the rioters were the "criminal element in Watts" yet informs us that of the 3,438 adults arrested, 1,164 had only minor criminal records and 1,232 had never been arrested before. Moreover, such statistics are always misleading. Most Negroes, at one time or another, have been picked up and placed in jail. I myself have been arrested twice in Harlem on charges that had no basis in fact: once for trying to stop a police officer from arresting the wrong man; the second time for asking an officer who was throwing several young men into a paddy wagon what they had done. Both times I was charged with interfering with an arrest and kept overnight in jail until the judge recognized me and dismissed the charges. Most Negroes are not fortunate enough to be recognized by judges.

Having accepted Chief Parker's view of the riots, the report goes on to absolve him of the charge of discrimination: "Chief Parker's statements to us and collateral evidence, such as his fairness to Negro officers, are inconsistent with his having such an attitude ['deep hatred of Negroes']. Despite the depth of feeling against Chief Parker expressed to us by so many witnesses, he is recognized even by many of his vocal critics as a capable Chief who directs an efficient police force and serves well this entire community."

I am not going to stress the usual argument that the police habitually mistreat Negroes. Every Negro knows this. There is scarcely any black man, woman, or child in the land who at some point or other has not been mistreated by a policeman. (A young man in Watts said, "The riots will continue because I, as a Negro, am immediately considered to be a criminal by the police and, if I have a pretty woman with me, she is a tramp even if she is my wife or mother.") Police Chief Parker, however, goes beyond the usual bounds. He does not recognize that he is prejudiced, and being both naive and zealous about law and order, he is given to a dangerous fanaticism. His reference to the Negro rioters as "monkeys," and his "top . . . and bottom" description of the riots, speak for themselves, and they could only have further enraged and encouraged the rioters. His insistence on dealing with the outbreak in Watts as though it were the random work of a "criminal element" threatened to lead the community, as Martin Luther King remarked after the meeting he and I had with Chief Parker, "into potential holocaust." Though Dr. King and I have had considerable experience in talking with public officials who do not understand the Negro community, our discussions with Chief Parker and Mayor Samuel Yorty left us completely nonplussed. They both denied, for example, that there was any prejudice in Los Angeles. When we pointed to the very heavy vote in the city for Proposition 14, they replied, "That's no indication of prejudice. That's personal choice." When I asked Chief Parker about his choice of language, he implied that this was the only language Negroes understood.

The impression of "blind intransigence and ignorance of the social forces involved" which Dr. King carried away from our meeting with Chief Parker is borne out by other indications. The cast of his political beliefs, for example, was evidenced during his appearance last May on the Manion Forum, one of the leading platforms of the radical right, in which (according to newspaper reports) he offered his "considered opinion that America today is in reality more than half pagan" and that "we have moved our form of government to a socialist form of government." Such opinions have a good deal of currency today within the Los Angeles police department. About a month before the riots, a leaflet describing Dr. King as a liar and a Communist was posted on the bulletin board of a Los Angeles police station, and only after the concerted efforts of various Negro organizations was this scurrilous pamphlet removed.

Certainly these were "aggravating factors" that the McCone Report should properly have mentioned. But what is more important to understand is that even if every policeman in every black ghetto behaved like an angel and were trained in the most progressive of police academies, the conflict would still exist. This is so because the ghetto is a place where Negroes do not want to be and are fighting to get out of. When someone with a billy club and a gun tells you to behave yourself amid these terrible circumstances, he becomes a zoo keeper, demanding of you, as one of "these monkeys" (to use Chief Parker's phrase), that you accept abhorrent conditions. He is brutalizing you by insisting that you tolerate what you cannot, and ought not, tolerate.

In its blithe ignorance of such feelings, the McCone Report offers as one of its principal suggestions that speakers be sent to Negro schools to teach the students that the police are their friends and that their interests are best served by respect for law and order. Such public-relations gimmicks, of course, are futile—it is hardly a lack of contact with the police that creates the problem. Nor, as I have suggested, is it only a matter of prejudice. The fact is that when Negroes are deprived of work, they resort to selling numbers, women, or dope to earn a living; they must gamble and work in poolrooms. And when the policeman upholds the law, he is depriving them of their livelihood. A clever criminal in the Negro ghettos is not unlike a clever "operator" in the white business world, and so long as Negroes are denied legitimate opportunities, no exhortations to obey the rules of the society and to regard the police as friends will have any effect.

This is not to say that relations between the police and the Negroes of Watts could not be improved. Mayor Yorty and Police

Chief Parker might have headed off a full-scale riot had they refrained from denouncing the Negro leaders and agreed to meet with them early on. Over and over again—to repeat the point with which we began—the rioters claimed that violence was the only way they could get these officials to listen to them. The McCone Commission, however, rejects the proposal for an independent police review board and instead recommends that the post of Inspector General be established—under the authority of the Chief of Police—to handle grievances.

The conditions of Negro life in Watts are not, of course, ignored by the McCone Report. Their basic structure is outlined in a section entitled "Dull, Devastating Spiral of Failure." Here we find that the Negro's "homelife destroys incentive"; that he lacks "experience with words and ideas"—that he is "unready and unprepared" in school; and that, "unprepared and unready," he *slips into the ranks of the unemployed*" (my italics).

I would say, *is shoved*. It is time that we began to understand this "dull, devastating spiral of failure" and that we stopped attributing it to this or that characteristic of Negro life. In 1940, Edward Wright Bakke described the effects of unemployment on family structure in terms of the following model: The jobless man no longer provides, credit runs out, the woman is forced to take a job; if relief then becomes necessary, the woman is regarded even more as the center of the family; the man is dependent on her, the children are bewildered, and the stability of the family is threatened and often shattered. Bakke's research dealt strictly with white families. The fact that Negro social

scientists like E. Franklin Frazier and Kenneth Clark have shown that this pattern is typical among the Negro poor does not mean, then, that it stems from some inherent Negro trait or is the ineluctable product of Negro social history. If Negroes suffer more than others from the problems of family instability today, it is not because they are Negro but because they are so disproportionately unemployed, underemployed, and ill-paid.

Anyone looking for historical patterns would do well to consider the labor market for Negroes since the Emancipation. He will find that Negro men have consistently been denied the opportunity to enter the labor force in anything like proportionate numbers, have been concentrated in the unskilled and marginal labor and service occupations, and have generally required wartime emergencies to make any advances in employment, job quality, and security. Such advances are then largely wiped out when the economy slumps again.

In 1948, for example, the rates of Negro and white unemployment were roughly equal. During the next decade, however, Negro unemployment was consistently double that of whites, and among Negro teenagers it remained at the disastrously high figure which prevailed for the entire population during the Depression. It is true that the nation's improved economic performance in recent years has reduced the percentage of jobless Negroes from 12.6 per cent, which it reached in 1958 (12.5 per cent in 1961) to roughly 8.1 per cent today. Despite this progress, the rate of Negro unemployment continues to be twice as high as white (8.13 per cent as against 4.2 per cent). In other words, job discrimination remains constant. These statistics, moreover, conceal the persistence of Negro youth unemployment: in 1961, 24.7 per cent of those Negro teenagers not in school were out of work and it is estimated that in 1966 this incredible rate will only decline to 23.2 per cent. What this figure tells us is that the rise in Negro employment has largely resulted from the calling of men with previous experience back to work. This is an ominous trend, for it is estimated that in the coming year, 20 per cent of the new entrants into the labor force will be Negro (almost twice as high as the Negro percentage of the population). Approximately half of these young Negroes will not have the equivalent of a high-school education and they will be competing in an economy in which the demand for skill and training is increasing sharply.

Thus there is bound to be a further deterioration of the Negro's economic—and hence social—position, despite the important political victories being achieved by the civil-rights movement. For many young Negroes, who are learning that economic servitude can be as effective an instrument of discrimination as racist laws, the new "freedom" has already become a bitter thing indeed. No wonder that the men of Watts were incensed by reports that the poverty program was being obstructed in Los Angeles by administrative wrangling. (As I write this, the New York *Times* reports that political rivalries and ambitions have now virtually paralyzed the program in that area.)

How does the McCone Report propose to halt this "dull, devastating spiral of failure"? First, through education—"our fundamental resource." The commission's analysis begins with a comparison of class

size in white and Negro areas (the latter are referred to throughout as "disadvantaged areas" and Negro schools, as "disadvantaged schools"). It immediately notes that classes in the disadvantaged schools are slightly smaller; on the other hand, the more experienced teachers are likely to be found in the *non*-disadvantaged areas, and there is tremendous overcrowding in the disadvantaged schools because of double sessions. The buildings in the "disadvantaged areas are in better repair"; on the other hand, there are "cafeterias in the advantaged schools" but not in the disadvantaged schools, which also have no libraries. This random balance sheet of "resources" shows no sense of priorities; moreover, despite the alarming deficiencies it uncovers in the "disadvantaged schools," the McCone Report, in consistent fashion, places its emphasis on the Negro child's "deficiency in environmental experiences" and on "his homelife [which] all too often fails to give him incentive. . . ."

The two major recommendations of the commission in this area will hardly serve to correct the imbalances revealed. The first is that elementary and junior high schools in the "disadvantaged areas" which have achievement levels substantially below the city average should be designated "Emergency Schools." In each of these schools an emergency literacy program is to be established with a maximum of 22 students in each class and an enlarged and supportive corps of teachers. The second recommendation is to establish a permanent pre-school program to help prepare three- and four-year-old children to read and write.

W. T. Bassett, executive secretary of the Los Angeles AFL-CIO, has criticized the report for its failure to deal with education and training for adolescents and adults who are no longer in school. Another glaring omission is of a specific plan to decrease school segregation. While most of us now agree that the major goal of American education must be that of quality integrated schools, we cannot, as even the report suggests, achieve the quality without at the same time moving toward integration. The stated goal of the McCone Commission, however, is to "reverse the trend of defacto segregation" by improving the quality of the Negro schools; in short, separate but equal schools that do not disturb the existing social patterns which isolate the Negro child in his "disadvantaged areas."

That the commission's explicit concern for Negro problems falls short of its implicit concern for the status quo is also evident in its proposals for housing. It calls for the liberalization of credit and FHA-insured loans in "disadvantaged areas," the implementation of rehabilitation measures and other urban-renewal programs and, as its particular innovation, the creation of a "wide area data bank." Meanwhile it refuses to discuss, much less to criticize, the effect of Proposition 14 or to recommend a new fair-housing code. To protect the Negro against discrimination, the McCone Report supports the creation of a Commission on Human Relations, but does not present any proposals that would enable it to do more than collect information and conduct public-relations campaigns.

The most crucial section of the report is the one on employment and, not unexpectedly, it is also the most ignorant, unimaginative, and conservative—despite its dramatic recommendation that 50,000 new jobs be created. On the matter of youth unemployment, the report suggests that the existing federal projects initiate a series of "attitudinal training" programs to help young Negroes develop the necessary motivation to hold on to these new jobs which are to come from somewhere that the commission keeps secret. This is just another example of the commission's continued reliance on public relations, and of its preoccupation with the "dull, devastating spiral" of Negro failure. The truth of the matter is that Negro youths cannot change their attitudes until they see that they can get jobs. When what they see is unemployment and their Economic Opportunity programs being manipulated in behalf of politicians, their attitudes will remain realistically cynical.

Once again, let me try to cut through the obscurantism which has increasingly come to cloud this issue of Negro attitudes. I am on a committee which administers the Apprenticeship Training Program of the Workers Defense League. For many years the League had heard that there were not enough Negro applicants to fill the various openings for apprenticeship training and had also repeatedly been told by vocational-school counselors that Negro students could not pay attention to key subjects such as English and mathematics. The League began its own recruitment and placement program two years ago and now has more than 500 apprentice applicants on file. When, last fall, Local 28 of the Sheetmetal Workers Union—to take one example—announced that a new admission test for apprentices was to be given soon, the League contacted those applicants who had indicated an interest in sheetmetal work. The young men came to the office, filled out a 10-page application form, filed a ten-dollar fee, and returned it to the Local 28 office. Then, five nights a week for three weeks, they came to Harlem, in many cases from Brooklyn and Queens, to be tutored. Most of the young men showed up for all fifteen sessions, and scored well on the test. At their interviews they were poised and confident. Eleven of these men finally were admitted to a class of 33. The WDL doesn't attribute this success to a miraculous program; it merely knows that when young people are told that at the end of a given period of study those who perform well will obtain decent work, then their attitudes will be markedly different from those who are sent off to a work camp with vague promises.

To cut the cost of job training programs, the McCone Commission avers that compensation "should not be necessary for those trainees who are receiving welfare support." Earlier in the report the authors point out that welfare services tend to destroy family life by giving more money to a woman who lives alone; yet they have the audacity to ask that the practice of not allowing men who are on family relief to earn an additional income be maintained for young men who are working and being trained. How is a young man to be adequately motivated if he cannot feel that his work is meaningful and necessary? The McCone Report would have us say to him, "There, there, young man, we're going to keep you off the streets—just putter around doing this make-work." But the young man knows

that he can collect welfare checks and also hustle on street corners to increase his earnings. A man's share of a welfare allotment is pitifully small, but more than that, he should be paid for his work; and if one is interested in his morale, he should not be treated as a charity case.

Continuing with the problem of employment, the report recommends that "there should immediately be developed in the affected area a job training and placement center through the combined efforts of Negroes, employers, labor unions and government." In the absence of actual jobs, this would mean merely setting up a new division, albeit voluntary, of the unemployment insurance program. "Federal and state governments should seek to insure through development of new facilities and additional means of communication that advantage is taken of government and private training programs and employment opportunities in our disadvantaged communities." Perhaps the only thing the Job Corps program doesn't lack is publicity: last summer it received ten times as many applications as it could handle. Nor can new types of information centers and questionnaires provide 50,000 new jobs. They may provide positions for social workers and vocational counselors, but very few of them will be unemployed Negroes.

The report goes on: "Legislation should be enacted requiring employers with more than 250 employees and all labor unions to report annually to the state Fair Employment Practices Commission, the racial composition of the work force and membership." But an FEP Commission that merely collects information and propaganda is powerless. And even with the fullest cooperation of labor and management to promote equality of opportunity, the fact remains that there are not enough jobs in the Los Angeles area to go around, even for those who are fortunate enough to be included in the retraining programs. As long as unions cannot find work for many of their own members, there is not much they can do to help unemployed Negroes. And the McCone Report places much of its hope in private enterprise, whose response so far has been meager. The highest estimate of the number of jobs given to Los Angeles Negroes since the Watts crisis is less than 1,000.

The Negro slums today are ghettoes of despair. In Watts, as elsewhere, there are the unemployable poor: the children, the aging, the permanently handicapped. No measure of employment or of economic growth will put an end to their misery, and only government programs can provide them with a decent way of life. The care of these people could be made a major area of job growth. Los Angeles officials could immediately train and put to work women and unemployed youths as school attendants, recreation counselors, practical nurses, and community workers. The federal government and the state of California could aid the people of Watts by beginning a massive public-works program to build needed housing, schools, hospitals, neighborhood centers, and transportation facilities: this, too, would create new jobs. In short, they could begin to develop the $100-billion freedom budget advocated by A. Philip Randolph.

Such proposals may seem impractical and even incredible. But what is truly impractical and incredible is that America, with its enormous wealth, has allowed Watts to become what it is and that a commission empowered to study this explosive situation should come up with answers that boil down to voluntary actions by business and labor, new public-relations campaigns for municipal agencies, and information-gathering for housing, fair-employment, and welfare departments. The Watts manifesto is a response to realities that the McCone Report is barely beginning to grasp. Like the liberal consensus which it embodies and reflects, the commission's imagination and political intelligence appear paralyzed by the hard facts of Negro deprivation it has unearthed, and it lacks the political will to demand that the vast resources of contemporary America be used to build a genuinely great society that will finally put an end to these deprivations. And what is most impractical and incredible of all is that we may very well continue to teach impoverished, segregated, and ignored Negroes that the only way they can get the ear of America is to rise up in violence.

Note: This article was written previous to the March 1966 disturbances in Watts.

Maria Angelina Soldatenko

Organizing Latina Garment Workers in Los Angeles

Chicanas and Latinas have a long history of organizing; however, surrounded by non-Latino unions dominated by males, they are kept out of the unions. Their workplace is racially and ethnically stratified. Most supervisors in the garment industry are White male, while the workers are female. The state also plays a huge role in the exploitation of Latina working women and the Los Angeles garment workers especially. Hence, California's government constantly failed to protect immigrant workers and instead implemented stronger immigration laws and labor restrictions that impacted the Latina working woman's life negatively. (*IJ*)

Recent literature on Chicanas and organized labor celebrates Chicanas' participation in unions and its links to family, community, and ethnicity. Ruiz's and Zavella's work demonstrates the creation of a work culture and system of networks among Mexicana and Chicana cannery workers. Both trace the participation and leadership roles of Mexicanas and Chicanas in United Cannery, Agricultural, Packing and Allied Workers of America and the way in which active participation in organized labor had an impact on the lives of these women (Ruiz 1987; Zavella 1987; Ruiz 1990). The picture I will paint of Latinas[1] in the Los Angeles garment industry is very different. Workers are still not formally organized, and women are excluded from leadership positions in the union.[2] In fact, the long- and short-term strategies of the International Lady's Garment Workers Union, in conjunction with the nature of the industry, have effectively disenfranchised Latinas from their right to organize.[3] This situation rests on the racist and sexist nature of organized labor in the Los Angeles garment industry. My aim in this essay is to demonstrate how race and gender have been used to keep Latinas from organizing.

Before describing any research on Latinas, I would like to posit a theoretical and political position. In the particular case of garment workers, Latina *costureras* must be placed at the center of our analysis. This means two things: First, we must consider their lived experiences and their conditions of work; and second, we must examine these within the construct of standpoint methodology.

Latina costureras do not exist in a vacuum. Political and social structural factors have an impact on the conditions of Latinas' working lives. In the particular case of the Los Angeles garment industry, a mutual relationship exists between the existence and development of sweatshops and the availability of undocumented Latina workers in Los Angeles (Soldatenko 1990). The garment industry in Los Angeles did not arise by chance. The historical move from the Northeast was triggered by a desire for cheaper nonunionized labor (Lamphere 1987; NACLA 1980). Latinas are locked into an industry that offers little possibility for advancement yet represents one of the few options in a gender/ethnic stratified labor market. We therefore need to understand the position of Latinas in the structure of the industry and their immigrant status if we are to understand why Latinas remain without union representation. This does not mean that our understanding of the costureras is subsumed by a purely economic study. Gender, race/ethnicity, class, and immigrant status are essential in any study of Los Angeles costureras.

Second, if we place women at the center of the analysis, we need to step away from traditional academic approaches. The work of Dorothy Smith provides an excellent point of departure. She vigorously argues that women must stand at the center of any analysis intended to understand them:

> We have not known, as poets, painters, and sculptors have known, how to begin from our own experience, how to make ourselves as women the subject of the sociological act of knowing (Smith 1987, 69).

In the process of placing women at the center, we necessarily open to question epistemological issues in the social sciences. Women of color are excluded, not only from the social sciences, but from the conceptualizations of Euro American feminists as well.[4] Traditional approaches must be reformulated in order to account for women who have been either excluded or reduced to stereotypical accounts. It is simply not good enough to use existing mainstream methodologies uncritically. When interpreting Latinas' lived experience, pertinent cultural knowledge must be brought to bear (Stanfield 1988). Oppositional ethnographies and life histories can assist in this task to give voice to these women by recording their perspectives on their experiences (hooks 1990; Mani 1990; Chabram 1990).[5]

Costureras and Theories of Work

To get an idea of the problems Latinas face, we can begin by looking at a recent study of the history of ILGWU in Los Angeles by Laslett and Tyler. The book opens with a remarkable observation:

When people refer to the ladies' garment industry, they tend to assume that it is composed exclusively of female workers . . . the overwhelming majority of employees in the industry have always been women. . . . In the West, the majority have nearly always been Latinas. But the . . . industry has also employed men, mostly in skilled positions; and men have always dominated the officer cadre of the union (Laslett and Tyler 1989, 3).

This statement demonstrates the typical exclusion of Chicanas, Mexicans, and Latinas within the ILGWU. Women of color do the work; white men lead.[6] We should not simply reject this situation as inequitable; we need to understand how this sexist and racist view permeates both Latinas' reality and the analyses of Latinas. We therefore need to explain, on one hand, how the ILGWU in Los Angeles has been and continues to be controlled by white males, while the vast majority of workers are unorganized Latinas.[7] On the other hand, we need to be aware that research that does not include standpoint methodology is flawed. The only way to find answers is to begin to openly discuss the racist and sexist nature of organized labor from the point of view of Latinas

themselves. I will begin by examining some of the theories of work.

The participation of women of color in unions must be put in the context of particular job settings and historical periods. By looking at particular case studies of working women of color, it is possible to discern the main factors that contribute to their participation, or lack of it, in organized labor. I would like to look at four issues that have appeared in the recent literature concerning women and unions: gender segregation, work culture and resistance, the exclusionary practices of unions, and the role of the state in organized labor.

Historically, a fragmentation of jobs considered appropriate for women and men arose out of patriarchal practices within particular economic and social contexts (Walby 1986; Milkman 1987). This gender segregation at work has been detrimental to women. As Tilly and Scott explain:

From the preindustrial period to the present, jobs have been segregated by sex, and women's work has persistently been associated with low skill and low pay. Sex-segregated labor markets are not simply differentiated markets, they are also asymmetrical; women's work is consistently ranked lower than men's (Tilly and Scott 1987, 2).

This separation must be addressed at the outset of any discussion about work. This process justifies and legitimizes the existence of men's and women's work and the inferiority of the latter. The debate on gender segregation has recently been extended to account for the gender/race segregation in the lowest occupations. Gender/ethnic-specific occupations have appeared and been assigned to women of color in the United States.[8] These occupations, such as jobs in the service industry, electronics, and garment manufacturing, are accompanied by terrible working conditions and extremely low wages. In the case of Latinas in the garment industry, their undocumented status further restricts their job options. The interlinking of gender, race, class, and immigrant status has led to the creation of an industry that operates like any other industry in underdeveloped societies.

Organized labor must therefore be studied in the context of gender/ethnic segregation at work. The level of segregation by gender and ethnicity affects the character of the labor organizing that can take place and its ultimate success or failure. Some scholars argue that it is possible to create a work culture on the shop floor. Networks are developed among women in the same ethnic group or across ethnic lines. These networks created at work extend from work to lifecycle and family events celebrated at the workplace. Solidarity arises among workers, resulting in some cases in effective union participation and resistance against management (Lamphere 1987; Sacks 1988; Ruiz 1990; Zavella 1987; Westwood 1984). Ruiz, for instance, argues that in some cases the ghettoization of an ethnic group and crowded conditions at work, as in the case of Mexican cannery workers, might result in effective unionization (Ruiz 1990, 281).

For Latinas in Los Angeles's sweatshops, the development of a work culture did not occur. This does not disprove the existence of work cultures among women workers; rather it illuminates the pervasive effect that a particular set of working conditions, and a fragmented and extended community, has on the possibility that Latina costureras could effectively resist management and deteriorating working conditions. Even though Latinas sit next to each other, they are completely absorbed in their sewing machines. The noise level does not allow for conversation and exchange at work. Furthermore, these women are constantly forced to compete for the good bundles that are distributed according to the supervisor's criteria—sometimes unfairly—to particular groups of women.

Though Latinas come into contact during work breaks, the conditions of work are so competitive that they must always be on guard. Moreover, new workers who will eventually take the place of the senior garment workers are constantly entering the shop. The working conditions are complicated by the high turnover rate; women do not stay long enough at the shop to establish networks. New immigrant workers constantly replace those already on the line. Another factor that retards the development of networks is the geographical character of Los Angeles. Latina garment workers do not live close to each other in a differentiated community. They are spread across multiple communities throughout the city and beyond its limits. Their family and coworker networks are not connected by geographic immediacy. As a result, my research did not corroborate the findings of those who reported community ties among women workers (Lamphere 1987; Sacks 1988; Zavella 1987; Westwood 1984).

Many scholars have analyzed the sexist practices of union officials and rank-and-file males in U.S. labor (Ruiz 1990; Zavella 1988; Lamphere and Grenier 1988; Bookman and Morgen 1988; Sacks 1988). It has been pointedly argued that men have kept women out of unions because women were seen as competitors in the labor market. Together with a patriarchal ideology in which women were assigned roles as mothers and wives, men kept women without options by marginalizing them in the labor market (Kessler-Harris 1975; Walby 1988; Bradley 1989).

In the case of working-class Chicanas and Latinas there exists little question as to their long history in the labor market. Latinas have been relegated to the lowest-paying and most onerous of occupations in the labor market, placing them in "ethnic niches" (Ruiz 1990; Phizacklea 1988). In Los Angeles, the garment industry represents one of these niches that has been sustained and exists because of the available pool of immigrant Latina and Asian working women.[9]

The state plays an important role as well in the marginalization of women in both employment and union organizing. The efforts of the unions to confine women to certain "unskilled" jobs is compounded by the passage of certain types of labor legislation. For example, some protective labor legislation excluded women from performing certain jobs considered dangerous and "immoral."[10] As Strom notes, women did not receive the kind of assistance that men did through labor legislation in the 1930s. Married women were constantly under attack, were condemned for working outside the home, and were not allowed to fully participate in government and union policies (Strom 1983).

In the case of the Los Angeles garment industry, we can observe the role of the state through the failure of the labor department and labor legislation to effectively protect immigrant Latina working women. There are few inspectors in the garment industry, and their numbers appear to be decreasing. Abuses on the part of garment contractors have rarely been stopped. The National Labor Relations Board's process of complaints is long and complicated; it might take from thirty months to three years for a complaint to be resolved (Douglas 1986, 207). A recent attempt at implementation of new state legislation, the Hayden initiative, to make manufacturers jointly liable with contractors and subcontractors for violations against workers was vetoed by Governor Deukmeijian in August 1990. Thus the state, through the lack of protection and labor violation regulation, leaves Latinas vulnerable to all forms of abuse.

The lack of a protective state policy for worker rights is further evident in the implementation of immigration laws and labor restrictions that effectively segregate immigrant women into underground shops in the garment industry (Laslett and Tyler 1989; Phizacklea 1988). In the sweatshops it is the employers who suggest that workers purchase false work permits. Delia, a Mexican garment worker, describes such an incident:

El dueño me daba para . . . [The owner offered me some money to buy fake papers. My husband did not let me . . . the owner offered me the minimum wage with fake papers. He got fake papers for this other guy at the shop . . . he used to say that even if the papers were not good, he would take them.]

Many Latinas remain silent about these abuses. They are afraid to lose their meager salaries. There are, however, some Latinas who are ready to risk deportation by complaining. Adela, a Mexican garment worker, reported her employer. She knows that she is going to face deportation, but she explains why she had to do it:

No le hace que me deporten . . . [It doesn't matter if they deport me, I will just go away. This is a vicious circle, there should be a law . . . they should deport the drug addicts, to me (sigh) . . . I cannot see my people, humiliating themselves for money . . . I leave and there will be someone else to take my place.]

Even though Chicanas and Mexicanas have a long history in union organizations, they are kept outside of union leadership. They were always circumscribed by the manipulations of non-Latino male-dominated unions who in the end did not integrate them into the different unions. Union leaders continue to be shortsighted as to the possibilities and the subsequent prospects for organizing if Chicanas, Mexicanas, and Latinas are included in real leadership positions (Ruiz 1990; Zavella 1987; Durón 1984). The ILGWU in Los Angeles, for example, unlike the ILGWU in San Francisco, which has an Asian woman as manager of the Pacific North West District Council, hires Latinas but never to positions of importance.

The ILGWU has not been able to accommodate Latinas in leadership positions even though the majority of garment workers are Latinas. The union typically hires Latinas to positions of minor importance when their expertise is needed to deal directly with Latina garment workers. In general, however, Latinas are excluded from positions of power, leadership, and decision making, even though it is clear that their opinions and leadership could be valuable to any attempts at unionization.

The structure of the garment industry, management, the state, and organized labor have worked in harmonious ways to the detriment of immigrant Latina workers in the garment industry of Los Angeles. The garment industry in Los Angeles illuminates the processes by which immigrant women, who historically have this occupation in this industry, are left completely unprotected by any form of regulation from the state via the board of labor relations or by labor organizations such as the ILGWU. This situation by which garment workers are attempting to survive is taking place at the same time that the state is enforcing a new immigration law (Immigration Reform and Control Act, IRCA). This immigration law is supposed to sanction employers who hire undocumented workers. In practice it has exacerbated a situation in which undocumented workers have to work in illegal contractor shops where there is no regulation or enforcement of basic labor laws, such as minimum wage, hours of work, and industrial homework, not to mention unsanitary and dangerous working conditions.

Latina Garment Workers in Los Angeles

While it is a very legitimate issue to discuss lack of representation of Latinas in leadership positions in unions, I want to argue that our point of departure must be the masses of Latinas. I propose that in order to study Latina garment workers in Los Angeles and their lack of participation in unions we must start from the lived experiences of Latinas themselves. It is no longer enough to focus on the unions, the ILGWU, and its officials and organizers. We already know that unions are heavily male and non-Latino and that racist perceptions are common among the leadership of the AFL-CIO.[11] The ILGWU in no way reflects the population of Latina garment workers who form the majority of that labor sector in Los Angeles. If we want to understand the problems of unionization we must explore the life histories of Latinas who are nonunionized, concentrated in contractor's shops, and doing industrial homework. The future of the garment workers in Los Angeles depends on that majority of Latinas who continue to be exploited and are nonunion. The life history approach is important in looking at Latinas and their participation in the industry. We need to know where Latinas are located in the structure of the garment industry. How do Latinas look at unions? What do Latinas need in terms of organizing, from their own perspective?

Methods

From 1987 to 1990 I did participant observation at the ILGWU and sewing schools where Latinas are trained and placed in shops at the end of their training. Working in a contractor's shop in order to accurately assess the working conditions, I learned to operate industrial sewing machines and worked piece rates, in an effort to learn what it means to be a garment worker in Los Angeles. Later, I interviewed key informants and collected the life histories of some Latina garment workers of various ages working at shops or doing industrial homework.

Through participating with Latina garment workers in Los Angeles, it is clear that one of the main problems that Latinas face in the apparel industry is the lack of unionization. This lack of unionization has usually been explained by union officials and scholars as a result of Latinas' (1) naiveté and lack of past union experience in their country of origin;[12] (2) their lack of English skills; (3) their lack of schooling and ignorance about U.S. social institutions; and (4) the *machismo* of Latino husbands.[13] I intend to debunk these myths reproduced by both scholars and union officials.

Many scholars argue that immigrant European garment workers back East at the turn of the century were able to organize because they had a history of struggle behind them (Asher 1984). According to Schlein, regarding the case of the garment industry in Los Angeles:

The original Los Angeles garment workers and union leaders were transplanted New Yorkers with European roots. They came replete with the tradition of socialist ideas and a strong regard for unions. As the labor force changed in favor of Latin American workers the union lost much of its force. Its efforts to communicate and organize among people who could not relate to unions became frustrated, leading to the present situation (Schlein 1980, 116).

Given the worker struggles of late-nineteenth-century Europe, some scholars point to the rapid unionization in certain industries on the East Coast. They carried over, if you wish, a culture and history of unionization. In contrast, their argument continues, Latinas in the twentieth century lack this culture and history. Latinas are again depicted as less sophisticated, more ignorant, and politically inferior to their European counterparts.

To begin with, Latinas who come to the United States and participate in the apparel industry are a heterogeneous population. It is difficult to establish their class origins, levels of education, and labor experience in their countries of origin. In fact, we encounter a collage of experiences: Latinas come from urban and rural areas; some garment workers have worked in various types of industrial settings, including the garment industry, while others were rural laborers.[14] For all, the apparel industry offered the only entry into the U.S. labor market.

Many of the Latinas had a sixth- to eighth-grade education or higher but due to lack of English skills chose to enter the garment industry. Some Latinas I talked to were secretaries, teachers, or nurses in their countries of origin. If they wanted to continue their own professions in this country, they would have had to take exams and learn English. It would be too costly and time-consuming, and their economic situation did not allow them to opt for this choice.

More important, these women are not ignorant of unions and labor organizing. They know that the United States has labor laws and are aware of the existence of the ILGWU. The Spanish-language media, furthermore, informs them about daily labor events—strikes, boycotts, state or federal investigations, and the like. Many of these women clearly understand or have experienced some type of labor organizing, especially if they came from urban areas. Ignorance about Latin American countries' labor histories greatly hampers scholars, union officials, and anyone interested in organizing Latinas. Latinas do not come to the United States as blank slates; they already have experienced or witnessed the repressive forces used by governments against legitimate unionization efforts on the part of workers. It is common in Mexico or El Salvador to make use of the police or the military to suppress any attempt by independent unions to organize.[15] Furthermore, Los Angeles has a labor history in which Mexican garment workers since the 1930s have actively participated (Laslett and Tyler 1989; Pesotta 1945; Vásquez 1980; Monroy 1980; Durón 1984).

It was Chicanas who worked closely with Rose Pesotta and the ILGWU. Rose Pessota was a Jewish immigrant worker from Ukraine who became a union organizer and vice-president of the ILGWU from 1934 to 1944. Because Pesotta had a vision for the ILGWU, she advocated the inclusion of women in different ethnic groups as union organizers. Her strategy worked with Mexican-origin women in Los Angeles during the 1930s and 1940s. Pessota drew influence from her ability to work with Mexican-origin women. She saw them as equal workers with the potential for organizing—unlike her male counterparts who saw Mexican women as unorganizable.[16] Even though Pesotta was able to communicate with Chicanas, her interactions revealed a paternalistic bent (Monroy 1980). Nevertheless, we must recognize that she was more effective than anyone else at that time.

Therefore, the question we need to ask is why these Latinas have not organized. No simple answer exists. One aspect of the problem lies in the organizational structure of the garment industry and the place that Latinas occupy within this structure.[17] For an illustration we have the case of a Salvadoran garment worker who has been in the industry for nine years. This is what she told me when I asked if she knew about a garment workers' union:

Sí, yo ya sabía que había un sindicato . . . [Yes, I already knew about the union, and I wanted to become a member. But then I found out that the ILGWU only accepts membership from stable shops or large manufacturers who can respond to union demands.]

She was working for a small contractor shop where a large number of Latinas are concentrated. She continued:

Y pensar . . . [And to think that people like us that really need the union cannot be part of it! . . . I have worked in less than human conditions. I have been exposed to thievery, they (the owners) have stolen from me, they have not paid me for work that I have done. . . . I would talk about all these things to people in the union. But the union people would tell me that those were shops that could close overnight and open somewhere else.)

Thus the decision of the ILGWU not to get involved with workers in small contracting shops affects a large number of Latinas who have no hope for fair representation. At the same time, a large number of unscrupulous contractors take advantage of this situation. The ILGWU has a valid claim when its leadership points out that as soon as they try to organize small shops the owners threaten to inform immigration officials,[18] or they move to a different location and leave the workers out of work again. The structure of the garment industry lends itself to this type of intimidation and manipulation of immigrant workers. The big manufacturers subcontract their work; it is hard to trace them—though not impossible. A couple of Latinas who were not paid for their work traced a label from a contractor's shop in downtown Los Angeles all the way to a manufacturing firm in Santa Monica. They asked the manager to give them any lead on the unscrupulous contractor who had made them work for a week without any remuneration. The manager understood the situation but never called them on the phone as she promised to do when that contractor came back to the factory.

Latinas are doing industrial homework throughout Los Angeles County even though a ban exists on industrial homework in California. Walking through the Latino communities in and around downtown Los Angeles one hears the roar of industrial machines running at any time during the day or night and sees garbage dumpsters close to apartment houses filled with fabric remnants from the overlock sewing machines.[19] During the last week of March in 1988, hearings with the Labor Relations Board took place in Los Angeles, and many people from the garment industry, unions, and community organizations testified, as did Latina homeworkers. The deplorable work conditions for homeworkers and their children were denounced; however, as one Latina homeworker asked me after two days of hearings:

Ahora ya les dijimos a todos . . . [Now we have told everyone how bad it is doing homework, and now what? What are the unions and community groups going to do about it? What about us, the women who are still working at it?]

If it is difficult to organize in contractors' shops, it is even more difficult to organize homeworkers. These women are isolated, working day and night, because the factory is their home. These Latinas understand that homework is illegal, but one homeworker explained why she preferred staying home:

Tengo que cuidar . . . [I have to look after my grandson and my younger daughter who is going to school. My

older daughter is working, and I have to babysit for her. Before I used to pay for gas and lunch in order to go to the factory. I had to pay for a babysitter as well. Now I can be with my family.]

When I asked her how much was she getting paid, she assured me that it was the minimum wage. However, when I began to ask for the hours that she had worked and how much money she got the week before, she was no longer sure. She showed me a finished cocktail gown with a lot of work and fancy pleats, for which she was paid only $3.75 apiece. It took her about two hours to do the whole garment.

At another level the immigrant status of some Latinas inhibits union organization. For Latinas, their ethnicity, gender, class, and often their immigrant status are interrelated. A garment worker explained it to me this way.

Organizarse para la gente . . . [To get organized for some people will be a double-edged sword; some people have no documents, and it is precisely these types of shops (referring to small contractor's shops) that accommodate people who do not have papers; some people prefer to earn one dollar an hour to deportation.]

From my own experience as a participant observer I can attest to the anonymity and easy entrance into contractors' shops, the lack of regard for new immigration laws, and the way in which they operate to accommodate immigrant workers. I was admitted with no questions asked; they did not even know my name. My sewing machine had a number, and I was referred to as "number four." The converted warehouse had a heavy metal screen door that remained locked at all times, partly to prevent INS officials from just walking in. There was a garage exit at the other end of the building.

I asked Olga, a Salvadoran garment worker, if Latinas could be organized without the help of a union. She responded:

Sí se podría hacer . . . [It could be done, but people who have no documents are very vulnerable. Even people with documents do not get organized. I do know that they are not interested in getting organized. Why do we not get organized? . . . I would like to test that idea. I think that we could come up with some norms of work that we could present to the employers. But we have to study this carefully. This should be studied. . . . There are possibilities, but this would not benefit the organizers, only the people that are being organized.]

She came up with ideas for how to go about organizing, always aware of the discrepancy between those with documents and those who did not have them. The documented workers are very sensitive regarding the position of their undocumented peers and avoid exposing them to the possibility of deportation or economic hardship. Olga was infuriated by all her experiences as a garment worker in the United States. She summarized it this way:

En mi país . . . [Back home they said that over here we were going to sweep dollars with the broom . . . that is a big lie! Over here we are going to sweep,

and we will not see any dollars. . . . Since I came to this country I have worked and I have not seen any money. . . . It is totally unfair.]

To exclude Latinas from important positions in union leadership has repercussions for the future of predominately Latina unions and working Latinas. The following example illustrates the lack of gender/ethnic awareness on the part of the union's cadre. In 1990, the ILGWU opened a new center for legal aid. It is located in the heart of the garment district. Free legal aid is available to garment workers who want to complain about employers. I asked one of the ILGWU leaders if Latinas had been consulted on the usefulness of the center in addressing their complaints. He explained that the question of the center was decided among the leadership (mainly male). The ILGWU intention is to encourage Latinas to complain to the NLRB about employers who commit labor violations. This center might function to deter unscrupulous contractors and to attract Latinas to the ILGWU. It remains to be seen if this will be the net result. One major problem remains—undocumented Latinas who avail themselves of the center's services risk deportation.

When I asked Latinas what their immediate needs were and how the ILGWU could best serve them and effectively attract the women as members, they cited child care issues. The lack of child care is one of the major problems for Latinas and an issue that produces a great deal of anxiety and family instability. As Pilar, a Mexican trimmer, explained:

Mi problema más grande . . . [My biggest problem is child care for my little girl. One goes to work, and the child stays in this environment (referring to the inner city area). . . . We want to move out of this area. Yesterday at six in the afternoon there was a shooting. . . . I am going to send my daughter to Mexico with her grandparents.]

And according to Dolores, a Mexican trimmer and mother of five children ranging in age from eighteen to two years old.

Mi hija, la grande . . . [My oldest daughter has to stay and take care of her two little sisters . . . she goes to school at night to learn English . . . the other day one of the little ones went out into the street, and we found her at the police station.]

In ignoring those issues of greatest concern to Latinas, their largest constituency, the union diminishes its effectiveness as a political force. The union effort to aid Latinas with free legal advice and support must be recognized as a legitimate strategy by the potential membership. Yet by not taking into consideration the needs of Latinas, the process of organizing is retarded.

Conclusion

In order to analyze the lack of unionization among Latina garment workers in Los Angeles, we have to understand the complexity of issues that Latinas face in the industry. Inadvertently, the union has worked in harmony with the state through labor legislation and immigration laws. Not organizing the sector of the industry in which the majority of Latinas are concentrated negatively affects Latinas.

We must note that the garment industry has became an "ethnic niche" for immigrant Latinas in Los Angeles. In this niche, they suffer the terrible labor conditions and miserable wages of the piece-rate system. The segregation at work along gender/ethnic lines occurs simultaneously with the gender/racial exclusionary practices of organized labor and the sanctions of the state that exacerbate the exploitation of Latina garment workers.

We need to understand the lived experiences of Latinas in the apparel industry in Los Angeles if we want to understand the issues of gender, race, and ethnicity in trade unions. The histories of the women who have been in this industry since the 1920s have not been sufficiently documented or studied. It is already assumed that this population is ignorant and culturally unsuited to unionization. We need to ask Latinas what problems they face as women of color outside of and in the union—and what is it that Latinas want from community organizations and unions. In many ways the working conditions for these immigrant women have deteriorated; proportionately, their wages have decreased in the last forty years. There is a qualitative difference between the conditions of work in the 1980s and the 1960s. Unionization efforts have died down as compared to earlier years, a phenomenon closely related to the present structure of the garment industry and the Union's decision not to organize shops where Latinas are concentrated. The

ILGWU could organize as it did under the leadership of Pesotta in the 1930s when the union advertised on Spanish-language radio stations. The majority of garment workers then were Mexican women who were willing to strike and demand fair wages and hours of work. Perhaps in the 1990s Latinas are not a priority on the agenda of union organizers and leaders in Los Angeles.

Notes

1. Historically in the garment industry in Los Angeles, the majority of sewing machine operators were Chicanas and Mexicanas. At the present time, younger Chicanas have moved to other occupations, and many older Chicanas have retired or are in the process of retiring from this industry. Immigrant Mexicanas remain the majority of garment workers in the different types of shops—though there is an increasing number of women from other parts of Latin America. Here "Latinas" refers to the group of women that I studied in the Los Angeles garment industry. It does not mean, however, that they form a homogeneous group.

2. In 1988, the ILGWU claimed membership of only 1 percent of the total number of garment workers, estimated by the ILGWU at around 100,000 workers (Ferraro 1988).

3. The ILGWU can trace its history back to 1910–1911 (Laslett and Tyler 1989, 15).

4. Several feminists have demonstrated how research by Euro American feminists has attempted to subsume the experience of women of color into their own theories and agendas (Spelman 1988; hooks 1984; Collins 1990).

5. I do not want to argue that ethnography is the method that will allow us truly to give marginalized populations their voices. This is not the case. Ethnography, whatever its variant, began as and continues to be the tool of colonization; it restricts voice. As a tool for domination, it is never neutral. I simply want to argue that when we approach ethnography critically, understanding its deficiencies, we can use it to initiate our study.

6. The hidden assumption is that immigrant and minority women are traditional and familistic and therefore incapable of organizing. This position has been effectively critiqued by Zavella (1988), Durón (1984), Bookman and Morgan (1988), and Ruiz (1990).

7. Scholars have documented the ways in which the ILGWU in Los Angeles has excluded Mexicanas and Latinas from leadership positions (Laslett and Tyler 1989; Monroy 1980). At best the leadership in the ILGWU have paternalistically tried to "guide" Latina workers (Monroy 1980).

8. This also occurs in Great Britain (Phizacklea 1990).

9. Asian women represent a smaller significant sector of the garment workers in Los Angeles. At the beginning they were only Chinese concentrated in Chinatown, but they have extended geographically to other areas. There are other groups as well, such as

Koreans, Vietnamese, Thai, and Cambodians.

10. In the 1800s some critics believed that women who spent long hours at the pedal sewing machine were sexually aroused (Chapkis and Enloe 1983, 69).

11. According to some observers, people of color are unwelcome and misunderstood by organized labor in Los Angeles. In the words of Miguel Machuca, an ex-ILGWU organizer, "I remember attending meetings at the AFL-CIO . . . when the tone of the meetings was very antagonistic towards Mexicans, or wetbacks, a term I heard very often. I heard organizers saying, 'what are we going to do about the damn wetbacks? . . . why don't we call immigration on them?'" (Machuca 1988, 8–11).

12. According to Laslett and Tyler 1989, "Latino workers tended at first to be swayed by the paternalistic blandishments of the contractors." Latinos also looked upon white organizers with suspicion. "ILGWU organizers, most of whom were still white, were sometimes wrongly seen by the newcomers as 'agents of authority,' who may also seek to have them deported" (Laslett and Tyler 1989). Also note Schlein 1980, who argues that only European workers have a trade unionist tradition.

13. "The machismo associated with Latino culture could also make it difficult to organize the married women in the trade" (Laslett and Tyler 1989).

14. Lourdes Arguelles argues that Mexicanas who migrate to the U.S. Southwest are not the landless and/or the poorest of their society (Arguelles 1990). There is little information on women from Central and South America (Peñalosa 1986).

15. The labor history of women in Mexico is extensive (Ruiz-Funes 1990). For a short account of Mexican garment workers in Mexico see Arbalaez 1990.

16. According to the ILGWU regional representative in Los Angeles, in the early 1980s married Latinas could not get organized because of the machismo among Latino husbands (Laslett and Tyler 1989, 108). These culturalist explanations demonstrate the racism inherent in perceptions of the ILGWU's leadership.

17. The garment industry in Los Angeles is structured to function at several levels. We first have the manufacturers where designing, cutting, sewing and finishing are done in the same place. The "jobbers" do designing and cutting and contract out the sewing of garments. The contractors, who may or may not be licensed, do the sewing themselves; sometimes they subcontract as well. At the bottom are the homeworkers who can work for all of them in their own homes.

18. The Immigration and Naturalization Service has been involved in union organizing drives by the ILGWU. In the strike of Lilli Diamond Fashions in 1977, the INS was pivotal in the demoralization and deportation of activist Latina workers (Vásquez 1980).

19. The Bush administration pressed to have that ban lifted throughout the nation, but it was not lifted on garment production.

References

Arbalaez, A. Marisol. 1990. "Impacto social del sismo, Mexico 1985: Las costureras." In *Between Borders: Essay on Mexicana/Chicana History,* ed. Adelaida R. Del Castillo. Encino, Calif.: Floricanto Press.

Arguelles, Lourdes. 1990. "Undocumented Female Labor in the United States Southwest: An Essay on Migration, Consciousness, Oppression, and Struggle." In *Between Borders: Essay on Mexicana/Chicana History,* ed. Adelaida R. Del Castillo. Encino, Calif.: Floricanto Press.

Asher, Nina. 1994. "Dorothy Jacob's Bellanca: Women Clothing Workers and the Run Away Shops." In *A Needle, a Bobbin, a Strike: Women Needle Workers in America,* ed. Joan M. Jensen and Sue Davidson. Philadelphia: Temple University.

Bookman, Ann, and Sandra Morgen. 1988. "'Carry It On': Continuing the Discussion and the Struggle." In *Women and the Politics of Empowerment,* ed. Ann Bookman and Sandra Morgen. Philadelphia: Temple University Press.

Bradley, Harriet. 1989. *Men's Work, Women's Work: A Sociological History of the Sexual Division of Labor in Employment.* Minneapolis: University of Minnesota Press.

Chabram, Angie. 1990. "Chicana/o Studies as Oppositional Ethnography." *Cultural Studies* 4, No. 3.

Chapkis, Wendy, and Cynthia Enloe, eds. 1983. *Of Common Cloth: Women in the Global Textile Industry.* Amsterdam: Transnational Institute.

Collins, Patricia Hill. 1990. *Black Feminist Thought: Knowledge Consciousness, and the Politics of Empowerment.* Boston: Unwin/Hyman.

Douglas, Sara U. 1986. *Labor's New Voice: Unions and the Mass Media.* Norwood, N.J.: Ablex Publishing Corporation.

Durón, Clementina. 1984. "Mexican Women and Labor Conflict in Los Angeles: The ILGWU Dressmakers' Strike of 1933." *Aztlán* 15, No. 1.

Ferraro, Cathleen. 1988. "Fragmentation, Competition Inhibit L.A.'s Union Growth." *California Apparel News* (February): 12–18.

hooks, bell. 1984. *Feminist Theory: From Margin to Center.* Boston: South End Press.

____. 1990. *Yearning: Race, Gender and Cultural Politics.* Boston: South End Press.

Kesser-Harris, Alice. 1975. "Where Are the Organized Women Workers?" *Feminist Studies* (fall).

Lamphere, Louise. 1987. *From Working Daughters to Working Mothers: Immigrant Women in a New England Industrial Community.* Ithaca, N.Y.: Cornell University Press.

Lamphere, Louise, and Guillermo J. Grenier. 1988. "Women's Unions, and 'Participative Management': Organizing in the Sun Belt." In *Women and the Politics of Empowerment,* ed. Ann Bookman and Sandra Morgen. Philadelphia: Temple University Press.

Laslett, John, and Mary Tyler. 1989. *The ILGWU in Los Angeles 1907–1988.* Inglewood, Calif.: Ten Star Press.

Machuca, Miguel. 1988. "Organizing Asian and Latino Workers." In

Organizing Asian Pacific Workers in Southern California, ed. June McMahon. Los Angeles: Institute of Industrial Relations.

Mani, Lata. 1990. "Multiple Mediations: Feminist Scholarship in the Age of Multi-National Reception." *Feminist Review 35.*

Milkman, Ruth. 1987. *Gender at Work: The Dynamics of Job Segregation by Sex during World War II.* Urbana: University of Illinois Press.

Monroy, Douglas. 1980. "La Costura en Los Angeles, 1933–1939: The ILGWU and the Politics of Domination." In *Mexican Women in the United States: Struggles Past and Present,* ed. Magdalena Mora and Adelaida R. Del Castillo. Los Angeles: Chicano Studies Research Center.

NACLA Report of the Americas. 1980. "Capital's Flight: The Apparel Industry Moves South." In *Mexican Women in the United States: Struggles Past* and Present, ed. Magdalena Mora and Adelaida R. Del Castillo. Los Angeles: Chicano Studies Research Center.

Pesotta, Rose. 1945. *Bread Upon the Waters.* New York: Dodd, Mead and Company.

Phizacklea, Annie. 1988. "Entrepreneurship, Ethnicity, and Gender." In *Enterprising Women: Ethnicity, Economy, and Gender Relations,* ed. Sally Westwood and Parminder Bhachu. London: Routledge Press.

____. 1990. *Unpacking the Fashion Industry: Gender, Racism and Class in Production.* London: Routledge Press.

Ruiz, Vicki L. 1987. *Cannery Women, Cannery Lives.* Albuquerque: University of New Mexico.

____. 1990. "A Promise Fulfilled: Mexican Cannery Workers in Southern California." In *Between Borders: Essays on Mexicana/Chicana History,* ed. Adelaida R. Del Castillo. Encino. Calif.: Floricanto Press,

Ruiz-Funes, Concepción and Enriqueta Tuñón. 1990. "Panorama de las luchas de la mujer mexicana en el siglo XX." In *Between Borders: Essays on Mexicana/Chicana History,* ed. Adelaida R. Del Castillo. Encino, Calif.: Floricanto Press.

Sacks, Karen Brodkin. 1988. *Caring by the Hour: Women, Work, and Organizing the Duke Medical Center.* Urbana: University of Illinois Press.

Schlein, Lisa. 1980. "Los Angeles Garment Industry Sews a Cloak of Shame." In *Mexican Women in the United States: Struggles Past and Present,* ed. Magdalena Mora and Adelaida R. Del Castillo. Los Angeles: Chicano Studies Research Center.

Smith, Dorothy E. 1987. *The Everyday World as Problematic: A Feminist Sociology.* Boston: Northeastern University Press.

Soldatenko, Maria. 1990. "Made in the U.S.A.: Latina Garment Workers in the Sweatshops of Los Angeles." Paper presented at Stanford Law School at Palo Alto, Calif., in October.

Spelman, Elizabeth V. 1988. *Essential Women: Problems of Exclusion in Feminist Thought.* Boston: Beacon Press.

Stanfield II, John. 1988. "Not Quite in the Club." *The American Sociologist* (winter).

Strom, Sharon Hartman. 1983. "Challenging 'Women's Place':

Feminism, the Left, and Industrial Unionism in the 1930s." *Feminist Studies* (summer).

Tilly, Louise A., and Joan W. Scott. 1987. *Women, Work, and Family.* New York: Methuen Press.

Vásquez, Mario F. 1980. "The Election Day Immigration Raid at Lilli Diamond Originals and the Response of the ILGWU." In *Mexican Women in the United States: Struggles Past and Present,* ed. Magdalena Mora and Adelaida R. Del Castillo. Los Angeles: Chicano Studies Research Center.

Walby, Sylvia. 1986. *Patriarchy at Work: Patriarchal and Capitalist Relations in Employment.* Cambridge, Mass.: Polity Press.

____. 1988. "Segregation in Employment in Social and Economic Theory." In *Gender Segregation at Work,* ed. Sylvia Walby. Philadelphia: Open University Press.

Westwood, Sally. 1984. *All Day, Every Day: Factory and Family in the Making of Women's Lives.* Urbana: University of Illinois Press.

Zavella, Patricia. 1987. *Women's Work and Chicano Families: Cannery Workers of the Santa Clara Valley.* Ithaca, N.Y.: Cornell University Press.

____. 1988. "The Politics of Race and Gender: Organizing Chicana Cannery Workers in Northern California." In *Women and the Politics of Empowerment,* ed. Ann Bookman and Sandra Morgen. Philadelphia: Temple University Press.

James Diego Vigil

Barrio Gangs: Street Life and Identity in Southern California

Gangs have a long-standing presence in Southern California, especially in the Los Angeles Chicano community. Vigil used a multi-dimensional approach to explain both the presence and persistence of gangs, and explored why young men and women continue to find gangs both attractive and a rational choice. His approach combines history, anthropology, and sociology in explaining this phenomenon. A major factor of the attractiveness of gangs is the "multiple marginality" that young Chicanos in California's barrios are forced to endure. Vigil argues that lack of opportunities for achieving the "Californian Dream," conflict within the family, difficulties in adapting to mainstream culture, and other factors are responsible for the marginality. This is a useful perspective in both analyzing why gangs exist and why young Californian people join gangs. *(LH)*

In this brief introduction to the book Barrio Gangs, *cultural anthropologist Vigil draws on historical, cultural and underclass theory to frame his notions about the development and persistence of Hispanic, or Cholo, gangs. Multiple marginality results from cultural accommodation to Anglo-American lifestyles, intergenerational culture clashes, and limited opportunities for social mobility in barrio communities. The barrio street gang is a social adaptation to the economic and cultural stressors confronting young men of Mexican descent. It is instructive to consider Vigil's position relative to the criticisms of subcultural theory presented by Bursik and Grasmick. Can the concept of multiple marginality be*

171

applied to the development of other ethnic gangs and female gang membership (as described in the articles presented in Section I)?

A look behind the scenes of Chicano youth gang behavior is long overdue. It is important to know how the streets have become such a strong socializing force in the barrios of Southern California and why certain adolescents and youth there are particularly motivated to identify with the street gang. Many of the street gang habits and customs make better sense when considered in the context of street pressures and group identification processes. To survive in street culture, one must have a street identity. It will be revealed in this study that there are many intricacies and complexities to this street identity.

Chicano street gangs in Los Angeles and Southern California have been around for several decades (Bogardus 1926). Over the past forty years they have been viewed as a menace to society, wreaking crime and violence on the rest of the populace, or as a serious social problem with roots in the urban experience of low-income minority groups. Several explanations of Chicano gangs (McWilliams 1968; Griffith 1948; Tuck 1956; Heller 1966; Rosenquist and Megargee 1969; Klein 1971; Snyder 1977; J. Moore 1978; Horowitz 1983) advanced our understanding of the problem. However, the complexity of the street gang requires a careful separation of the cluster of factors that contribute to its formation and persistence. The lives of the street youths who comprise the barrio gang reflect multiple stresses and pressures, which result in a multiple marginality. This multiple marginality derives from various interwoven situations and conditions that tend to act and react upon one another. Although interrelated, the unfolding and interpretation of these ecological, economic, social, cultural, and psychological features of the street gang suggest a developmental sequence.

All of these considerations are integral to the relationship between multiple marginality and gang patterns. In particular, it will be clear that barrio children whose lives are most intensely affected by marginality in these dimensions are more at risk to become gang members. Moreover, use of the concept will permit an examination of gang violence and related behavior within the context of a cumulative, additive experience. My self-reflexive life history involvement with various facets of street and gang life and the life histories of different types of contemporary gang members provide insights and nuances and shifting levels of insider/outsider analysis to this perspective. This combination of ways of examining and describing the street gang will promote theory building and the integration of more narrowly focused explanations for gang phenomena that have emerged over the years.

Anyone who regularly works with street gangs can learn the answers to such questions as, Where they are located? Who are the members? What do they do and how do they do it? However, even after having gained such knowledge, few observers understand what the sources of this behavior are or when in a person's life such behavior emerges. It is these and other such questions that should guide our discussion if we are to better comprehend the gang phenomenon. Partial, incomplete, and narrow assessments do injustice to the general public as well as to the communities where gangs are common. As an example of this narrow attitude, I once inquired of a city official, the director of community programs and affairs, what recreational and social programs were offered to the local barrio youth and whether he was familiar with some of the conditions that caused the formation of the gang. He gave a testy response: "We don't want to understand the problem, we just want to stop it." While desiring to "stop it" is understandable, such lack of analysis can only impede the official's desire.

Chicano gangs are made up largely of young males, from 13 to 25 years of age. The gang subcultural style is a response to the pressures of street life and serves to give certain barrio youth a source of familial support, goals and directives, and sanctions and guides. Although gang members typically constitute a small minority of the young in a barrio, they represent a street style that both conforms and contrasts with familiar youth patterns (Klein 1969). On the one hand, most of their time is spent in the usual cohort activities found in any neighborhood where adolescents and other youth congregate. They talk, joke, plan social events, and exchange stories of adventure and love. Their alcohol consumption and drug use shows some parallels with that of other American adolescents. Yet it is their other, violent, socially disruptive activities that distinguish gang members from most adolescents.

Reflecting the tendency among adolescents to develop new modes of dress and speech, Chicano gang members have adopted a distinctive street style of dress, speech, gestures, tattoos, and graffiti. This style is called *cholo,* a centuries-old term for some Latin American Indians who are partially acculturated to Hispanic-based elite cultures (Wolck 1973). The term also reflects the cultural transitional situation of Mexican Americans in the southwestern United States; it is a process strongly affected by underclass forces and street requisites. Many of the cholo customs symbolize an attachment to and identification with the gang, although many individuals copy the style without joining the gang. As we will note, there is a wide difference among members in degree of commitment to the gang, but generally it is those members with the most problematic lives and intense street experiences who become regular members. Over the decades, the gang has developed a subculture, that is, a social structure and cultural value system with its own age-graded cohorts, initiations, norms and goals, and roles. These now function to socialize and enculturate barrio youth. Though the emergence of a gang subculture initially resulted from urban maladaption among some segments of the Mexican immigrant population, it is now a continuing factor to which new Latino immigrants must adapt. To understand developments in this area we must look to the starting point, the inception of this country's urban revolution.

Gangs in Urban Immigrant Communities

Gangs have been an urban problem in the United States since the beginning of large-scale immigration to this country before the turn of the century (Thrasher 1963; [1927]). The processes and patterns of immigrant adaption, although different in important ways, stemmed from remarkably similar sources. The early groups were European immigrants especially from southeastern Europe, who came to this country to find work and a better life. Most of them settled in urban areas and established their own communities. The process of finding work, locating a place to live, and adjusting to urban life was repeated many times over for different ethnic groups, and the Mexican immigrant population is no different in this regard.

What characterized most of these groups was their poverty, their lack of skills. As a result, they were treated as a cheap source of labor. In addition they came from different cultural and (by contemporary definition) racial backgrounds that contrasted sharply with the dominant Anglo-American one. Anglo native-born Americans tended to view the ethnically different newcomers' appearance, behavior patterns, and poverty as a single entity; the immigrants thus faced discrimination from the native born. Their cultural difference acted in two ways to affect them. One stemmed from the changes they had to make in their own cultural values, beliefs, and patterns to adjust and acculturate to Anglo-American lifestyles. The other was a result of how the dominant Anglo culture received and accommodated them. Their own attitudes and behaviors and those of the predominant society operated to affect where they would live, what they would do for a living, and how, when, and even whether they would become "Americanized" (Handlin 1951). Exploitation and discrimination, in particular, dominated the early period after their arrival and extended to the lives of their children. The pressures and anxieties of urban poverty, of the struggle toward a better life, and of overcoming feelings of ethnic and racial inferiority made immigrant cultural adaptation problematic. Such an experience often resulted in gangs.

Throughout most of this century, researchers and writers have compiled evidence on urban gangs. The focus of these accounts varies as to ethnic group, time, and place and the theoretical emphasis. Nonetheless, there is widespread agreement among writers that gangs are an urban phenomenon, particularly so in the cases of ethnic minorities (Clinard 1968), and they represent a pattern found among lower-class adolescents (Cloward and Ohlin 1960). In fact, there is a complex of other factors that make the urban experience so remarkably uniform: a breakdown in social institutions, especially the family and schools (which often impede rather than accommodate adjustment); a first- and second-generational conflict within each ethnic group, which creates loyalty discord and identity confusions; and a noted predisposition among youth to gravitate toward street peers for sources of social associations and personal fulfillment.

Within a generation or two, most members of each early ethnic immigrant group improved their standard of living and stabilized themselves as wage earners and homemakers. Problems associated with urban adaptation, such as youth gangs, crime, poor housing, and unemployment, were initially severe. Eventually, these problems were worked through and became less serious as each group acculturated. Hence, after two generations of severe culture clash both within the ethnic community (intergenerational) and between it and the other communities, the issues that sometimes became a source of national concern, such as culture conflict, economic exploitation, and associated social disruptions, tend to dissipate.

The Nature and Persistence of Chicano Gangs

Although Mexican Americans in urban settings largely share with earlier, mostly eastern U.S. ethnics a similarity in how adaptation proceeds, there are also distinct differences between them. For one thing, Chicano youth gangs (unlike those of other immigrant groups) have shown a remarkable longevity. Moore, Vigil, and Garcia (1983) suggest reasons, for this difference: "the gangs are long-lasting, not transitory phenomena. . . . With few exceptions, the Chicano communities of Los Angeles never have been invaded by another ethnic group, nor has another ethnic group succeeded them, nor has there been total cultural disintegration. Instead, there has been more or less continuous immigration of yet more Mexicans, with a reinforcement of some of the traditional culture" (p. 183). Mexican Americans remained more visu-

ally distinct from the majority than did the third generation descendants of European immigrants, and the continued presence of fully unacculturated Mexicans made their communities more culturally distinct.

Many families and their children experience acute poverty and limited social mobility opportunities in these barrios, and thus, over time, there developed an underclass with its own set of problems. It is from among these children that the youth most intensely involved in the gangs tends to come. As members of a persistent underclass within the Mexican American population, these youths come from households with even lower incomes than those of other barrio families and a higher incidence of stressful family situations. (This is perhaps reflective of what Auletta [1982] refers to as the 9 million, a subgroup of the 25 million below the national poverty level, who experience a grinding cycle of poverty. Recent reports seem to support the existence of this strata in urban centers [Bearak and Meyer 1985:14; NALEO 1985].) Poor school records and limited job options have combined to make them even more street oriented. As part of their survival on the streets, especially during adolescence, they adopt cultural values and customs that help shape their personal identities.

The youth gangs of Mexican Americans have arisen in the context of the broader pattern of Mexican adaptation to urban life in the United States. Mexican immigration has been the primary factor in the growth of the Mexican American population. The first large wave (1920s) brought anywhere from 1.5 million to 2 million immigrants, doubling the native Mexican

American population (Samora 1971). In subsequent waves in the periods from 1940 to 1964 (4 million) and from 1969 through the 1970s (anywhere from 6 to 12 million), the population has continued to swell (Cornelius 1978). Throughout these decades of immigration, the population increasingly settled in urban areas, and today close to 90 percent of the Mexican American (native and immigrant alike) population is in urban areas (Alvírez, Bean, and Williams 1981). A recent report (Muller 1984) on foreign immigration to California since 1970 found that, of over 2 million who have legally settled there, "at least 1.3 million of them have settled in its seven southern counties" (p. 1); and this figure excludes the uncounted and undocumented (Cornelius, Chávez, and Castro 1982). Southern California, and Los Angeles particularly, is the urban area that has received most of these immigrants. Their adjustment and its social and cultural developments have taken different forms, depending on the work opportunities, places of settlement, and, generally, the standard of living attained by immigrants. Such continuous waves of immigrants ensure that there is always a large pool of second-generation Mexican Americans.

Bogardus (1926) noted that in the early years of Mexican immigration there was a "boy" gang problem and characterized it as an incipient form that could be remedied. However, in the following decades it was clear that the gang problem was becoming a serious one, with a formal structure and emerging set of norms and rules to attract and guide members (Bogardus 1943). Cultural change over the years was affected by barrio and under-

class life and was particularly acute during the Depression, when even more Mexican youths experienced the intense pressures of urban poverty, especially the second generation. It is a second-generation urban American experience that, in the Chicano case, is a continually renewed phenomenon because of continued immigration. The second generation in the 1930s–1940s originated the *pachuco* lifestyle (a label created for those who wore zoot suits and spoke a mixed English-Spanish slang language that borrowed heavily from *caló*–this, in turn, was a continuation of what the Gypsies had started in Spain and later was diffused, by bullfighters it seems, to Mexico [McWilliams 1968; G. C. Barker 1950]). Pachucos were a group who strove to reconcile the conflicting values and nascent pressures that urban adaptation brought; prolonged lower-class status and immobility shaped how Mexican culture was relinquished and American culture integrated into a street style. This style served as a mechanism of adaptation for many youth who needed a source of personal identification and human support, especially during the adolescent self-identification process where ego and peer groups merge to simplify age/sex identification. Pachucos were more than a "boy" gang of loosely aligned street children who participated primarily in street mischief. They had passed the incipient phase of gang formation, as pride in barrio affiliation, barrio conflicts, and some amount of drug use and abuse became a part of their lifestyle. Because most pachucos preferred to look "cool" in their zoot suits and have a good time, these damaging group activities were not as widespread or intense as those practiced in more recent decades. As the practice of negative group activities has escalated, the early generations of gang members, even most pachucos, can be viewed as a transitional form of gang.

A gang subculture eventually formed and became a pressing force in barrio life. Earlier, youths would join the boys on the street for play or mischief. Later, pachucos began to add their distinctive elements to the emerging street gang style. With the passage of time, and the perpetuation of situations, conditions, and social practices that helped to create it, the street style now works to socialize and enculturate youth to a rooted gang subculture with its own group norms and cholo role fronts. The street violence and other debilitating activities that are common features of barrio life can only be understood in terms of this subcultural socialization and its appeal to barrio youths with particular types of personal backgrounds that give rise to particular forms of self-identification processes.

In the 1980s, Chicano gangs comprise at least one-half of the four hundred gangs that exist in Los Angeles County (Decker 1983). This number, of course, is larger when the counties adjacent to Los Angeles are included. Notwithstanding the absolute number of Chicano gangs, however, only a small percentage of Chicano youth, perhaps only 4 to 10 percent of most barrios, are affiliated with gangs (Morales 1982). Of this relatively small percentage, there are subcategories (based upon degree and level of commitment) of regular, peripheral, temporary, and situational. For the most part, gang affiliation and gang-related behavior are primarily male phenomena, although many barrios also have smaller female cliques. The great majority of youths, as in other ethnic groups (cf., e.g., Whyte 1973), find other sources of identification and emulation.

The cultural style of the gang subculture arose partly as a response to street life. However, its major cultural forms are a reforging of Mexican and American patterns. This recombination, of course, borrowed heavily from the earlier pachuco syncretic formulation of creating a culture of mixed and blended elements (e.g., language). Cholos (the present term identifying the style as well as its bearers), share a cultural orientation that makes them distinct from other barrio youth. Although cholos are Americanized, either by accident or by design, they refuse or are unable to be totally assimilated (Vigil 1979, Buriel et al. 1982). In important ways they consider themselves traditionalists and retain certain Mexican customs, however attenuated, as part of their cultural repertoire. For example, they have retained the caló idiom of expression; the strong sense of group as family; the adolescent *palomilla* cohorting tradition (Rubel 1966), which includes many daring and bravado male patterns; and an antiauthority attitude, which is, perhaps, a reaction against *gabacho* (originally a term used for foreigners, such as the French in Mexico during the 1860s intervention, but now designating Anglos) racism (Vigil 1984).

The gangs that have been addressed by researchers range from those that began in the 1940s, and that have over time established more than a dozen identifiable age-graded cohorts (Moore 1978), to those of more recent vintage. An individual gang might include as many as two hundred or more, or as few as ten or twelve, members.

It is mainly in the suburbs that the newer, smaller gangs are found. Older, larger gangs, on the other hand, are usually located in long-established urban and semirural barrios. Semirural barrios, and the gangs associated with them, have often been engulfed in recent years by rapidly expanding suburban growth. The deep-rooted presence of older barrio gangs has become a model and a stimulus for gang formation in other areas, as well as a major socialization factor throughout the barrio and nearby areas.

Acculturation is a major factor in a large urban region, such as the greater Los Angeles metropolitan area. Barrio and underclass life has shaped each new immigrant population in different ways, however, creating generational contrasts. As the decades pass, each generation, depending on sociocultural environment and historical conditions, becomes part of a process of cultural change and accommodation. What once began as a Mexican subculture is now transformed into different subcultures. It is in the second generation where the children of Mexican immigrants undergo acculturation shifts resembling a transitional (cholo subculture) phase. Sometimes the phase involves culture conflict, whereby both the donor culture and the host culture become problematic. This ambivalent cultural (and personal) identity makes the gang subculture attractive for a small but significant minority of barrio youth. Their lives are often regulated by the age-graded *klikas* (cliques, or cohorts within the gang). Older gang members also lend some sense of order to their often confused interpersonal interactions by providing vertical lines of organization (Klein 1971); and the gang's involvement in some forms of criminal behavior affords avenues for prestige and income to those who have limited chances of acquiring meaningful jobs (Moore 1978; Chicano Pinto Research Project 1979, 1981). Increasingly, in recent years, both immigrant youths from Mexico and third-generation Mexican Americans have become peripherally involved with street gangs. The Chicano Pinto Research Project (1979, 1981) has found small numbers of third-generation Chicanos, who are themselves offspring of gang members, involved in the core membership of some younger age cohorts.

Multiple Marginality and Street Adaptation

The Chicano youth gang began and grew in ecologically marginal areas of the city and surrounding countryside. It was fed by pressures generated by a marginal economic role. It is peopled by youths with marginal ethnic and personal identities. Each feature of gang life merits scrutiny by itself, but once this task is completed the next step is to search for the links between these features. For example, the interrelationships between socioeconomic condition (e.g., mother-centered households) or social event (e.g., sex identity strivings) must be assessed to understand why gangs are so important during adolescence. A multiple research strategy employing the concept of multiple marginality, which is especially useful with broad and in-depth self-reflexive and life history information, will enhance this understanding. This type of information reflects various times, places, thoughts, and events that must be unpeeled layer by layer, and thus a multiple construct facilitates such a discussion. It is a construct that views reality as a constellation of forces tending to act and react upon one another.

Multiple marginality encompasses the consequences of barrio life, low socioeconomic status, street socialization and enculturation, and problematic development of a self-identity. These gang features arise in a web of ecological, socioeconomic, cultural, and psychological factors. The use of such a concept in an analysis of Chicano youth gangs will help to avoid the difficulties stemming from single-cause examinations of previous gang studies; Cartwright et al. (1975, 25-45) have addressed such problems in the second chapter of their review of juvenile gangs. The use of the concept multiple marginality can lead to what Geertz (1973, 3) has called a "thick description." Looking at various circumstances and forces in a combinative way increases our understanding of the similarities and variations found within and across groups. It also affords an opportunity to make use of an analyst's personal experiences when merited. Having watched gangs and gang members for many years as an insider has enabled me to chart the flow of events and decision-making processes of street gangs.

An eclectic multiple marginality analysis makes it possible to integrate key elements of the several theories that have been formulated to explain gang delinquency that emerged in the middle 1950s to early 1960s. (This is no coincidence, as the post-World War II urban explosion led to the development of problems among new minority groups, such as Puerto Ricans, blacks, and Mexican Americans, that were perhaps even more threatening than what had transpired earlier with white ethnics. These new phenomena led, in turn, to the reformation of old theories and the development of new theories.) In summary fashion, these theories are (1) male maturation process, "becoming a man" (e.g., Bloch and Niederhoffer 1958); (2) subcultural, collective solution of lower-class boys to acquire status (e.g., Cohen 1955); (3) lower-class cultural values (e.g., W. B. Miller 1958); (4) lower-class means and upper-class goals disjunctures or simplified means-goals discrepancy (e.g., Cloward and Ohlin 1960); and (5) sociopathic personalities that make "near-group" (e.g., Yablonsky 1959). There are several ways to assess these theories: they can either be reclassified as sociogenic (e.g., 3, 4) and psychogenic (e.g., 1, 2, 5) or, examined another way, as fitting within explanations that focus on strain (2, 4), cultural deviance (1-4), and (in varying degrees, all five) social control (Edgerton 1973; Dembo et al. 1984; Cartwright et al. 1975). Although the authors argue that their particular theory is most salient to the gang phenomenon, each theory accounts for only an aspect of the gang pattern. Yet, all the authors in fact rely on a number of related factors to arrive at their theoretical formulation. For example, Bloch and Niederhoffer (1958) maintain that the gang outlet for becoming a man results because society (through such phenomena as poverty, family stress, and urban disorganization) has failed them; and Cloward and Ohlin (1960), working on a variation of Merton's (1949) means/goals disjunctures, elaborate on the nature of low-income slum life to explain gang sub-cultural variations. This suggests that a cluster of factors needs to be examined to understand gang delinquency; Cloward and Ohlin say as much with these words: "gangs, or subcultures . . . are typically found among adolescent males in lower-class areas of large urban centers" (p. 1; cf. Short and Strodtbeck 1965, 19).

The multiple marginality framework better allows for descriptions and interpretations of particular (and perhaps peculiar) facts of people, time, and place. Such a larger framework simultaneously provides for a broader and more in-depth portrayal of the various realities that gang members experience. The intensity and duration of the individual or group experience in gangs as such are better gauged in this broadly integrative way. There are several marginal situations and conditions that are a part of the Mexicans' overall adaptation to urban life. In such circumstances of "long duration . . . the individual can be born into it and live his whole life in it," becoming a participant in "even the development of a 'marginal culture'" (Dickie-Clark 1966, 24).

Some researchers have noted that the concept of marginality should be carefully applied because it tends to diminish the important role of lower-income workers in a capitalist economy (Peattie 1974). Perlman (1976), in providing a sweeping critical summation of marginality theory, nevertheless recognizes the need for a construct that looks "to some set of circumstances outside individual control," such as one that "explains these conditions as expressions of the social structure and the historical process" and that looks at "different dimensions of marginality and

seeks rather to examine the specificity of their interaction in each instance" (251).

Mexican and Mexican American labor has definitely been significant in the economic development of the southwestern United States, for example, in mining, farming, railroading, and so on. These contributions, however, have not assured them of commensurate political and economic power, as they are excluded by leaders from decision-making processes. This marginality, moreover, is maintained by structural features in the environment to which they must adapt (Kapferer 1978; Lomnitz 1977; Barrera 1979).

The background to the current gang situation is also important, for multiple marginality has cumulative, diachronic sources, especially in group history. A *macro* (group history), *meso* (family history), and *micro* (life history) descending order of analysis is undertaken to show through time how ecological and economic conditions create sociocultural stresses and ambiguities, which, in turn, lead to subcultural and psychological mechanisms of adjustment. Descriptions of group and family history are well documented in the archives (Bogardus 1926, 1934) and in such studies as the longitudinal investigations of Moore and her *pinto* (ex-convict) associates (Moore 1978; Chicano Pinto Research Project 1979, 1981; Moore and Mata 1981). Moreover, my personal life experiences with numerous families who exemplify the multiple processes that lead to gang patterns provide for a unique insider/outsider interpretive perspective to inform these life histories and to show how these personalized events of places and living actions are refracted through the prism of multiple marginality. For example, I have gone through many experiences similar to those of gang youths . . . including being set upon and beaten by gang members into whose "turf" I had strayed. Such personal experiences inform my interpretation of such events.

A macroexamination of Mexican adaptation provides the backdrop for understanding Chicano youth gangs, for there are several areas that need to be traced. Clearly, a key focus is to examine how an emergent underclass life has affected many Mexicans. The underclass phenomenon entails the longitudinal effects of poverty. The youth groups that are produced in such nascent circumstances are quite different from, for example, the earlier non-violent "street corner" groups reported by Whyte (1973). In fact, endemic racial barriers and cultural strains have combined with status to make this so (Wolfgang et al. 1972; Bogardus 1943). The historical record of cultural and social disparagement experienced by Mexicans is indicative of such developments (Moore and Pachón 1976; Acuña 1981; Vigil 1984).

Urban adaptation for immigrant Mexican families was problematic initially and continues to be so today. Low-paying jobs led to residence in older, run-down interstices of the city, such as sections of East Los Angeles (Gustafson 1940, 25–40; Ginn 1947, 18–19). Such circumstances created repercussions in other social, cultural, and psychological realms. Moreover, and similar to the experience of other immigrant groups (Feldstein and Costello 1974; Shaw and McKay 1942), schools and law enforcement often operated to aggravate rather than ameliorate problems in Mexican cultural adaptations (U.S. Commission on Civil Rights 1970, 1971). This segmented integration into American society and subsequent fragmenting of traditional social practices and cultural customs resulted in a new cultural orientation. In short, economic hardships undermined social control institutions: family life became stress ridden and schooling and contacts with law enforcement were problematic. The streets and older street youths became the major socialization and enculturation agents, with the gang representing a type of street social control institution by becoming in turn a partial substitute for *family* (providing emotional and social support networks), *school* (giving instructions on how to think and act), and *police* (authority and sanctions to enforce adherence to gang norms). The experience created a new social identity and thus a need for a new personal identity, and for street youth, the gang, both good and bad features, became a coping mechanism to ameliorate social pressures and develop avenues for personal fulfillment.

References

Acuña, Rudy, 1981. *Occupied America: A History of Chicanos.* 2nd ed. New York. Harper and Row.

Alvírez, David, Frank D. Bean, and Dorie Williams, 1981. "The Mexican American Family." In *Ethnic Families in America: Patterns and Variations,* Charles H. Mindel and Robert W. Hobenstein (eds.), pp. 269–292. New York: Elsevier.

Auletta, Ken, 1982. *The Underclass.* New York: Random House.

Barker, G. C., 1950. *Pachuco, an American-Spanish Argot and Its Social Function in Tucson, Arizona.* Tucson: University of Arizona Press.

Barrera, Mario, 1979. *Race and Class in the Southwest. A Theory of Racial Inequality.* Notre Dame: University of Notre Dame Press.

Bearak, Barry and Richard E. Meyer, 1985. "No Tactic Yet Found to Wm Poverty War." *Los Angeles Times,* August 1. [Five-part series, America and Its Poor]

Bloch, H. A. and A. Niederhoffer, 1958. *The Gang: A Study in Adolescent Behavior.* New York: Philosophical Library.

Bogardus, Emory S., 1926. *The City Boy and His Problem.* Los Angeles: House of Ralston, Rotary Club of Los Angeles.

____ 1934. *The Mexican in the United States.* USC Social Science Series, No. 8. Los Angeles: University of Southern California Press.

____ 1943. "Gangs of Mexican American Youth." *Sociology and Social Research* 28:55–56.

Buriel, Raymond, Silverio Calzada, and Richard Vasquez, 1982. "The Relationship of Traditional Mexican American Culture to Adjustment and Delinquency among Three Generations of Mexican American Male Adolescents," *Hispanic Journal of Behavioral Sciences* 4(1):41–55.

Cartwright, Desmond S., B. Tomson, and H. Schwartz, 1975. *Gang Delinquency.* Monterey, Calif: Brook/Cole.

Chicano Pinto Research Project, 1979. *A Model for Chicano Drug Use and for Effective Utilization of Employment and Training Resources by Barrio Addicts and Ex-Offenders.* Los Angeles: Final Report for the Department of Labor and National Institute of Drug Abuse.

____ 1981. *Barrio Impact of High Incarceration Rates.* By Joan W. Moore and John Long. Los Angeles: Final Report for National Institute of Mental Health.

Clinard, Marshal B., 1968. *Sociology of Deviant Behavior.* New York: Holt, Rinehart and Winston.

Cloward, R. A., and L. B. Ohlin, 1960. *Delinquency and Opportunity: A Theory of Delinquent Gangs.* New York: Free Press.

Cohen, Albert K., 1955. *Delinquent Boys: The Culture of the Gang.* Glencoe, IL: Free Press.

Cornelius, Wayne A., Leo R. Chávez, and Jorge G. Castro, 1982. *Mexican Immigrants and Southern California: A Summary of Current Knowledge.* University of California, San Diego, Center for U.S.-Mexican Studies, Research Report Series, No. 36.

Decker, Cathleen, 1983. "Gang-Related Murders Fall by 38% in Los Angeles." *Los Angeles Times,* January 7.

Dembo, Richard, Nola Allen, and Harold J. Vetter, 1984. *A Framework for Understanding Nondelinquent and Delinquent Life Styles in the Inner City. [N.p.]*

Dickie-Clark, H. F., 1966. *The Marginal Situation.* London: Routledge, Keagan Paul.

Edgerton, Robert B., 1973. *Deviant Behavior and Cultural Theory.* Addison Wesley Module in Anthropology, No. 37. Reading, Mass: Addison-Wesley Publishing Co.

Feldstein, S., and L. Costello (eds.), 1974. *The Ordeal of Assimilation: A Documentary History of the White Working Class.* New York: Anchor Press/Doubleday

Geertz, Clifford, 1973. *The Interpretation of Culture.* New York: Basic Books.

Ginn, M.D., 1947. "Social Implications of the Living Conditions of a Selected Number of Families Participating in the Cleland House Program." M.A. thesis, University of Southern California, Department of Sociology.

Griffith, Beatrice, 1948. *American Me.* Boston: Houghton Mifflin Company.

Gustafson, C. V, 1940. "An Ecological Analysis of the Hollenbeck Area of Los Angeles." M.A. thesis, University of Southern California: Department of Sociology.

Handlin, Oscar, 1951. *The Uprooted.* New York: Grosset and Dunlap.

Heller, Celia S., 1966. *Mexican American Youth: Forgotten Youth at the Crossroads.* New York: Random House.

Horowitz, Ruth, 1983. *Honor and the American Dream: Culture and Identity in a Chicano Community.* New Brunswick, NJ. Rutgers University Press.

Kapferer, Bruce, 1978, "Structural Marginality and the Urban Social Order." *Urban Anthropology* 7(3):287–320.

Klein, Malcolm W., 1968. "Impressions of Juvenile Gang Members. *Adolescence* 3(9):3–78.

_____ 1971, *Street Gangs and Street Workers.* Englewood Cliffs, NJ: Prentice-Hall.

Lomnitz, Larissa A., 1977. *Networks and Marginality: Life in a Mexican Shantytown.* New York: Academic Press.

McWilliams, C., 1968. *North from Mexico—the Spanish-Speaking People of the United States.* New York: Greenwood Press.

Merton, Robert K., 1949. *Social Theory and Social Structure.* Glencoe, IL: Free Press.

Miller, Walter B., 1958. "Lower Class Culture as a Generating Milieu of Gang Delinquency." *Journal of Social Issues* 14(3):519.

Moore, Joan, 1978. *Homeboys: Gangs, Drugs, and Prison in the Barrios of Los Angeles.* Philadelphia: Temple University Press.

Moore, Joan, and Alberto Mata, 1981. *Women and Heroin in Chicano Communities.* Los Angeles: Chicano Pinto Research Project.

Moore, Joan W., and Harry Pachón, 1976. *Mexican Americans.* Englewood Cliffs, NJ: Prentice-Hall.

Moore, Joan W., James Diego Vigil, and Robert Garcia, 1983. "Residence and Territoriality in Gangs." *Journal of Social Problems* 31(2):182–194.

Morales, Armando, 1982. "The Mexican American Gang Member: Evaluation and Treatment." In *Mental Health and Americans,* Rosina M. Becerra, Marvin Karno, and Javier I. Escobar (eds.). New York: Grune and Straton.

Muller, Thomas, 1984. *The Fourth Wave: California's Newest Immigrants.* Washington, D.C.: Urban Institute Press.

National Association of Latino Elected and Appointed Officials (NALEO), 1985. *Poverty's Invisible Victims: Hispanic Children; Number of Latino*

Poor Children Doubles in California in Past Decade. Washington, D.C.: NALEO News Release.

Peattie, Lisa R., 1974. "The Concept of 'Marginality' as Applied to Squatter Settlements." In *Latin American Urban Research: Anthropological Perspectives on Latin American Urbanization,* vol. 4, ed. Wayne A. Cornelius and Felicity M. Trueblood (eds.). Beverly Hills: Sage Publications.

Perlman, Janet, 1976. *The Myth of Marginality.* Berkeley: University of California Press.

Rosenquist, C. M., and E. I. Megargee, 1969. *Delinquency in three Cultures.* Austin: University of Texas Press.

Rubel, A. J., 1966. *Across the Tracks: Mexican Americans in a Texas City.* Austin: University of Texas Press.

Samora, J., 1971. *Los Mojados: The Wetback Story.* Notre Dame: University of Notre Dame Press.

Shaw, C., and R. McKay, 1942. *Juvenile Delinquency and Urban Areas.* Chicago: University of Chicago Press.

Short, James F., Jr, and Fred L. Strodtbeck, 1965. *Group Process and Gang Delinquency.* Chicago: University of Chicago Press.

Snyder, P. Z., 1977. "An Anthropological Description of Street Gangs in the Los Angeles Area." [A working note, prepared for the Department of Justice, by the Rand Corporation, Santa Monica, California.]

Thrasher, Frederic M., 1963. *The Gang.* Chicago: University of Chicago Press. [Originally published in 1927.]

Tuck, R., 1956. *Not with the Fist: Mexican-Americans in a Southwest City.* New York: Harcourt, Brace.

United States Commission on Civil Rights, 1970. *Mexican Americans and the Administration of Justice in the Southwest.* Washington, D.C.: U.S. Government Printing Office.

____ 1971. *Report I: Ethnic Isolation of Mexican Americans in the Public Schools of the Southwest.* Washington, D.C.: U.S. Government Printing Office.

Vigil, James Diego, 1979. "Adaptation Strategies and Cultural Life Styles of Mexican American Adolescents." *Hispanic Journal of Behavioral Sciences* 1(4):375–392. [UCLA Spanish-Speaking Mental Health Research Center.]

____ 1984. *From Indians to Chicanos. The Dynamics of Mexican American Culture.* Prospect Heights, IL: Waveland Press. [Originally published as *From Indians to Chicanos: A Sociocultural History.* St. Louis: C. V. Mosby Co., 1980.]

Whyte, William F., 1973. *Street Corner Society.* Chicago: University of Chicago Press. [Originally published in 1943.]

Wolck, Wolfgang, 1973. "Attitudes toward Spanish and Quechua in Bilingual Peru." In *Language and Attitudes.* Roger Shuy and Ralph W. Fosold (eds.). Georgetown: Georgetown University Press.

Wolfgang, Marvin, Robert M. Figlio, and Thorsten Sellin, 1972. *Delinquency in a Birth Cohort.* Chicago: University of Chicago Press.

Yablonsky, L., 1959. "The Delinquent Gang as a Near-Group." *Social Problems* 7:108-117.

Maria P. P. Root

Contemporary Mixed-Heritage Filipino Americans: Fighting Colonized Identities

This article raises important issues of racial and ethnic identity at a time when increasing numbers of Americans are of mixed ancestry. Maria P. P. Root discusses the history of miscegenation and intermarriage of Filipinos with other groups, and relates the changing ethnicity to both European and American colonialism and Filipino emigration to California. She also examines how gender differences and factors influence a high rate of intermarriage among Filipino Americans and why this trend is likely to continue.

The development of a positive and meaningful self-concept of Filipino American children in relation to their mixed origins is analyzed by Root, as well as the importance of and acquisition of ethnic identity. As more and more people in America, especially in California, are identified as multi-ethnic or multi-racial and more people choose partners outside their own racial or ethnic groups, it is essential that we openly discuss how this affects individuals and impacts California's communities. *(LH)*

Whether planful or accidental, centuries of invasion and visitation by traders, seafarers, missionaries, warfarers, and colonists guaranteed that Filipinos across the archipelago would fuse multiple ethnic influences and physical features. Across families, the family portrait defies neatly delineated boundaries; Filipinos belong to no race[1] and belong to all. Skin tones range from the strongest coffee color to the creamy color of banana flesh. Hair texture ranges from coarse to smooth, kinky to straight, light brown to blue-black. Short to tall, thin to large, and everything in between exists. Likewise, eye shapes and color and noses vary. In short, physical appearance cannot be the definitive marker defining or identifying Filipinos or Filipino Americans. This chapter outlines the evidence and impact of the colonizing tool of racialization on Filipino American ethnic identity through the experiences of contemporary mixed-heritage Filipinos.

Background

Four hundred years of combined colonization, first by Spain and then by the United States, widened the Filipino gene pool with the possibilities of lighter skin, hair, and eyes. The tools of colonization gave meaning to the variation in physical appearance among Filipinos. Spain introduced colorism; preferential treatment was clearly associated with lighter skin color. Centuries of this education primed the Filipino for vulnerability to internalize American rules of race. Colorism and then racism inculcated the notions "White is beautiful," "White is intelligent," and "White is powerful" in the psyches of many brown-hued Filipinos, thus inferiorizing the Filipino.

Countries colonized by light-skinned people of European origin (e.g., the United States, Puerto Rico, Brazil) have developed elaborate terms to denote color gradients or racial mixing (e.g., Comas-Diaz, 1996; Daniel, 1992). In the Philippines as in Mexico, the term *mestizo* or *mestiza* signified a cross between the indigenous people and the Spaniard. In the Philippines, its meaning was extended to refer to mixtures between Filipinos and

white Americans. Its use in the United States continues to be extended, much as the term used in Hawai'i to describe mixture, *hapa*, has transcended its original meaning. Originally connoting a mixture between Hawaiian and foreigner, usually white, *hapa* now generically refers to all phenotypic mixes in Hawai'i, even if not of Hawaiian ancestry. Likewise, the term *mestizo* has been extended to almost all mixes of Filipino heritage. Contemporarily, it is a term that has a mixed reception in the United States. It carries unjustified connotations of superiority in the Philippines and, ironically, the connotation of imposterhood or inauthenticity in this country.

Unfortunately, Filipinos are acquiring the rules that guide domestic race relations. First, some Filipinos are accepting the notion of a racial hierarchy with white at the top and black at the bottom. If Filipinos had not accepted the concept of a racial hierarchy, the term *mestizo* would have been abandoned; pejorative terms would not exist for those Filipinos now of contemporary African ancestry (even though, as a Malayan people, we were recipients of the African diaspora). Second, lacking an appropriate road map to negotiate race relations in this country, Filipino Americans are basing ethnic authenticity on fictional and toxic notions of racial purity. For example, in one of my classes, a student talked about how affronted she felt when people thought she was of "mixed" heritage rather than "full-blooded" Filipino.

Consider the confluence of two historical processes for further understanding Filipinos' susceptibility to a racialization process: the civil rights movements of the

1960s and 1970s and the post-1965 immigration wave of Filipinos. The largest number of Filipinos are immigrants; most Filipino Americans arrived after the change of immigration laws in 1965. Unlike previous Filipino immigrant cohorts, a large portion of the post-1965 cohort came from an educated and privileged class that had and often retains some status (San Juan, 1992). They advocate for their children to become Americans—and to maintain or achieve status for the family. Furthermore, they enter this country as beneficiaries of the civil rights legislation that removes some obstacles to upward mobility for some people of color. The lessons around race are no longer as harsh, but they are nevertheless insidiously present.

This period of time also coincides with the contemporary civil rights movements in this country, in which culture and ethnicity were largely reduced to race (Omi & Winant, 1994). Subsequently, Filipino American ethnic solidarity has been increasingly racially defined. In this transformation, ethnic solidarity has acquired and required the application of oppressive racial authenticity tests (Root, 1990, 1992), by which some Filipino Americans reject mixed-heritage Filipinos. At a time when Filipino Americans are continuing to try to define who and what is Filipino American, this narrow definition constructs a divisive reality inconsistent with the facts of Filipino history. Filipinos have forever been and forever will be undefinable by race. Contemporary mixed-heritage Filipino Americans are potential and unfortunate casualties in this transformation of ethnicity. Denying one's cultural relatedness testifies to the colonization of

identity suffered by most visible ethnic oppressed groups in this country (Atkinson, Morten, & Sue, 1989; Cross, 1991). Self-protection results in rejecting all that is perceived as part of the colonizer; mixed-heritage Filipinos are the physical embodiment of the Filipino's contact with the colonizer. Thus, in the contemporary context, more so than in previous moments in history, the mixed-heritage Filipino is placed in a liminal position between two cultures (Hill, 1994), which are basically in tacit agreement that American is better than Filipino and which continue to define "American" as white.

This conceptual analysis also suggests a juxtaposition of positions on mixed-heritage Filipinos. On one hand, mixed-heritage Filipinos who inherit African, Latino, and/or Native American ancestry may be more easily welcomed as Filipinos by some because they inherit another legacy of oppression. On the other hand, when the racial hierarchy is invoked, these members of community are deemed even less valuable Filipinos. Those Filipinos of immediate European heritage may be regarded as less authentic by some, yet enviable by others.

Despite the diversity of physical appearance embodied in looking Filipino, many children of Filipino descent of cross-cultural and/or interracial marriages in the United States experience gatekeeping comments such as "But you don't look Filipino" or "You're American, not Filipino."[2] What are the costs of these comments to those persons who are the object of scrutiny for the moment? What might be the costs to the Filipino American community? Such statements suggest that an insidious process of translating ethnicity into race prevails with the assimilation of American values. Thus, the colonizing of the Filipino continues in the United States. A brief analysis and summary of Filipino intermarriage is essential to placing the emergence and experience of contemporary Filipinos of mixed heritage in context.

Filipino Intermarriage

The U.S. military presence in the Philippines from 1890 through the 1990s guaranteed continued racial and cultural mixing for Filipinos. In a patriarchal structure, the colonized is constructed as a female to be dominated by the superior colonizing male. Consider that the Philippines and all other colonized countries are referred to in the female gender. And consider that patriarchy constructs itself as heterosexual, possessive, and aggressive; it will possess the women (Young, 1995). It constructs men of color in the female gender to reduce their threat to the colonizer (Lerner, 1986) and assumes that the colonizer is a more attractive mate to the colonized woman. In reality, she is property; thus, she does not necessarily have free choice to refuse the colonizer as a lover or partner.

Unlike the Chinese, Japanese, and Koreans before them, Filipino men would be open to marriage with American women other than Filipinos. Filipino male intermarriage in the United States, primarily with white women, would have occurred because of uneven sex ratios between Filipino men and women in the United States due to patterns of sojourn-

ing and immigration, availability and proximity of white women, and some familiarity with and positive regard for American European-originated culture. More insidiously, primed to prize light skin, and without Filipina women, Filipino men could be expected to find white women particularly attractive. For example, in Chicago from the early to mid 20th century, Filipino men mixed with daughters of other recent immigrants of Polish, Irish, and German descent (Posadas, 1989). However, Filipino men mixed with other racially visible ethnic groups with whom they found some cultural affinity when there was proximity. In the Northwest, Filipino men mixed with American Indian women; in San Diego and Imperial counties of California, Filipino men mixed with Mexican and Mexican American women.

The mixing of Filipino men with white women brought the wrath of white citizens and politicians intent on keeping the line between white and not-white well defined. Specific legislation was introduced to prevent Filipino men from marrying white women. For example, although California had antimiscegenation laws that prevented whites and blacks and whites and Asians from intermarrying, it was not clear if Filipinos were Asians. However, in a landmark case, *Roldan v. Los Angeles County* in 1933, Filipinos were classified as Malays and quickly added to the list of persons prohibited from intermarriage with whites. Several states eventually added Filipinos (Malays) to their list of persons prohibited from intermarriage with whites. Nevertheless, intermarriage continued in states in which laws did not prohibit it.

Furthermore, marriages between U.S. servicemen stationed in the Philippines and Filipinas continued.

Several historical factors have sustained Filipino American intermarriage since World War II. The presence of American military in the Pacific, specifically with military bases in the Philippines during World War II, the Korean War, the Vietnam War, and onward, guaranteed there would be interracial mixing and, subsequently, children (Root, 1997). The Immigration and Nationality Act of 1965 amended the previous immigration law and opened the door to increased immigration. The repeal of the remaining antimiscegenation laws in 1967 paved the road for an increase in interracial marriage in general. Since then, the numbers of Filipinos in the United States have multiplied, and their rates of intermarriage have increased.

The profile of contemporary children and young adults of mixed Filipino heritage has changed in the United States during the course of the century Prior to World War II, the majority of mixed-heritage Filipinos had Filipino fathers and white American mothers. These men were primarily employed as laborers, though they might have initially come to this country as *pensionados* to study at universities. With the limitation imposed on Filipino migration with the Tydings-McDuffie Act of 1934, sex ratios remained imbalanced, and similar marriages continued where they were legal. However, following World War II, and particularly the Korean War, the Filipina war bride entered the United States exempted from immigration quotas through the Soldier Brides Act of 1947. During this period of time, a generation of Filipinos, many of whom were born in the Philippines of white American fathers, emerged. With the 1965 Immigration and Nationality Act and the consequent growth and transformation of Filipino communities in the United States, the majority of young people of mixed heritage under 20 may have either a Filipino mother or father who may indeed have been born, if not raised, most of his or her life, in the United States.

International marriages still occur, largely through military contact and the mail-order bride business. Each year, thousands of women leave the Philippines in search of better economic opportunities than the local economy offers. Unfortunately, the bridal export business has changed cross-cultural and cross-national marriage from a romantic event to a suspect catalog business in which the Philippines is the largest supplier of international brides via this industry (Lin, 1991; Mochizuki, 1987; to Germans, Danes (Ravn & Trier, 1980), Australians (Boer, 1988), Japanese (Samonte, 1986), and Americans (Glodava & Onizuka, 1994) in the past decade. Denigrating stereotypes of Filipinas as exotic, childlike, subservient, and gold-digging maintain an attitude that dismisses the validity of a majority of these relationships and the children from them. When these women have children and are unmarried, separated, or divorced, negative stereotypes are extended to their mixed-race children.

Though few contemporary studies of intermarriage in the United States for Filipinos exist compared to studies of intermarriage for Japanese and Chinese (Kitano, Yeung, Chai, & Hatanaka, 1984;

Sung, 1990), two pilot studies suggest that rates of intermarriage for Filipinos will continue at a high rate. Revilla (1989) surveyed Filipino American college students in the Los Angeles area. In 1996, Bergano and Bergano-Kinney surveyed East Coast and Northwest Filipino college students involved in Filipino organizations. Despite some geographic and gender differences, the two studies share two findings. First, a considerable number of college students in these samples do not feel compelled to marry Filipinos. And second, although the rates vary by region, both young men and women are open to interracial dating and marriage. Agbayani-Siewert and Revilla's (1995) survey of studies on Filipino intermarriage underscores these findings.

Agbayani-Siewert and Revilla (1995) observed that although studies confirm the tendency of Filipinos to intermarry white partners as consistent with Asian American intermarriage patterns, there are two distinct differences for Filipinos as compared to other Asian Americans. First, the men intermarry as often as the women in California, where the second-largest population of Filipinos exists in the United States. On the basis of 1980 census data for California, Jiobu (1988) found that although Filipinas tend to marry non-Filipinos more frequently than the men do, when women married to U.S. military men are excluded from the figures, the rates for men and women are similar and high: 20% or greater. This rate of intermarriage places Filipinos as a group with the highest rate of intermarriage for the four groups that Jiobu examined (Japanese, Chinese, Korean, Filipino). Their second observation is that

Filipinos intermarry with other Asian Americans (e.g., Japanese, Chinese, Vietnamese) less frequently than Japanese, Chinese, and Koreans who intermarry. Using Jiobu's analysis, Filipinos in California married persons of Latino or Hispanic descent next most frequently. This is an ethnic group that has some cultural similarity to Filipinos.

Several factors currently suggest that intermarriage for Filipinos will continue at a high rate, if not actually increase. First, the removal of legal barriers to intermarriage throughout the United States in 1967, in tandem with other civil rights legislation such as fair housing and equal employment practices, ensures the likelihood that most Filipinos will live, work, and play in neighborhoods where there are non-Filipinos. Furthermore, the educational level of many post-1965 immigrants will place them in neighborhoods and workplaces that are middle class and primarily white. Although there is concern for the cultural preservation that inmarriage more likely ensures, many Filipinos wanting success for their children encourage them to be as American as possible; this wish for their children may stem from vestiges of colonialism that increase the acceptability of intermarriage with white Americans. (The high rates of Japanese Americans' intermarriage with white Americans have in part been attributed to the push to become Americanized at a more accelerated pace after their incarceration during World War II.) Whereas not all Filipino intermarriage with whites is driven by these factors, this factor would certainly make the Filipino more willing to look on a white partner favorably over other non-Filipino partners.

Simultaneously, affinity through oppression and class similarity opens the door for intermarriage with other ethnically oppressed groups who are not white.

Growth of the Filipino American Community

The high rates of intermarriage for Filipinos in the United States suggest that the physical diversity of appearance among Filipinos and those of Filipino descent in the United States will only increase. Although Filipinos are perhaps most similar in appearance to persons of Latino and Native American and Native Hawaiian heritage, defining and identifying who is Filipino cannot rest predominantly on physical appearance. However, without articulation of what is Filipino, without recognition of the injurious process of racialization, and without positive role models of Filipinos for some persons, young people are subject to using the template by which people struggle with racial identity in a limited, monoracial paradigm. Thus, they may deny their Filipino heritage to be accepted and fit in with their white peers. According to researchers, this rejection is common to persons who are members of devalued groups and have internalized a devalued sense of self and have internalized a white reference group (e.g., Atkinson et al., 1989; Cross, 1991). With exposure to eye-opening experiences that suggest that there are structural and attitudinal barriers to being wholly accepted by white dominant culture, individuals are thrust back into examining their roots and reacquainting themselves with and immersing themselves in what is positive about their culture of origin. Eventually, they may appreciate the positive attributes of different people and critically evaluate what is negative or positive on an individual basis. At times, this is at the risk of either rejecting being Filipino or absorbing some other identity that is articulated more clearly for them.

Psychological and social alienation seems to be part of the experience associated with American adolescent individuation from family. Contemporary mixed-race Filipinos, particularly during adolescence and young adulthood, may be unable to untangle their feelings of alienation from the typical adolescent experience, marginality as a person of color in a society in which race matters, and difference as an ambiguous Filipino.

With their parents' cross-cultural union, at least one parent is likely to be indoctrinated into the racial system. Thus, their Filipino parent may at times be viewed as racially distinctive from their non-Filipino parent by the non-Filipino parent. Or the children may be constructed as superior or inferior because they are similar to one parent or the other; ethnicity and race are likely to be confused. The subtlety of this process constructs race and constructs the child as mixed race. In a society that is racially diverse and stratified, one's race is a social address for many contexts. Thus, individuals symbolically become the embodiment of differences, often striving to make meaning out of their unique social position as bicultural and biracial.

Ironically, centuries of colonization have left a multiracial people without an appropriate road map in a system that subscribes to a monoracial ideology that values pure race. The Filipino struggle with identity bears much resemblance to the process of working out a mixed racial identity, particularly when one group is oppressed or subjugated by the other (Bradshaw, 1992; Chao, 1995; Hall, 1992; Root, 1992, 1996c). We must reexamine the paradigms by which we seek our identity. If they do not fit our history, we will be forever lost trying to find our way home with a map that does not have our address. The dominant frameworks, even within Asian America, do not fit Filipinos well. Contemporarily, multiethnic and multiracial paradigms are emerging that fit the Filipino American experience better.

Being contemporary mixed heritage of Filipino ancestry in the United States adds a complexity to the struggle with identity that is both similar to and different from being of mixed race of other Asian descent such as Japanese, Chinese, Vietnamese, or Korean. In general, there is not a defamation of physical appearance or assumed defect of character associated with mixing gene pools. As self-identified mixed-heritage people, to empower ourselves we must refuse to account for ourselves in fractions—one half Filipino, one half something else (Root, 1996a)—which is an act of colonizing identity; we must refuse to be gatekeepers of racial authenticity; we must refuse to participate in divisions originating in class, phenotype, education, dialect, and nativity. That we have not and may not attain a singular resolution of identity pathologizes Filipinos. We must redefine solidarity and resolution in light of our history as a people colonized, invaded, and spread out geographically in the archipelago and now internationally. We must respect the diversity in our community rather than strive to eliminate or ignore it.

Implications for the Filipino American Community

Given the high rates of intermarriage for Filipino American men and women, we are going to raise a large generation of people who are mixed race by the American definition of race. Furthermore, the Filipino American population will grow more rapidly through intermarriage if those of mixed heritage are welcomed and encouraged to identify as Filipino. Our community will be stronger if we do not require people to pass "blood quantum" tests such as those generated by the U.S. government for determining who is American Indian or Native Hawaiian. Our community will also be stronger if we can accommodate the distinct possibility that many of our young people will be multiethnic: that is, Filipino *and* something else, such as Japanese, Chicana/o, Indian, African, or Jewish. Historically, Filipinos have been able to do this. Researchers of multiethnic and multiracial identity note that a normal part of possessing multiple affiliations is that in some contexts one aspect of identity will be more prominent while others are background (Hall, 1992; Root, 1992, 1996a, 1996b; Stephan, 1992).

Ramirez's (1983) work on Mexican American bicultural identity suggests that the ability to switch or be both increases flexibility of thinking and problem solving. Ultimately, this flexibility may be a survival skill in the twisted world of racial paradigms.

The lack of articulating and valuing what diversity means in the Filipino American community places the multiethnic or multiracial Filipino at risk of being alienated by and from the Filipino community. For those already likely to be misidentified as belonging to another ethnic group, such as Chicana/o, American Indian, or some more familiar Asian group, depending on the part of the country, rejection from the Filipino community is particularly meaningful, and therefore hurtful. Multiheritage Filipinos will frequently be asked the question asked of racially ambiguous people, "What are you?" The frequency with which some individuals receive these questions informs them about how race is conducted and confounded with ethnicity in the United States.

Young people react to ethnic inquisition differently. Some, very secure in their identity, may refuse to prove they are Filipino; they are likely to be living in a community of friends that recognize them as Filipino. Others will try to be more Filipino than Filipino, absorbing every aspect of Filipino and Filipino American knowledge that comes their way; they establish their belonging by their cultural expertise. Still others will interpret the inquisition as a rejection. They may turn their back on the community as a defense against repeated scrutiny and rejection.

This latter response concerns me. With the first alternative, it is possible to be Filipino identified and proud and to accept that people are having a difficult time adjusting to the expanding diversity of the contemporary Filipino community. The second alternative is developmentally predictable; having to demonstrate cultural expertise eases up as one feels more secure in one's sense of who one is even if others do not reflect one's identity accurately. Unfortunately, the third alternative is a worst-case scenario. The rejected one may invoke an equally oppressive attitude toward the inquisitor: The inquisitor is defective. Both parties are casualties of racial colonization.

There are some actions parents can take to help their children claim their Filipino heritage proudly. These recommendations are gathered from the literature on the empowerment of mixed-race persons and the current knowledge of factors affecting ethnic identity (Root, 1992, 1996c, 1997). First, give your child a first or middle name that is connected with their Filipino heritage. Particularly for a female child who through marriage may relinquish her maiden name, a given name becomes that much more important. Although children may be embarrassed by this name at different times in their life, it also reassures them that they are Filipino; it may also be part of their passport into Filipino communities in which the family is unknown. Second, talk positively about what you value about being Filipino. Children may make fun of you for feeling or talking so positively about things that are Filipino, but they are likely to absorb some positive feeling from these reflections. An absence of comment may speak as strongly as negative comments about Filipinos. Third, connect them to the Filipino community through stories of relatives and family roots in the United States, the Philippines, and elsewhere. Creating a family tree may be a way to make this connection. Reading Filipino and Filipino American literature may be another avenue for connection. Being connected to the past is a foundation for knowing who you are in the present. Fourth, if you live in or near a community where there are Filipino community gatherings, go to some of these. Role models, sense of similarity, and exposure to the diversity of behavior, attitudes, accents, and physical appearance can help children subsequently counter stereotypes they may hear about Filipinos. It will also probably expose them to other young people who have contemporary multiethnic or multiracial origins. Fifth, do not make disparaging comments about Filipinos in general or other groups of people of color. A child may identify with those persons you denigrate. Last, inquire if your child has encountered any of the gatekeeping, curiosity questions. Some children will wonder if they are "real" Filipinos or "what" they are. Help them develop answers that maintain their sense of control over who they are. Such discussions can help them recognize and fight the racial colonizing of their identity.

Conclusion

The profile of the mixed-heritage Filipino in the United States has changed and diversified through this century. Predominantly fathered by Filipino American men prior to Philippine independence from the United States, then subsequently and predominantly birthed by international brides of U.S. servicemen after World War II and particularly through the Korean and Vietnam war eras, the contemporary Filipino of mixed heritage emerges in a different historical context post civil rights and in a different class context post 1965. Subsequent to the 1965 Immigration and Nationality Act, contemporary mixed-race people may be fathered or mothered by a Filipino parent and, increasingly, American born.

The American social system is littered with dangerous interpretations of physical, behavioral, and social differences among people. Unfortunately, many Filipinos attempting to compete economically and be accepted as Americans uncritically accept the American rules of race. They are not aware of alternative road maps or frameworks for identity. Consequently, they relinquish the fight against the colonization of Filipino identity.

The Filipino of mixed heritage is positioned liminally and symbolically in the psychological space that confronts the larger community What does it mean to be Filipino in America? What does it mean to be American of Filipino heritage? If Filipino Americans emphasize race-based markers in determining and defining who is Filipino, our community will suffer. We will use the colonizer's tool against each other.

With high rates of intermarriage for both genders, the phenotype of the Filipino American will continue to diversify. As our community works to define who is Filipino, it is incumbent to our viability, solidarity, and health to be as inclusive as possible and to embrace the growing cohort of contemporary Filipinos of mixed heritage. Many contemporary Filipinos of mixed heritage have resisted a colonized identity. They are evidence that the juxtaposition of Filipino and American is resolvable but requires a different road map. Ultimately, the health, viability, and resilience of the Filipino community will depend on our ability to resist becoming casualties of colonized racial identities. In Paulo Freire's (1970) words, "The solution . . . is not to become 'beings inside of,' but . . . [people] . . . freeing themselves: for, in reality, they are not marginal to the structure, but oppressed . . . within it" (10-11).

Notes

1. Race is used as a social construction throughout this chapter.
2. Some of this gatekeeping is experienced by American-born Filipinos from Philippine-born Filipinos.

References

Agbayani-Siewert, P., & Revilla, L. (1995). Filipino Americans. In P. G. Min (Ed.), *Asian Americans: Contemporary trends and issues* (pp. 134-168). Thousand Oaks, CA: Sage.

Atkinson, D. R., Morten, G., & Sue, D. W. (Eds.). (1989). *Counseling American minorities: A cross-cultural perspective.* Dubuque, IA: William C. Brown.

Boer, C. (1988). *Are you looking for a Filipino wife? A study of Filipina-Australian marriages.* Sydney, Australia: General Synod Office.

Bradshaw, C. K. (1992). Beauty and the beast: On racial ambiguity. In M. P. P. Root (Ed.), *Racially mixed people in America* (pp. 77-88). Newbury Park, CA: Sage.

Chao, C. M. (1995). A bridge over troubled waters: Being Eurasian in the U. S. of A. In J. Adleman & G. Enguidanos (Eds.), *Racism in the lives of women: Testimony, theory, and guides to antiracist practice* (pp. 33-44). New York: Harrington Park.

Comas-Diaz, L. (1996). LatiNegra: Mental health issues of African Latinas. In M. P. P. Root (Ed.), *The multiracial experience: Racial borders as the new frontier* (pp. 167-190). Thousand Oaks, CA: Sage.

Cross, W E., Jr. (1991). *Shades of black: Diversity in African-American identity.* Philadelphia: Temple University Press.

Daniel, G. R. (1992). Passers and pluralists: Subverting the racial divide. In M. P. P. Root (Ed.), *Racially mixed people in America* (pp. 91-107). Newbury Park, CA: Sage.

Freire, P. (1970). *Cultural action for freedom.* Cambridge, MA: Harvard Educational Review Press.

Glodava, M., & Onizuka, R. (1994). *Mail order brides: Women for Sale.* Fort Collins, CO: Alaken.

Hall, C. I. I. (1992). Please choose one: Ethnic identity choices for biracial individuals. In M. P. P. Root (Ed.), *Racially mixed people in America* (pp. 250-264). Newbury Park, CA: Sage.

Hill, R. C. (1994). Liminal identity: Clinical observations. *Journal of the American Association for Philippine Psychology, 1,* 55-68.

Immigration and Nationality Act of 1965. 8 U.S.C. § *1101 et seq.*

Jiobu, R. (1988). *Ethnicity and assimilation.* Albany: State University of New York Press.

Kitano, H. H., Yeung, W.-T., Chai, L., & Hatanaka, H. (1984). Asian American interracial marriage. *Journal of Marriage and the Family, 46,* 179-190.

Lerner, G. (1986). *The creation of patriarchy.* New York: Oxford University Press.

Lin, J. L. (1991). *Marital satisfaction and conflict in intercultural correspondence marriage.* Unpublished doctoral dissertation, University of Washington.

Mochizuki, K. (1987, May 7). I think Oriental women are just great. *International Examiner,* p. 13.

Omi, M., & Winant, H. (1994). *Racial formation in the United States from the 1960s to the 1990s* (2nd ed.). New York: Routledge.

Posadas, B. M. (1989). Mestiza girlhood: Interracial families in Chicago's Filipino American community since 1925. In Asian Women United of California (Ed.), *Making waves: An anthology of writings by and about Asian American women* (pp. 273-282). Boston: Beacon.

Ramirez, M., III. (1983). *Psychology of the Americas: Mestizo perspectives on personality and mental health.* New York: Pergamon.

Ravn, M., & Trier, B. (1980). *Asian heart.* New York: Filmmakers Library.

Revilla, L. (1989). Dating and marriage preferences among Filipino Americans. *Journal of the Asian American Psychological Association, 13,* 72-79.

Roldan v. Los Angeles County, 129 Cal. App. 267, 18 P2d 706 (1933).

Root, M. P. P. (1990). Resolving "other" status: Identity development of biracial individuals. In L. S. Brown & M. P. P. Root (Eds.), *Diversity and complexity in feminist therapy* (pp. 185-206). New York: Harrington.

Root, M. P. P. (1992). *Racially mixed people in America.* Newbury Park, CA: Sage.

Root, M. P. P. (1996a). A bill of rights for racially mixed people. In M. P. P Root (Ed.), *The multiracial experience: Racial borders as the new frontier* (pp. 3-14). Thousand Oaks, CA: Sage.

Root, M. P P. (1996b). The multiracial experience: Racial borders as a significant frontier in race relations. In M. P. P. Root (Ed.), *The multiracial experience: Racial borders as the new frontier* (pp. xiii-xxviii). Thousand Oaks, CA: Sage.

Root, M. P. P. (Ed.). (1996c). *The multiracial experience: Racial borders as the new frontier.* Thousand Oaks, CA: Sage.

Root, M. P P (1997). The biracial baby boom: Understanding ecological constructions of racial identity in the twenty-first century. In R. H. Sheets & E. Hollins (Eds.), *Race, ethnic and cultural identity formation.* New York: Lawrence Erlbaum.

Root, M. P P. (1997). Multiracial Asian Americans: Changing the face of Asian America. In L. C. Lee & N. W. Zane (Eds.), *Handbook of Asian American psychology.* Thousand Oaks, CA: Sage.

Samonte, E. L. (1986). *Filipino wives with Japanese husbands: Communication variables and marital satisfaction.* Unpublished doctoral dissertation, University of the Philippines.

San Juan, E., Jr. (1992). *Racial formational critical transformations: Articulations of power in ethnic and racial studies in the United States.* Atlantic Highlands, NJ: Humanities.

Soldier Brides Act of 1945. 59 Stat. 659.

Stephan, C. W. (1992). Mixed-heritage individuals: Ethnic identity and trait characteristics. In M. P. P. Root (Ed.), *Racially mixed people in America* (pp. 50–63). Newbury Park, CA: Sage.

Sung, B. L. (1990). *Chinese American intermarriage.* New York: Center for Migration Studies.

Tydings-McDuffie Act of 1934. 48 Stat. 456.

Young, R. J. C. (1995). *Colonial desire: Hybridity in theory, culture and race.* New York: Routledge.

David Van Leer

Visible Silence: Spectatorship in Black Gay and Lesbian Film

As California has evolved it has often provided a refuge for the world's non-conformists and America's most adventurous. These non-conforming residents were once called '49ers, then later "beatniks," bikers," and "hippies." Citizens of the Golden State have a well-deserved reputation of tolerating, if not always welcoming, those who might be understood as "cultural outlaws." This is a legacy so appreciated that our urban communities have pockets of migrant "deviants" that have sometimes become a city's "majority." Among the most visionary of those with an outsider's point of view have been California filmmakers. Members of the film industry have been crucial to people of the world developing both dreams and fears of California.

David Van Leer describes in his article the artistic focus of Marlon Riggs and those who embraced or rejected his "body" of work. While homosexuals have always been a part of California, few have become as notorious or important as Riggs. Though the scourge of the AIDs epidemic prematurely shuttered his camera, debates about Riggs' films continues. Van Leer's article presents some of the themes that insure that the community Riggs portrayed will remain better understood if not always embraced. (SMM)

No one was surprised at the controversy surrounding the broadcast of Marlon Riggs' *Tongues Untied* on national public television's *P.O.V.* in the summer of 1991. The film had been in release for two years, applauded in America and Europe at festivals of black, gay, and independent films, and even telecast three times on local PBS affiliates. But Riggs' powerful celebration of African American gay male subjectivity with its attendant criticism of U.S. racism and homophobia was less likely to please a national audience. More than half of the 284 stations carrying the show canceled this episode, while others moved it to a less visible time slot. Nobody could have anticipated the specific criticisms from conservative politicians—Pat Buchanan's unauthorized use of footage from the film in a campaign commercial to illustrate George Bush's supposed sympathy for homosexuals; or Jesse Helms' citation of it in the U.S. Senate as a purported misuse of NEA funds (of which the film had very little, and none directly from the Endowment). But such hysteria and opportunism were of a piece with other attacks on experimental artists.[1]

In some senses the screening upstaged the film. Shifting attention from the particular invisibility of black male homosexuals to more general (less racialized) issues of pornography and government funding for the arts, the broadcast did not so much untie tongues as set them wagging. Decrying homosexuality as sin, fundamentalists substituted moral categories for the sociological ones the film used to explore a minoritized subculture within the predominantly white middle-class (and implicitly racist) gay ghettos of New York and San Francisco. Even liberal defenses dealt more with the abstract issue of discrimination than with Riggs' specific representation of it. Emphasizing the film's criticism of black heterosexuals and white homosexuals, straight white culture emerged comparatively unscathed. Public Broadcasting was deemed heroic and *P.O.V.*, a series not previously attentive to race or sexuality, established its concern for minority issues, while using the controversy to cancel future gay programs.[2]

Celebrity is a dubious distinction; to be lionized is to be domesticated. The acclaim that singles out Riggs as "first" or "best" reduces the many voices of *Tongues* to the lone cry of a solitary victim, who is then seen to speak for all gay African Americans. Such a reduction, unfair in itself, misunderstands the dynamic process by which minoritized filmmakers position themselves within cinematic traditions affording little space to issues of race or sexuality. However unique (and stable) his voice seems to the dominant culture, Riggs' work is in ongoing dialogue with representations of homosexual African Americans throughout film and culture. Endlessly interactive, his films can only be understood in terms of their adaptation of the generic conventions of the documentary to the tradition of black gay and lesbian self-representation of which they are a part.[3]

I

Like all doubly minoritized artists, black homosexuals must make choices about how to characterize their dual participation in an African American culture usually assumed to be heterosexual and a gay culture usually thought to be white. In part this choice is determined by those communities' willingness to receive them as equal participants. In this regard neither black or gay filmmaking has been especially receptive. The ruthless exclusion of images of black homosexuals from most films is matched by the careful regulation of those few depictions that do appear. And as preliminary to their own speaking out, homosexual African American directors feel it necessary to remind audiences how flawed are the representations of black gays and lesbians within both traditions.

The homophobia of straight African Americans is the more obvious (or more regularly denounced) of the two. In *Tongues Untied,* Riggs singles out the monologues of Eddie Murphy and the "Gamma/Fag" chant in Spike Lee's *School Daze* (1988) as particularly demeaning characterizations of gay men. Elsewhere he expands the list to include *In Living Color's* "Men on Film" skits, while other critics have called attention to the jailhouse sequence in Reginald Hudlin's *House Party* (1990).[4] Depictions of African American lesbians, though probably less frequent than those of gay men, are equally unsatisfactory. A particularly unflattering sequence in Lee's *She's Gotta Have It* (1986) introduces a lesbian only to suggest that homosexuality is not one of the things his heroine has to have. Even the most positive gay figures remain isolated from the community. The self-confident Lindy in Michael Schultz's *Car Wash* (1976)—who responds to a co-worker's taunts with the claim to be "more man than you'll ever be and more woman

than you'll ever get"—is marginalized both by his effeminacy and by his irrelevance in a plot that grants to its other characters political or sexual lives outside work.

The evident homophobia of some African American films is matched by the less explicit racism of white gay films.[5] Many groundbreaking scripts—like Mart Crowley's *The Boys in the Band* (1970) and Harvey Fierstein's *Torch Song Trilogy* (1988)—use black characters only as window dressing, while the most mainstreamed gay film on AIDS—Norman René's *Longtime Companion* (1990)—includes no people of color, despite their statistical prominence in the lists of those gay men infected or dead.[6] Even those films that do acknowledge race as an element of gay sexuality rarely give a voice to the racialized other. Gus Van Sant's *Mala Noche* (1986) views skeptically its white protagonist's fascination with Mexican youth. Yet by denying access to the Latino youth's points of view, the film implies that their bisexuality is more circumstantial and less interesting than the hero's unambiguous homosexuality.[7]

More painful than these insensitive silencings and omissions is the way in which sexuality often subsumes color in apparently well-meaning white narratives. Some works treat sexuality and race as interchangeable. In *Home of the Brave* (1949), gay playwright Arthur Laurents rewrites his stage drama about an anti-Semitic slur within the military as a racial incident. Denying the black character a separate identity, Laurents' plot merely substitutes racism for anti-Semitism, which itself symbolizes the more important but unmentionable problem of homophobia.[8] Lesbian directors offer more subtle depictions of the intersections between race and sexuality. Unlike its gay male counterpart, white lesbian cinema regularly examines the role of blacks within the homosexual community, and films like Lizzie Borden's *Born in Flames* (1983) and Sheila McLaughlin's *She Must Be Seeing Things* (1987) afford central roles to lesbians of color. Yet although these works explore in detail the consciousness of their black characters, some viewers still experience the films' subordination of racial categories to sexual ones as a form of tokenism and fetishization.[9]

If silenced or objectified in fictional narratives about white sexuality, people of color regularly speak in white gay documentaries. Yet here too black speech is restricted by the predominantly white conversation surrounding it. In chronicling the pre-liberation history of homosexual culture, Greta Schiller's *Before Stonewall: The Making of a Gay and Lesbian Community* (1985) includes the testimony of at least five people of color, most notably that of poet Audre Lorde. Yet to assert the unity of homosexual culture, the film downplays the differences, treating the black gay subculture about which the blacks reminisce as if it were the same culture referred to by the whites. Lorde's tonally ambiguous critique of the appropriation of civil rights political tactics by white feminists and gay activists is juxtaposed to (and implicitly equated with) a white gay man's dewy-eyed recollections of voter registration campaigns in the South. Mabel Hampton's account of her partying with "Ethel, Bessie, and Alberta" and other performers "in the life" is followed by (and used to validate) an optimistic distinction between the white homosexuals welcomed in Harlem and the fashionable heterosexuals who went slumming there. Racial differences are reinforced by the mise-en-scène. Although the white characters are often depicted in groups and at recognizable locales, the blacks are (except for Lorde and her companion) photographed one at a time in anonymous rooms. Cut off from all visible markers of communal experience or social environment, they become merely deracinated images of gay white tolerance. However much they are in the life, that life is not in the film.

The ambiguity of gay black representations in white documentary derives less from directors' insensitivity than from the conventions of the genre itself. In disseminating knowledge, documentary affects an objective point of view. Such realism is of course manufactured through a host of fictive and cinematic techniques: narrative, juxtaposition, pacing, editing, framing, camera placement. Yet viewers too conscious of cinematic techniques might become distracted from a film's argument or even distrustful of it. To learn anything, audiences must repress the material conditions of the film's production and projection to accept provisionally what they see as reality. Bracketing questions of positioning, motivation, and evidence, and pretending to transparent and unmediated vision, documentaries implicitly argue that their testimony, while perhaps incomplete, is "realer" than the silence and ignorance it is offered to counter. In most cases this argument seems defensible, and we treat the filmmaker as unbiased and the camera as invisible.[10]

When the camera looks across boundaries, however, the gaze seems more embattled, the medium less transparent. The very act of looking that the documentary posits as neutral has historically been a tool of racial oppression.[11] Intended as an act of identification, documentary looking at others is epistemologically indistinguishable from the voyeurism with which racial bodies have traditionally been sexualized and controlled. Such differences in the politics of the gaze are articulated in and epitomized by the Mariposa Group's *Word Is Out: Stories of Some of Our Lives* (1977). An anthology of gay coming-out stories, the film crosscuts interviews with more than two dozen individuals to demonstrate the variety of homosexual experience. The white interviewees are characterized by differences of geographic region, class, politics, education, and occupation, as well as those of sexual orientation. These characters tell a wide variety of stories—about former marriages, child custody suits, adolescent sexual experiences. Although sympathetically portrayed, the people of color speak more narrowly as people of color, as if race were their story. The Latina whose interviews open and close the film is a compelling presence, but not a vocal one. Her individuality is established not through anecdotal narratives but through her accented speech, her halting rhythms, and finally her silence. Even Betty Powell, the black lesbian who resoundingly challenges her ability to "represent," speaking *of* her discomfort at being forced to speak *as*, cannot escape appropriation. Despite her objection in the film's first minutes, her subsequent appearances cooperate fully with the film's project of representation. Nothing follows methodologically from her initial protest, which becomes just one

more instance of the film's inclusive "honesty."[12]

The moral ambiguity of racial looking and racial learning lies at the heart of Shirley Clarke's *Portrait of Jason* (1967). The film is surely the most complex white representation of a black gay male, and Jason the least silent homosexual in cinema. The film's 100-plus minutes are entirely filled with his nonstop musings, and his body is the only human image that appears on screen (until in the final seconds the director appears out of focus to call a halt to the filming). Jason is not in any simple sense objectified by the filmmakers' probing questions and unflinching gaze. Though the film is formally cinema verité, Jason himself characterizes that verité as a performance. Moving through a range of ironic voices—most notably black hip, white gay camp, and black gay camp—he dodges Clarke's wheedling and her (black) boyfriend's harangues, much as he recalls playing with his psychiatrists. He similarly theatricalizes his body, through costumes, cabaret turns, and flamboyant postures, in a frenetic dance that evades the camera's gaze. Yet ultimately Jason is captured on film, and in robbing Clarke of her control he may lose his as well. At the very least his diversionary tactics make for very uncomfortable watching, and this documentary fails to explain anything. For whom is Jason performing and why? Does the movie escape its manipulations by recording them at every step, zooming in on the drugs and liquor with which the filmmakers spur Jason on to greater self-revelation? And why do audiences watch—how can we bear to?

II

It is incorrect (even generous) to say that before the work of Marlon Riggs African American male homosexuality was invisible in U.S. film. The problem is not the lack of a tradition of black gay representation but what that tradition had taught. Hostility, neglect, tokenization, and objectification are Marlon Riggs' inheritance from previous black and gay films and his points of reference as gay black director. The meagerness of that inheritance marks not simply the moral biases of previous directors but problems of stereotyping and objectification built into the very concept of minority representation. Focusing on the tensions between seeing and knowing, Riggs' mature work plays the ideological limitations of what dominant culture is willing to see off against the epistemological limitations of spectatorship itself as a process of learning through looking.

His concern with representation as process was not immediately evident. Riggs' first full-length documentary, the Emmy-winning *Ethnic Notions* (1986), seems a conventional "realistic" survey of the stereotypic images by which white society constructed the "notions" of the African American that it used to authorize its brutality and to undermine black self-respect. Surveying a wealth of racist illustrations, photographs, films, music, and material objects, the film contrasts these "distortions" with the reality of the black experience in the United States. Riggs himself has underscored this conventionalism by characterizing the film as dues-paying, a straightforward historicist reading of racism that prevented critics from rejecting his nonlinear argument and multi-voiced narration in *Tongues* as just "a faggot going off."[13]

There is no reason to question Riggs' sincerity either in *Notions* or in his subsequent evaluation of the work as preliminary. Yet some of the visual contradictions Riggs will later examine explicitly are already implicit in this early piece. As in many works documenting cultural misrepresentation, the film's overt catalog of inaccurate images is at odds with its tacit assumption that its own images are accurate. The argument depends on a series of visual contrasts—between true images and false images, between false images and true narrative voice-overs between false images and false musical backgrounds, between (usually) false drawings and (usually) true photographs, between historical images and living academic commentators. These dichotomies are neither equivalent nor stable. Although certain cinematic components, especially the narrative voice-over and the scholarly analyses, seem entirely reliable, there is no one-to-one correlation between modes of representation and accuracy of images. It is at least suggestive that the harshest charges of misrepresentation are directed against the genre that Riggs employs to tell truth—that of film itself.

In part these tensions merely suggest the trivial paradox of trying to take an accurate picture of an inaccurate picture. Yet the film's explicit claim that images are never innocent requires that its own images be examined. There is a tension between the film's politics and its aesthetics: racist cookie jars and children's books are lovingly photographed with the clarity and brilliant colors of a museum catalog.

Even more ambivalent is the film's tone toward those performers who enacted cultural stereotypes. An earlier television documentary on a similar topic—*Black History: Lost, Stolen, or Strayed* (1968)—had been so dismissive of Stepin Fetchit that the actor sued CBS. Riggs' account is never so directly critical. Yet the clips of Fetchit and especially Hattie McDaniel display these accomplished performers at their worst. And the sequence crosscutting Ethel Waters' performance of the song "Darkies Never Dream" with King's "I have a dream" speech judges the singer deficient by measuring her against an impossibly high standard.

The film's tendency to blame actors for their complicity with cultural stereotypes is matched by a complementary desire to mask its participants' function as performers. Although the commentators seem merely to present the truth, our acceptance of their truthfulness depends as much on how the scholars look as on what they say. Despite the film's clear insistence that contemporary images continue to remain politically problematic, the commentators act as if the problem of stereotyping has been solved—both through their exclusive focus on former representations and for the ease with which they can today explicate such errors. Particularly interesting in physical terms is the film's first—and most famous—commentator, the Berkeley historian Lawrence Levine. One of the most respected historians of African American culture, Levine speaks throughout the film with unimpeachable authority. Yet as one of the film's "token" whites, his own image is more complicated. White bodies in black documentaries do not stick out as

do black bodies in white ones. Called "Larry" on the screen and "Lawrence" in the credits, Levine's folksy white presence does not need to examine its position, as did the black lesbian in *Word Is Out*. This very absence of difference among the scholars raises questions about how the images of the commentators misrepresent (or at least suppress) some of the very racial constructions the film studies. Watching Levine express impatience and dismay at the white entitlement that allowed Al Jolson without qualm to black his face for *The Jazz Singer,* the viewer is uncertain how to read the potential discontinuity between Levine's image and his words.[14]

Similar ambiguities inform the use of Esther Rolle, the film's narrator. Speaking her scripted part in measured tones that contrast with Levine's offhand analysis, she stands as the film's most commanding contemporary voice, as he is its most intellectualized contemporary body. Yet Rolle's invisibility, however traditional in such voice-of-God narrations, is itself an absent image. Rolle's voice-overs attacking the mammy figure cannot entirely erase the ways in which she herself has unwillingly perpetuated it. A classically trained actress who has performed Shakespeare, Hansberry, and Baldwin, Rolle is still best remembered (and recognized) as Beatrice Arthur's maid and Jimmie Walker's mom. Her career has been hampered by the same racial preconceptions that hurt McDaniel. There is even a visual continuity between the two. Rolle's stately carriage and personal demeanor recall the ways McDaniel in her public appearances distanced herself from her screen persona. And the absence of Rolle's image in the documentary marks the continuing difficulty film has in representing the black female.

The careful visual use of Levine, McDaniel, and Rolle suggests that the film's realism is not effortless. At three points, *Notions* admits the film's conventionality to be a pose, by examining its methods of representation. In the final credits, the film acknowledges its dual use of images as aesthetic objects and as markers of racism by praising Jan Faulkner, "whose collection of black memorabilia inspired this documentary." It is perhaps overscrupulous to worry that the characterization of the historian of material culture as "muse" reinforces the paradox of the true imaging of false images that underlies documentary realism. But it is surely true that the process by which demeaning stereotypes become "inspirational" collectibles defines the transformative power of representation—that images can themselves be framed and thus redefined.

Even more striking than this brief moment of methodological self-reflection are two scenes in which the film, anticipating the disjunctions between image and sound in *Tongues,* explicitly announces its performances to be performed. Throughout the film, the history of white actors playing African Americans is rejected as demeaning, whether in the trivializing comedy of the minstrel show or the brutalizing melodrama of *The Birth of a Nation.* Morally more complex is the process by which black actors, to gain a hearing, themselves donned blackface and adopted the stereotypes of their white predecessors. As Leni Sloan sympathetically explains, the actors saw degradation

as a doorway, and the perpetuation of stereotypes also created a new black workforce.

To illustrate the doubleness of this activity, Riggs employs—for the only time in this film—the distancing techniques associated with postmodern performance art. In the simpler of the two sequences, Sloan himself blacks up and performs a monologue in the voice of Bert Williams, the most successful of the blacks in blackface. The doubling effect, which treats Williams as image and imager, allows for the kind of sympathy not afforded Waters or McDaniel. As the one moment not scripted by Riggs, the passage calls attention to the sensibility elsewhere unifying the film's diverse images, introducing in Sloan's prose a voice not identical to (even at odds with) that of Riggs as documentarian. To underscore this difference director Riggs chooses an unusual camera angle, filming the scene over Sloan's shoulder into a mirror where Sloan's reflection talks as he blacks himself up to become Williams in the process of Williams becoming his stage persona. This self-conscious staging of the subjectivity of viewpoint identifies as equally staged the film's unobtrusive use of traditional headshots to represent the truthfulness of its analysis.

If the staging of Sloan's monologue admits the fictiveness of Riggs' realistic presentation, the second scene questions our own complicity as spectators. Two black actors with clown-white lips (but no visible blackface) re-create the vaudevillian comedy of the minstrel dance. Their performance is crosscut with images of a third black musician—also in clown costume—slapping out a rhythm on his knees and chest. Unlike the historicizing realism of the rest of the film, this sequence is clearly modern. The costumes blend period and modern styles. The music is a contemporary re-creation (rather than an archival recording as elsewhere in the movie). Though the knee-slap serves as sound track for the dance, the dancers do not coordinate their movements to its beats. The effect is surreal, more akin to the modernist choreography of Merce Cunningham or Alvin Ailey than to minstrel dance. Internalizing the film's hostility within the dance, this reframed performance shifts our relation for the material. Usually the film encourages us to identify with the filmmaker, as if looking at an exposé of racism were the same as writing one. Here, however, we are asked not to be angered by the object but to become the audience for and object of its anger. This ethnic "notion" stares angrily back out at our gaze, to ask whether in watching Riggs' outrage we have not assumed ourselves innocent of discriminatory image-making.

III

In challenging the purported realism of the documentary tradition, *Ethnic Notions* avoids one of the pitfalls of minority art—what Kobena Mercer has called the "burden of representation."[15] As Betty Powell complains in *Word Is Out*, minority voices are expected not only to present their views, but to present them as characteristic of a group—the representation must also be representative. In his first full-length statement, Riggs evades such pigeon holing by offering as "his"

view images of the ways in which blacks were viewed over time. Through the neutralizing conventions of the historical survey, Riggs prevents his account from being reduced to his positioning, and reading ethnicity as merely "notional"—someone else's idea of who you are—he implies that there is no group of which he can be taken as representative, virtually no thing for a representation to represent.

Such a deconstruction resolves only some of the difficulties in figuring race. A minority defined solely in terms of its images has no voice of its own. Those underrepresented within the group remain invisible, and in *Ethnic Notions* black gays appear only as stereotypes in white gay greeting cards. To give voices to both race and sexuality, Riggs' next film *Tongues Untied* abandons other people's notions for direct testimony. Riggs admits his polemic intentions:

> Tongues Untied *is explicitly a point-of-view work. It does not attempt to address questions of so-called "balance" or "objectivity." I am a black gay man. I made the work from that perspective. . . .* Tongues Untied *tries to provide people growing up with an image of the possibilities of life. I want them to know it is possible to live life fully, happily, and joyfully with the full understanding and the full affirmation of who you are.*

He further insists that to represent the diversity of black gay experience the film "crosses many boundaries of genre."

> *What I wanted to do with* Tongues Untied *was to start the dialogue, and*

preserve our lives in a form that people can see and address, not only now, but in years to come. People will see there was a vibrant black gay community in these United States in 1989.[16]

In speaking directly to black gay men, however, Riggs must negotiate carefully his relation to the "people" with whom he "dialogues" only indirectly—his white and straight black audiences. Autobiography is customarily the genre in which dominant cultures first permit minorities to speak. Yet untying tongues comes with strings attached, and the popularity of minority autobiography depends on empowered readers' limited expectations for it as a literary form. Traditional autobiography presents a narrative of individual triumph—how I became rich and famous, for example, or how I won the war—and implicitly promises that through imitation the reader may become as wealthy/celebrated/decorated as the author. Minority autobiography, however, asserts not one's achievements but only one's presence: though neither rich nor famous, I too exist. As representatives of a victimized group, minority autobiographers do not stand as models or exemplars but only as counterexamples; they instruct dominant culture not how it can become "like me" but how it remains irrevocably "not us." Minority autobiographers are repeatedly disassociated from their lives, defining themselves in terms of past oppressions rather than present accomplishments. "Slave" narrators, permitted to publish only under the supervision of white editors, were further required to prove their stories were "written by him/herself." Preconceptions about such authors' skill

were so strong that success in self-presentation was occasionally offered as evidence that they could not be what they claimed.[17]

This "burden of self-representation"—minority autobiography's subordination of individuals to their positioning—lies at the heart of Powell's objection in *Word Is Out*. In refusing to "represent" others, she primarily celebrates the diversity of black lesbian culture; she cannot speak for all. Yet in objecting that she is not everyone, she also asserts that she is herself, an individual whose virtues are not reducible to her affiliations. The inability of minority autobiographers to serve as exemplars is not a function only of race. All the lesbians and gay men interviewed in the film are similarly representative; the subgroups they represent—debutante, sissy, butch—are just less clearly articulated than are racialized ones. Yet it is possible to wonder with Powell whether the visibility of people of color within gay documentaries is a virtue. What seems one minority's sympathy for comparable positions may mark only the extent to which minority autobiography has already internalized the sense of inferiority by which dominant cultures subordinate racial minorities.

Tongues Untied undercuts the self-deprecating implications of minority self-representation by divorcing voice from personality and representativeness. Riggs' refusal of autobiography is clear from the film's title. Recalling minority autobiographies' reversals of previous silences, the phrase "Tongues Untied" suggests that something has not yet been heard. Unlike the positioned statement with which a minority artist traditionally announces a new voice, however, *Tongues* pluralizes the noun, refusing to cast its account as an authenticating statement from a reliable "inside" source.[18] "Tongues Untied" is not "Black Elk Speaks" or even Frederick Douglass's *Narrative . . . written by himself.* From the opening chant of "brother to brother," voices layered on top of each other speak in a disorienting mix of genres—poetry, song, monologue, skit. There is little concern for narrative continuity. Voice-overs contradict images, which are themselves often superimposed on each other. Nor is there much correlation between narrators and authors: Riggs recites Hemphill's poetry, Hemphill recites Audre Lorde's prose, as if all the voices of black homosexuality were interchangeable.

Such multiple voicings dramatize the act of speaking up while frustrating viewers' desire for personal revelation. Although such layering might have rendered the individual voices anonymous, however, Riggs' performers retain their separate identities. Some of the conventions of the confessional documentary remain. Unlike the scholarly authorities of *Notions,* the speakers are not identified by title cards. The camera angles suggest immediacy: avoiding the three-quarter shot of traditional documentary, the performers often look straight at the viewer, a gaze usually reserved for intimate revelation (and commercial hardsell). Yet these personalizing tactics only underline the film's disinterest in the most important convention of the. minority autobiography—the realistic reproduction of conversation and thought. In *Word Is Out* or *Portrait of Jason* the interviewees banter with the production crew, and even in *Notions* the academics make their analy-

ses appear natural and off-hand.[19] In *Tongues,* however, where voices often play over images of still lips and every word is self-consciously scripted, there is no illusion of spontaneity: all is performance. In the theatricality of their authority, the speakers of *Tongues* recall less the storytellers of *Word* than the scholars in *Notions,* using their credentials as black gay men to recite positions that may or may not be identically their own.

Tongues does not merely cast its "representatives" as authorities. It insists on their individuality as well. From the first we are reminded that the film's performers have identities outside this particular untying. The title cards read "Tongues Untied/by Marlon Riggs/featuring Essex Hemphill." Although Frederick Douglass had to prove that he wrote his own words, Riggs' anthology of many tongues is unambiguously "by" him. In openly acknowledging the poet Hemphill, the film alludes indirectly to its use of such other celebrated figures as dancer Willie Ninja, poet Donald Woods, playwright Reginald T. Jackson, and Brian Freeman, founder of the performance art troupe Pomo Afro Homos. These highly claimed individuals are not silenced or invisible, and the absence of the name cards *Notions* used to identify its authorities measures not the lesser importance of the performers in *Tongues* but their greater fame. Quite simply Essex Hemphill is more recognizable than Larry Levine and at moments, especially in the vogueing sequence, we are even encouraged to stargaze. *Tongues* never degenerates into popular autobiography's self congratulatory hints about how to become a famous poet or meet Madonna. Yet the film does admit, as *Before Stonewall* does not in its similar use of Audre Lorde, that Hemphill is famous.

The film's refusal to reduce its performers to the merely representative status of the minority autobiography is clearest in Riggs' treatment of his own image, voice, and words. In one sense, of course, his approach is autobiographical. Riggs is a black gay male and draws on his own experiences for voices and images. At the same time, it is not their autobiographical authenticity that makes the arguments true. Riggs' nude dance beneath the opening credits epitomizes the irony of his self-presentation. One of the film's few controversial images, the dance skillfully (and erotically) exposes a beautiful muscled body. Yet the choreography, in which Riggs' hands repeatedly cover his face, suggests that openness can mask as well as reveal, offering confidences merely to direct attention from the significant. Coming so early in the film, the scene implies that sexualizing the black body is a very preliminary way of breaking silence. And of course the penis—defining icon of male nudity and taboo of Hollywood censors—is only fleetingly visible in Riggs' underlit movements: in this film, lips—not genitals—are the visual focus of homoeroticism.

Riggs' theatricalization of his body explores the epistemological difference between exposure and revelation, nudity and visibility. Filming himself as if naked and natural, Riggs asks viewers to question the categories of realness or immediacy by which any autobiography is judged authentic. When Riggs reads from a poem about his adolescent love for a white boy while the camera slowly zooms in on a photograph of a blond youth, documentary conventions ask viewers to accept the photo as evidence of the event's reality. Yet our acquiescence mostly measures Riggs' craft as poet, actor, and filmmaker. His impassioned delivery of the poetic cadences makes us believe his account; and it is the relentlessness of the zoom more than the blandness of the photo that lends the moment its air of tragic inevitability. We do not believe the story from the evidence of a poem and a picture, or even because we have come to "trust" Riggs. We believe it because we are predisposed to the poem's moral. Images and narrative only add substance to what we have already accepted in principle.[20]

It is in the context of the film's resistance to autobiography that we must read the most controversial moment—the film's closing statement (both written and recited) that "BLACK MEN LOVING BLACK MEN IS *THE* REVOLUTIONARY ACT." Many have read the statement as an attack on interracial love, and the film's final transitions from AIDS to civil rights as Riggs' privileging of his racial identity over his sexual one. Some have pointed out the contradiction between the claim and Riggs' long-term relationship with a white partner, whose "loving support" is acknowledged in the film's final title card. Yet such debates misread the sentence, both linguistically and in terms of the film's use of speech. Not original with Riggs, the statement quotes Joseph Beam, who sees it as merely (in a phrase Riggs quotes) "an acknowledgment of responsibility" and (in phrases not cited) "an autonomous agenda for the eighties, which is not rooted in any particular sexual, political, or class affiliation."[21] Nor is it clear what Riggs means by italicizing Beam's "the": does black male love become "the" revolutionary act because it is a very radical activity or because it is the only acceptable one?

The controversy's narrow understanding of the relation between politics and sex is less troubling than its attempt to resituate the film within the very traditions of documentary realism and minority autobiography that Riggs explicitly rejects. To avoid the trivialization and fetishization that plague the genres, Riggs insists that there are many voices, none identically his. Viewers who emphasize one title card—"BLACK MEN LOVING BLACK MEN IS *THE* REVOLUTIONARY ACT"—over another— "and the loving support of Jack Vincent"—impose their own priorities on the film's multiple narratives, and the objection "But Jack is white" recasts a group performance as simple self-revelation. The film's truth does not depend on what a particular Marlon may be doing offscreen, and like the sex "scandals" that attend many performers whose public behavior is at odds with their screen personae (Pee-wee Herman and Woody Allen, to mention only the most recent), the debate marks the audience's overidentification with Riggs' screen image.[22] Perhaps what makes one kind of loving seem "the" revolutionary act lies less in the differing characters of acts than in society's strident claim that sex has no political content: it is the (anticipated) denial of Beam's statement that makes it both true and revolutionary.

However misguided, the "problem of Jack" reveals the film's manipulation of its audience's need to (mis)identify with its images. Traditionally the film viewer (implicitly white, male, and heterosexual) assumes the camera's eye to be his own. *Notions* questioned the moral complacency of this identification, implying that looking at misrepresentations was not the same as analyzing their inaccuracy. *Tongues* more simply denies that most of us are the camera. Minority autobiography teaches nonminority readers to know another culture; Riggs confronts them with their inability to read it. The film makes great demands on our knowledge: refusing to explain its images and words, it expects viewers simply to understand cultural settings and recognize the famous participants. Unable to fulfill these expectations, viewers are repeatedly brought up short by the incompleteness of their knowledge—misinterpreting the source of a passage familiar to gay African Americans, or invited to think an image means one thing when it really means another. Opening in the masculine black environment of the basketball court, the film reveals the sexuality of its images only after some straight male viewers have mistakenly identified with the homosexuals on the screen. Other moments, like the stock footage of the Castro Street Fair, similarly ask white gay audiences to see that purported images of sexual liberation actually record the absence of black bodies.

In looking "as" a black gay man, blacks and gays experience the errors of their spectatorship. For straight white viewers, the movie does not even offer the possibility of misidentification by which black straights and white gays are included in the conversation. Offering no coming-out narratives or debates about the psychosocial origins of sexual object-choice, the film refuses to reproduce the traditional arguments used to "explain" homosexuality to a mainstream audience. Ignoring white racism and homophobia, it forestalls the tendency of liberal guilt to refocus attention on itself by reducing minority experience to oppression by dominant culture. In Riggs' representations dominant culture is not the audience, the standard, or the villain, and to view his "other" images, white heterosexuals abandon the very spectatorial privilege whose primacy is the foundation of traditional cinema.[23]

Only when considering aspects of black gay culture familiar to the general public does the film acknowledge the existence of a straight white gaze—documenting how the appropriation of black gay male culture transforms untied tongues into marketable goods. Though a comic sequence, the "lesson in snap" at "the Institute of SNAP!thology" darkly hints that the desire to know black gays may only be the latest form of radical chic. Mimicking the conventions of television hucksterism—complete with title cards, "greatest hits" lists, everything but the 800 number—Riggs refuses to distinguish the cultural motives of PBS from those of the Home Shopping Network. Equally self-deflating is his presentation of vogueing, the most commercialized aspect of black gay culture. The photography's "realistic" vocabulary—street setting, grainy color, unsteady camera, lack of cuts—places the dance within a specific social context denied it in Madonna videos. Yet in finally employing the documentary style absent elsewhere, the sequence questions viewers' equation of visual crudity with minority truth. Like the blackface dancers in Notions, Willie

Ninja in his staginess calls attention to our gaze, and his mimed powdering of his nose recalls Riggs' ambivalence toward the similarly mirrored depiction of Bert Williams in blackface. This most commercialized image in Tongues is also the most hostile and silent, asking viewers not only by what right they look but whether looking automatically silences.[24]

IV

New voices can be heard only when old views are obstructed, and in Tongues Untied the immediacy of speech is tempered by the self-consciousness of sight. To all but the black gay men identified as the film's primary audience, spectatorship offers an eye not I, and the film's overlooked images become visible only through resistance to established modes of looking. Yet Riggs' cautions have largely been ignored by the mainstream viewers they address, and the film absorbed by the very traditions it critiques. Debates around the work reinstate the dichotomies—gay/straight, black/white—attacked by the film's pluralist tongues. Riggs' alienating theatricalizations are recast as personal autobiography, and his eroticized men as quickly fetishized as had been Josephine Baker. After such a taming of Tongues, black gay and lesbian directors have sought more drastic strategies to make images irreducible as well as visible.

As we would expect, Riggs' subsequent work revises the misreadings of his position. Two short pieces explicitly continue Tongues, employing the same performers, narrative techniques, and even footage to modify its argumentation and appearance.

A visually unassuming postscript to *Tongues, Affirmations* (1990) tempers the earlier film's most controversial arguments, offering in two brief episodes a more hopeful account of interracial love and a more pessimistic one of black solidarity. Reworking form rather than content, *Anthem* (1991) adopts avant-garde film techniques to recast the earlier film as a frenetic collage of sound and color. With narrative and characterization obliterated, movement and pacing take precedence, and sexual sequences that seemed perfunctory in *Tongues* are eroticized by the sensuality of the whole.[25]

Riggs' longer pieces since *Tongues* appear to reembrace documentary realism. Though not explicitly revisionist, however, these films exploit absence and the unsaid to challenge viewer expectations through ominous omissions. *Color Adjustment* (1991), his first full-length film after *Tongues,* surveys the development of television images of African Americans—from the gross oversimplifications of "Amos and Andy" and "Beulah," through the incomplete liberalism of "Julia," "Good Times," and "Roots," to more complex incarnations like "The Cosby Show" and "Frank's Place." Yet, as Riggs knows, greater availability of minority images does not automatically solve the problem; his own appearance as the single most visible gay television image (black or white) encouraged voyeurism as fully as gay pride. Throughout *Adjustment, the* charge that television images do not portray the reality of the African American experience is overshadowed by a greater uncertainty about what would constitute an appropriate image. The accuracy with which an image shows our experience depends on who defines the constituency of the "our"; and the documentary's analysis is compromised by its exclusive focus on heterosexuality. Perhaps the praise of "Frank's Place" for its broad range of blacks need not worry the series' depiction of a New Orleans without homosexuality. But when one scholar asserts that "Cosby represents everyone's fantasy; everyone wants to live that way," it is hard to believe the tongues of Riggs' previous three films would agree.

The film critiques its silence about heterosexism in structuring its material. The narrative is framed by quotations from James Baldwin, a writer most famous for his dual identity as African American and homosexual. The failure to mention the homoeroticism of shows like "I Spy" may be unintentional, but Riggs' HIV status makes the film's fleeting allusions to AIDS all the more painful for being understated. Most important, a sexual bias informs the film's most original argument—its linking of racial stereotyping to the myth of the family. Treating the incorporation of black actors into the American dream family as a form of cooptation, the authorities and film clips demonstrate that the family has been the site of racial stereotyping. Riggs' narration pushes this observation further to insist that the fault lies less with the particular content of the images than with the choice of the social unity of the family to measure African American achievement. Although from "Beulah" to "Cosby" depictions of the black family have become more accurate, racial misrepresentation will continue as long as television locates its images "all in the family."

The documentary's implicit claim for the "natural" antipathy between race and the family originates in an argument about the documentable tension between the family, by definition heterosexual, and a homosexuality that purportedly foreswears procreation and seduces children. Although black culture is not itself anti-family, the normative use of the family model to define gays as abnormal bodes ill as well for any minority group. Despite his authorities' naive faith in the possibility of better black images, Riggs warns that television's transformation of (straight/white/male) social structures into (universal) oral norms prevents any serious consideration of cultural difference. Using a gay trope to unsettle (perhaps undo) a media analysis reproducing the sexual conventionality of that medium, Riggs argues that until minorities cooperate in rethinking all the structures of representation, the normalizing potential of imagery will betray each group in turn.

As *Color Adjustment* must be read in dialogue with its own heterosexism, so Riggs' final completed film—the beautiful but austere *Non, Je Ne Regrette Rien (No Regrets)* (1992)—can only be appreciated in comparison with AIDS representation more generally. Weaving together five interviews with seropositive black males, the film argues powerfully for our fellowship with those affected, while ending the silence that still ties tongues concerning African American losses (of, for example, designer Willi Smith and choreography Alvin Ailey). Combining high-gloss photography with the static camera of the "talking heads" format, the narrative reinvents traditional mise-en-scène to correct gay documentary's customary penchant for entertaining characterization and low production values. Presenting comparatively subdued figures, the film avoids the epigrammatic wit and the class and gender stereotypes—salty butch, drag savant, streetwise tough, smug capitalist—by which gay documentary from *Word Is Out* to *Paris Is Burning* has made its interviewees lovable. The photography similarly reconceives the conventional imaging of AIDS.[26] In contrast to the debilitating lesions and sunken cheeks marking the seropositive as "victim," the absence of visible illness in the film depicts the strength (and longevity) of those infected with a virus falsely read as death. To counter the erotophobia surrounding infection, the camera imitates pornography's fondness for close-up body parts, sexualizing its bodies without the depersonalization often attending such dismemberments. The film calls no attention to its revisions; Riggs does not wish technique to upstage the immediacy of the testimony. But the minimalism of his staging redefines what it means to look at the diseased body, challenging spectatorial presuppositions as completely as does the more confrontive postmodernism of *Tongues*.[27]

After the success of Riggs' *Tongues* (and black British director Isaac Julien's *Looking for Langston*), increasing attention has been paid to representations of African American sexuality by such talented U.S. directors as Aarin Burch, Christopher Leo Daniels, Cheryl Dunye, Thomas Harris, Melanie Nelson, Michelle Parkerson, Sylvia Rhue, Catherine Saalfield, Dawn Suggs, Jocelyn Taylor, Jack Waters, Yvonne Welbon, and Jacqueline Woodson. Although this work is too rich to reduce to a single analytic model (or a few pages), these films extend Riggs' critique of documentary realism and personal revelation by incorporating into their narratives self-conscious reflections on their cinematic antecedents, photographic methods, and modes of production. Jack Waters' *The Male Gayze* (1990), for example, addresses familiar problems of white appropriation and objectification in its tale of a black dancer whose nude photograph was illegally marketed by a European choreographer. The film's ambiguous images, however, stand in ironic relation to the straightforward narrative. Just as modern dance dissociates movement from music, the film's images proceed independently of its narration: some intersect with it, like the shots of a postcard that may be an incarnation of the offending photograph; others—of a father and a child, a family picnic, or grazing horses—have no discernible relation to the tale. The disjunction between sounds and images questions the process by which we unify the diverse elements of any cinematic gaze. Viewers equate the postcard with the photograph, just as they assume the narrator to be the dancer, the dancer to be the director, and the film to be autobiography. Yet nothing requires such an ordering of cinematic images, which uses spectatorial privilege to control the film's irregularities much as the older choreographer uses his power and position to seduce and commodify the young black dancer. According to the film's ironic title, not only can gay male desire reproduce straight racism, but any gaze may involve a similar "mastery" in its "male" unification of flickering light and noise into narrative.

Black lesbian directors have probably even less access to funding and audiences than do African American gay males. Not surprisingly, their work maintains close formal ties to the marketable genres of documentary and autobiography. Yet highly sensitive to the inequities of cultural positioning, these triply minoritized artists scrutinize the techniques of realism and immediacy by which they gain viewers.[28] Yvonne Welbon's *Sisters in the Life* (1993), for example, dramatizes a conventional reminiscence of "first love." Yet the contrast between the staged representations of the woman's adolescent memories and the improvised scenes in which Wellbon as director "interviews" the adult woman and a "grown-up" lover undermine the dichotomies of innocence/experience, past/present, actor/director, and fiction/truth on which such reminiscences depend. After an imagistic meditation involving isolation, violence, and a masculinized woman in *Chasing the Moon* (1990), Dawn Suggs in her subsequent *I Never Danced the Way Girls Were* Supposed *To* (1991) recasts the same anger as a running commentary on lesbian images by a comically bemused narration. Wondering whether lesbians have abnormal relations to shoes and sandwiches, the narrative comes to realize the arbitrariness of any attempt to define normalcy. Acceptable behavior depends on who judges, and by its end the film's opening footage of stereotyped lesbians has been comically redefined to gaze not with contempt but with envy.

In *Among Good Christian People* (1991), Catherine Saalfield and Jacqueline Woodson examine the intersection of religion with race and homosexuality, largely in terms of Woodson's recollections of her youth as a Jehovah's Witness. Yet the documentary's variety of narrative styles—archival footage framed by a black border, improvised interviews by anonymous choir members, Woodson's scripted autobiography-calls attention to the staged character of all such authenticating realism. Though endorsing Woodson's narrative as true, the film also admits the theatricality of that truth, offering alternative readings of the same lines of script, and photographing the same objects on contemporary videotape and artificially aged "archival" film stock. Bringing fiction and reality even closer together, Saalfield's *Bird in the Hand* (1993), codirected with Melanie Nelson, tells the fictional story of a breakup between a student (played and scripted by Nelson) and her filmmaker lover. Hyperrealistically photographed, the film walks a narrow line between narrative and polemic, using its slight plot to debate issues of spousal violence and codependency. In its preoccupation with cars and Manhattan streets, it initiates along with white director Su Friedrich's *Rules of the Road* (1993) a lesbian inversion of the buddy/road picture. And its epilogue offering a date with the (now available) filmmaker breaks through the wall narrative establishes between image and audience.

As signaled by *Bird in the Hand,* the return to narrative within black gay and lesbian film does not impede the tradition's scrutiny of its modes of representation. Employing the traditional cinematic vocabulary of commercial Hollywood, Michael Mayson's *Billy Turner's Secret* (1990) energetically recounts the learning and liberation resulting from an urban black's coming-out to his African American and Latino friends. The very

conventionality of Mayson's storytelling makes his political innovations more effective. He imitates Spike Lee's verbal wit, multiethnic characters, and use of Brooklyn exteriors to tell the story Lee's films most fear, even like Lee casting himself in a pivotal role (as the homophobe). The film gets too much comic mileage out of ethnic and sexual slurs and reinscribes a masculinist ethos of violence in the climactic brutalization of the homophobe by homosexual characters. Yet Mayson not only preaches tolerance with more energy and wit than the solemn uplift of PBS's *American Playhouse.* The guilelessness of his hybrid position as the straight-identified actor/director in a gay-identified film expands traditional definitions of what makes cinema gay.

A more sustained examination of the limits of narration is evident in the films of Michelle Parkerson. Although Parkerson's work is primarily within documentary, her focus on singers in *But Then, She's Betty Carter* (1980) and *Gotta Make This Journey: Sweet Honey in the Rock* (1983) and especially on a male impersonator in *Storme: The Lady Of the Jewel Box* (1987) has placed questions of performance and theatricality at the center of her realism. Her science fiction mini-epic *Odds and Ends* (1993) confronts directly the symbiotic relation between artifice and verisimilitude. Unlike science fiction novels, where imagination can roam to the very limits of language, sci-fi films are at the mercy of their production values. Yet the special effect only epitomizes the dependency of all cinematic images on technological manipulation, and Parkerson's satire directs its deconstructive (not to say camp) gaze not only at Hollywood gargantuanism but at the more general exclusions of realistic narrative. Inverting the imperialism, and racism, and misogyny of traditional sci-fi plots, she tells a story of a galactic liberation from a culture of white male clones as undertaken by black females in the name of interplanetary Afrocentrism. Building on the gay absurdist techniques of Charles Ludlam's Theater of the Ridiculous and of Pomo Afro Homos, she experiments with fractured chronology and hyperbolic performance to loosen the stranglehold of realistic representation on plot and character as well. Thus while introducing new characters and ideas into a genre where they had been invisible, she continues to warn that old forms unmodified may not permit speaking the new.

Perhaps the most promising model for minority self-representation lies in recent work by Cheryl Dunye. In *Janine* (1990), Dunye recalls a troubled high school friendship with a patronizing rich white girl. An adept reading of how power inequities reinforce personal insecurities, the narrative, like Riggs' memories of the white boy in *Tongues,* leaves relatively unexamined the conditions of its retelling. In her *She Don't Fade* (1991), Dunye situates a similar consideration of lesbian relationships within a self-reflexive exploration of filmmaking in general. Appropriating the title, photography, mock documentary style, and character asides of Spike Lee's *She's Gotta Have It,* Dunye not only lambastes Lee's anti-Lesbianism, but explores more generally the interdependence of sexuality and narrative. Moving effortlessly between her personae as director Cheryl and character Shae, Dunye teases audience readiness to

accept as authentic any personalizing narrative, whether of Shae or of Janine. White technician Paula, reluctantly acting the part of Shae's confidante Paula, dramatizes the arbitrariness of our markers of difference in her incoherent character accent, half Brooklyn Jew, half black snap queen. And the intimacy and solemnity viewers impose on all sex scenes is prohibited by the film's sound tract, in which crew members, including technician Paula, offer advice to the nude actresses until all collapse in laughter. In dialogue with Lee, storytelling, and audiences' needs for identification and verisimilitude, Dunye's *Fade* suggests that a romance can ironize its conventions without sacrificing in the final fadeout the narrative satisfaction of the passionate embrace.

Beginning with the work of Marlon Riggs, black lesbian and gay male directors have made homosexuality visible in film. They have done so not simply by imaging it through traditional modes of filmic representation but by using sexual invisibility to define what realism and autobiography are unable to represent. In these films speech both announces its former silencing and tests the boundaries of its newfound permission to speak. Their self-reflexivity marks not only an abstract commitment to theory but a practical instinct for survival. Those not aware how to address an audience will never appear before one; those inattentive to the conditions by which they are tolerated will be coopted by the very process of their screening. The methodological skepticism of the minority artists is a hard lesson to those for whom conventional representation has been adequate, because it was created for them. Yet only by examining the conditions that deny reality to others can our reality have meaning. When communication knows its limits, we may be able to end language's ability to silence—to hear along with tongues no longer tied tongues never tied at all.

Notes

1. For a comprehensive overview of the debate surrounding the PBS screening, see Gary Rivlin and Sara Catania, "A Tongue Untied," *East Bay Express* 16, No. 31 (May 15, 1992): 10-14, 18-21.

2. It is suggestive that Buchanan's footage from the movie showed white homosexuals rather than the African Americans more central in Riggs' account. For an example of the process by which Riggs' film passes out of liberal discourse, see Eve Kosofsky Sedgwick, "Socratic Raptures, Socratic Ruptures: Notes Toward Queer Performativity," in *English Inside and Out: The Places of Literary Criticism,* ed. Susan Gubar and Jonathan Kamholtz (New York: Routledge, 1993), pp. 122-36. Here Sedgwick's participation in the "protest-function" following one station's refusal to screen the video affords her the occasion to muse about AIDS, chemotherapy, queer performance, and (white) theory without ever attending to the work itself.

3. By so placing Riggs *in* a context, I do not wish to reduce him *to* a context— to make him a "symptom" of (not to say "credit to") his cultural position. For a sensitive account of the limitations of the "comparativist" approach and especially of the problematic relation between individual talent and popular assessment, see Wahneema Lubiano, "But Compared to What?: Reading Realism, Representation, and Essentialism in *School Daze, Do the Right Thing,* and the Spike Lee Discourse," *Black American Literature Forum* 25, No. 2 (Summer 1991): 253-82.

4. See, for example, Riggs, "Black Macho Revisited: Reflections of a Snap Queen," *Black American Literature Forum* 25, No. 2 (Summer 1991): 389-94. For similar readings by other directors and critics, see Michelle Parkerson, "Birth of a Notion: Towards Black Gay and Lesbian Imagery in Film and Video," in *Queer Looks: Perspectives on Lesbian and Gay Film and Video,* ed. Martha Gever, Pratibha Parmar, and John Greyson (New York: Routledge, 1993), pp. 234-37; and Lubiano, "But Compared to What?"

5. For an excellent overview of the use of race by white gay and lesbian filmmakers, see B. Ruby Rich, "When Difference Is (More Than) Skin Deep," in *Queer Looks,* pp. 318-39.

6. Even after Riggs, white filmmakers remain oblivious to their racism. As an account of the sexual revolution in San Francisco, Armistead Maupin's *Tales of the City* books (1978-89) show their age. Yet when in 1994 PBS aired a film version of the first volume, it not only included no people of color, gay or straight; it

unashamedly "featured" Dorothea, Maupin's black lesbian character who turns out to be a WASP in blackface.

7. Gus Van Sant's subsequent, more commercial films dealing with similar material—*Drugstore Cowboy* (1989) and *My Own Private Idaho* (1991)—have been even less explicit on the racial dimensions of street culture. The films of Rainer Werner Fassbinder, and especially his filmic use of his real-life lover the Moroccan actor El Hedi Ben Salem, offer a more complicated though not fully satisfactory account of the intersection between sexuality and race. In *Fox and His Friends* (1975), Salem plays an African hired to service Fassbinder's Fox, a working-class homosexual being taught the privileges of the German tourist by his upper-middle-class boyfriend. In *Ali—Fear Eats the Soul* (1974), Salem is part of a working-class, interracial heterosexual relationship, but his body is fetishized for the camera in a way that might be characterized as homosexual spectatorship. On Van Sant and Fassbinder, see Rich, "When Difference Is (More Than) Skin Deep," in *Queer Looks*, pp. 423–25; Judith Mayne, "Fassbinder and Spectatorship," *New German Critique* 12 (1977): 61–74; and Kaja Silverman, *Male Subjectivity at the Margins* (New York: Routledge, 1992), pp. 125–56, 214–96. For more general considerations of the place of race within white film, see Richard Dyer, "White," *Screen* (1988); rpt. in his *The Matter of Images: Essays on Representations* (New York:

Routledge, 1993), pp. 141–63; and Judith Mayne, *Cinema and Spectatorship* (New York: Routledge, 1993), pp. 142–72.

8. James Baldwin comments indirectly on Laurents' conflation of race and sexuality in his reading of the film in *The Devil Finds Work* (New York: Dell, 1976), pp., 81–82. The problem of sexual substitution informs much of Laurents' work. In his play *The Time of the Cuckoo* (filmed as *Summertime)* a female spinster on vacation stands in for the gay man cruising Venice. Such conglomerate identities come to a head (comically) in Laurents' script for *West Side Story,* in which homoeroticized chorus boys, arbitrarily divided into Polish and Puerto Rican, sing and dance a mix of ballet and Broadway, all under the sign of updated Shakespeare. For a general (generous) reading of *Home,* see Donald Bogle, *Toms, Coons, Mulattoes, Mammies, and Bucks: An Interpretive History of Blacks in American Films,* new expanded edition (New York: Continuum, 1990), pp. 144–47. For skeptical accounts, see Thomas Cripps, *Making Movies Black: The Hollywood Message Movie from World War II to the Civil Rights Era* (New York: Oxford University Press, 1993), pp. 221–26; and Michele Wallace, "Race, Gender, and Psychoanalysis in Forties Film: *Lost Boundaries, Home of the Brave,* and *The Quiet One,"* in *Black American Cinema,* ed. Manthia Diawara (New York: Routledge, 1992), pp. 257–71. For a more general discussion of gay

male appropriations of minority identity, see my *The Queening of America: Gay Culture in Straight Society* (New York: Routledge, 1995).

9. For complementary reactions to white lesbian representations of African Americans, see Parkerson, "Birth of a Notion," and Rich, "When Difference Is (More Than) Skin Deep," in *Queer Looks,* pp. 237, 318–39. For a debate on these issues in terms of the pivotal work of Sheila McLaughlin, see the discussion following Teresa de Lauretis, "Film and the Visible," in *How Do I Look?: Queer Film and Video,* ed. Bad Object-Choices (Seattle: Bay Press, 1991), pp. 264–76. For McLaughlin's own evaluation of her use of race, see Alison Butler, *"She Must Be Seeing Things:* An Interview with Sheila McLaughlin," in *Queer Looks,* pp. 368–76. More ambiguous in its implications is the way in which some narratives, like Nella Larsen's novel *Passing* (1929) and Julie Dash's film *Illusions* (1982), seem to figure racial passing as "like" homosexuality.

10. Much recent theory explores the fictionality of nonfiction film. See, for example, Bill Nichols, *Representing Reality: Issues and Concepts in Documentary* (Bloomington: Indiana University Press, 1991), pp. 32–75, 165–98; and Michael Renov, ed., *Theorizing Documentary* (New York: Routledge, 1993).

11. Minority film criticism has repeatedly problematized the role of "realness" in delineating difference. See, for example, Lubiano, "But Compared to What?"; Kobena Mercer, "Diaspora Culture and the Dialogic Imagination: The Aesthetics of Black Independent Film in Britain," in *BLACKFRAMES: Critical Perspectives on Black Independent Cinema,* ed. Mbye B. Cham and Claire Andrade-Watkins (Cambridge, Mass.: MIT Press, 1988, pp. 50–61; Trinh T. Minh-ha, "The Totalizing Quest of Meaning," in *When the Moon Waxes Red: Representation, Gender and Cultural Politics* (New York: Routledge, 1991, pp. 29–50; Valerie Smith, "The Documentary Impulse in Contemporary U.S. African American Film," in *Black Popular Culture: A Project by Michele Wallace,* ed. Gina Dent (Seattle: Bay Press, 1992), pp. 56–64; and Ana M. López, "(Not) Looking for Origins: Postmodernity, Documentary, and *America,"* in *Theorizing Documentary,* pp. 151–63.

12. For a more optimistic reading of Powell's objection, see Isaac Julien and Kobena Mercer, "Introduction—De Margin and De Centre," in *The Last "Special" Issue on Race?,* ed. Isaac Julien and Kobena Mercer, *Screen* 29, No. 4 (Autumn 1988): 2–10.

13. For the conventionality of *Notions,* see Bill Nichols, "'Getting to Know You,' Knowledge, Power, and the Body," in *Theorizing Documentary,* pp. 186–88; and Riggs' own evaluation in Rivlin and Catania, "A Tongue Untied," p. 18.

14. In discussing Paul Robeson's popularity with both white and black audiences, Richard Dyer argues that however much they may seem to value the same things, "black discourses see

(these virtues] as contributions to the development of society, white as enviable qualities that only blacks have." In light of this difference, Levine's explanation that blackface liberated whites to adopt purported black freedoms may not only be accurate, but repeat the error by internalizing white envy for the uniquely black. See Dyer, *Heavenly Bodies: Film Stars and Society* (New York: St. Martins Press, 1986), p. 79.

15. Kobena Mercer, "Black Art and the Burden of Representation," *Third Text* 10 (Spring 1990): 61–78.

16. Ron Simmons, *"Tongues Untied: An Interview with Marlon Riggs,"* in *Brother to Brother: New Writings by Black Gay Men,* ed. Essex Hemphill, conceived by Joseph Fairchild Beam (Boston: Alyson, 1991), pp. 191–92, 193. Kobena Mercer cites an even more telling description by Riggs: "What films like *Tongues Untied* do, especially for people who have had no images of themselves out there to see, is give them a visible and visual representation of their lives." Kobena Mercer, "Dark and Lovely Too: Black Gay Men in Independent Film," in *Queer Looks,* p. 244.

17. The pressures exerted by white editors is a repeated theme in the scholarship of the slave narrative. See, for example, William L. Andrews, *To Tell a Free Story: The First Century of Afro-American Autobiography, 1760–1865* (Urbana: University of Illinois Press, 1986), pp. 19–22; and James Olney, "'I Was Born': Slave Narratives, Their Status as Autobiography and Literature," in *The Slave's Narrative,*

ed. Charles T. Davis and Henry Louis Gates Jr. (New York: Oxford University Press, 1985), pp. 148–75. On the epistemological paradoxes of the slave narrative see my "Reading Slavery: The Anxiety of Ethnicity in Douglass's *Narrative,"* in *Frederick Douglass: New Literary and Historical Essays,* ed. Eric J. Sundquiust (New York: Cambridge University Press, 1990), pp. 118–40.

18. Kobena Mercer has dealt widely with the limitations of authenticity as a measure of documentary realism. See his "Diaspora Culture and the Dialogic Imagination," in *BLACK-FRAMES,* pp. 50–61; and on *Tongues* itself, "Dark and Lovely Too: Black Gay Men in Independent Film," in *Queer Looks,* pp. 238–56. For a critique of the use of a "narrative informant" to understand another culture, see James Clifford, The *Predicament of Culture: Twentieth-Century Ethnography, Literature, and Art* (Cambridge, Mass.: Harvard University Press, 1988), especially pp. 21–54.

19. On the importance of this "interactive model, of documentary discourse, with passing reference to *Notions,* see Bill Nichols, *Representing Reality,* pp. 44–56.

20. The boundary between truth and literature becomes even less distinct when Riggs publishes his "autobiographical" poetic fragments under the title "Tongues Untied" in *Brother to Brother: New Writings by Black Gay Men.* Conceived by the late Joseph Beam and edited by Essex Hemphill, this volume is obviously in symbiotic

relation to the film, from whose opening chant it draws its own title. The interpenetration of the two works—and their continuity with Beam's earlier volume *In the Life: A Black Gay Anthology* (Boston: Alyson, 1986) and with Isaac Julien's film *Looking for Langston* (1989)—suggests the extent to which the project, however differently realized by Beam, Hemphill, Julien, and Riggs, is in some very real sense a communal one.

21. See "Brother to Brother: Words from the Heart," in *In the Life,* pp. 230–42. Like Riggs' poem "Tongues Untied," Beam's essay joins together various ideas originally published separately. The incendiary sentence appears several times in the last three pages of the essay; the qualifying phrases are from p. 242. Riggs himself explicates the line in a similarly abstract way: "Many people do interpret "black men loving black men" solely in terms of a sexual, romantic affinity, and love. But what I meant was love in the sense of friendship, community, family, and fraternity, which was far more important, in nurturing me as a black gay man, than the love of a particular lover who is white"; Simmons' interview, *"Tongues Untied,"* in *Brother to Brother,* p. 194. Riggs agrees with Simmons' sense that "a love relationship, it's not a political act per se" (p. 194). For a balanced overview of the debate in both the black and white gay presses, see Rich, "When Difference Is (More Than) Skin Deep," in *Queer Looks,* pp. 331–39.

22. A similar misreading has informed criticism of Isaac Julien's *Looking for Langston.* Released shortly before *Tongues,* Julien's film employs not documentary analysis but the objectivizing conventions of the high art film to explore black gay culture. Nevertheless critics as different as Mercer and Gates insist on relocating Julien within a personalizing tradition. Each concludes, in virtually identical formulations, that though "we look for Langston, we find Isaac." Though, offered as praise, the formulation nevertheless attests to the force of autobiography as minority authentication even in a work whose mode is objective and historicist. See Mercer, "Dark and Lovely Too," p. 250; and Henry Louis Gates Jr., "The Black Man's Burden," in *Black Popular Culture: A Project by Michele Wallace,* ed. Gina Dent (Seattle: Bay Press, 1992), p. 77. On Julien's film more generally, see as well Manthia Diawara, "The Absent One: The Avant-Garde and the Black Imaginary in *Looking for Langston,"* *Wide Angle,* 13, Nos. 3/4 (July–October 1991): 96–106; and Henry Louis Gates Jr., "Looking for Modernism," in *Black American Cinema,* ed. Manthia Diawara (New York: Routledge, 1992), pp. 200–207. The general critical preference for high art over documentary realism hurts Julien himself when, in his subsequent film *Young Soul Rebels* (1991), he experiments with popular narrative forms closer to those of *Tongues.* See Isaac Julien's claim that in the concept of "black popular culture" the first adjective overshadows the second: "Black Is, Black Ain't: Notes

on De-Essentializing Black Identities" [with discussion], in *Black Popular Culture: A Project by Michele Wallace*, pp. 255-75.

23. For models of alternative spectatorship in minority film, see Manthia Diawara, "Black Spectatorship: Problems of Identification and Resistance," in *The Last "Special" Issue on Race?*, ed. Isaac Julien and Kobena Mercer, *Screen* 29, No. 4 (Autumn 1988): 66-76; rpt. in *Black American Cinema*, ed. Manthia Diawara (New York: Routledge, 1992), pp. 211-20;,and Teresa de Lauretis, "Film and the Visible," in *How Do I Look? Queer Film and Video*, pp. 225-76.

24. For an excellent discussion of Riggs' deconstructive use of snap and vogueing, see Marcos Becquer, "Snap!thology and Other Discursive Practices in *Tongues Untied*," *Wide Angle* 13, No. 2 (April 1991): 6-17. For a general consideration of the representation of vogueing in white film, with some reference to Riggs, see bell hooks, *Black Looks: Race and Representation* (Boston: South End Press, 1992), pp. 145-64.

25. For a general discussion of how avant-garde forms function within black gay film, see Manthia Diawara, "The Absent One: The Avant-Garde and the Black Imaginary in *Looking for Langston*," *Wide Angle*, 13, Nos. 3/4 (July-October 1991): 96-106.

26. On the general problems of representing AIDS, see the articles of Douglas Crimp, especially "Portraits of People with AIDS," in *Cultural Studies*, ed. Lawrence Grossberg, Cary Nelson,

and Paula Treichler (New York: Routledge, 1992), pp. 117-33. On the relation of the African American community to such representations, see Phillip Brian Harper, "Eloquence and Epitaph: Black Nationalism and the Homophobic Impulse in Responses to the Death of Max Robinson," *Social Text* 289, no. 3 (1991): 68-86.

27. The haunting posthumous *Black Is . . . Black Ain't* (1995) is Riggs' most extended attempt to reconcile sexuality and race. The film claims that identity categories only limit African Americans, and it offers homosexuality as a central example of the kind of thing excluded from traditional definitions of blackness. It is difficult, however, to be more specific about the film's reconciliation of the two identities, for Riggs did not of course have total control over the final form of the film, completed after his death in 1994.

28. Positioning is the explicit topic of the first celebrated film by an American lesbian of color, *Ten Cents a Dance (Parallax)* (1985), by the Japanese Canadian director Midi Onodera. In a controversial formalist innovation, Onodera symbolizes the ostracization of the lesbian of color through a narrative boxed into three sets of paired stationary images, only one of the six including an "actual" lesbian, played by the director. For analyses of this groundbreaking work, a masterpiece of modern feminist filmmaking and implicit touchstone for subsequent work by African American lesbians, see Judith Mayne, *The Woman at the*

Keyhole: Feminism and Women's Cinema (Bloomington: Indiana University Press, 1990), pp. 225–27; and idem, "A Parallax View of Lesbian Authorship," in *Inside/Out: Lesbian Theories, Gay Theories* (New York: Routledge, 1991), pp. 173–84.

Leland T. Saito

Asian Americans and Latinos in San Gabriel Valley, California: Ethnic Political Cooperation and Redistricting 1990–92

Suburban dynamics often dominate life in today's California. Though young adults revel in weekend car cruising along hot drags such as Sunset Boulevard and Cesar Chavez Avenue [formerly Whittier Boulevard] in Los Angeles, Story Road [San Jose], Mission Street [San Francisco], and Kearny Street [Fresno], many do so after driving in from suburbs. Life there sometimes bores youth. Yet politicians and marketers know that important and "new" majorities inhabit suburban valleys all over California. While not as famous as the San Fernando Valley, communities east of Los Angeles known as the San Gabriel region may better indicate where California is heading. Including the cities of Azusa and Duarte in its eastern region to Montebello and Alhambra in the western boundaries, this area reflects the complexities of contention and change in today's suburbia.

Once these were locations of sleepy truck farms for residents of the City of Los Angeles, now the Valley's local politics and ethnic dynamics are fodder for social scientists hoping to understand where California and the American West are heading. In the article that follows, Leland Saito describes early 1990s relations between Latinos and Asian Americans in that setting. Change has continued since Saito's report, but his choice of this suburbia remains where some of the most important of California's interethnic relations are taking place. Much can be learned, by reflecting on what occurred so recently in this representative setting. *(SMM)*

After the racial turmoil of the 1960s and 1970s, the relative calm of the 1980s seemed to indicate that the United States was entering a period of improved race relations. However, the racial rhetoric of politicians such as Jesse Helms, the popularity of ex-Ku Klux Klan member David Duke in the Louisiana elections, and the rise in racial hate crimes once again brought race and ethnic relations to the forefront of public attention. In addition to the conflicts of Anglos versus African Americans that have long dominated the discourse on race and ethnic relations, conflict between ethnic groups, such as Korean small business owners and their African American clientele, have now emerged.

Interethnic struggle reached a high point following the acquittal of the four Los Angeles police officers accused of using violent force against Rodney King, an African American. Following the verdict, hundreds of businesses owned by Koreans and other ethnic groups were looted and burned down by African Americans and Latinos.

Against this backdrop of racial tension, I examine political relationships between Asian Americans and Latinos in the San Gabriel Valley, located in Los Angeles County. I examine an Asian American organization that was established around the issue of redistricting and reapportionment and how the group formed an alliance with its Latino counterpart in the region. In this case, the Asian American and Latino organizations were able to reach agreement on plans that accomplished the complex task of protecting the political interests of Latinos and Asian Americans.

What were the circumstances in the San Gabriel Valley that led to cooperation in the redistricting process between Asian Americans and Latinos? The Asian American and Latino communities overlap in the region so that district plans would affect both groups.

The San Gabriel Valley is an ideal place to study ethnic relations because of its demographics. Beginning in the 1970s, the formerly Anglo population experienced rapid change when large numbers of Asian Americans and Latinos entered the region. For example, Monterey Park has become the first city outside of Hawaii with a majority (57.5 percent) Asian American population.[1] At the regional level, Latinos have become the majority population in the valley and they hold all elected state and federal offices that cover Monterey Park. Yet, vestiges of Anglo political dominance remain on the local level in the form of Anglo control of some city councils.

This study primarily uses data from ethnographic fieldwork and interviews collected from 1990 to 1992. Census and voter registration data were also utilized. Ethnographic fieldwork was critical for documenting and analyzing events emerging from the historical and contemporary factors that formed the context for ethnic relations in the San Gabriel Valley.

This paper differs in three ways from other studies in race and ethnic relations. First, community studies traditionally examine one ethnic group, or compare an ethnic group with Anglos; this study examines two groups, Asian Americans and Latinos.[2] Second, most studies examining ethnic relations examine conflict,[3] whereas my research examines the circumstances around the volatile process that led to ethnic cooperation rather than conflict. Third, while one school of thought suggests that ethnicity is decreasing in importance politically, my study supports the persistence of ethnicity in politics.

Theoretically, one school of thought suggests that economic class is increasing in importance with a relative decline in ethnicity. Milton Gordon, in his formulation of assimilation theory, believed that ethnicity, "defined or set off by race, religion, or national origin," was a temporary condition which would disappear as groups "assimilated" into the mainstream.[4] In politics, Robert Dahl focused on the overlap of generation and economic class, concluding that ethnic politics would lose its meaning when an ethnic group made the transition from an immigrant group which is economically homogeneous to the third generation which becomes economically heterogeneous.[5] As a result, economic interests among members of the ethnic group would vary tremendously and would take precedence over ethnic group interests. Nathan Glazer's and Daniel Moynihan's work showed that ethnic groups in New York city continue to have importance as "interest groups" and refocused attention on the political consequences of ethmcity.[6] This paper examines the conditions supporting the persistence of ethnicity in politics, using redistricting as an example.

Redistricting: Asian Americans

After each decennial census, the state political districts (assembly, senate, and congressional) are reconfigured to reflect changes in population. Redistricting is critical for ethnic politics because it creates state and federal districts from which officials are elected. Historically, politicians have divided geographic concentrations of ethnic groups into many districts, diluting their political influence.

Organizing along ethnic lines is made possible through legal precedent and federal laws. The Voting Rights Act of 1965 and 1982 amendment prohibit minority vote dilution by fragmenting communities.[7] Recent court cases have established the legal basis for creating electoral districts that preserve the political integrity of ethnic groups by keeping communities intact within districts. One of the most important for the Los Angeles region was the 1990 case of *Garza* v. *County of Los Angeles,* which ruled that Latinos had been consistently divided into separate districts. As a result, the Los Angeles County supervisorial districts were redrawn and a Latina, Gloria Molina, was elected to office in the newly created district where Latinos became the majority population group. Oral and written testimony submitted by Asian Americans to the state senate and assembly committees on redistricting focused on these laws and court rulings, stressing the need to keep Asian American communities whole within a district, rather than fragmented in a number of districts.

In their oral and written testimonies submitted to the state assembly and senate committees on redistricting, the Coalition of Asian Pacific Americans for Fair Reapportionment outlined the issues that followed ethnic lines and established the fact that there was such an entity as an "Asian American" community. Anti-Asian

American activities, such as hate crimes and English-Only movements, employment discrimination, lack of social service funding, immigration policy, discriminatory admission policies of California state universities, and racist rhetoric by politicians linking immigration to social problems were some of the issues mentioned in the testimony.

Judy Chu, former mayor of Monterey Park and a current member of the city council, addressed some of these issues in her testimony before the Senate committee on elections and reapportionment:

> *Without concentrated districts, the ability for Asian Americans to express their concerns about issues will be diluted. For instance, Monterey Park faced an anti-immigrant movement in the mid to late 1980s. There were attempts to restrict languages other than English from being spoken in public, from being written on city materials that went to the public, and from being on commercial signs. There were attempts to prevent foreign-language books from being in our library. While these efforts have been defeated in Monterey Park, some of the issues are still being pushed in other parts of the San Gabriel Valley where there is no organized opposition. . . . Asians need advocates for programs that will help Asian immigrant children and adults learn the English language and make the transition to American society successfully. Unfortunately, those programs are sparse or have long waiting lists.[8]*

Leland Saito, in testimony submitted to the assembly committee, cited employment discrimination in Alhambra, the city that borders Monterey Park to the north:

> *In 1990, the United States Justice Department sued the city of Alhambra and its Fire and Police Departments with charges of employment discrimination against minorities. The U.S. Justice Department does not sue a city unless there is strong evidence of discrimination in hiring and employment procedures and an egregious disparity between the ethnic makeup of the department and surrounding region.[9]*

Redistricting was a key issue for Asian Americans, given that no Asian American had been elected to the state legislature in over a decade. The basis for any claim starts with the raw numbers of population and the 127 percent increase of California's Asian American population over the last decade due primarily to immigration. The increase during the past ten years of the Asian American population in cities in the San Gabriel Valley was dramatic. Monterey Park's Asian American population increased by 90.6 percent, bringing the Asian American population to 57.5 percent of the city's population. Similarly, in the nearby cities of Alhambra, Rosemead, and San Gabriel, the Asian American population increased between 289 to 372 percent, forming between 32 to 38 percent of the population in those cities.[10]

The statewide Coalition of Asian Pacific Americans for Fair Reapportionment was formed in 1990 to advocate the interests of Asian Americans and Pacific Islanders to the state legislature which is in charge of the redistricting and reapportionment process.

The Southern California part of the coalition targeted three areas in Los Angeles County with large and rapidly growing Asian American and Pacific Islander populations. They were the Central Los Angeles, South Bay, and San Gabriel Valley areas. Regional coalitions were organized and the San Gabriel Valley Asian Pacific Americans for Fair Reapportionment was established.

The goals included reversing the fragmentation of Asian American and Pacific Islander communities into separate political districts, educating the community about the politics of redistricting and reapportionment, and establishing working ties between ethnic groups in the Asian American and Pacific Islander community as well as with Latinos and African Americans.

Judy Chu, speaking on behalf of the San Gabriel Valley coalition about the fragmentation of the community in testimony to the Senate Committee on Reapportionment, stated:

> Our votes are fractionalized. The cities (in the west San Gabriel Valley). . . . are divided into two supervisorial districts, three assembly districts, three senatorial districts, and three congressional districts. It is no wonder that Asians in California are virtually unrepresented anywhere beyond the local level.[11]

Reflecting the demographic mix of the area, most of the members of the San Gabriel Valley group were Chinese American, along with some Japanese American. Republicans and Democrats were active in the non-partisan organization.[12]

The statewide and regional coalitions established themselves before the state legislature as the voices of the Asian American and Pacific Islander community in the redistricting process. However, over time the agenda appeared to be controlled primarily by the native-born and established immigrants, while the more recent immigrants supplied their numbers to give the coalitions legitimacy as representatives of the different communities. Experience with politics, networks with political activists in the different ethnic communities, technical skills needed for the analysis of data, and the knowledge required to testify at government hearings were resources that existed largely among certain members of the community. Employees of social service agencies, college students and professors, staff workers of elected officials, and attorneys were the primary participants in the coalitions.

As a result, negotiations between Asian Americans and Latinos were carried out by a small group of highly-educated professionals who were acutely aware of the need for coalitions because of the tremendous amount of work and resources required to counter the history of gerrymandering that fragmented ethnic communities.

Asian Americans and Latinos

There were major problems to overcome in the development of an alliance between the two ethnic groups. Asian

Americans were well aware of the large numbers of Latinos in the San Gabriel Valley and of the fact that Latinos held all county, state, and federal elected offices that included Monterey Park. The needs of Asian Americans could easily be lost in an alliance.

Latinos were concerned about the rapidly growing number of Asian Americans and the threat this posed to growing Latino political power. In fact, when the Southwest Voter Registration and Education Project, a Latino organization, held one of the first voter registration drives in the area for Asian Americans, some Latinos in the region complained about it, saying that resources should be used only for Latinos.[13]

However, despite their differences, several factors encouraged the development of an alliance. Each group recognized the strengths of the other. As newcomers to the process, Asian Americans involved in redistricting were well aware of the need to work with the more experienced Latinos. Asian Americans had much to learn from Latino organizations that had gained political and legal knowledge through their successful court cases, such as *Garza v. County of Los Angeles*. Latinos also had the support of organizations with much larger budgets, such as the Mexican American Legal Defence and Education Fund and the Southwest Voter Registration and Education Project. Even though the Asian American population is growing rapidly in the San Gabriel Valley, Latinos are still the largest population group in the area. Also, there were Latino members in the state legislature who would be open to listening to the Latino coalition.

During the first meeting between the two statewide groups in May 1991, an Asian American stated that we were new to the game and looked to Latinos for guidance:

> *Asians and Pacific Islanders are at an early stage. We look to the Latino community for help. We want to nurture the relationship, I am encouraged by the sensitivity expressed at this table. We would appreciate your guidance, steps we should take, direction to go in; it's a new process for many of us. Someone later added that we (Asian Americans) are where the Latinos were in the 1960s or 70s.*[14]

Latinos were well aware of the tremendous growth of the Asian American population in the valley documented by the 1990 census. Latinos were also aware that this growth was translating into a political force represented by recent successful campaigns to elect Asian Americans to local city councils and school boards. Also, as the late Jesse Unruh reportedly said, "money is the mother's milk of politics'" and Asian Americans had a strong record of donating money. Don Nakanishi writes that Asian Americans have become "a major new source of campaign funds, a veritable mountain of gold."[15] In fact, Nakanishi notes that Asian Americans "In the 1988 presidential election. . . . were second only to the American Jewish population in the amount of campaign money raised by an ethnic or minority group."[16] The fact that this money could also flow to Latino candidates had already been proven in past campaigns when Asian Americans held fund raisers for state

Senator Art Torres in his bid for Los Angeles County Supervisor in the newly created San Gabriel Valley district and for Xavier Becerra and his campaign for the Assembly in 1990.

Although they are the majority of the population, Latinos and Asian Americans still lack representatives in elected offices. For example, in 1991, the city council of Rosemead was all Anglo, despite the fact that Asian Americans and Latinos combined were over 80 percent of the population. In August 1991, during one of the Latino and Asian American meetings to discuss plans, one Latino began to talk about the necessity of building links between Latinos and Asian Americans at all levels.

> We have to work together. In local neighborhoods, cities, the region. Working together, Asians and Latinos can offset the disproportionate amount of political power held by Anglos. We can work together on a project, or elections. The perception among Latinos is that Asians have a lot of money, are organized. The newspapers have given this a lot of coverage. I have all the articles since this began. We can pool our resources, Asians have money and we have numbers.[18]

Asian Americans responded by saying that they were committed to working together because of common issues. Realistically, political realities dictated that Asian Americans must work with Latinos. In fact, Asian Americans already had a long history of working with Latinos and they listed a number of examples.

> I can say that Asians are committed to working with Latinos because the political reality is that Asians need Latinos more than Latinos need Asians because our population is smaller and we have a low number of registered voters. We know we need Latino support to win. In fact, we have already started making links. Tomorrow, the local Asian Pacific Democratic Club, many of the members of the coalition are part of that, are meeting with the San Gabriel Valley LULAC to discuss redistricting. The Asian Democratic club walked for Xavier Becerra's campaign. Asians volunteered for Art Torres during his last campaign. One of the Latinos replied that this was true, he had worked on Becerra's campaign and was impressed by the Asian turnout.[18]

Asian Americans and Latinos understood that the political clout of both groups supporting one set of redistricting plans for the region would increase the possibility of the legislature adopting the plan. Most important, they also knew that if Asian Americans and Latinos were pitted against one another, both groups could end up losing.

In conclusion, Latinos and Asian Americans recognized that each group could benefit through combined efforts. The enemy was the political establishment and its history of political gerry-mandering which fragmented each community, diluting political power and leaving them with leaders who did not have to respond to issues of the Asian American and Latino communities.

Building a State Assembly District

The main concern of the Asian American group was keeping their population together and getting as many Asian Americans as possible into an assembly district. The group checked the 1990 census data and picked out the cities with the largest numbers of Asian Americans. Using this rough guide, the group drew a line around Monterey Park, Alhambra, Rosemead, San Gabriel, South Pasadena, San Marino, and Temple City. To achieve the required amount of about 370,000 people for an assembly district, the group experimented with portions of cities to the north, such as Arcadia, and cities to the east and south, such as El Monte, and Montebello. The group ended up with districts where the Asian American population ranged around 35 percent.

Checking political parties, the districts varied from slightly more Democratic to slightly more Republican. The major difference was going north and east into cities like Arcadia which included more Anglo Republicans while going south brought in more Latino Democrats.

What really interested the group was the voting record in the 1990 California secretary of state election. Flores, an Anglo Republican, was a Los Angeles City Council person for the southern area and little known in the San Gabriel Valley. It is possible that Latinos may have thought that she was Latina because of her last name, acquired through marriage. Checking the data, in the Republican northern cities such as San Marino, Flores won by a wide margin whereas in the Democratic Latino cities, Eu won by a wide margin. The group thought that this was interesting because even though Flores had a Latino last name, incumbency and political party seemed to be more important to the Latino vote. The group was concerned about the northern cities. What did it mean when a very popular moderate Asian American Democrat could not win? After all, Eu had won some past elections with the highest vote totals of anyone running for a statewide office.

Examining the areas of population concentration and growth collided with several political realities. First, creating a district that would maximize Asian American political influence does not necessarily result from just grouping the largest number of Asian Americans possible in one district. The northern cities were areas of heavy Asian American growth but also contained large numbers of politically conservative Anglos who may not support issues important to Asian Americans, such as more open immigration policies and bilingual voting materials. Discussion during a meeting of the Asian American coalition brought out these points as members expressed their concern:

Some residents in the northern cities were very conservative and the John Birch Society was active there. Another person added, it goes beyond political partisanship because the anti-Asian activity in the north was scary. A recent newspaper article in the Los Angeles Times *listed a number of incidents, including cross-burnings on lawns of Asian homes. What will inclusion of these areas mean for Asian political interests? Will our interest be served best by someone responding to the interests of conservative Anglos or moderate to liberal Latinos? If a moderate Democrat like March can't win (in the northern cities), what chance does another Asian have? Maybe even an Asian Republican with a strong record with the party may not have a chance.[19]*

As one Latino mentioned:

If the cities with high Asian concentrations were put in one district, would we be creating a district which will not be an Asian influence district? It could possibly be a district where the Asian population would be high, but Anglo registered voters may be the dominant group. If that is so, then an Asian or Latino influence district would be lost in the area.[20]

Second, there was difficulty in reconciling the political rights of the Asian American population, which was under the protection of the Voting Rights Act, and the Latino assemblyman, who as a minority elected official, also came under the Voting Rights Act. He lived in Monterey Park and had expressed his desire to stay there. How would you create a single district which protected his rights as an ethnic incumbent, and also protected the rights of Asian Americans? Adding cities like South Pasadena and San Marino would be out of the question because along with Asian Americans were high numbers of Anglo Republicans who were not likely to vote for a Latino Democrat. Also, the Asian American group did not want to ignore the concerns

of the Latino group and damage efforts to build a coalition.

Also, the possibility of a lower voter turnout in the southern cities as compared to the northern cities may favor an Asian American candidate.

If we go north, we get Republican, high propensity voters, people who may not vote for an Asian. Going south or east, we get Latinos, Democrats. They may not vote for an Asian either, but even in areas like Montebello which are considered middle-class Latino strongholds, their voting frequency may be less than in northern areas. Because their voter turnout is less, it may be better to go south than north.[21]

The group studied the current 59th district and discussed ways to modify it. Adding Rosemead and San Gabriel would keep the core Asian American population together. The four cities (along with Monterey Park and Alhambra) with the largest and fastest growing Asian American populations would be together. At the same time, by going south, a Latino majority population would be maintained. Solidly Democratic, the area did support March Fong Eu.

With these proposals in mind, the Asian American and Latino groups got together to work out a final plan. One Latino said that they were working hard to develop a plan that considered the concerns of the Asian American community. Therefore they moved Rosemead from the 60th to the plans for the 59th Assembly district. The Latinos agreed that because of its large (34.3 percent) and rapidly growing (371 percent over the past decade) Asian American population, it should go along with Monterey Park. This would also benefit Latinos because it would weaken the Anglo incumbent (assembly district) by taking away a city where she received many of her votes.[22] The strength of the Anglo vote in the city was clear since all the city council members at that time were Anglo.

Adding San Gabriel was tougher for the Latino group. Not currently in the 59th Assembly district, it would add yet another city to Xavier Becerra's Latino district, an additional burden for his reelection campaign. Although there was a solid middle-class community of Latino voters, there was also a large number of high propensity Republican Anglo voters.

Ultimately, adding the four cities of Asian American concentration and growth to the 59th district could be done while still maintaining a district where Latinos and Democrats were well over 50 percent of the population, giving the Latino incumbent a strong base to run on if he decided to seek reelection.

On August 30, 1991, the San Gabriel Valley Latino and Asian American groups, along with representatives from both statewide organizations, held a press conference in Monterey Park's city hall to announce that they had reached agreement on plans for districts in their region. In September, a group of Latinos and Asian Americans went together to Sacramento and met with a number of elected officials to lobby for their joint plan.

The Governor of California, Pete Wilson, vetoed the plans submitted by the state legislature. The state Supreme Court took over the redistricting task and appointed a "special masters" committee to create a new plan. The San Gabriel Valley Asian American and Latino groups coordinated their testimonies to support one another when they spoke before the masters committee.

The state Supreme Court adopted the new plan on January 27, 1992. The plan created a new assembly district, 49, which followed the recommendations of the valley coalition by grouping the four cities of Asian American concentration. The San Gabriel Valley was the only region in the state where such close working ties existed between Asian Americans and Latinos.

Conclusion

Perhaps one of the reasons why Asian Americans and Latinos were able to reach agreement over plans was the demographic balance of the San Gabriel Valley. Clearly, although the Asian American population was rapidly growing, their numbers in terms of registered voters were too small to be a threat to a strong Latino candidate. Therefore, Latinos could agree to the Asian American plan of grouping four cities together without endangering the reelection chances of the incumbent Latino assemblyman. As the Asian American population continued to grow and gain political power, changing the balance of power in the region, forging an alliance could prove to be a much more difficult task.

Asian Americans understood that they were newcomers to the redistricting process and that they would benefit from an alliance with Latinos who had the experience of winning major battles in court which established political rights, had powerful organizations backing their efforts, held all major political offices in the region, and had the largest ethnic population in the state to give them a strong foundation for their claims. In the year 2000, when the next census is taken and the redistricting process occurs again, Asian Americans will no longer be newcomers to the process. The question is, will Asian Americans find it necessary to form a coalition with Latinos? Uniting two groups proved to be much easier when a common enemy existed, the state legislature, which was interested in pitting the two groups against one another. Judging from the experience of the 1990s and the fragmentation of many Asian American and Latino communities throughout the state in the final redistricting plans, the common goal of protecting the political rights of their respective communities could again prove to be a powerful inducement for forming a coalition.

Latinos and Asian Americans also have similar concerns which should continue to provide a basis for a coalition. With large numbers of immigrants in both groups, some of the issues they share include bilingual voting materials, English language classes, and immigration policy. As ethnic groups, they both face employment discrimination as shown in cases filed against the city of Alhambra. Although Latinos had made some headway in terms of electing officials, both groups were faced with politicians who were unresponsive to their concerns.

Unlike the conditions in Los Angeles that sparked the events following the Rodney King decision, such as class divi-sions following ethnic lines, an educational system in crisis, high unemployment, few services, and deteriorating housing stock, the San Gabriel Valley had a significant middle class population. Also, there were a number of Latino and Asian American individuals and organizations in existence that had a history of working together.[23] The difficult task of building working relations was made easier because of such existing ties. Politically experienced and economically stable, the residents were able to get involved with what is for the average person, an abstract political concept that seemed to have little to do with the reality of their day-to-day lives.

In contrast to the San Gabriel Valley coalitions around a set of plans, the Los Angeles downtown Asian American and Latino groups basically agreed to disagree and not attack one another. Major differences between Los Angeles and the San Gabriel Valley might explain why agreement was reached in one place but not the other. First, the Asian American population mix in downtown was much more complex, with well developed Japanese, Chinese, Korean, and Filipino communities as compared to the San Gabriel Valley which was dominated by Chinese and Japanese Americans.[24] Organizing the individual Asian American communities and then meeting together as a unified group was a more complicated and lengthy process.[25] In addition, the San Gabriel Valley Asian American population was more experienced politically because of its longer history of working on the campaigns of local Asian American candidates. Networks and organizations were already in place which could begin work on redistricting.

Second, the downtown Asian American and Latino populations were spread out over a much larger area, with miles separating some of the communities as compared to the four contiguous cities in the San Gabriel Valley Asian American plan. Third, the overall demographic mix of the downtown area was more complicated with a large population of African Americans who were nearly absent (about 1 percent) in the San Gabriel Valley. This required taking into consideration the political rights of another group, making the process much more complex. Fourth, downtown Los Angeles contained some of the most expensive real estate in the state, making it the site of much larger political battles than in the San Gabriel Valley. As a result of these four factors, Los Angeles presented a more complex set of circumstances that had to be worked out among more participants.

In summary, organizing along ethnic lines was made possible by federal law and legal precedent which established the political rights of communities as defined by ethnicity. Understanding the political nature of redistricting, Asian Americans and Latinos put aside their differences and combined their resources to fight the common enemy, the political establishment and its history of political gerrymandering, which had fragmented Asian American and Latino communities for so long.

Notes

This research was supported in part by a Rockefeller Foundation Fellowship in the Humanities administered by the UCLA Asian American Studies Center and an American Sociological Association Minority Fellowship funded by the National Institute on Mental Health.

1. Paul M. Ong, *Asian Pacific Islanders in California, 1990* (Los Angeles: Asian American Studies Center, University of California, Los Angeles, 1991).
2. Illsoo Kim, *New Urban Immigrants: The Korean Community in New York* (Princeton, New Jersey: Princeton University Press, 1981); Peter Kwong, *The New Chinatown* (New York: Hill and Wang, 1987); S. Frank Miyamoto, *Social Solidarity among the Japanese in Seattle* (Seattle, Washington: University of Washington Press, 1984); Victor G. Nee, and Brett de Bary Nee, *Longtime California: A Documentary Study of an American Chinatown* (Stanford: Stanford University Press, 1986).
3. Edward Chang, "New Urban Crisis: Korean-Black Conflict in Los Angeles" (Ph.D. Dissertation, University of California at Berkeley, 1990); Melvin L. Oliver and James H. Johnson, "Inter-Ethnic Conflict in an Urban Ghetto: The Case of Blacks and Latinos in Los Angeles," *Research in Social Movements, Conflict and Change* 6 (1984):57-94.
4. Milton M. Gordon, *Assimilation in American Life* (New York: Oxford University Press, 1964), 27.

5. Robert A. Dahl, *Who Governs? Democracy and Power in an American City* (New Haven, Connecticut: Yale University Press, 1973).

6. Nathan Glazer and Daniel P. Moynihan, *Beyond the Melting Pot* (Cambridge, Massachusetts: MIT Press, 1986), 17.

7. Chandler Davidson, editor, *Minority Vote Dilution* (Washington D.C.: Howard University Press, 1984).

8. Judy Chu, March 9, 1991. Testimony delivered in Los Angeles to the California Senate Committee on Elections and Reapportionment.

9. Leland Saito, June 28, 1991. Testimony delivered in Los Angeles to the California Assembly Committee on Elections, Reapportionment and Constitutional Amendments.

10. Ong.

11. Chu, March 9,1991.

12. Don Nakanishi, "The Next Swing Vote? Asian Pacific Americans and California Politics" in Byran O. Jackson and Michael B. Preston, eds. *Racial and Ethnic Politics in California* (Berkeley: IGS Press, 1991).

13. Jose Z. Calderon, "Mexican American Politics in a Multi-Ethnic Community: The Case of Monterey Park: 1985-1990." Ph.D. dissertation, UCLA, 1991.

14. Statement of a member of the Los Angeles Asian American Coalition during a meeting in Los Angeles on May 24, 1991.

15. Nakanishi, 47.

16. Nakanishi, 47.

17. Statement of a member of the San Gabriel Valley Latino Coalition during a meeting between the Valley groups on August 8, 1991.

18. Statement of a member of the San Gabriel Valley Asian American Coalition during a meeting between Valley groups on August 8, 1991.

19. Discussion during a San Gabriel Valley Asian American Coalition meeting on July 30, 1991.

20. A member of the Latino California state coalition during a meeting with the California state Asian American coalition on June 26, 1991, in Los Angeles.

21. A member of the San Gabriel Valley Asian American coalition during a meeting on June 27, 1992.

22. Discussion during meeting between the Asian American and Latino San Gabriel Valley coalitions on August 8, 1991.

23. Leland T. Saito, "Politics in a New Demographic Era: Asian Americans in Monterey Park, California." Ph.D. dissertation, UCLA, 1992.

24. ____. "Japanese Americans and the New Chinese Immigrants: The Politics of Adaptation," *California Sociologist* 12 (1989):195–211. Leland T. Saito and John Horton, "The Chinese Immigration and the Rise of Asian American Politics in Monterey Park, California" in Edna Bonacich, Paul Ong, and Lucie Cheng, eds. *Struggles for a Place: The New Asian Immigration in the Restructuring Political Economy* (Philadelphia: Temple University Press, 1993).

25. Yen Le Espiritu, *Asian American Panethnicity: Bridging Institutions and Identities* (Philadelphia: Temple University Press, 1992).

Sirathra Som

The Donut Queen

Cambodian refugees in California do not share the same discrimination and exclusion from the dominant society that Chinese and Japanese immigrants experienced. Many Cambodians reached California after 1975 through the United States Refugee Settlement Program after the end of the Vietnam War. Practically non-existing before 1975 in the United States, the Cambodian refugees were far dispersed throughout the country for settlement based on sponsorship. With the first wave of Cambodian refugees many U.S. government employees reached America. They were the youngest immigrants to reach America; their average age was in the mid twenties. California's largest Cambodian community is located in the Long Beach area of Los Angeles County, but a large number of Cambodians also settled in San Jose. To succeed in the "American dream," Cambodians pool their resources and start their own business ventures. Many are successful, however, according to the U.S. Census from 1990, over fifty percent of the Cambodians still received public assistance. (IJ)

We meet at one of her donut shops. She is wearing a very stylish black jumpsuit, her hair pulled back tight, gold accessories, and very large sunglasses. Her new black BMW car is parked outside the window. She exudes an air of confidence and has a series of amusing anecdotes concerning cross-cultural experiences.

I was born in the capital, Phnom Penh, and led a very comfortable life. I can still see the school I went to as a child. I see the trees on the street and I think of the familiar things that made my life happy. I grew up a happy child with friends and school to keep me busy. My parents were educated but we were not what you would call rich. We never talked about money. Things just happened with my life, that's how I describe it—things just happened. That was the way with the war and leaving, it just happened.

What is the role of women in Cambodia?

The role of women in Cambodia is very defined. A woman is supposed to act in a certain way. Women are wives and mothers—those are the roles. We never questioned any of it. Not me, not my mother—we accepted it. If you grew up in a society where the rules are established and the community obeys them, then you just go along with it. You ask no questions—just go with it. I suppose it was expected. I would go to university and get an education, but more important, I would get married and have children. Those were my duties. I gave up university when I married. My marriage, of course, was arranged. I was young, and before we left the country I had two babies. I fit the traditional role of a good wife and mother and listener.

No one can forget the final days in Cambodia. It was only yesterday in my mind. Cambodia fell before Vietnam, and by early April we had to leave. My husband worked for the U.S. Agency for International Development, so we would be in a dangerous position if we stayed. No question about it, we would have been killed. I was twenty-two then. We left on April 7, 1975, and went to Camp Pendleton and were released to a sponsor in Texas three weeks later.

All of my family and my husband's family were killed, all of my friends. No one was left. It was like a plague of death and everyone is gone. The Khmer Rouge killed everyone. All of my family were educated people—those were the ones that Pol Pot wanted most to destroy.

We arrived in California with nothing, nothing. Only the clothes we were wearing. I could not speak English and everybody looked threatening to me. Simple things seemed complicated. Colors were different, sounds were different. Each day was filled with more questions than answers.

Tell me about your first job.

My first job was at the Sheraton Hotel in San Francisco as a domestic, and I earned $2.50 an hour. I was lucky to get the job—there were a lot of people who wanted it. We lived in Oakland and the job was in San Francisco. To be without a car in California is like being a bird without wings. You can live but then you can't really live. So I commuted by bus with several transfers. I remember the first day when I had to transfer from the first bus to the second one and I got lost. I panicked. I could not speak and I used hand signals. A nice man took my hand and took me to the bus. He had a wonderful smile and it was that smile I will never forget.

I learned English but not in a classroom. That's too much wasted time, it's too tiring. If you want to learn, you listen to people on the street, listen to the radio and TV, but also you force yourself to speak. After I learned what I thought was English, although it wasn't so good, I registered for sixteen units of accounting at night school—but I had no time—work and family forced me to quit.

For me there was no question of whether I should work or stay at home.

One of the first things you learn in America is that you need money. You can't be without money. There is no one then to help you. So we needed two incomes and I went to work. I know my husband did not like it, but it could not be helped. The journey here created problems for us and this work situation was one of them. I could work easier than he could and I began to do well and I supported the family. I became the breadwinner.

He had bad feelings about this, I understood this, but the feelings got worse. It's hard for me to talk about it. I understood his pain but there was nothing I could do about it to help him. Eventually, we were divorced. Divorced! This would be unheard-of in Cambodia where you are married once and that is it for life. But he could not make the changes here. The money was always a problem. Now he has a master's degree and works as a counselor in San Francisco. That part of my life is completed.

What do you think of American women?

I find that American women think too much about things which complicate their lives, and it seems strange to me. I suppose all women have been raised to follow, but you must take the chances while they are there. Too many American women also lack patience. They want everything so quickly and they want the impossible. No patience. Life is not that way, and it only leads to unhappiness. Our Buddhist tradition teaches us patience. Maybe it cannot be learned. When I got divorced, I felt sick; I lost twenty pounds. Silly? Well, I had three children to care for and I could

not have the luxury of worrying and wasting time. So I accepted my situation and made peace.

Tell me how you started here in business.

Before the U. S., I had never worked. In 1976, I persuaded Winchell's Donuts to give me a manager franchise and to work off the $5,000 fee. Then I started a small Winchell's shop in Berkeley and was able to pay off the franchise fee in four months. I built up one business and sold it in five months. I doubled the money I had paid for it. In 1982, when I was visiting some friends in Stockton, I noticed a run-down Oriental food store being mismanaged, and the owners were glad to sell it. The Asia food store is doing very well today. The store is ideally located in a busy shopping center within a few blocks of a new housing subdivision full of Asian refugee farm workers.

I began with nothing and now I have something. For me, that's what is great about America. I know the Cambodian men say I am tough—so what? By American standards you need to be good at business to survive. So maybe I am tough. But it is very hard work. I am working every morning at four-thirty in one of my six donut stores. I want to buy that McDonald's hamburger store next door, that is my next investment.

Have you experienced discrimination in the United States?

I know about discrimination against Cambodians. It was not so long ago that hate groups wanted to burn down the section of Stockton where the Cambodians lived. The KKK was here, you know. I suppose we remind people of the war. But then, too, we get discrimination among our own refugee groups. Most people think we are Vietnamese, they only talk about Vietnamese refugees. Well, we are different. The Vietnamese get better training programs and other services. They are more forceful than Cambodians, but that is part of our history.

I have no problems as a working mother. I am remarried now. My three children are happy, and I spend time with them every day. I am at a point that if I want to take a few days off or take a vacation with them, I can do it. just knowing you can do that is a good feeling. My kids are doing very well in school. They get rewards. For every A on the report card they get ten dollars. Anything less than an A, then they must do housework for me. It is my incentive system.

I care deeply about my fellow Cambodians here. I know their lives are miserable and painful. I have helped thirteen families start their own businesses around here. I share my experiences and the lessons I have learned. I get upset with refugees who live too long on welfare if they are able to work. I get upset with the welfare caseworkers, too, who encourage a lot of people to take cash assistance and to stay on welfare. They need their clients. I feel that anyone can achieve success here if they are smart and willing to work hard. I encourage people to start a business.

I have no regrets; how could I? I want to get my M.B.A. and I worry about the first time my twelve-year-old daughter brings home her first boyfriend. No, I have not seen *The Killing Fields* movie about Cambodia. I am not ready for that.

Robert Alvarez

Los Re-Mexicanizados: Mexicanidad, Changing Identity and Long-term Affiliations on the U.S.-Mexico Border

All humans grapple with issues of self-concept as we discover our identity. The processes of self-discovery are usually gradual and guided by family, peers, media, education, and a variety of other sources. In this society individuals also "discover" their racial and/or ethnic identity. This can be an affirming moment or it can be associated with trauma, shame, anger or even self-rejection.

In the article that follows, Robert Alvarez describes the intricate dynamics of identity discovery among California's Mexicanos. The importance of speaking Spanish [Mexican style] is examined, as are the specific anchors of life in nearby Mexican towns. Alvarez weaves into his article evolutionary trends from a California town named Lemon Grove. One of the most important educational court cases in California's modern era emerged from this town and these positively self-identified Mexicanos. All can learn about themselves and others by reading the stories of those who refuse to be defined by an international border. (SMM)

I don't know how to put it in words but, to me it's an outstanding feeling. And being a true Mexican. . . . You know. I don't really like the word Chicano. But it's alright. I think it's Mexican. Mexico. Viva Mexico. Y el chile atras. Yea, you feel proud of being a Mexican . . . of your race. I think that's the way it should be. Even if you live here, even if you were born here . . . you're a Mexican. . . .

Antonio Urcino Alvarez Castellanos

In December of 1999, my great-uncle, Tiburcio Castellanos, passed away at the age of 93. Tiburcio, known as Tom by many and Guero by the family, was born in the small mining town of Julio Cesar, now long abandoned, just south of the U.S.-Mexico border in the territory of Baja California. Tiburcio was the last of six children born to Cleofas Gaxiola and Narcisso Castellanos. His birth took place in Mexico at the insistence of his father, Don Narcisso, who with his wife and family had previously trekked across the U.S.-Mexico boundary into the United States and eventually settled in Lemon Grove, California. Like Tiburcio, another son, Chicho (Narcisso) was born under similar circumstances. Cleofas once again returned to Mexico to give birth. These boys, like the rest of the family, were born *Mexicanos* but spent their entire lives along the border in the United States. When Tom passed away at 93, he was still a Mexican citizen, though in all, he had spent only four years of his life in Mexico (Mexicali) where he had attended grammar school and where he had met his wife, Refugio—a.k.a. Ruth.

Tom's life in the United States illustrates an accommodation to American society that exemplifies what social scientists define as acculturation. He spoke fluent English—but never lost his Spanish, worked his way into a regular position as a skilled paint mixer, and retired from Benson Paint Company in San Diego, California. His work at Benson Paint was deemed important to the national interest during World War II, and thus he was exempted from military service.

Tom was a good "citizen" known for his honesty, punctuality, and accountability.

As a youth, he played baseball and learned to caddie and play golf at the local Lemon Grove Golf Club where he was the keeper of the greens. In essence he was a law-abiding person, an exemplary good "American" who contributed to and participated in U.S. society.

Tom Castellano's life raises questions concerning the popular belief that in the long run, Mexicans, like other immigrant-origin peoples, lose specific identities as they become assimilated into American society. Stories like Tom's are known throughout the U.S.-Mexico Borderlands. Although born in Mexico, he was raised in the United States among a cohort of first-generation American citizens, many of which, now octogenarians, continue to emphasize a certain "Mexicanness"—a *Mexicanidad*—that contrasts sharply with sociological and anthropological depictions concerning identity and accommodation of immigrants to the U.S.

Curiously, some of these individuals, who have lived their entire lives in the United States, in the later stages of their lives have *re-identified* with Mexico and with *being* Mexican. Paradoxically, these folk grew up in formative periods in U.S. history, such as the Great Depression, and were tested patriotically, as in WWII, but although they partook of and often immersed themselves in "American" life, they never lost their sense of identity as *Mexicanos*. The numerous "Mexican-American" Veterans of Foreign War chapters, like the Don Diego Chapter in San Diego, and the strength of the GI Forum are good examples of the maintenance of this "ethnic" pride.

Studies of Mexican immigration and settlement have focused on the slow accommodation/acculturation of Mexicans to the U.S., yet there has been little work illustrating and examining the *re-identification* of border folk toward previous national inclinations. It is assumed that most Mexicans who settle in the U.S. will sometime in the future become Americanized—become part of the social-cultural makeup of the U.S. in varying degrees. The long-term U.S. settlement and natural U.S. citizenship of *Mexicanos* and others often preclude the Americanization process, as individuals and communities partake and engage in life in the United States. Yet current border policy and contemporary political-economic venues influence new forms of identity for U.S. citizens of Mexican descent. For example, Chicanos and Chicanas, no longer stigmatized by Mexicans as *"pochos"* (half Mexicans), are finding open arms in intellectual circles throughout Mexico; similarly, U.S. Mexicans range the border and the interior of Mexico in new-found bicultural aptitude. The glory of Mexico, beyond the border, has captivated the cultural essence, the history, and the genealogy of the past for a new breed of folk influenced by the presence not of the border, but of Mexico, our neighboring nation-state. The border, the line in the sand, has influenced the re-crossing and made Mexico not just a nation for sojourning, but a place of re-identifying. These border people are "returning" to Mexico, becoming *Mexicanizados,* and expressing *Mexicanidad,* regardless of having been born and having lived their full adult lives in the United States.

Contrary to much of the current sociological literature that continues to rely on an acculturative model, the maintenance and re-identification of U.S citizens with Mexicanness is an important phenomenon that points to the diverse and eclectic nature of "Borderlands" identity and questions a long-term model that ends with assimilation. This is due in part to the scant studies, especially anthropological ethnographies, that have incorporated long-term ethnohistorical and sociological documentation of life on the border. The *Longue Durée,* with the analytical emphasis on the importance of changing social scenarios over time so emphasized by Fernand Braudel in *On History,* is hard to find on the border. In contrast, the observations herein are based on long-term ethnographic work (and life) in a single community—Lemon Grove, California. As a native son, I first documented the initial entrance of pioneer migrants to this border town (see Robert Alvarez, *Familia: Migration and Adaptation in Baja and Alta California, 1800–1975,* University of California Press, 1991), and over the last 20 years have continued to interview and document the history and life of my grandparents' and parents' generations.

The "community" on which I focus is defined by the descendants of pioneer Mexican immigrants who settled in Lemon Grove. The town is now a unified city of more than 23,000 people, just 15 miles east of San Diego, approximately 15 miles north of the U.S.-Mexico border. To most of Lemon Grove's residents, its history as an agricultural community and site of the first segregation court case in the United States is unknown. It was the original group of Mexican immigrants who had challenged a 1930 school board decision to segregate the Mexican students of the public school into a "Mexican" school for the instruction of English and Americanization studies. This case, named for my father—*Roberto Alvarez vs. the Lemon Grove School Board,* has been documented in ethnography and film as an important precedent in Mexican American history and in U.S. desegregation legislation.[1] The Mexican community, through the assistance of the Mexican Consul, won the court case—the first school desegregation victory in the United States.

As depicted in the film, there is a glorious finale in which justice prevails. The school children, numbering 75 first-generation American citizens, were allowed reentrance into the regular school. The popular consensus is that with the victory, these children were finally able to engage American life fully. This episode with greater America, it was believed, ensured a successful accommodation to society and to "being" American.

However, my work in the Lemon Grove community illustrates a profound dissonance and marginality that prevailed during the years following the court case among the first-generation Mexican Americans, as well as with the succeeding generation, my own. These Mexican American youth did indeed return to the "regular" school, but ironically, they returned to segregated classrooms. This division of Mexican American and Euro American youth continued for at least the next 20 years. And in a pattern that continues today, only 5 percent of these first-generation Mexican American children finished high school.

The Great Depression served both as an entry point for jobs in the greater American society and as an impetus to exploring the world outside of Lemon Grove. Young Mexican American men and women worked in the Civilian Conservation Corps and in the Works Progress Administration of Franklin Roosevelt during the Depression. Later, most Mexican American men patriotically signed up for the draft in the Second World War as infantry or as Navy personnel. The final outcome for the majority of the Mexican American adults of this Lemon Grove generation was an economic marginality, compared to the lives of their peers throughout the United States. Limited by education and a broader social-economic discrimination, only a minute percentage of this Mexican American generation was economically "successful"; most did not experience social mobility, nor did they "succeed" in the American Dream.

The next Lemon Grove generation, my own, is sprinkled with complex social and cultural resonance that bespeaks an outright period of both social marginality and changing identity. However, as this second generation matures (now past the half-century mark), the realization of a past seems to be reasserting itself—in Lemon Grove and other Mexicano Barrios in San Diego, on the border, and in Mexico. As stated by a member of this second generation:

> *At first we all wanted to be Americans because they [Anglos] didn't want us, so we fought like hell to prove that we were more American than even them. Now that we're older, that doesn't seem to matter. What's important is that we all want to be Mexicans!*

This conflict and process in identity formation illustrates a profound contradiction in our social science and popular belief about acculturation and assimilation. The case of Lemon Grove not only challenges the broad-brush strokes of "Americanization," but illustrates the unique variation of identity along the U.S.-Mexico border. Importantly, this also questions our assumptions that it is the geopolitical border and the dual-identity of both American and Mexican culture that influences a "Borderland identity."

In at least one instance, it is Mexico, the neighboring nation-state, that incurs a "deep territorialization" and identification with specific locales and histories. It is an identity associated not with the border but with Mexico. This identification invigorates identity tied to specific history and place.

There is interesting evidence that the process of "Mexicanization" and the incurred sentiment of being Mexican is not a solitary, isolated phenomenon. James Diego Vigil illustrates this process among current Chicano high school students in Los Angeles.[2] Vigil's study compares 20-year educational achievement patterns among Mexican and Mexican American high school students in two Los Angeles communities. Vigil studied these neighborhoods first in the early 1970s, then returned in the late 1980s. What he found contrasted sharply. In the late 1960s and early 1970s being "Mexican" was viewed by high school-age cohorts as a stigma to be shed. For these students, becoming "American" was the goal. During the late 1980s, however, high school cohorts in the same communities expressed a specific *Mexicanidad*—an iden-

tification with being Mexican. They continued to strive for economic parity and class standing in "greater America," but being Mexican did not carry the stigma of the past. Of particular significance here is that one of these cohorts is located outside of the "barrio," in a second-generation suburban middle-class neighborhood.

Vigil's book is instructive because it deals specifically with American high school populations in Los Angeles. This ethnic identity is also recognized in a 1996 University of California Linguistic Report, which indicates that in Southern California, a "Mexicanization" process has provided the Mexican American population with a sense of pride and dignity in things ethnic or Mexican.[3]

New social process and identification associated with ethnicity are not solely germane to California or the U.S.-Mexico Borderlands. The current cultural diasporas of new immigrant populations in Europe and throughout the U.S. indicate not a new "ethnicity," but a pronounced ethnic maintenance and re-identification. Arjun Appadurai has eloquently discussed these phenomena in *Modernity at Large*.[4] Appadurai argues that this is in part a new social imagination expressed in our contemporary globalized world, wherein the media, transportation, communication, and migration have come together in a manner that bind people to home communities in ways that were impossible in the past. And rather than being restricted because of territorial separation from homes, new (and old) immigrants are tied in novel and hybrid ways to their places of origin. With the contemporary advantage of the global media, transportation, and historical processes of immigration, people imagine and create new and different scenarios that are not tied to the bounded communities of the past. The multiple and regular instances of new immigrant enclaves throughout the major cities of the U.S. that not only maintain but create new ties and identity to home regions and countries are a testament to the assertion of national and ethnic pride.

For newcomers—first generation immigrants—the ethnic essence is always strong. But this sentiment, tied to ethnic identification, is expected to whither as time goes by, especially as these people become part of the American fabric. Lemon Grove, however, illustrates the maintenance and perseverance of such ethnic sentiment and emphasizes the reconditioning and re-engagement with ethnic identity based on a return and "re-imagining" of ancestral ground—in this case Mexico.

The *place* of the border is important here, because Lemon Grove is situated along the immediate borderlands with Mexico. Yet to the folk of Lemon Grove, the reference is not the geopolitical line, but the towns and places south of the border—Tijuana, Tecate, Ensenada, places that form part of an historical and present identity tying first-generation immigrants—parents—with current residents of San Diego county—offspring and first- and second-generation U.S. citizens. The identity is not to a generic "Mexico," but to a Mexico that is made up of particular histories and memories, specific towns and individuals.

There has been a recent onslaught of redefinition in current social science literature aimed at addressing the contemporary processes of migration in globalism and transnationalism. This has been important in understanding current social processes in migration influenced by new technology, new forms of rapid transit and travel, media, and communication. It is the media, technology, and people's "imagining" new identities that spur new communities across geographic space, linking home and host societies in fundamentally new ways. Most of the immigration literature today outlines not only the settings to which migrants travel (as in the past) but also highlights and includes original home communities. Such work illustrates the continuing connections and social-cultural processes that tie migrants to new sites of settlement and to communities of origin. New terms that stress the overall processes of migrant agency, identity, and community stress the extensions of social process that include both home and host community across national boundaries. Hence, "de-territorialization" and "re-territorialization" are terms that redefine community processes across space and place, and are inclusive of home and host society that often cross national geopolitical boundaries such as the U.S.-Mexico border. Although these perspectives have been invaluable in redefining how social science, and anthropology in particular, have interpreted the process of migration and settlement, there has been little focus on the importance of place along the U.S.-Mexico border.

The border is continually presented as a place of social "hysteria," where individuals are confronted with multiple identities and conflicting nation-state prerogatives. Much of the popular literature links border identity, duality, and multiplicity in culture and language; it is the Mex-

America of Carlos Fuente and the Nine Nations of Joel Garreau;[5] it is an amalgamated mongrel that is constantly shifting. But for most of us who have lived this experience, the border offers more than the political/cultural divisions portrayed in much of the literature. There has been a dearth of work focusing on the actual agency (i.e., action) and praxis (i.e., practice) of individuals as knowers and agents of their own destiny in Borderlands research. The border has come to be and to signify an oppressive structure controlled by the state and its agencies.

But there is along the border a specific belonging, a "deep territorialization," that is connected not to the border as such, but to the communities, the histories, and the people that make up this range of social life. Carlos Vélez-Ibáñez, in describing the U.S.-Mexican border population, states that "the border crossed us" essentializing the geographic-historical belonging of many border communities.[6] Donna K. Flynn, in "We Are the Border," offers a very apt contrast to the "de-" and "reterritorializing" of border people in discussing the case of the Shabe on the Nigerian border, which is an appropriate comparison for communities of the U.S.-Mexico border.[7] For the Shabe, as for Lemon Grove and other sites on the U.S.-Mexico Borderlands, people express a local sense of deep placement instead of displacement, a local sense of deep territorialization instead of de-territorialization. Such sense of place forges strong sentiments of rootedness in the Borderlands themselves.

An important consideration here is the variation of behavior along the U.S.-Mexico Boderlands. As illustrated by Heyman in his discussion of "Border Culture," the *interactions* of individuals in specific contexts create culturally significant behavior. It is precisely because people use (often strategically) their cultural identities that it is difficult for social scientists to identify what border folks "are." Border folk are notorious for shifting and negotiating identities in the range of "American" to "Mexican," depending on specific conditions and situations. Yet, although border folk do indeed utilize and "negotiate" identities in social circumstances, there is specific adherence to particular identities based on place, history, and belonging

The people of Lemon Grove, California, illustrate not just the pride of being Mexican, of being from the border, but the essence and process of *"re-Mexicanidad."* The particular essence of identity here is focused in the sentiment of *being* Mexican. It is rooted in specific knowledge about particular persons, specific places, and specific histories tied to current realizations of ethnicity.

> *It's something about being a Mexican, that you don't forget that you're a true Mexican.* No le hace donde naciste, *even if you were born here in the United States from Mexican parents. You know you're Mexican. Nothing else. . . . And not only that. You're proud of being a Mexican.* No chingaderas *["no screwing around"].* It's one thing knowing, and not being one.[8]

Lemon Grove during the Depression and World War II was composed of a large working-class Mexicano community that stemmed primarily from the adjacent

Mexican state of Baja California. Many of the settlers had come north via a mining circuit of booms and busts that led across the border into San Diego County. Lemon Grove provided a wealth of working-class jobs before and after the Depression in the lemon orchards, a citrus packing shed, and a gravel mining quarry.

For most residents, and especially for the first-generation American born, the Lemon Grove *barrio* was a safe haven where parents and *parientes* made up the social world. Relatives often crossed into Mexico to Tijuana, Tecate, and Mexicali. In fact, many of the original settlers of Lemon Grove eventually returned to these Mexican border towns in the early '30s, where they settled and remained. Family members fostered bonds between each other across the border through tightly woven extended families that shared a variety of important family affairs. Birthdays, baptisms, funerals, and weddings became events that helped the Mexican Americans maintain ties to both sides of the geopolitical line. The picture painted by the surviving first U.S.-born generation is one of contentment and community cohesiveness, marked by the cultural identity of *Mexicanidad*—fostered by their parents and the community—not of the border.

Yea, pues, casi toda la gente en Lemon Grove era pura unida as far as being Mexican. Yea, I would say so. Yea. Muy unida. Todo muy (unida). Era muy importante vivir como un Mexicano, pensar como un Mexicano. . . . We were all living here, al pie del cañon.

(Yea, well just about all the people in Lemon Grove were very united as far as being Mexican. Yea, I would say so. Yea. Very united. Always very (united). It was very important to live like a Mexican, think like a Mexican. We were all living here, at the foot of the canyon).[9]

My father, Roberto R. Alvarez Castellanos, illustrates the essence of *re-Mexicanizado*—a success story in social and economic terms, specifically through the accommodation of an American lifestyle. However, his life illustrates a profound engagement with *Mexicanidad*, especially during his later life. His story has meaning that goes beyond his success in American society.

Roberto Alvarez was chosen as litigant for the school desegregation case. As a child, he spoke excellent English, did well in school, and was known as a punctual and diligent worker. He was the catcher for the local softball team, and in high school played football. During the Depression (and time of the school desegregation case), he (and his brother and sisters) held a number of odd jobs, contributing to the family's welfare. He worked at the local grocery store, cleaned chicken coops, and even tutored non-Mexican students. During World War II, he joined the U.S. Navy, learned bookkeeping, and served aboard ship in the Pacific. He was in Tokyo just after the surrender of the Japanese, and witnessed the ceremonial surrender of Japanese forces aboard his vessel. On his return from the Pacific, together with his cousin Henry Castellanos, he began a fruit distribution company with money saved from previous jobs and the service. As the years went by, the business grew, and today, 50 years later, it includes branches throughout California, Texas, and Mexico. Of specific importance here is the essence of identity: first as child, then later in the service, and as a businessman and entrepreneur, Roberto Alvarez was an exemplary "American." Yet as the years went by, a certain Mexicanness flourished.

About 20 years ago, when my father was around 60, he began frequent business sojourns into Mexico. These visits and interactions connected him with new and previous friends and relatives, influencing a rather dramatic celebration of *Mexicanidad.* He always had fostered and maintained close relations with his extended family on both sides of the geopolitical border. His closest friends and allies were Mexican Americans, but he moved gracefully in the Anglo business world. This strategic "American" profile was aimed at "success" in society. I recall that because of the strong discrimination my sister, Guadalupe, had encountered in her first year of grammar school, my father insisted that we speak English at home—a strong break from many of the previous generations' insistence that Spanish be the home language. My father was intent on our survival and success in the American domain. He believed, practiced, and preached the American work ethic in which the individual is in control of his or her own destiny. However, the Mexicanness that was once kept primarily to interaction with *parientes,* friends, and family, became a public symbol in both the United States and Mexico.

Today, Roberto Alvarez is known as Don Roberto Alvarez throughout Mexican business domains. His regular dress includes a broad-brimmed "tejana" (a Texas-style cowboy hat), the symbol of the *norteño,* the northern Mexicano. The wearing of a "tejana," what many would argue is symbolic practice, began when Don Roberto began frequenting Mexico. Today, at the age of 81, he continues working in the produce industry and travels frequently to a variety of fruit regions throughout Mexico. Although he is the only person among his cohorts from Lemon Grove who dons the "tejana," folks from Lemon Grove embrace this symbol. It is a recognition of *Mexicanidad* and representation of success for the community.

In addition to a resurgence of *Mexicanidad* in Lemon Grove, there are cases of Lemon Grove offspring crossing the border to live in Mexico. Such returns are not isolated events, as illustrated by a number of accounts,[10] and include the "return" of both first- and second-generation U.S. citizens to Mexico, after adulthood and life in the United States. Manuel Smith, like his father, Manuel Smith Mesa, who was born in Baja California,[11] became a police officer. (Manuel, Sr., had been the first Mexican American in the San Diego Police Force.) Because of Manuel's knowledge of the border and of Spanish, he worked as a liaison for the Tijuana and San Diego Police Departments. He married and settled in San Diego, but also through his wife, a Mexican citizen, established himself in a ranch in El Valle de la Trinidad, close to his father's birthplace, El Alamo, east of Ensenada, about 100 miles south of the U.S.-Mexican border. In El Valle, his uncle (and mine), Guillermo Simpson, had also bought a ranch. The fathers of Guillermo and Manuel had roamed this region of Baja California as young men, after the migration of their parents into the U.S. This is an area in which two important mines, El Real del Castillo and El Alamo, flourished when the original pioneer migrants meandered north to San Diego. It was here that my great-grandparents, Los Smith, also Manuel's grandparents, first arrived to the north. And it was here that Manuel's father was born.

Again the irony of "being" American meets the essence of identity. Manuel became a homicide detective and retired from the San Diego Police Force with honors. Although both his name (Smith) and his career and life in the U.S. bespeak the role and model of a good American, Manuel prides himself and his family on being *Mexicano,* with a history of Mexican immigrants, and a strong sentiment of *Mexicanidad.*

Today Manuel continues to live in San Diego, but he frequents the ranch in El Valle de la Trinidad. His sentiment and identity are tied to this place, its memories and presence.

In my own life I have come to know Mexico from differing persuasions. As a scholar of the border, of Mexico, I initially wrote of the past and present couched in the literary markers of the anthropological. I grew up struggling to be an American, and at times shed my Mexicanness for a particular recognition as a "regular" American high school student, a surfer, a "college man" in the strictest of stereotyped senses. However, as I grew to realize that my role "changes" from *vato-loco*—"crazy dude"—to American boy, from Bob to Roberto, essentialized

the shifting patterns of socialization pressure, I too reconnected with a Mexican past and present. During the years 1984 to 1989 I worked in Tijuana—"on the border," in the fruit trade, with my father. During that period I discovered a certain Mexicanness that I believed I had never denied, but in reality had never really known. Although I had grown up "on the border," experienced a lifelong engagement in the U.S., procured a Ph.D. with a focus on Mexico, I can say now that I had not fully experienced *Mexicanidad.* The rekindling of identity tied to a Mexican reality in Baja California, in Tijuana, in Mexico, stirred my specific re-identification, not with a borderness, but with a certain Mexicanness.

Mexicanidad can be seen as more than a recognition and sense of identity; it is evident that *Mexicanidad* should be viewed as a process. And the process of *Mexicanidad,* especially when viewed historically, and with reference to specific places and specific communities, raises new and important questions.

Lemon Grove illustrates the importance of place. However secure place becomes, a particularly significant force is the United States. The sociological boundaries of American society, the discrimination and forced "acculturation," serve to first accentuate the need to identify with U.S. society. But then, as David Guitiérrez illustrates in *Walls and Mirrors, ethnic distinctiveness,* in this case Mexican American, is constantly reinforced by discriminatory treatment, as in Los Angeles and the greater Southwest.[12]

We must remember that the geopolitical border and Mexico have had differing influences in the Borderlands. Joe

Alcozer, a current resident of San Diego, but born of Mexican parentage from Piedras Negras, tells of growing up in South Texas without ever entering Mexico until he joined the Navy during World War II. Along with other Tejanos, he was shipped out of Texas on the railroad that passed into Baja California (Mexico) and into the small town of Tecate, before arriving in San Diego. Even today, Mexico does not evoke the identity of his past and present.

The variation of experience and histories in specific places of the Borderlands indicates that the specific patterns of behavior and identity of people along the U.S.-Mexico border are closely tied to interpreted histories, cultural space, and social process.[13]

Notes

1. Robert R. Alvarez, "The Lemon Grove Incident: The Nation's First Successful Desegregation Court Case," *Journal of San Diego History*, 32 (Spring 1986): 116–136. The film by the same name was produced by KPBS San Diego in 1984.
2. James Diego Vigil, *Personas Mexicanas. Changing High Schoolers in a Changing Los Angeles: Case Studies in Cultural Anthropology* (New York: Harcourt Brace College Publishers, 1997).
3. B. McLaughlin, *Linguistic, Psychological and Contextual Factors in Language Shift* (Santa Barbara: University of California Linguistics Minority Research Institute, 1994): 3, 4.
4. Arjun Appadurai, *Modernity at Large: Cultural Dimensions of Globalization* (Minneapolis: University of Minnesota Press, 1996).
5. Carlos Fuentes in the novel *Christopher Unborn* (New York: Farrar, Straus and Giroux, 1986) discusses Mex-America, a zone of the future, now occupied by the U.S.-Mexico border. Joel Garreau, in *The Nine Nations of North America* (New York: Houghton Mifflin, 1981), also posits a Mex-America that blends two cultures on the U.S.-Mexico border.
6. Carlos Vélez-Ibáñez, *Border Visions: Mexican Cultures of the Southwest United States* (Tucson: University of Arizona Press, 1996).
7. Donna K. Flynn, "'We are the Border': Identity, Exchange, and the State Along the Benin-Nigeria Border," *American Ethnologist*, 24, 2 (May 1997): 311–354.
8. Interview with Antonio Urcino Alvarez Castellanos, Jan. 4, 2000, Phoenix, AZ.
9. Ibid.
10. For example, see Oscar Martinez, *Border People: Life and Society in the U.S. Mexico Borderlands* (Tucson: University of Arizona Press, 1994), and Vélez-Ibáñez, *Border Visions*.
11. Los Smith are primarily from the town of Comundu in the state of Baja California del Sur, Mexico. English and other European surnames are common in this part of the state because of early settlers that came with the whale and sea otter trade during the mid to late 1800s.
12. David G. Guitiérrez, *Walls and Mirrors: Mexican Americans,*

Mexican Immigrants, and the Politics of Ethnicity (Berkeley: University of California Press, 1995).

13. Interview with José Alcozer, San Diego, California, Mar. 15, 2000. Importantly, his motivation for joining the service was ". . . to show the Americans that we were as good as them." Throughout his life he worked at social equality as a union leader for Mexicanos in San Diego County. He was also instrumental in founding the Don Diego Post of the VFW in San Diego). The profoundness of the subjectivity of local peoples' behavior in the general milieu of the Borderlands is also illustrated by Oscar Martinez's *Border People.* Martinez goes to great length in classifying and typologizing this complexity.

Louis M. Holscher and Celestino Fernández

Contrabando y Corrupcion: The Rise in Popularity of Narcocorridos

This article discusses and analyzes a category of recent popular songs (performed in Spanish) that are regularly heard throughout Mexico and in much of the United States, particularly the Southwest. These songs, known as *corridos* (ballads), are factually based and deal with a variety of cultural themes important to Mexicans and Chicanos. Those *corridos* that deal with themes and issues involving drugs, particularly trafficking, have come to be commonly known as *narcocorridos* (narcotics ballads). These story-telling songs portray, and some critics argue glorify, the culture of drug smuggling and the exploits of drug traffickers and related criminals.

Included in this article is a brief historical overview of *corridos*, Mexican and Chicano popular songs that describe and comment on current political and social events, and depict the exploits of both famous and infamous individuals. A number of *narcocorridos* are presented and discussed as examples of currently (or recently) popular songs that deal with drugs and related topics such as drug lords and smuggling. The paper concludes with a discussion of the societal response (both favorable and unfavorable) to *narcocorridos*, and the songs' potential impact on young people and society in general. *(LH)*

The Corrido Tradition

Critics and the media have labeled recent Mexican and Chicano (Mexican American) songs dealing with drugs "narcocorridos" (narcotics-ballads). This type of music, both in terms of lyrical content and music, comes out of the *corrido* (ballad) tradition, which has been popular in Mexico and the Southwestern United States since the early to mid-19th century (Roberts, 1999; Simmons, 1951). The Mexican civil war (1846–48), for example, is well preserved in *corrido* texts (Roberts, 1999). Although they originated in central Mexico and have long been popular throughout all of Mexico and the American Southwest, *corridos* are a principal variant of *norteña* music and one of the main musical fares in northern Mexico. The *corrido* genre is generally based on a rather declamatory melody and their singers stretch the last line of each verse distinctively. *Corridos* can be in polka, waltz, or march time; conventionally, a 2/4 time is used for upbeat topics and waltz time for all others (Roberts, 1999). They are often sung in duet with one voice slightly dominating, often in parallel thirds and sixths—the most basic Spanish-derived harmonic approach. In terms of music, *corridos* are usually "sing-songy" and repetitive, with a relatively simple up-and-down cadence, with an accordion, guitar, and other instruments accompanying a vocalist. This paper broadly defines the term "*corrido*," and examines recent compositions in this genre that express views or comment upon matters related to drugs and crime.

During the past 20 years, *corridos* greatly gained in popularity throughout Mexico and the U.S., selling particularly well in markets throughout the Southwest and northern Mexico. *Corridos*, however, have a long history. In the 1500s their likely ancestors were the Andalusian romantic verses (known as *romances*) brought to Mexico by Spanish conquerors (Herrera-Sobek, 1998). In the late 1800s and early 1900s, they served as a popular form of news bulletin by traveling musicians (*trovadores*). Assassinations, revolutions, natural disasters, accidents, elections, immigration, strikes, family feuds, folk heroes and shoot-outs between bandits and the police were all popular themes for *corridos*. In fact, almost any event that touches the public sentiment can serve as inspiration for a *corrido* (Griffith and Fernández, 1988). *Corridos* are deeply ingrained in Mexican and Chicano culture, and are a standard form of marking major events in both public and daily life. They have covered events ranging from the coming of the railroads to Sputnik, from romantic entanglements to bank robberies. The facets of Mexican life that can be studied through the *corrido* are practically unlimited, and these ballads can be used as historical documents of important aspects of modern Mexican and Chicano life, as well as of the daily trials and tribulations of the *pueblo* (the popular or common classes). There are *corridos* about natural disasters (hurricanes, earthquakes, flood, etc.), traffic accidents, wars (e.g., the U.S.-Mexico War, WW II, Vietnam and the Persian Gulf War) and joyous events like weddings and winning the lottery (Fernández and Officer, 1989). President John F. Kennedy's assassination is documented in over fifteen *corridos* (Dickey, 1978), for example, and the athletic achievements of Fernando Valenzuela, the ace pitcher for the Los Angeles Dodgers of the 1980s, can also be found in several ballads, e.g., Lalo Guerrero's *Olé Fernando* and *Fernando, El Toro* (*Fernando, The Bull*). There were also *corridos* about smuggling prior to the 1970s, including at least one from the Prohibition era. *Los Tres Tequileros* tells about the deaths of three tequila smugglers who were killed in an ambush by the Texas Rangers (Wald, 2001). Although *corridos* are essentially ballads that tell a story, they often contain beliefs, values, attitudes and commentary on many topics, much like the editorial page of the modern newspaper (Griffith and Fernández, 1988). Simmons (1951), for example, uses *corridos* to trace agrarian, political, and religious reform, as well as relations with foreigners and foreign nations in 20th century Mexico. He also discusses the treatment of Mexican leaders, and the Mexican national personality through this genre.

Corridos on specifically Chicano themes—often on political and cultural clashes—have been sung since the 19th century, and still continue to be composed. The earliest known complete U.S. *corrido*, *El Corrido de Kiansas* (Kansas), describes the cattle drives from Texas to Kansas in the late 1860s and early 1870s, and was sung in Brownsville by 1870 (Roberts, 1999). *El Condenado a Muerte* (*The One Condemned to Death*) was discovered in New Mexico and laments the author's coming execution for an unnamed crime, and actually gives an exact date, Wednesday, July 20, 1832 (Roberts, 1999). Possibly the earliest Texas *corrido* is *Corrido de Leandro Rivera*,

which dates from 1841. Paredes (1958) labeled the period from 1836 to the late 1930s the "corrido century" on the U.S.-Mexico border (although given the popularity of *corridos* in this region during the past 20 years, a rival "*corrido* century" may be in the making). An early Texas *corrido* hero was Juan Nepomuceno Cortina, who in 1859 shot a Brownsville, Texas, city marshal who had been mistreating his mother's servant, and with his followers briefly occupied the town before fleeing across the border. The most famous *corrido* from that period was about Gregorio Cortéz, whose exploits and problems resulting from the shooting of a Texas Ranger have also been documented in a recent popular film, *The Ballad of Gregorio Cortéz*, starring James Edward Olmos. Numerous *corridos* are available about the late César Chávez, the founder and long-time leader of the farm workers' movement. One of the first ballads on César Chávez was by Felipe Cantú (Burciaga, 1991), one of the original actors in El Teatro Campesino (The Campestral Theatre), a highly popular theatre that performed plays with social and political themes of interest to farm workers and other laborers. There is even a 1995 *corrido* mourning the death of Selena, the popular Tejana star who had recently been murdered by the president of her fan club.

Corridos are often intensely serious, and they have always mirrored social and political concerns. They are repositories of both myth and history for a people not often served by mainstream newspapers and other media. A few such examples are: *Los Rinches de Texas* (*The Texas Rangers*) which tells the story of how Texas Rangers brutally beat poor farm workers. This song is featured in the film *Chulas Fronteras* (*Beautiful Borders*) and describes an incident during a strike of melon-pickers in Star County, Texas, in June 1967; the *Corrido de Juan Reyna* (*The Ballad of Juan Reyna*) recounts his conviction for manslaughter (for killing a police officer while allegedly being beaten up in a squad car) and sentence to prison; a sequel tells of Reyna's apparent suicide in jail five months before his release; and *La Tragedia de Oklahoma* (*The Tragedy in Oklahoma*) deals with a famous case in which two students from Mexico, one of whom was related to the president, were shot by deputies near Ardmore, Oklahoma. One overt protest song is *El Deportado* (*The Deportee*) which bluntly describes Anglos as very evil, and who treat Mexicans without pity.

A relatively recent song, *El Corrido de César Chávez* (*The Ballad of César Chávez*) by Los Pinguinos del Norte (The Penguins of the North), reflects the rise of Chicano political and ethnic consciousness in the 1960s and 1970s. The death of eighteen undocumented workers who died of heat asphyxiation while locked in a boxcar was widely reported in the mainstream press, but was also recorded in a *corrido*, *El Vagon de la Muerte* (*The Boxcar of Death*). Hence, *corridos* have acted as not only a reflection of political and social consciousness but also as a stimulus to it.

Simmons (1951) is careful to point out that the views and events described in *corridos* are not always entirely correct (but no means of popular expression is always fully accurate); however, *corridos* are generally quite accurate in documenting the names, dates and locations of specific events. They also provide an important point of view on events and people from the composer's perspective and others who may share his point of view. Much of *corrido* music is working class in origin, and provides an analysis of events and people from the perspective of "*el pueblo*" (the common folk); thus, although *corridos* may not always present a complete picture, they do present views that may not reflect elite or even middle-class interests. The values espoused are most often ones of bravery, loyalty to friends, machismo, independence, disrespect for the law (but respect for a Higher Law) and a love of justice for the common man. Women are either generally not mentioned, or are the subject of strong emotions of love, anger, scorn, etc. There are a few notable *corridos*, however, that favorably refer to the love and good advice of mothers. There are literally thousands of *corridos*, and this article only touches on one small aspect of popular and representative tunes that deal with drugs. The article analyzes and comments on the extent to which these songs provide an expression of how a sizeable segment of the working class population has viewed drugs and drug smugglers during the past thirty or so years. In that respect, it may provide a view of public/popular opinion not otherwise found in the media or other sources—similar to the role of rap music in the U.S. The popularity of these *corridos* is one indication that many people, particularly young people, have not accepted the official anti-drug message of the Mexican and United States governments.

Drug Trafficking and Mexican Music

In 1972 Los Tigres del Norte (The Tigers of the North) released *Contrabando y Traición* (*Contraband and Betrayal*), at a time when drug use had increased dramatically in less than a decade, and Mexican immigrants were seeing drug trafficking daily as they crossed the border. The song, about drug runners, was a huge hit, and was a critical factor in Los Tigres becoming major stars in Spanish-language pop music. Their music continues to be very popular at Mexican and Chicano *fiestas* and dances. Since 1972, Los Tigres, whose members are originally from Mexico, but who have made the San José, California, area their home since the late 1960s, have made 30 records and 14 movies, won a Grammy, and have changed Mexican/Chicano pop music at least twice—first with songs about drug smuggling and more recently with immigration songs (Quinones, 1997). Still largely unknown outside the Chicano community, they are revered within the Mexican-immigrant and Chicano communities in the United States and among Mexicans throughout Mexico. Los Tigres has also modernized the *corrido*, infusing their music with *cumbias*, rock rhythms, and sound effects of machine guns and sirens. With their popularity they have broadened the appeal of the accordion-based music of Northern Mexico (*música norteña*). Over time, they have added a full drum set and an electric bass, and thus modernized *norteño* music. Besides their "drug" songs, common themes in their music include machismo, desires and the values and beliefs that are the essence of the Mexican and Chicano working class such as dignity, respect, family, and Christianity.

Contrabando y Traición became a *norteño* classic and has been recorded by many other bands, plus it was the title of a popular commercial film. (In the U.S., popular books, both fiction and nonfiction, frequently serve to inspire feature films; *corridos* have often done the same in Mexico.) The two main characters of *Contrabando y Tracíon*, Emilio Varela and Camelia, "La Tejana" (The Texan), are now part of Chicano folklore. This *corrido* was also the first hit song about drug smuggling, and thus the first *narcocorrido*. The song *El Corrido de Camelia La Texana* (*The Ballad of Camelia "The Texan"*) spawned a number of movies, including one titled *Mataron a Camelia La Texana* (*They Killed Camelia, "The Texan,"* 1976) and *Ya Encontraron a Camelia* (*They Found Camelia*, 1979) (Herrera-Sobek, 1998). Los Tigres followed *Contrabando y Traición* with *La Banda del Carro Rojo* (*The Red Car Gang*) also a *corrido* about drug smuggling. These tunes essentially sparked a trend that is currently undergoing immense popularity in Mexican music. In a sense, the *narcocorrido* is an update, both in terms of music and theme of the traditional *corrido*, and emphasizes drug smugglers, shoot-outs between drug gangs and the police, corruption, and betrayal. Most *norteño* bands today play a selection of *narcocorridos*, and many bands play almost nothing else. Like gangster rap in the U.S., *corridos* recount violence and crime and have achieved immense popularity without the benefit of radio airplay in many areas. Even in areas where *narco-corridos* are played regularly, disc jockeys often will warn listeners about language and content when such *corridos* are particularly graphic.

Criticism of *narcocorridos* has come from leaders within the Catholic Church, business leaders, and from at least one political party, the conservative National Action Party (PAN) in Mexico, the party of Mexico's current president. They have been labeled as part of a "culture of death" for emphasizing drugs and murder. *Newsweek* (April 23, 2001) notes that, "Critics on both sides of the border are attacking Mexican pop songs that glorify drugs. *Los Tucanes de Tijuana* and *Los Tigres del Norte*, in particular, are targets for their *narcocorridos* . . . Tijuana's city council and a national business coalition are urging stations to stop playing these songs." Jorge Hernández of Los Tigres, like many rap artists, responds that, "The only thing that we do is sing about what happens every day. We're interpreters, then the public decides what songs they like" (Quinones, 1997).

Since the early 1970s, the Chicano community and Mexican working class have decided they like *narcocorridos*. Los Tigres regularly includes two or three on each album. In 1989, they released *Corridos Prohibidos* (*Prohibited* or *Banned Corridos*), an entire album about drug smuggling. Numerous other less well known singers and bands have followed suit with their own *narcocorridos* CDs and cassettes which can be purchased in almost any store that sells music, from small specialized music shops that cater to Mexicans and Chicanos to large chain department stores such as Target and K-Mart. This album was very controversial in both the U.S. and Mexico, and was reported to be very popular among the drug smugglers themselves. Los Tigres, however, is not really a "narcoband"; it is a *norteño* band that plays all varieties of *norteño* music, including *corridos* dealing with various themes; one of these themes is drug trafficking. Los Tigres, for example, won a Grammy for *America,* a rock tune that preaches the universal brotherhood of Latinos. Also, unlike younger bands today, Los Tigres rarely mention the names of real drug smugglers, are not photographed with handguns or assault rifles, and usually refer to marijuana and cocaine as *hierba mala* (bad weed) and *coca*. In addition, Los Tigres have achieved a more respectable cultural claim with their songs about the immigration experience; for example, *Vivan Los Mojados* (*Long Live the Wetbacks*) and *El Otro Mexico* (*The Other Mexico*) which deals with the undying desire of Mexican immigrants to return home.

The title song of *Jefe de Jefes* (*Boss of Bosses* or *Chief of Chiefs*), which has a number of pictures in the CD booklet of the members of Los Tigres at Alcatraz, was released in the summer of 1997 and is about a fictional drug kingpin. The album features several *narcocorridos*, including one about drug lord Hector "*El Güero*" Palma, who was arrested in 1996 after a plane crash. *El Prisionero* (*The Prisoner*) is about recent political assassinations in Mexico. One song on *Jefe de Jefes, Ni Aquí Ni Allá* (*Neither Here nor There*), captures the feelings of many Mexican immigrants today. It is a pessimistic tune that captures the anti-immigrant sentiments in the U.S. and the corruption, scandals, and economic crisis in Mexico. The song concludes that immigrants are unlikely to receive justice or be able to improve economically in either country. In a previous song, *La Jaula de Oro* (*The Golden Cage*), an immigrant who years earlier had outwitted *La Migra* (The Border Patrol) does not feel at home in the country he worked so hard to enter. Even worse, he notes, his children now speak English and reject his *Mexicanidad*, his "Mexicaness." And while the protagonist would love to return to Mexico, he cannot leave his house and job for fear of being apprehended and deported because he needs the job in the U.S. in order to provide for his family. Thus, Jorge Hernández notes that the U.S. is like a "cage made of gold"—immigrants may live well and be able to afford some nice things, but it is not home, it is not as relaxing and peaceful as living in Mexico. Also, the family is no longer as important and one is certainly not free to move about, particularly if one is an undocumented immigrant; although the bird/immigrant lives in a "golden cage," it is a cage nonetheless (Quinones, 1997).

Perhaps one explanation for why *narco* and immigration *corridos* are so popular is because they capture the essential reasons as to why so many Mexican immigrants come to the U.S. Namely, the lack of employment and economic opportunity in Mexico and the availability of work in the U.S., as well as because these songs document and help people cope with the discrimination and lack of equality experienced in the U.S., for example, as expressed in *Ni Aquí Ni Allá*. Undoubtedly, these are some of the critical factors (employment and income) as

well that make the drug trade lucrative for many young working class Mexican men. As Cortese notes, "The Mexican-U.S. border is the only place where one can leap from the First World to the Third World in five minutes" (Cortese, 1990).

The 1990s experienced a resurgence of the *corrido*'s popularity. At the request of listening audiences, Spanish-language radio stations throughout the Southwest and Mexico offered daily hour-long *corrido* programs (in some cases the "*corrido* hour" was offered twice daily, usually during early morning and late evening). Without a doubt, during the 1990s the single favorite theme of *corridos* became drug trafficking. When Mario Quintero, the lead singer of the popular group Los Tucanes de Tijuana, takes the stage he often sings about drug lords, cocaine shipments and shoot-outs. They have one of the hottest bands in Northern Mexico and are equally popular with Chicanos in the United States. One of their recent two-CD releases, *Tucanes de Plata*, has sold a million copies in the U.S. and over 2 million copies worldwide. They have been criticized for glorifying the drug trade and drug lords, and the question has been raised whether the message of Los Tucanes and dozens of other bands and *corrido* singers may be changing the values of a generation of young Mexicanos and Chicanos (Collier, 1997). One of their popular new songs is called *La Piñata* (*The Piñata*) and tells of a drug lord's party that included a *piñata* full of bags of cocaine. Two other songs from their new CD are El Primo (*The Cousin*) which adopts the voice of a narcotics boss and *The Little Colombian Rock* which refers to cocaine. While it is an open question whether these tunes and others like them actually change beliefs and behavior, they regularly describe the potential riches and pitfalls of the drug trade. Often these *corridos* speak of betrayals, murders and assassinations among those involved in drug trafficking, and the listener could easily conclude that this is a highly dangerous enterprise, one not worth entering. Yet, this was not the common interpretation during the 1900s. Drug trafficking, while highly dangerous, is a most lucrative business. A report issued by the United Nations (1997) documents that "drug trafficking has grown to a $400 billion-a-year enterprise." The same report notes that worldwide, "illegal drugs are reported as a bigger business than all exports of automobiles and about equal to the international textile trade." Drug traffickers "are successful 85–90% of the time" (Cortese, 1990).

Besides Los Tucanes and Los Tigres del Norte, other known (and many relatively obscure) groups like Los Huracanes and Los Dinamicos del Norte have also had success with *narcocorridos*. Popular titles include: *Contraband of Júarez, Terrible AK-47, Partners of the Mafia, The Cellular Phone,* and *Sacred Cargo.* Like rap music in the U.S., *narcocorridos* have been widely criticized in Mexico as having a negative influence on young people and a negative impact on society in general. Rene Villanueva, a prominent music historian and a member of Los Folkloristas (a band that has played *corridos* and other traditional regional Mexican music since the 1960s) calls *narcocorridos* a "horrible perversion of Mexican culture," and "a sign of how the power of money amid poverty has diverted people's interest to

the most vulgar aspects of our society" (Collier, 1997). In two northwest Mexican states, Chihuahua and Sinaloa, government officials have banned *narcocorridos* from the radio and television, and many other individual stations have done the same. (Of course, banning them has not made them disappear or any less popular.) A common complaint is that they glorify criminal behavior and should be banned everywhere. Interestingly, it is commonly believed/known that these two states are home to numerous individuals involved in the drug trade. There is a shrine in Culiacán, the capital of the state of Sinaloa, dedicated to a Jesús Malverde where traffickers go (literally at all hours of the day and night) to pray for protection during drug trips and to thank him when such trips have been successful. It is common knowledge that Malverde has come to be known as "the saint of the drug traffickers." There are numerous *corridos*, incidentally, about Malverde and some of these very specifically refer to drug trafficking.

There have not been calls for similar actions in California, Arizona, or Texas, for example, although *narcocorridos* remain very popular on Spanish-language stations in these states. Vicente Romero, program director of KRAY-FM in Salinas plays *rancheras* and other popular forms of Mexican music, but he also plays *narcocorridos*, commenting that, "Maybe Los Tucanes and the other *narcocorridos* are a bad influence, but we have to play them because everybody asks for them, and no one complains" (Collier, 1997). It may be that they arouse less concern than rap music because they have a much softer touch musically, and lack the aggressiveness and harder edge of many rap tunes. Plus, *narcocorridos* are part of the long and extensive *corrido* musical and cultural tradition and are almost always sung in Spanish, and thus rarely heard outside the Chicano and Mexican immigrant communities. Additionally, *narcocorridos* are performed by individuals and groups who look "normal," that is, they dress in clothes normal to the *norteño* music tradition, unlike rappers who project a distinct "look" (e.g., tattoos, baggy clothes, and lots of large jewelry). *Narcocorridos*, at times, almost seem to make drugs and drug trafficking a positive, lucrative, and charming experience. While they share drug and crime themes with gangster rap, they are still very popular with a large segment of the Spanish-speaking population.

Quintero, the lead singer and guitarist from Los Tucanes, responds to critics in much the same way as many rap artists, that they are simply reporting on a popular aspect of contemporary life, and that by prohibiting drugs the government has actually contributed to their popularity and to the development of a multi-billion dollar underground business. One of the most controversial aspects of Los Tucanes' songs is that some of their lyrics read as if they might have been written for the drug lords and gangs themselves. For example, the group's song about *"El Güero"* (Whitey) Palma, a Sinaloa drug lord now serving time in Mexico's high-security Almoloya prison, calls him "a respectable gentleman" and concludes in a warning to the police: "Don't go over the line, because the king isn't dead . . . Don't sleep soundly. The orders are the same, and will be carried out to the letter. Even your pillow could explode on you." Quintero argues that their songs are about what they have seen or what people tell us. *La Piñata* is about a real, he claims, drug lord's cocaine party that someone told him about. Whether *corridos* are always completely accurate or not is somewhat irrelevant. What is accurate, however, is that illegal drugs have been part of American popular culture since the 1960s and drug smuggling, drug wars, and other activities endemic to the drug trade and drug use have touched the lives of most Americans, including Chicanos and *Mexicanos*. Given the role of the *corrido* in Chicano and Mexican cultures, its role in capturing and commenting on the daily experience, particularly that which shocks, it is no accident, nor should it be surprising, that we find so many *corridos* about drug trafficking and that these *corridos* have become so popular.

Conclusion

Narcocorridos seem to indicate a change in heroes or, if you will, anti-heroes to some extent. While drug smugglers and dealers do fight the government, they rarely do it to benefit the community or the oppressed. Their popularity with young working class Mexicanos and Chicanos should not be surprising, however, given the poverty and inequality that continues to be a common phenomenon in both countries. As Cortese (1990) notes, "Profit and poverty explain why Mexico has become the source of large quantities of illicit drugs . . . They [poor Mexicans] literally have nothing to lose and much to gain by cultivating or trafficking in illicit drugs."

References

Anderson, Sean E., and Howard, Gregory J. (1998). *Interrogating Popular Culture: Deviance, Justice, and Social Order*. Albany, New York: Harrow and Heston Publishers.

Burciaga, José Antonio (1993). *Drink Cultura: Chicanismo*. Santa Barbara, CA: Joshua Odell Editions.

Collier, Robert. (1997) "Drugs Muscle into Mexican Music Mix: Trafficking Theme Hits Popular Nerve." *San Francisco Chronicle*, October 17, p. 1.

Cortese, Anthony J. (1990). "Claims-Making and Drug Trafficking: The Mexican Connection." *Nanzan Review of American Studies*, 12:1026.

Dibble, Sandra (1998). "Tijuana Band Has Fans Hooked on Drug-war Ballads." *The San Diego Union-Tribune*, March 30, p. A-1.

Dickey, Dan W. (1978). *The Kennedy Corridos: A Case Study of the Ballads of a Mexican American Hero*. Austin: Center of Mexican American Studies, University of Texas.

Fernández, Celestino and James E. Officer (1989). "The Lighter Side of Mexican Immigration: Humor and Satire in the Mexican Corrido." *Journal of the Southwest*, vol. 31:471–496.

Griffith, James S. and Celestino Fernández (1988). "Mexican Horse Races and Cultural Values: The Case of *Los Corridos del Merino*." *Western Folklore*, vol. 47:129–151.

Herrera-Sobek, Maria (1998). "*The Corrido as Hypertext: Undocumented Mexican Immigrant Films and the Mexican/Chicano Ballad*." In *Culture Across Borders: Mexican Immigration & Popular Culture*. Edited by David R. Maciel and Maria Herrera-Sobek, Tucson: The University of Arizona Press.

Paredes, Américo (1958). *With His Pistol in His Hand*. Austin: University of Texas Press.

Peña, Manuel H. (1985). *The Texas-Mexican Conjunto: History of a Working Class Music*. Austin: University of Texas Press.

Quinones, Sam (1997/8). "San Jose's Los Tigres del Norte Have Remade Mexican Pop Music Twice Over." *Metro*, December 21–January 7, 1998, p. 23.

Reyna, José R. (n.d.). "*Conjunto Music*." Liner notes to CD, Texas-Mexican Border Music.

Roberts, John S. (1999). *The Latin Tinge: The Impact of Latin American Music on the United States* (2nd ed.). New York: Oxford University Press.

Salazar, Rubén (1970). "Pachuco Folk Heroes—They Were First to Be Different." *Los Angles Times*, June.

Simmons, Merle E. (1951). *The Mexican Corrido as a Source for Interpretive Study of Modern Mexico (1870–1950): With a Consideration of the Origins and Development of the Corrido Tradition*. Ph.D. dissertation, University Microfilms, Ann Arbor, Michigan.

United Nations (1997). *World Drug Report*. 332-page report issued by the United Nations in June.

Wald, Elijah (2001). *Narcocorrido: A Journey into the Music of Drugs, Guns, and Guerrillas*. New York: HarperCollins Publishers.

Ybarra-Fausto, Tomás (1977). "The Chicano Movement and the Emergence of a Chicano Poetic Consciousness." *New Scholar*, vol. 6: 81–109.

Appendix A

Antonine Tibesar, ed.

Juniperro Serra Reports on the Missions of California

By 1769, the Spanish crown sent an expedition from Mexico to Upper California to establish a colony. The Franciscan missionary Junipero Serra was a member of the first Spanish "settlers" in California. Between 1769 and 1823 the missionaries founded twenty-one missions between San Diego and San Francisco, all close to the Pacific coast or rivers. Father Serra, living at the mission in Monterey, was the support seeker for all missions between San Diego and Monterey. In 1773, back in Mexico, he politely complained in this mission report to the Spanish Viceroy about the inadequate maintenance of the missions by the presidios and the Spanish commissary. He declared the missions in dire need of provisions and Indian laborers. Complaints about the officers in the presidio, who did not consider the missions their first priority, are also expressed. *(LH)*

To Antonio María de Bucareli y Ursua

Report on the general condition and needs of the missions of Upper California; thirty-two suggestions for improvement in the government of the missions. Written at Mexico City, March 13, 1773. Accompanying memorandum lists the church furnishings needed in some of the missions.

Jesus, Mary, Joseph!

Most Excellent Sir:

Fray Junípero Serra of the Order of our Seraphic Father Saint Francis, Apostolic Missionary of the College de *Propaganda Fide* of San Fernando of this Court of Mexico, President of the missions of the gentiles of Monterey, and those annexed to it; in obedience to orders emanating from my Superior, which are enclosed herewith; and, at the same time, being inspired with confidence and edification at the great zeal with which Your Excellency—as Viceregent of our Catholic and Sovereign Monarch, whom God keep—desires the stability and the daily advancement of that new center of Christianity, that has already been started in five missions, and where there are proposals to increase the number by further foundations; and appreciating the great favor Your Excellency deigns to show me, without any merit on my part, because I have had a share in all that has been accomplished in these new establishments, since the first day they were begun;

and, in that I have been an eyewitness of all the events which have taken place there, and can explain to Your Excellency everything that, in my judgment seems necessary and fitting to procure the fulfillment of the pious projects of our Great Monarch—whom God prosper—who is desirous of introducing, and spreading, in these extensive territories our Holy Catholic Faith, I, with all submission due to Your Excellency, wish to present the following suggestions.

1. As soon as possible, it is imperative that there be procured, from Vera Cruz, a shipmaster, and a pilot's mate, to sail the packet boat *San Carlos* to Monterey. The reason is that, if Your Excellency grants Don Miguel Pino permission, as he requests, to return to Cádiz, his home country, where he has a wife and mother he left many years ago, there are in San Blas no other navigating officers except the Frigate Ensign and Commandant Don Juan Perez and the Pilot's Mate Don Joseph Cañizares. The latter, being a mere youth, does not seem qualified to be entrusted with the responsibility of being chief, and only navigating officer, for the said boat. But he could be used as assistant, or second officer, to relieve the watch with the chief. It is, as you know, a very weighty matter to carry the whole responsibility, as was the case in the last trip with our friend Don Juan Pérez. I lay emphasis on the "as soon as possible" because the new frigate[1] is almost in readiness for sailing; and so another master, and his mate, are needed. All of which, briefly, is what I told Your Excellency in our talk about the necessity of two more navigators, and two more pilot's mates.

2. I consider it most advisable that the new frigate should be got in readiness with the utmost speed possible, because, seeing how large it is—I myself have been on board, and was amazed at its enormous capacity—one trip with it, added to what the two packet boats can carry, might save from the pangs of famine and starvation both the presidio and the missions— whether already in being or yet to be founded—and bring content and happiness to the hearts of all, a condition of things which will best serve the advancement and progress we are all so eager to see.

3. I might call the attention of Your Excellency to the fact that this year no *sínodo* has been received by me; it has been paid for the twelve religious, and no more. In other words, it has been paid for the ten that are at present in various places, and who administer, two in each of them, the said five new missions,[2] as is vouched for in the affidavit I am enclosing herewith, made out by the Officer of the presidio; and likewise, for the two others who are, at present, staying in San Diego, waiting for the foundation of San Buenaventura. Now since it is my intention—as soon as Your Excellency shall have decided what measures should most properly be taken—to take the road back to my San Carlos Mission, it does not seem the right thing that my brethren should have to maintain me with what they need for themselves.

And even though the objection might be raised that in such a case three ministers will have to be maintained in one mission, I reply that I see nothing extraordinary in that, since the third is the President. It is most advisable that the President be considered as supernumerary, so that he may be free to go here and there on his visitations of the missions, and be present at the foundation of the new ones. In carrying out these duties, he should be able to leave two Fathers for days of obligation, when one has to say Mass at the presidio, and the other at the mission. Or, in other words: the third may be maintained with the title of Captain of the Presidio—and his *sínodo* could well be four hundred pesos—the minimum, I believe, that would be given a secular priest, should he be appointed to the post. In any case, his residence should be at the mission. But about this point I wish to speak at greater length to Your Excellency.

The two religious staying in San Diego while they wait for the foundation of the San Buenaventura Mission are Father Preacher Fray Ramón Usón, and Father Preacher Fray Juan Figuer.[3] They have been there since the beginning of November of last year, 1772.

4. Various pious people of Tepic, Compostela, and thereabouts, having heard something of the hardships we have had to undergo, promised me that, on my return to Monterey, they would send supplies of corn and other provisions for us and the newly converted Christians. I ask Your Excellency, then, that you would kindly give orders to the Commissary at San Blas to put on board what is sent to me as alms, along with an itemized account. The invoices should state that all such supplies belong solely to the missions, and are not to be inspected by the Officer of the presidio.

This same might be said concerning some cases that are awaiting shipment in Loreto, which contain books, images, crucifixes for the missions, and other minor objects, such as tools—all personal effects belonging to the religious of our College, who have left, or are about to leave, the old missions of California. In consideration of freight charges, since they were being returned to Mexico, where there is no shortage of such articles, they gave them all to the new missions, where everything is needed. All these cases were carefully examined, both inside and out, by the Reverend Dominican Fathers, a formality which allowed them to verify, with their own eyes, how unfounded was the claim, made and publicized by Governor Don Felipe Barri,[4] that all these packing cases were full of furnishings stolen from the missions. If these cases cannot be taken by land to San Diego, Your Excellency might order the said Governor to send them on board ship to the Port of San Blas; and address them to the Commissary there, who might put them aboard the ship sailing for Monterey, and with the same stipulation on the invoices, that they belong solely to the missions.

5. It seems to me most appropriate that Your Excellency should authorize the Captain of the Tubac Presidio to undertake the expedition he was anxious to start, to discover a route to the Port of San Diego or of Monterey. Furthermore, for this reason, Your Excellency should not omit, in accordance with your own good judgment, to give also the order to some outstanding man from New Mexico to undertake the same exploration. According to the best of my information, if they start straight west from Santa Fe, with a slight deviation to the south, they will strike Monterey, since it is on the lati-

tude of 36 degrees and 36 minutes; and Santa Fe, according to Don Pedro de Rivera's diary, is on the 37th degree and 28 minutes. Most assuredly, if, for our good fortune, a line of communication should be opened up from one or both of these ports to the aforementioned regions, and especially with New Mexico, their conquest would thus be hastened to a most notable degree, assuring a harvest of many souls for heaven.[5]

6. A measure that seems to me of special importance is the removal, or recall, of the Officer Don Pedro Fages from the command of the Presidio at Monterey, and the appointment of another in his place. Otherwise there will be no stopping the desertions of soldiers and others, who, up to the present time, have caused so much trouble and will continue to do so. Nor can matters remain as they are, as far as those who still stay on are concerned—they stay because they can not get away. Every one of them is extremely wrought up. Their grievance is not only because of long hours of work and a lack of food—as I have on numerous occasions heard them declare— but because of the harsh treatment, and unbearable manners, of the said officer.

Independently of what I already knew from long experience, I have just received, along with my last bundle of letters, copies of what, on the one hand, the volunteer soldiers of that presidio write to their Captain, Agustín Callis,[6] whom they suppose to be at your Court, and, on the other hand, what the leather-jacket soldiers think, as they write to their officer, Don Fernando de Rivera—whom, also, they suppose to be in Mexico. Both groups of men ask their respective Officers to free them in any manner they can from such harsh treatment and oppression. In the said writings there is no other complaint except that they have over them Don Pedro Fages.

If I were called upon to tell, not of the annoyances he has caused me, and the rest of the religious—a story that shall remain untold—but of the damage his conduct has continually done to the missions, it would be a long story. If details are required to supply further arguments to bring about the result desired, Your Excellency has only to say the word. But if what has already been said, as well as the information given in writing by the Reverend Father Guardian of our College, and by me, by word of mouth, be sufficient for the purpose we have in mind, I beg and beseech Your Excellency that he may be discharged honorably, and without any humiliation whatsoever; and I pray God to bless him.[7]

7. My opinion is that, at the present time, it is inadvisable that the Officer to be put in command of the said presidio should be an officer of the regular troop, because they are not trained in the duties of leather-jacket soldiers—a totally different branch of the service—and we might find ourselves in the same predicament as before.

Appreciating fully the great compliment Your Excellency pays me in permitting me to suggest a candidate suitable for the place, I say that, as far as I can judge, among those belonging to the company, there is no more suitable man than the company Sergeant, Don José Francisco Ortega.[8]

The reasons for my choice are his record, and his ability to take charge of such a command.

First, his record. After he had served the King for some years as a leather-jacket soldier in California during the time of the Jesuits and was promoted to the rank of sergeant, he left the service to spend all his time in the mines in the southern part of the peninsula. At that time, he, being clearly the man best suited for the post in that department, was appointed Associate Judge for all the King's mines there and administered justice with equity for a number of years.

When the new Governor, Don Gaspar de Portolá, came to take command of the province, at the time the Jesuits were expelled, he met him for the first time, and had numerous dealings with him, and insisted that he join the service once more with rank as sergeant. Ortega accepted and went in the Governor's company to Loreto. He served the said Governor and the King in the management of the royal warehouse, being put in charge of all correspondence, accounts and administration for more than a year, while the said royal hacienda was under the control of Señor Portolá.

Then the new Commissary Don Francisco Trillo came, who employed him as secretary as long as he needed him. When the expedition to Monterey got under way, the Sergeant was appointed to the second part of it, with which I went myself, as well as the Governor. We set out on our way, and when we began to enter the gentile country we received the last letters from the Most Illustrious Inspector General. In the letter addressed to the Governor, which was read in my presence, His Most Illustrious Lordship said that Sergeant Ortega should follow the expedition with the assurance that, on his return, he was keeping for him his promotion as Lieutenant Officer of the company, for Don Blas Somera was leaving this post, having asked for his retirement. We all celebrated the good news and promise, repeatedly offering him our congratulations.

When the expedition started on its way, as soon as the short stretch of the road, familiar to some of the soldiers who had passed that way before, came to an end, the Governor instructed the Sergeant, accompanied by only one soldier, to explore ahead daily the road we had to follow the following day. And so, for more than a month that our journey lasted, he continued to go ahead the whole time, covering more than three times the distance that the rest of the expedition had to cover. He forged ahead in search of watering places and camping spots; then he would come back with the information, and guide us to the spots he had discovered. The single soldier who was his companion was sometimes changed, but the Sergeant never.

The risks he ran in going among so many gentiles, which became evident by what we saw later, kept me in continual anxiety; and, as a matter of fact, at times, it was only thanks to the protection of his favorite saints that he escaped unscathed.

After our arrival at San Diego, every one was elated, telling one another what a marvellous trip we had made. At that time the search for the Port of Monterey was decided upon. The Sergeant went along with the others. Fathers Crespí and Gómez, who accompanied the expedition as far as the Port of San Francisco, told me that, during all the trip, the part taken by Señor Ortega was most remarkable. Even

though Captain Rivera was appointed as first explorer, always was the Sergeant employed in the same capacity, especially when they tried to find the port in various directions. And he was the man that went the farthest in exploring the estuaries of San Francisco, in search of a crossing to the other side, which was never found.

When the expedition came back to San Diego, the Governor was informed of what had happened to us on the Feast of the Assumption of Our Lady—that the gentiles had killed one of our men, wounded others, and tried to kill all of us. And while the return to Monterey was under consideration—as actually happened after the arrival of the boat—he decided it was desirable that a man especially adapted to the work should take command of the escort, and remain in the Mission of San Diego. Accordingly the Governor appointed the said Sergeant. As for me, since I was going to Monterey with the greatest anxiety at leaving the two poor Fathers exposed to so many dangers and as many hardships, the greatest consolation I had, as regards their dangerous position, was that the Sergeant was there to defend them; and my confidence was not misplaced.

The expedition being at an end, he was sent to California. The Governor employed him in carrying provisions from Sinaloa, in going to and from San Diego, and in discovering and pointing out the proper sites for the five missions that are to be founded in the stretch in between. During these explorations, while he was climbing mountains and crossing valleys, over and above what he had principally in mind, he discovered a way from Velicatá to San Diego which saves a distance of some fifty leagues; and this he will soon shorten still more, I assure you.

This, Most Excellent Lord, is a short sketch of the record of the man I am recommending to Your Excellency.

Now as regards his fitness for the position, I can say that, as far as I have seen, in command of soldiers he is firm without rigidity, and has prudence and common sense. I believe they will love him without ceasing to fear him; they will fear him sufficiently without ceasing to love him. Since, in all the duties with which he has been entrusted, and which I have just now described, he has acquitted himself with honor, I feel confident that he will do the same with all future appointments. In his youthful days, in the town of Zelaya, his native place, he had the management of a storehouse and shop; he is alert and capable in the management of business. He writes a good hand, and I am sure that the storehouse will be well administered; and since he is most conscientious, the accounts will be as the law requires. When Pedro Fages got his appointment to the office in question, he had only the title of Lieutenant. With the same title this most deserving man could be given the same office. But let it be as Your Excellency shall decide; in any case you will decide what is for the best.

8. I suggest that Your Excellency give strict orders to the Officer who will be sent, that, as soon as the Missionary Father of any mission requests it, he should remove the soldier or soldiers who give bad example, especially in the matter of incontinence; he should recall them to the presidio and send, in their place, another or others who are not known as immoral or scandalous. And even when the Father does not specify the sin of the soldier, his request for removal should always be heeded, since, in certain cases, it is not advisable to give the reason, either to prevent making public a hidden sin, or for other reasons that can easily be imagined. As for the soldier who does not give grounds for complaint at the mission, you may be very sure the Father will not ask for his removal; and if the request is made, it is very evident that there are good reasons; and so it is right that his request should be granted. This is what a number of the most excellent predecessors of Your Excellency have decided upon, at the suggestion of our College.[9]

9. Your Excellency should notify the said Officer and the soldiers that the training, governance, punishment and education of baptized Indians, or of those who are being prepared for Baptism, belong exclusively to the Missionary Fathers, the only exception being for capital offenses. Therefore no chastisement or ill-treatment should be inflicted on any of them whether by the Officer or by any soldier, without the Missionary Father's passing upon it. This has been the time-honored practice of this kingdom ever since the conquest; and it is quite in conformity with the law of nature concerning the education of the children, and an essential condition for the rightful training of the poor neophytes. Having these as his basic reasons, as well as others that might be adduced, the Most Illustrious Inspector General gave instructions to this effect before leaving California. Yet, on the contrary practice has prevailed, which has resulted in the worst of evils. I had intended to explain myself at greater length on this most important topic but I leave it for

later, should circumstances make it necessary.[10]

10. Concerning the number of soldiers required in the missions as escort, I give my opinion as follows:

For Mission San Carlos de Monterey, established on the banks of the Carmel River, in consideration of its proximity to the presidio, eight leather-jacket soldiers are sufficient.

For San Antonio de Padua de los Robles: ten leather-jacket soldiers.

For San Luis Obispo de los Tichos: ten leather-jacket soldiers also.

For San Gabriel de los Temblores: likewise ten leather-jacket soldiers.

And for San Diego of the Port: thirteen or fourteen leather-jacket soldiers also. The reason for this increase in number is that, from this mission, very frequently a courier has to start, either for California, or for Monterey. If the number were less, what occurred when the boat last came there might happen again. Captain Don Juan Pérez found so few soldiers in the mission, that he deemed it advisable to order a number of sailors to disembark for the proper protection of the mission. This I mentioned in my letter to Your Excellency, if my memory serves me well.

As for the Missions of San Buenaventura and Santa Clara, at first sight it would seem to me that there should be twenty for the first mentioned, on account of its closeness to the Santa Barbara Channel, and for Santa Clara, fifteen.

With regard to the Mission of our Seraphic Father San Francisco, in his famous Port, I say nothing, because I am unaware of the manner and place in which Your Excellency has decided that it should be established.

The conclusion of all this seems to me to be as follows: that, for the presidio, and the missions already established or yet to be founded, it will be necessary and most suitable that the number of a hundred leather-jacket soldiers be realized, and that they be attached as a separate unit to the Presidio of Monterey, and should not be linked up, in any way, with those of Old California.

11. For these soldiers there should be in the Presidio of Monterey a store, with the merchandise they need, and a list of prices—something they have not had up to the present—and a regular accounting of their pay. They should be cut off from all dependence on the store at Loreto, which, because of its being so far away, is only a source of continual trouble. And, seeing that most of their salary has to be taken in kind from the royal warehouse, it should be allowed the usual percentage of profit, but the soldiers' pay should be increased. The last issuance of regulations decreased it considerably, while more work was exacted of them. The result will be that those who are there will be content to remain; and others, with their families, will wish to go there. The facts of the matter are that not long ago the career of a soldier was one that was sought for, and the family of such a man made out quite well. But today there is no one who is eager for it, or on the lookout for it.

It seems to me that, if things were put on a more satisfactory basis, some captain or other from Sinaloa, or from one of the other provinces, might be commissioned to recruit from thirty to forty leather-jacket soldiers; and, of their number, as many as possible with their families. They should be Spaniards with a good record, and they should be guaranteed the same treatment they have been receiving for the past years in California. Brought there by boat, they could continue by land to Monterey. They should have a supply of animals, arms and other things that are part of the service. And thus these missions would be well provided for, the land would be well settled, and the interests of all, whether spiritual or temporal, served the more efficiently.

Furthermore, it seems to me not at all necessary for all to be married men; provided that, at least, two such families be stationed in each mission, I think it is most probable that the others would not be long before marrying also. Even as it is, quite a number of them have come to me with that in mind.

As for pay in coin, my opinion is that when they ask for it, it should be given. After all, it all goes back to the store, except perhaps a little that they spend with those on board when the ship arrives. Then business could be put on a cash basis, as is done at Loreto. It might turn out in this way better for the treasurer, and for themselves. As it is, I fear they spend more for food and clothes, but get less for their money. I wanted to get to the bottom of the matter from exact figures. But I realized that it was impossible, because I did not know what was the cost price, and what the selling price, of the goods. And so I could not figure what profit was made. Yet, if there is any way at all to arrive at so desirable a goal, Your Excellency should not hesitate to order further appropriate measures to be taken.

12. It is of the utmost importance that the missions be provided with laborers, to till the land, and so raise crops for their maintenance and progress. We would already have made a start in so doing, were it not for the opposition of the Officer at the presidio—a situation I have described recently in a letter to the Reverend Father Guardian of our College, written about the middle of October, from San Diego. The original of that letter was turned over to the government offices of Your Excellency, where you may see it.

The easiest method seems to me the one we have presented from the beginning. I explained it in the said letter. It is this. Along with the sailors aboard ship, there should be a number of young men from the vicinity of San Blas. I should think that it would not be hard to find among them day laborers, cowboys and mule drivers. These should be divided among the missions—six to each, or four at least. But a rule should be made that the Officer of the presidio has no right to change them for a whole year; and that stipulation will inspire confidence in their minds. Otherwise, not a single one will be found to be willing to stay, especially as matters go now. Also, during the year their pay should be on the same basis as that of the sailors at San Blas; and in the missions they should receive free rations. And if at the end of the first year they wish to stay a second year, the same treatment should be continued. If they prefer to return to San Blas, by boat, they should be granted their request, and others should be provided to take their place.

13. It is of no less importance that, when the livestock arrives, which Your Excellency, in virtue of your decree, orders

to be forwarded from California for the equipment of the Monterey missions, some Indian families from the said California should come, of their own free will, with the expedition, and that they should receive every consideration from the officials. They should be distributed, at least two or three being placed in each mission. By taking such measures two purposes will be accomplished. The first will be that there will be an additional two or three Indians for work. The second, and the one I have most in mind, is that the Indians may realize that, till now, they have been much mistaken when they saw all men, and no women, among us; that there are marriages, also, among Christians. Last year, when one of the San Diego Fathers went to California to get provisions, which had run short in that mission, he brought back with him, along with the rest of his company, two of the said families. At his arrival, there was quite a commotion among the new Christians, and even among the gentiles; they did not know what to make of these families, so great was their delight. Just to see these families was a lesson as useful to them as was their happiness at their arrival. So if families other than Indian come from there, it will serve the same purpose very well—that is, if we can provide for them.

14. It was a practice of long standing in California that the Father maintained in each mission a soldier of his own choice, not so much as an escort but as a foreman; they called him the missionary-soldier. In his hands the Father would leave the responsibility both of the work to be done on the farm and any other business that might turn up. When the soldier turned out to be a man you could rely on, he often remained in that position till old age.

Today, just the reverse is happening. It is enough just to hear that a soldier is a good manager, and serves the Father well, to have him immediately dismissed, and sent elsewhere. "Because," says the Officer at Monterey, quoting the Governor of California, "when the soldiers see themselves beloved, and in good standing with the Father, they immediately get puffed up—and that leads them to lose respect for authority." If that line is followed, only those soldiers will be sent to the missions who care not at all what the Fathers think of them, and show them neither respect nor consideration.

If such be the case, I ask Your Excellency to be good enough to let the Commanding Officer of the presidio know that the old custom is to be re-established, and that the soldier whom, in each mission, the Fathers elect for said services should be relieved of guard and sentinel duty and the care of horses; that he is not to be removed without serious reason; and this removal—at least to keep peace and harmony—is to be made known to the Father in charge. Such an arrangement is of considerable importance for the progress and temporal prosperity of the missions. The Father minister is not able to take care of everything by himself; neither can he attend to all the varied occupations personally, because in the monastery he was not trained along those lines.

15. In my own name, and in the name of all the missionaries who are in that far land of exile, I ask Your Excellency that an invoice of everything that is sent by boat

to the missions for their upkeep during the following year should be sent also, and that it should be separate from what is sent to the Commanding Officer of the presidio and the escorts. That was the arrangement for the first year, and it gave no occasion for disagreement. The two following years, the Commissary at San Blas sent everything to the Officer of the presidio, for him to pass on to us, to keep us for a year, whatever he had a notion to give. Even the bells for which I asked the Most Excellent Marqués de Croix, as well as the two others I sent to San Blas to be recast—they were both cracked, and I wrote about them both to Your Excellency and to the Commissary at San Blas—arrived addressed to Don Pedro Fages, and Señor Trillo never wrote me a line about the whole matter. When I wanted to take them over, the Officer told me that they had come addressed to him, without any other instructions, and that he would do with them what he pleased.

Even our letters in San Blas are placed in the Officer's envelope, so that we should receive none except from his hand. The time and manner in which we received them I will tell you by word of mouth. The equipment that reaches us from our College, he says, is sent to him, and he is giving it to us. And so receipts are to be made out to him, and not to the Captain of the boat.

As regards our food supply—to last us a year, and to leave something over to give, at least, to the little Christian boys and girls—I intended to say a great deal, but will limit myself to this: that our sufferings are great; never have we, the religious, been in such dire straits, and never has the said Officer been living in such plenty, as

since the time he and we arrived in Monterey. May our poverty be accepted for the love of God, and may his plenty—I do not envy him it—do him good. What I do want and ask for is, that the missions be maintained, that there should be a mouthful over and above to give to our Christians and catechumens, and that Christianity be extended.

Only two Indians from California still remain at my San Carlos Mission. The rest I distributed among the other missions. When the Officer was partitioning out what was brought by pack train, and marked for Monterey, I asked him to make an entry in his accounts for the two said Indians, to which he replied that he would not give anything to any Indian, and that if I wanted to chase them away, I should do so.

To sum up the whole situation, my opinion is that, without a doubt, whatever, in your goodness, Your Excellency, or the King—whom God keep—sends us—and without it at the present time we could not keep going, nor could the missions be kept in existence—should be sent from here marked and addressed separately. I have already mentioned in the letter referred to, that this year the Missions of San Diego and San Gabriel are in poorer condition than last year, even though two boats arrived, while there was only one the year before. The explanation is that last year there was sent from here the full quota of supplies for San Diego, on the supposition that the packet boat *San José* had never reached there. And, in point of fact, it never did arrive.

16. Seeing that Your Excellency has already ordered a forge to be brought in the last shipload for San Diego Mission—which,

after many difficulties, I succeeded in having delivered by the Officer—one thing yet remains: that Your Excellency should send a blacksmith there. They are sadly in need of one there—both for the boats, which always need some shop repairs, and for the distant Monterey Mission. It will often happen that, while the men are at work, an ax head flies off the handle, a hoe or some other tool gets broken, and all they can do is to throw it aside. If they send it to the Monterey Presidio for repairs—and that is the only place where there is a forge and a blacksmith—it might be kept there a year. In my own mission, which is just a stone's throw away, it is quite usual for an ax, which could be mended in fifteen minutes, to be kept several weeks. And so the work has to wait.

17. In view of what I have just told you, I earnestly ask Your Excellency for an additional forge and blacksmith. If it were set up at the Carmel Mission it could also serve the Missions of San Antonio and San Luis. Not only would we get better service, but we would be able to have some of the newly converted youths learn the trade. This the Fathers of said missions, in their last letters, are most insistent upon. They are tired of dealing with the presidio, where the Officer does not absolutely refuse, but where repairs are done very slowly, and, all too frequently, a bad job is made of them. With a blacksmith in San Diego, the missions nearby can be served from there, and the one in Carmel can serve those of San Antonio and San Luis.

18. I beg of Your Excellency that, for the setting up of the two said forges, you order that there be sent and delivered to the two missions a goodly supply of iron—partly in bars, partly in sheets—and that it be clearly stated that it is sent for the missions. In that way, so as to get possession of it, we will avoid any further difficulties or counterclaims on the part of the presidio.

19. We are in as much need of two carpenters as we are of two blacksmiths, one for the missions near Monterey, and the other to be located at Mission San Gabriel de los Temblores, where San Diego and San Buenaventura can make use of him. Both of them should come equipped with the tools of their trade. All of these matters could easily be attended to, if Your Excellency would give whatever orders seem suitable to you to someone in Guadalaxara. There could easily be sent from there the two blacksmiths, the two carpenters, and all of their equipment. But they should be clearly given to understand that the equipment is not their own, but the property of the respective missions.

20. Keeping in mind that it is the practice of His Majesty—God bless him—to give to each of the newly founded missions two bells, a large and a small one, I make mention that, at the present time there are needed: two for the San Gabriel Mission, already founded, two for the Santa Clara Mission, and two others for that of San Francisco, when founded. And if of the four cast in San Blas, the Officer takes one for the presidio, there will yet be one needed for the San Luis Mission. Therefore, I ask Your Excellency to be so good as to order the four bells that were recently sent to Monterey to be handed over to me, and that three more pairs of bells be sent for the three said missions. And if it suits Your Excellency to send one more to be

placed at the presidio, to ring for Mass and the *Angelus,* etc., it seems a very fitting thing to do, and I will have it placed there without fail.

While we are on the subject, I might add that, having inspected those cast in San Blas, and comparing the expenses entailed with what it would cost to buy them in Mexico, plus the transportation—to have them cast in San Blas does not represent any great saving; therefore it would be better to have them sent from this city already cast. In addition, those made in San Blas are ugly and of poor quality. I am in no position to pass judgment on their tone, because I did not see them hung to test them.

21. Since it is the practice of His Majesty, whom God keep, to give the furnishings, the sacred vessels and the other church accessories connected with the administration of the Holy Sacraments to newly founded missions, the Most Excellent Marqués de Croix ordered each of the various commissaries to collect from the sacristies of the expelled Jesuits what had been assigned to each respectively and to put into large and adequate packing cases all the types of articles mentioned in the memorandum which His Excellency sent them.

The result was that when I inspected the five cases that came to me at Monterey for the five new missions, I found that two were not merely of the kind we needed, but that the articles were costly and valuable. Of these, one is for the Mission of our Father San Francisco, and the other for that of Santa Clara. But of the other three, which I gave to the Missions of San Luis, San Antonio and San Gabriel, the furnishings were all old, broken, and in a sad state, with the one exception that the commissary who prepared the case that fell to the lot of Mission San Antonio took the pains to have all the furnishings repaired, and the white linens washed and cleaned, so that the whole collection, while being poor and old, was at any rate passable.

But the furnishings in the other two cases are falling to pieces, and dirty—in a word, unusable. And so I was obliged to give from the Monterey vestments, three chasubles of considerable value to the three said missions: one to each, so that they may celebrate with some sort of decency. But antependia and chasubles, of the full range of colors, I cannot give, because I do not have them. And so I ask Your Excellency, out of those that may be distributed from the belongings of the Jesuit Fathers, or if new ones are being made on order, to be so good as to order that the said missions be provided with proper vestments. Also that, whatever Mission Santa Clara is still without, as can be seen from the list I am enclosing herewith, be sent along. I have no doubt that such action would be most conformable with the mind and wishes of our Catholic Monarch, who, always zealous for the splendor of Divine Worship, has never stopped at any expense in order to promote it.

22. Your Excellency might be so good as to give strict orders to the Officer in command not to put difficulties in the way of communications by letter between the religious in the missions and those of our College; to prohibit, under severe penalty, the opening of letters or sending them astray; to give orders likewise that, when there happens to be a courier, he should

notify us, and allow us sufficient time to write all we have in mind to write. Furthermore, I most humbly beg Your Excellency that the said letters from us be delivered to our College free, and without mail expense. The Reverend Father Guardian of this College tells me that he has to pay a large amount on that account. Seeing that the missions do not have any other funds than the *sínodo*—pure and simple—that my Lord the King—whom God keep—in his charity gives us, it seems to be an unnecessary hardship that we must pinch ourselves just to be able to get news of our own brethren and of activities in the missions. The worthy soldiers have that privilege. But who are more soldiers than we, who are continually on the battlefield, and as exposed as any soldier to the arrows of the enemy?

23. I suggest that the scales at San Blas should be regulated so that one fanega contains twelve almuds, as is the common rule, and that they should not give us, as they have until now, nine and a half or ten to the fanega; and in that way we have to certify that we have received such and such number of fanegas, so that in looking over the receipts here, it is a very different story from what we have in reality and in truth received.

24. When once this improvement of measures has been made, orders should be given that a whole series of weights be cast in San Blas, viz.: a half-fanega, quartilla, almud, half-almud and quartillo,[11] for each of the missions; the official stamp should be marked on them, as is usual in Mexico and everywhere in proof of their legality. Thus fortified, both for the present and the future, we will be on a firm ground as to the exact weight of what is given out and what is taken in; and fraud will be eliminated—an impossibility without taking such precautions.

25. It seems to me that it would be most helpful if Your Excellency were to give strict orders to the said Commissary at San Blas, that he take greater care than he has till now taken in the packing of provisions forwarded for the maintenance of these missions and presidio. If the corn is put on board when it has already been attacked by grubs, and is full of maggots— and the same goes for the rest of the supplies—what will be its state when it arrives at its destination, and what condition will it be in when the time comes to eat it? The corn that has been put on board fresh and in good condition has arrived there in the same good condition. But sometimes, when we received it with the kernels empty, the Captain of the boat answered that that was the way it was loaded in San Blas. Last year there was no meat; and this year, what did come, besides being small in quantity, was so maggoty and putrid that very reasonably it was said to be the same that was to have come the year before; and not having much room in the boat, our meat supply was neither much, nor little, but nil.

There is nothing in greater abundance in the countryside around San Blas than herds of cows. Counting this year, it will now be two years since our poor men have been promised—ever since we got there—as part of their daily ration, half a pound or six ounces of meat. They have practically not tasted any other meat than what they have obtained from the gentiles or from hunting.

But, this last year the greatest pity of all has been concerning the flour, which is, of all the things that are sent us or may be sent, the most helpful and most basic for the sustenance of life. It was put in plain sacks of poor material made of burlap or hemp, and consequently ran out at every motion or contact; and so the assignments arrived minus much that should have been there. And it is not hard to picture how much more they would be diminished when, after a lengthy journey, they arrived at their respective missions. How much money is thus thrown to the winds, both for what is lost—of the better quality—and for what is saved! If Your Excellency would kindly order the said article to be sent under the same stipulations that the Most Excellent Marqués de Croix laid down, such great losses would be avoided; and, with the same number of boatloads, there would be food to eat for a much longer time.

26. I wish once more to remind Your Excellency that all the missions are in the direst need of mules, so much so that those at some distance from the ports cannot possibly carry their provisions from them.

Had the Officer at the presidio not taken away from the two Missions of San Carlos and San Diego the mules given them by the Governor in the beginning, as I mentioned in my previous letter—and for which I am looking to Your Excellency for an adequate remedy—then these two missions would have been able to help their next-door neighbors. But the presidio took them all into protective custody; and with their ill-planned and, for the most part, purposeless transportation of goods, they are in a fair way to be the death of them all, a consummation helped on by the deserters, who stole

some of them, and by gentiles, who slaughtered others and ate their flesh. And, therefore, it seems to me a matter of the greatest importance that Your Excellency provide in this regard what you judge most fitting. Above all, a herd of mares and donkeys should be formed to breed mules; otherwise we will never emerge from our difficulties in this particular.

27. I earnestly beg of Your Excellency that the stock herd which, in the general distribution, was assigned to the two Missions of our Father San Francisco and of Santa Clara, together with the offspring from it, dating back to that day, should be handed over to me. I asked for it in the letter referred to, since there is every chance that we will take better care of the animals in the missions than they do in the presidio. This also will give us the chance to get a little more milk to help our little Christians—this being almost the only food we could afford to give them thus far.

28. May I recall to Your Excellency's memory that, at the time the expedition was setting out, a surgeon was appointed to it, by the name of Don Pedro Prat.[12] When we arrived at Monterey, the boat brought quite a supply of medicines for the use of the said surgeon, who was to keep what was needed for the presidio, and give to the missions what might be useful to them. He was to write down in a notebook the purpose for which each of the medicines was used, and how and when it should be used. But unfortunately it happened that on the day we found the Port of Monterey, the surgeon lost his mind. He remained a whole year at the presidio, completely out of his mind. Later, he was taken away, on board ship,

and finally he died at the hospital conducted by the Bethlehemite Fathers in Guadalaxara. The medicines are still there. Should Your Excellency graciously send another surgeon to take the place of the one deceased, we would have the satisfaction of having a patient bled, if necessary, and having someone to attend to a wound, a cut, a sore, or any other emergency which the skill and dexterity of such a practitioner could properly handle.

29. I ask Your Excellency for leave of absence for five soldiers, volunteers from Catalonia who reside at Monterey, who were married in Spain; for another who is uncertain whether he is a widower or not; and for another who is a total invalid. It will give the poor fellows much happiness. Here are their names:

Sergeant Puig, married.
Gerónimo Planes, married.
Pablo Ferrer, married.
Valentin Planells, married.
Francisco Bombau, married.
Domingo Clua, invalid.
Domingo Malaret, uncertain.

And of the leather-jacket soldiers, I ask the same favor for three who are married in faraway parts, and absent from their families for a long time.

The first is Miguel de Islas, an honest Spaniard, married in Mexico, where his wife and daughter are living; and he has been away from them for seven years.

The second, Juan Antonio Coronel, a mulatto, married in Sinaloa, and away from his wife for many years.

The third is married in San Luis Potosí; his surname is Sambrano; I do not remember his first name; I know only that he is married, and that he is a completely worthless fellow.

As regards these three, and also those mentioned above, it seems to me that it would be something most agreeable to God if Your Excellency would graciously allow them to return to their homes.

30. I also ask Your Excellency that you allow a bounty for those, be they soldiers or not, who enter into the state of marriage with girls of that faraway country, new Christian converts. On that point, the Most Illustrious Inspector General gave repeated orders to Don Pedro Fages, but I was not able to ascertain the exact terms and conditions.[13] However, whatever the case may be, it seems to me that anyone who marries after this fashion should be allowed to stay permanently attached to his wife's mission, without being removed to another; that he should be allowed an animal, immediately for his own use, if he is without one; and that, after he has worked a year or more on the mission farms, he be given from the royal herd two cows and a mule, or whatever may appear most suitable to Your Excellency. Lastly that, as time goes on, he might be assigned a piece of land for his own personal use provided he has nothing else to fall back upon.

31. I earnestly beg of Your Excellency that, when the new Commanding Officer shall be installed as Commandant of the Presidio of Monterey, he be allowed to publish, in the name of Your Excellency, a decree granting a general amnesty to deserters, if there are still any of them scattered among the gentiles. In this way, we will give peace of mind to the gentiles, and we will regain those wretched Christians who have gone astray. It would be a great

encouragement for all to see so striking an example of Your Excellency's good will and leniency towards those poor culprits.

Lastly—and as a conclusion to so many requests, all directed towards the one purpose which I outlined in the beginning of this lengthy document—I ask, with all due respect, that whatever measures Your Excellency will be pleased to adopt in reference to my recommendations, you will be good enough to see that a copy, or exact duplicate, of everything be given me, for my own future guidance, and that of the other missionaries. The reason is that, if I know precisely what Your Excellency has ordered the Commissary at San Blas to do, I will be able to remind him of it, if the necessity should arise. If I am acquainted, also, with what is required of the Governor of California[14] concerning such matters as the sending of livestock to the new missions; the arming and equipping of new soldiers, who will come from the other coast to Monterey—and they come at their own expense; the sending to San Diego or San Blas of the packing cases which are referred to in number 4 of this memorandum, and anything else that Your Excellency may order him, it will enable me to do the same thing.

But, first and foremost, and most emphatically, do I ask this as regards any order or instruction that may be given the Commanding Officer at the Presidio of Monterey; if we have any knowledge of the existence of such orders, Your Excellency may rest assured that neither I, nor any of my religious, will wish even in the slightest degree to do anything in opposition to such orders—a thing that might easily occur, if we were unaware of their existence.[15]

To sum up: Your Excellency, in this matter, as in all others, will graciously decide, order and command whatever may seem most fitting to you. As for myself, I feel perfectly confident, knowing your great prudence and zeal, that whatever appears the proper thing for you to do will always be what is for the best.

My wishes are that you arrive at these decisions as soon as possible, so that I may be able the sooner to take to the road once more to return to that poverty-stricken and far-distant vineyard of the Lord. And seeing that at present the state of my health is none too good, I will have to make the trip somewhat slowly.

And, so as not to stop asking for something right to the end, I beg Your Excellency to order some small allowance for the expenses of my trip. I would take it as a sign of your very special graciousness and favor towards me.

May our Lord God keep Your Excellency for as many years as my sincere affection wishes for you, in His holy love and grace.

Apostolic College of San Fernando of the Franciscan missionaries of this Court of Mexico, March 13, 1773.

Most Excellent Sir,

Kissing the hand of Your Excellency,

Your most humble servant and chaplain, who holds you in the highest respect, etc.,

Fray Junípero Serra

Notes

1. The *Santiago*, also called *Nueva Galicia*. When Serra passed through San Blas at the beginning of November, 1773, she was still under construction. She made her first trip in 1774 and carried Serra on his return voyage (Geiger, *Palóu's Life*, p. 144).

2. These were: San Diego, San Carlos de Carmelo (Monterey), San Gabriel, San Antonio, and San Luis Obispo.

3. Fathers Usón and Figuer had come to the Missions of Lower California in March, 1772, from the Franciscan Province of Aragon in Spain. Hardly had they received their first appointments, when these missions were ceded to the Dominicans. By September, 1772, they were already officially assigned to Upper California by the superiors of San Fernando.

4. Concerning the conduct of Barri (Barry) in this affair, see the chapter which Palóu had dedicated to it in his *Memoirs*, III, 314-352. Barry was to show the same hostile spirit towards the Dominicans, wherefore Bucareli had no other course but to accept Barry's resignation as Governor of California.

5. This recommendation of Father Serra was carefully considered by the authorities in Mexico City and is considered to have played an important part in gaining official consent for the expeditions which were conducted later by Juan Bautista Anza. (Herbert E. Bolton, *Anza's California Expeditions* [5 vols.; Berkeley, 1930], I, 58-59; IV, 96). Serra based his recommendation on a report by Pedro de Rivera, *Diario y Derrotero . . . de la Visita General de Presidios Situados en las Provincias Internas,* which was printed for the first time in Guatemala in 1836.

6. The Company of Volunteers of Catalonia was sent to Mexico in 1767 to help suppress the rebellion of the Sonora Indians. Gálvez detached Fages and a small number of men for Upper California. Later, Fages was to marry Eulalia, the daughter of Captain Callis. The document to which Serra refers is found in the Appendix.

7. This is not the only passage which proves that Serra harbored no resentment against Fages. When the captain was about to return to Mexico from his post in California, Father Serra wrote a letter from Monterey, July 19, 1774, to the viceroy in which he recommended Fages to the kind consideration of Bucareli as a good soldier who had acted frequently without reflection. The viceroy appreciated this gesture on the part of Father Serra and wrote to him, promising every consideration for Fages. Later Bucareli was to say that he repented having withdrawn Fages from California "after I had come to know him" (Instructions of Bucareli to Teodoro de Croix, March 20, 1777. Houghton Library, Harvard J. Spark's Collection, no. 98, vol. III, no. 15, art. 46). Perhaps Bucareli's reappraisal of Fages was aided by the knowledge that the captain enjoyed the special favor of the powerful Gálvez.

8. Palóu, *Memoirs*, II, 121-122, says that the viceroy did not grant this request on behalf of Ortega because his military rank was too low. However, Bucareli did promote him to the rank

of lieutenant with residence at San Diego, which certainly pleased both Serra and the missionaries. Serra's letters are filled with the kindliest references to the character of this good man, who was a native of California. His descendants continued to play important roles in many epochs of California history.

9. This request was granted by the authorities in Mexico. Gálvez, however, considered the request excessive and wanted the missionaries to explain their reasons to the commanding officer. Some modern authors seem to have misunderstood the meaning of this request when they say, for example, that "Serra took rather an extreme position in claiming authority" over the soldiers. It seems quite evident from Serra's words, that he was not requesting any authority over any soldiers, he was merely trying to protect his Indians from the scandalous conduct of some soldiers. Very frequently only the missionary would know of such conduct and he may have gained it through confidential sources.

10. This suggestion was also approved, although in general and quite cautious terms. However, the missionaries were satisfied with the approval.

11. Serra was dealing here with an evil which the viceregal government of Mexico had never been able to control, despite its best efforts. Merchants continued to use weights and measures of variable value long after the colonial period had come to an end, and the people endured the practice. Theoretically, there was a standard set of weights and measures in Mexico City, to which all others should have conformed. Actually, each city or region, almost without exception, seems to have set up its own standards. This custom confused not only Father Serra, but confuses historians as well. Some of the weights and measures mentioned more frequently by Father Serra with their official equivalents are:

fanega.................2.58 bushels
almud................6.88 dry quarts
quartillo............1.72 dry quarts

It is virtually impossible to give a trustworthy equivalent of the *teroio*, a measure mentioned so frequently by Father Serra (See Manuel Carrera Stampa, "The Evolution of Weights and Measures in New Spain," *The Hispanic American Historical Review*, XXIX [1949], 2-24).

12. This gentleman had merited the gratitude of Serra through his efforts on behalf of the scurvy-stricken sailors at San Diego in 1769. See Letter 10.

13. The authorities in Mexico preferred to delay a decision in this matter until they were prepared to issue a complete code of basic laws for the new settlements. Gálvez, however, favored giving those Spaniards or pure *mestizos*, who married converted Indian women, a double share of land. At the same time, Gálvez wished to have forbidden the marriage of the Indians with the other castes (AGI, Guadalajara, 514).

14. This was Felipe de Barri (Barry), who up to this time was still the governor of both Lower and Upper California.

15. Serra was indeed given a copy of all agreements and decisions reached as a result of the conferences in which he had taken part. This copy was certified by the secretary of the viceroy, Don José de Gorraez. Perhaps this was the copy used by Palóu in his *Memoirs*, II, 56, where such certification is included.

Appendix B

Treaty of Guadalupe Hidalgo

The Treaty of Guadalupe Hidalgo, ending the Mexican War, was signed on February 2, 1848, by Nicholas P. Trist for the United States and by a special commission representing the collapsed government of Mexico. Trist disregarded a recall to Washington, and negotiated the treaty in violation of most of his instructions. The U.S. Senate reluctantly approved the treaty.

Under the treaty, Mexico ceded to the United States Upper California and New Mexico (including Arizona) and recognized U.S. claims over Texas, with the Rio Grande as its southern boundary. The United States in turn paid Mexico $15,000,000, assumed the claims of American citizens against Mexico, recognized prior land grants in the Southwest, and offered citizenship to any Mexicans residing in the area.

TREATY OF PEACE, FRIENDSHIP, LIMITS, AND SETTLEMENT BETWEEN THE UNITED STATES OF AMERICA AND THE UNITED MEXICAN STATES CONCLUDED AT GUADALUPE HIDALGO, FEBRUARY 2, 1848; RATIFICATION ADVISED BY SENATE, WITH AMENDMENTS, MARCH 10, 1848;

RATIFIED BY PRESIDENT, MARCH 16, 1848; RATIFICATIONS EXCHANGED AT QUERETARO, MAY 30, 1848; PROCLAIMED, JULY 4, 1848.

IN THE NAME OF ALMIGHTY GOD

The United States of America and the United Mexican States animated by a sincere desire to put an end to the calamities of the war which unhappily exists between the two Republics and to establish Upon a solid basis relations of peace and friendship, which shall confer reciprocal benefits upon the citizens of both, and assure the concord, harmony, and mutual confidence wherein the two people should live, as good neighbors have for that purpose appointed their respective plenipotentiaries, that is to say: The President of the United States has appointed Nicholas P. Trist, a citizen of the United States, and the President of the Mexican Republic has appointed Don Luis Gonzaga Cuevas, Don Bernardo Couto, and Don Miguel Atristain, citizens of the said Republic; Who, after a reciprocal communication of their respective full powers, have, under

285

the protection of Almighty God, the author of peace, arranged, agreed upon, and signed the following:

Treaty of Peace, Friendship, Limits, and Settlement between the United States of America and the Mexican Republic.

ARTICLE I

There shall be firm and universal peace between the United States of America and the Mexican Republic, and between their respective countries, territories, cities, towns, and people, without exception of places or persons.

ARTICLE II

Immediately upon the signature of this treaty, a convention shall be entered into between a commissioner or commissioners appointed by the General-in-chief of the forces of the United States, and such as may be appointed by the Mexican Government, to the end that a provisional suspension of hostilities shall take place, and that, in the places occupied by the said forces, constitutional order may be reestablished, as regards the political, administrative, and judicial branches, so far as this shall be permitted by the circumstances of military occupation.

ARTICLE III

Immediately upon the ratification of the present treaty by the Government of the United States, orders shall be transmitted to the commanders of their land and naval forces, requiring the latter (pro-

vided this treaty shall then have been ratified by the Government of the Mexican Republic, and the ratifications exchanged) immediately to desist from blockading any Mexican ports and requiring the former (under the same condition) to commence, at the earliest moment practicable, withdrawing all troops of the United State then in the interior of the Mexican Republic, to points that shall be selected by common agreement, at a distance from the seaports not exceeding thirty leagues; and such evacuation of the interior of the Republic shall be completed with the least possible delay; the Mexican Government hereby binding itself to afford every facility in it's power for rendering the same convenient to the troops, on their march and in their new positions, and for promoting a good understanding between them and the inhabitants. In like manner orders shall be despatched to the persons in charge of the custom houses at all ports occupied by the forces of the United States, requiring them (under the same condition) immediately to deliver possession of the same to the persons authorized by the Mexican Government to receive it, together with all bonds and evidences of debt for duties on importations and on exportations, not yet fallen due. Moreover, a faithful and exact account shall be made out, showing the entire amount of all duties on imports and on exports, collected at such custom-houses, or elsewhere in Mexico, by authority of the United States, from and after the day of ratification of this treaty by the Government of the Mexican Republic; and also an account of the cost of collection; and such entire amount, deducting only the cost of collection, shall be delivered to the Mexican Government, at the city of Mexico, within three months after the exchange of ratifications.

The evacuation of the capital of the Mexican Republic by the troops of the United States, in virtue of the above stipulation, shall be completed in one month after the orders there stipulated for shall have been received by the commander of said troops, or sooner if possible.

ARTICLE IV

Immediately after the exchange of ratifications of the present treaty all castles, forts, territories, places, and possessions, which have been taken or occupied by the forces of the United States during the present war, within the limits of the Mexican Republic, as about to be established by the following article, shall be definitely restored to the said Republic, together with all the artillery, arms, apparatus of war, munitions, and other public property, which were in the said castles and forts when captured, and which shall remain there at the time when this treaty shall be duly ratified by the Government of the Mexican Republic. To this end, immediately upon the signature of this treaty, orders shall be despatched to the American officers commanding such castles and forts, securing against the removal or destruction of any such artillery, arms, apparatus of war, munitions, or other public property. The city of Mexico, within the inner line of intrenchments surrounding the said city, is comprehended in the above stipulation, as regards the restoration of artillery, apparatus of war, & c.

The final evacuation of the territory of the Mexican Republic, by the forces of the United States, shall be completed in three months—from the said exchange of ratifications, or sooner if possible; the Mexican Government hereby engaging, as in the foregoing article to use all means in its power for facilitating such evacuation, and rendering it convenient to the troops, and for promoting a good understanding between them and the inhabitants.

If, however, the ratification of this treaty by both parties should not take place in time to allow the embarcation of the troops of the United States to be completed before the commencement of the sickly season, at the Mexican ports on the Gulf of Mexico, in such case a friendly arrangement shall be entered into between the General-in-Chief of the said troops and the Mexican Government, whereby healthy and otherwise suitable places, at a distance from the ports not exceeding thirty leagues, shall be designated for the residence of such troops as may not yet have embarked, until the return 1i of the healthy season. And the space of time here referred to as, comprehending the sickly season shall be understood to extend from the first day of May to the first day of November.

All prisoners of war taken on either side, on land or on sea, shall be restored as soon as practicable after the exchange of ratifications of this treaty. It is also agreed that if any Mexicans should now be held as captives by any savage tribe within the limits of the United States, as about to be established by the following article, the Government of the said United States will exact the release of such captives and cause them to be restored to their country.

ARTICLE V

The boundary line between the two Republics shall commence in the Gulf of Mexico, three leagues from land, opposite the mouth of the Rio Grande, otherwise called Rio Bravo del Norte, or Opposite the mouth of its deepest branch, if it should have more than one branch empty-ing directly into the sea; from thence up the middle of that river, following the deepest channel, where it has more than one, to the point where it strikes the southern boundary of New Mexico; thence, westwardly, along the whole southern boundary of New Mexico (which runs north of the town called Paso) to its western termination; thence, northward, along the western line of New Mexico, until it intersects the first branch of the river Gila; (or if it should not intersect any branch of that river, then to the point on the said line nearest to such branch, and thence in a direct line to the same); thence down the middle of the said branch and of the said river, until it empties into the Rio Colorado; thence across the Rio Colorado, following the division line between Upper and Lower California, to the Pacific Ocean.

The southern and western limits of New Mexico, mentioned in the article, are those laid down in the map entitled "Map of the United Mexican States, as organ-ized and defined by various acts of the Congress of said republic, and construct-ed according to the best authorities. Revised edition. Published at New York, in 1847, by J. Disturnell," of which map a copy is added to this treaty, bearing the signatures and seals of the undersigned Plenipotentiaries. And, in order to pre-clude all difficulty in tracing upon the ground the limit separating Upper from Lower California, it is agreed that the said limit shall consist of a straight line drawn from the middle of the Rio Gila, where it unites with the Colorado, to a point on the coast of the Pacific Ocean, distant one marine league due south of the southern-most point of the port of San Diego, according to the plan of said port made in the year 1782 by Don Juan Pantoja, sec-ond sailing-master of the Spanish fleet, and published at Madrid in the year 1802, in the atlas to the voyage of the schooners Sutil and Mexicana; of which plan a copy is hereunto added, signed and sealed by the respective Plenipotentiaries.

In order to designate the boundary line with due precision, upon authoritative maps, and to establish upon the ground land-marks which shall show the limits of both republics, as described in the present article, the two Governments shall each appoint a commissioner and a surveyor, who, before the expiration of one year from the date of the exchange of ratifica-tions of this treaty, shall meet at the port of San Diego, and proceed to run and mark the said boundary in its whole course to the mouth of the Rio Bravo del Norte. They shall keep journals and make out plans of their operations; and the result agreed upon by them shall be deemed a part of this treaty, and shall have the same force as if it were inserted therein. The two Governments will amica-bly agree regarding what may be necessary to these persons, and also as to their respective escorts, should such be neces-sary.

The boundary line established by this article shall be religiously respected by each of the two republics, and no change shall ever be made therein, except by the express and free consent of both nations, lawfully given by the General Government of each, in conformity with its own constitution.

ARTICLE VI

The vessels and citizens of the United States shall, in all time, have a free and uninterrupted passage by the Gulf of California, and by the river Colorado below its confluence with the Gila, to and from their possessions situated north of the boundary line defined in the preceding article; it being understood that this passage is to be by navigating the Gulf of California and the river Colorado, and not by land, without the express consent of the Mexican Government.

If, by the examinations which may be made, it should be ascertained to be practicable and advantageous to construct a road, canal, or railway, which should in whole or in part run upon the river Gila, or upon its right or its left bank, within the space of one marine league from either margin of the river, the Governments of both republics will form an agreement regarding its construction, in order that it may serve equally for the use and advantage of both countries.

ARTICLE VII

The river Gila, and the part of the Rio Bravo del Norte lying below the southern boundary of New Mexico, being, agreeably to the fifth article, divided in the middle between the two republics, the navigation of the Gila and of the Bravo

below said boundary shall be free and common to the vessels and citizens of both countries; and neither shall, without the consent of the other, construct any work that may impede or interrupt, in whole or in part, the exercise of this right; not even for the purpose of favoring new methods of navigation. Nor shall any tax or contribution, under any denomination or title, be levied upon vessels or persons navigating the same or upon merchandise or effects transported thereon, except in the case of landing upon one of their shores. If, for the purpose of making the said rivers navigable, or for maintaining them in such state, it should be necessary or advantageous to establish any tax or contribution, this shall not be done without the consent of both Governments.

The stipulations contained in the present article shall not impair the territorial rights of either republic within its established limits.

ARTICLE VIII

Mexicans now established in territories previously belonging to Mexico, and which remain for the future within the limits of the United States, as defined by the present treaty, shall be free to continue where they now reside, or to remove at any time to the Mexican Republic, retaining the property which they possess in the said territories, or disposing thereof, and removing the proceeds wherever they please, without their being subjected, on this account, to any contribution, tax, or charge whatever.

Those who shall prefer to remain in the said territories may either retain the title and rights of Mexican citizens, or acquire those of citizens of the United States. But they shall be under the obligation to make their election within one year from the date of the exchange of ratifications of this treaty; and those who shall remain in the said territories after the expiration of that year, without having declared their intention to retain the character of Mexicans, shall be considered to have elected to become citizens of the United States.

In the said territories, property of every kind, now belonging to Mexicans not established there, shall be inviolably respected. The present owners, the heirs of these, and all Mexicans who may hereafter acquire said property by contract, shall enjoy with respect to it guarantees equally ample as if the same belonged to citizens of the United States.

ARTICLE IX

The Mexicans who, in the territories aforesaid, shall not preserve the character of citizens of the Mexican Republic, conformably with what is stipulated in the preceding article, shall be incorporated into the Union of the United States. and be admitted at the proper time (to be judged of by the Congress of the United States) to the enjoyment of all the rights of citizens of the United States, according to the principles of the Constitution; and in the mean time, shall be maintained and protected in the free enjoyment of their liberty and property, and secured in the free exercise of their religion without; restriction.

ARTICLE X

[Stricken out by the United States Amendments]

ARTICLE XI

Considering that a great part of the territories, which, by the present treaty, are to be comprehended for the future within the limits of the United States, is now occupied by savage tribes, who will hereafter be under the exclusive control of the Government of the United States, and whose incursions within the territory of Mexico would be prejudicial in the extreme, it is solemnly agreed that all such incursions shall be forcibly restrained by the Government of the United States whensoever this may be necessary; and that when they cannot be prevented, they shall be punished by the said Government, and satisfaction for the same shall be exacted all in the same way, and with equal diligence and energy, as if the same incursions were meditated or committed within its own territory, against its own citizens.

It shall not be lawful, under any pretext whatever, for any inhabitant of the United States to purchase or acquire any Mexican, or any foreigner residing in Mexico, who may have been captured by Indians inhabiting the territory of either of the two republics; nor to purchase or acquire horses, mules, cattle, or property of any kind, stolen within Mexican territory by such Indians.

And in the event of any person or persons, captured within Mexican territory by Indians, being carried into the territory of the United States, the Government of the latter engages and binds itself, in the most solemn manner, so soon as it shall know of such captives being within its territory, and shall be able so to do, through the faithful exercise of its influence and power, to rescue them and return them to their country. or deliver them to the agent or representative of the Mexican Government. The Mexican authorities will, as far as practicable, give to the Government of the United States notice of such captures; and its agents shall pay the expenses incurred in the maintenance and transmission of the rescued captives; who, in the mean time, shall be treated with the utmost hospitality by the American authorities at the place where they may be. But if the Government of the United States, before receiving such notice from Mexico, should obtain intelligence, through any other channel, of the existence of Mexican captives within its territory, it will proceed forthwith to effect their release and delivery to the Mexican agent, as above stipulated.

For the purpose of giving to these stipulations the fullest possible efficacy, thereby affording the security and redress demanded by their true spirit and intent, the Government of the United States will now and hereafter pass, without unnecessary delay, and always vigilantly enforce, such laws as the nature of the subject may require. And, finally, the sacredness of this obligation shall never be lost sight of by the said Government, when providing for the removal of the Indians from any portion of the said territories, or for its

being settled by citizens of the United States; but, on the contrary, special care shall then be taken not to place its Indian occupants under the necessity of seeking new homes, by committing those invasions which the United States have solemnly obliged themselves to restrain.

ARTICLE XII

In consideration of the extension acquired by the boundaries of the United States, as defined in the fifth article of the present treaty, the Government of the United States engages to pay to that of the Mexican Republic the sum of fifteen millions of dollars.

Immediately after the treaty shall have been duly ratified by the Government of the Mexican Republic, the sum of three millions of dollars shall be paid to the said Government by that of the United States, at the city of Mexico, in the gold or silver coin of Mexico The remaining twelve millions of dollars shall be paid at the same place, and in the same coin, in annual installments of three millions of dollars each, together with interest on the same at the rate of six per centum per annum. This interest shall begin to run upon the whole sum of twelve millions from the day of the ratification of the present treaty by the Mexican Government, and the first of the installments shall be paid at the expiration of one year from the same day. Together with each annual installment, as it falls due, the whole interest accruing on such installment from the beginning shall also be paid.

ARTICLE XIII

The United States engage, moreover, to assume and pay to the claimants all the amounts now due them, and those hereafter to become due, by reason of the claims already liquidated and decided against the Mexican Republic, under the conventions between the two republics severally concluded on the eleventh day of April, eighteen hundred and thirty-nine, and on the thirtieth day of January, eighteen hundred and forty-three; so that the Mexican Republic shall be absolutely exempt, for the future, from all expense whatever on account of the said claims.

ARTICLE XIV

The United States do furthermore discharge the Mexican Republic from all claims of citizens of the United States, not heretofore decided against the Mexican Government, which may have arisen previously to the date of the signature of this treaty; which discharge shall be final and perpetual, whether the said claims be rejected or be allowed by the board of commissioners provided for in the following article, and whatever shall be the total amount of those allowed.

ARTICLE XV

The United States, exonerating Mexico from all demands on account of the claims of their citizens mentioned in the preceding article, and considering them entirely and forever canceled, whatever their amount may be, undertake to make satisfaction for the same, to an amount not exceeding three and one-quarter millions of dollars. To ascertain the validity and amount of those claims, a board of commissioners shall be established by the Government of the United States, whose awards shall be final and conclusive; provided that, in deciding upon the validity of each claim, the board shall be guided and governed by the principles and rules of decision prescribed by the first and fifth articles of the unratified convention, concluded at the city of Mexico on the twentieth day of November, one thousand eight hundred and forty-three; and in no case shall an award be made in favour of any claim not embraced by these principles and rules.

If, in the opinion of the said board of commissioners or of the claimants, any books, records, or documents, in the possession or power of the Government of the Mexican Republic, shall be deemed necessary to the just decision of any claim, the commissioners, or the claimants through them, shall, within such period as Congress may designate, make an application in writing for the same, addressed to the Mexican Minister of Foreign Affairs, to be transmitted by the Secretary of State of the United States; and the Mexican Government engages, at the earliest possible moment after the receipt of such demand, to cause any of the books, records, or documents so specified, which shall be in their possession or power (or authenticated copies or extracts of the same), to be transmitted to the said Secretary of State, who shall immediately deliver them over to the said board of commissioners; provided that no such application shall be made by or at the instance of any claimant, until the facts which it is expected to prove by such books, records, or documents, shall have been stated under oath or affirmation.

ARTICLE XVI

Each of the contracting parties reserves to itself the entire right to fortify whatever point within its territory it may judge proper so to fortify for its security.

ARTICLE XVII

The treaty of amity, commerce, and navigation, concluded at the city of Mexico, on the fifth day of April, A. D. 1831, between the United States of America and the United Mexican States, except the additional article, and except so far as the stipulations of the said treaty may be incompatible with any stipulation contained in the present treaty, is hereby revived for the period of eight years from the day of the exchange of ratifications of this treaty, with the same force and virtue as if incorporated therein; it being understood that each of the contracting parties reserves to itself the right, at any time after the said period of eight years shall have expired, to terminate the same by giving one year's notice of such intention to the other party.

ARTICLE XVIII

All supplies whatever for troops of the United States in Mexico, arriving at ports in the occupation of such troops previous to the final evacuation thereof, although subsequently to the restoration of the cus-tom-houses at such ports, shall be entirely exempt from duties and charges of any kind; the Government of the United States hereby engaging and pledging its faith to establish and vigilantly to enforce, all possible guards for securing the revenue of Mexico, by preventing the importation, under cover of this stipulation, of any articles other than such, both in kind and in quantity, as shall really be wanted for the use and consumption of the forces of the United States during the time they may remain in Mexico. To this end it shall be the duty of all officers and agents of the United States to denounce to the Mexican authorities at the respective ports any attempts at a fraudulent abuse of this stipulation, which they may know of, or may have reason to suspect, and to give to such authorities all the aid in their power with regard thereto; and every such attempt, when duly proved and established by sentence of a competent tribunal, They shall be punished by the confiscation of the property so attempted to be fraudulently introduced.

ARTICLE XIX

With respect to all merchandise, effects, and property whatsoever, imported into ports of Mexico, whilst in the occupation of the forces of the United States, whether by citizens of either republic, or by citizens or subjects of any neutral nation, the following rules shall be observed:

(1) All such merchandise, effects, and property, if imported previously to the restoration of the custom-houses to the Mexican authorities, as stipulated for in

the third article of this treaty, shall be exempt from confiscation, although the importation of the same be prohibited by the Mexican tariff.

(2) The same perfect exemption shall be enjoyed by all such merchandise, effects, and property, imported subsequently to the restoration of the custom-houses, and previously to the sixty days fixed in the following article for the coming into force of the Mexican tariff at such ports respectively; the said merchandise, effects, and property being, however, at the time of their importation, subject to the payment of duties, as provided for in the said following article.

(3) All merchandise, effects, and property described in the two rules foregoing shall, during their continuance at the place of importation, and upon their leaving such place for the interior, be exempt from all duty, tax, or imposts of every kind, under whatsoever title or denomination. Nor shall they be there subject to any charge whatsoever upon the sale thereof.

(4) All merchandise, effects, and property, described in the first and second rules, which shall have been removed to any place in the interior, whilst such place was in the occupation of the forces of the United States, shall, during their continuance therein, be exempt from all tax upon the sale or consumption thereof, and from every kind of impost or contribution, under whatsoever title or denomination.

(5) But if any merchandise, effects, or property, described in the first and second rules, shall be removed to any place not occupied at the time by the forces of the United States, they shall, upon their introduction into such place, or upon their sale or consumption there, be subject to the same duties which, under the Mexican laws, they would be required to pay in such cases if they had been imported in time of peace, through the maritime custom-houses, and had there paid the duties conformably with the Mexican tariff.

(6) The owners of all merchandise, effects, or property, described in the first and second rules, and existing in any port of Mexico, shall have the right to reship the same, exempt from all tax, impost, or contribution whatever.

With respect to the metals, or other property, exported from any Mexican port whilst in the occupation of the forces of the United States, and previously to the restoration of the custom-house at such port, no person shall be required by the Mexican authorities, whether general or state, to pay any tax, duty, or contribution upon any such exportation, or in any manner to account for the same to the said authorities.

ARTICLE XX

Through consideration for the interests of commerce generally, it is agreed, that if less than sixty days should elapse between the date of the signature of this treaty and the restoration of the custom houses, conformably with the stipulation in the third article, in such case all merchandise, effects and property whatsoever, arriving at the Mexican ports after the restoration of the said custom-houses, and previously to the expiration of sixty days after the day of signature of this treaty, shall be admitted to entry; and no other duties shall be levied thereon than the duties established by the tariff found in force at such custom-houses at the time of the restoration of the same. And to all such merchandise, effects, and property, the rules established by the preceding article shall apply.

ARTICLE XXI

If unhappily any disagreement should hereafter arise between the Governments of the two republics, whether with respect to the interpretation of any stipulation in this treaty, or with respect to any other particular concerning the political or commercial relations of the two nations, the said Governments, in the name of those nations, do promise to each other that they will endeavour, in the most sincere and earnest manner, to settle the differences so arising, and to preserve the state of peace and friendship in which the two countries are now placing themselves, using, for this end, mutual representations and pacific negotiations. And if, by these means, they should not be enabled to come to an agreement, a resort shall not, on this account, be had to reprisals, aggression, or hostility of any kind, by the one republic against the other, until the Government of that which deems itself aggrieved shall have maturely considered, in the spirit of peace and good neighbourship, whether it would not be better that such difference should be settled by the arbitration of commissioners appointed on each side, or by that of a friendly nation. And should such course be proposed by either party, it shall be acceded to by the other, unless deemed by it altogether incompatible with the nature of the difference, or the circumstances of the case.

ARTICLE XXII

If (which is not to be expected, and which God forbid) war should unhappily break out between the two republics, they do now, with a view to such calamity, solemnly pledge themselves to each other and to the world to observe the following rules; absolutely where the nature of the subject permits, and as closely as possible in all cases where such absolute observance shall be impossible:

(1) The merchants of either republic then residing in the other shall be allowed to remain twelve months (for those dwelling in the interior), and six months (for those dwelling at the seaports) to collect their debts and settle their affairs; during which periods they shall enjoy the same protection, and be on the same footing, in all respects, as the citizens or subjects of the most friendly nations; and, at the expiration thereof, or at any time before, they shall have full liberty to depart, carrying off all their effects without molestation or hindrance, conforming therein to the same laws which the citizens or subjects of the most friendly nations are required to conform to. Upon the entrance of the armies of either nation into the territories of the other, women and children, ecclesiastics, scholars of every faculty, cultivators of the earth, merchants, artisans, manufacturers, and fishermen, unarmed and inhabiting unfortified towns, villages, or places, and in general all persons whose occupations are for the common subsistence and benefit of

mankind, shall be allowed to continue their respective employments, unmolested in their persons. Nor shall their houses or goods be burnt or otherwise destroyed, nor their cattle taken, nor their fields wasted, by the armed force into whose power, by the events of war, they may happen to fall; but if the necessity arise to take anything from them for the use of such armed force, the same shall be paid for at an equitable price. All churches, hospitals, schools, colleges, libraries, and other establishments for charitable and beneficent purposes, shall be respected, and all persons connected with the same protected in the discharge of their duties, and the pursuit of their vocations.

(2). In order that the fate of prisoners of war may be alleviated all such practices as those of sending them into distant, inclement or unwholesome districts, or crowding them into close and noxious places, shall be studiously avoided. They shall not be confined in dungeons, prison ships, or prisons; nor be put in irons, or bound or otherwise restrained in the use of their limbs. The officers shall enjoy liberty on their paroles, within convenient districts, and have comfortable quarters; and the common soldiers shall be dispose(in cantonments, open and extensive enough for air and exercise and lodged in barracks as roomy and good as are provided by the party in whose power they are for its own troops. But if any office shall break his parole by leaving the district so assigned him, or any other prisoner shall escape from the limits of his cantonment after they shall have been designated to him, such individual, officer, or other prisoner, shall forfeit so much of the benefit of this article as provides for his liberty on parole or in cantonment. And if any officer so breaking his parole or any common soldier so escaping from the limits assigned him, shall afterwards be found in arms previously to his being regularly exchanged, the person so offending shall be dealt with according to the established laws of war. The officers shall be daily furnished, by the party in whose power they are, with as many rations, and of the same articles, as are allowed either in kind or by commutation, to officers of equal rank in its own army; and all others shall be daily furnished with such ration as is allowed to a common soldier in its own service; the value of all which supplies shall, at the close of the war, or at periods to be agreed upon between the respective commanders, be paid by the other party, on a mutual adjustment of accounts for the subsistence of prisoners; and such accounts shall not be mingled with or set off against any others, nor the balance due on them withheld, as a compensation or reprisal for any cause whatever, real or pretended Each party shall be allowed to keep a commissary of prisoners, appointed by itself, with every cantonment of prisoners, in possession of the other; which commissary shall see the prisoners as often as he pleases; shall be allowed to receive, exempt from all duties a taxes, and to distribute, whatever comforts may be sent to them by their friends; and shall be free to transmit his reports in open letters to the party by whom he is employed.

And it is declared that neither the pretense that war dissolves all treaties, nor any other whatever, shall be considered as annulling or suspending the solemn covenant contained in this article. On the contrary, the state of war is precisely that for which it is provided; and, during which, its stipulations are to be as sacredly observed as the most acknowledged obligations under the law of nature or nations.

ARTICLE XXIII

This treaty shall be ratified by the President of the United States of America, by and with the advice and consent of the Senate thereof; and by the President of the Mexican Republic, with the previous approbation of its general Congress; and the ratifications shall be exchanged in the City of Washington, or at the seat of Government of Mexico, in four months from the date of the signature hereof, or sooner if practicable.

In faith whereof we, the respective Plenipotentiaries, have signed this treaty of peace, friendship, limits, and settlement, and have hereunto affixed our seals respectively. Done in quintuplicate, at the city of Guadalupe Hidalgo, on the second day of February, in the year of our Lord one thousand eight hundred and forty-eight.

N. P. TRIST
LUIS P. CUEVAS
BERNARDO COUTO
MIGL. ATRISTAIN

ADDENDUM:

The text of Article IX was modified by the U.S. Senate, and Article X was deleted in its entirety. The treaty, as it was ratified, is presented above. The original text of Articles IX and Article X appear below. The *Protocol of Queretaro,* also included below, clarified what was meant by the U.S. Senate modifications of the original treaty.

ARTICLE IX

The Mexicans, who, in the territories aforesaid, shall not preserve the character of citizens of the Mexican Republic, conformably with what is stipulated in the preceding Article, shall be incorporated into the Union of the United States, and admitted as soon as possible, according to the principles of the Federal Constitution, to the enjoyment of all the rights of citizens of the United States. In the mean time, they shall be maintained and protected in the enjoyment of their liberty, their property, and the civil rights now vested in them according to the Mexican laws. With respect to political rights, their condition shall be on an equality with that of the inhabitants of the other territories of the United States; and at least equally good as that of the inhabitants of Louisiana and the Floridas, when these provinces, by transfer from the French Republic and the Crown of Spain, became territories of the United States.

The same most ample guaranty shall be enjoyed by all ecclesiastics and religions corporations or communities, as well in the discharge of the offices of their ministry, as in the enjoyment of their property of every kind, whether individual or corporate. This guaranty shall embrace all temples, houses and edifices dedicated to the Roman Catholic worship; as well as all property destined to it's [sic] support, or to that of schools, hospitals and other foundations for charitable or beneficent purposes. No property of this nature shall be considered as having become the property of the American Government, or as subject to be, by it, disposed of or diverted to other uses.

Finally, the relations and communication between the Catholics living in the territories aforesaid, and their respective ecclesiastical authorities, shall be open, free and exempt from all hindrance whatever, even although such authorities should reside within the limits of the Mexican Republic, as defined by this treaty; and this freedom shall continue, so long as a new demarcation of ecclesiastical districts shall not have been made, conformably with the laws of the Roman Catholic Church.

ARTICLE X

All grants of land made by the Mexican Government or by the component authorities, in territories previously appertaining to Mexico, and remaining for the future within the limits of the United States, shall be respected as valid, to the same extent that the same grants would be valid, if the said territories had remained within the limits of Mexico. But the grantees of lands in Texas, put in possession thereof, who, by reason of the circumstances of the country since the beginning of the troubles between Texas and the Mexican Government, may have been prevented from fulfilling all the conditions of their grants, shall be under the obligation to fulfill said conditions within the periods limited in the same respectively; such periods to be now counted from the date of exchange of ratifications of this

treaty: in default of which the said grants shall not be obligatory upon the State of Texas, in virtue of the stipulations contained in this Article.

The foregoing stipulation in regard to grantees of land in Texas, is extended to all grantees of land in the territories aforesaid, elsewhere than Texas, put in possession under such grants; and, in default of the fulfillment of the conditions of any such grant, within the new period, which, as is above stipulated, begins with the day of the exchange of ratifications of this treaty, the same shall be null and void.

PROTOCOL OF QUERETARO

In the city of Queretaro on the twenty sixth of the month of May eighteen hundred and forty-eight at a conference between Their Excellencies Nathan Clifford and Ambrose H. Sevier Commissioners of the United States of America, with full powers from their Government to make to the Mexican Republic suitable explanations in regard to the amendments which the Senate and Government of the said United States have made in the treaty of peace, friendship, limits and definitive settlement between the two Republics, signed in Guadalupe Hidalgo, on the second day of February of the present year, and His Excellency Don Luis de la Rosa, Minister of Foreign Affairs of the Republic of Mexico, it was agreed, after adequate conversation respecting the changes alluded to, to record in the present protocol the following explanations which Their aforesaid Excellencies the Commissioners gave in the name of their Government and in fulfillment of the Commission conferred upon them near the Mexican Republic.

First

The American Government by suppressing the IXth article of the Treaty of Guadalupe and substituting the III article of the Treaty of Louisiana did not intend to diminish in any way what was agreed upon by the aforesaid article IXth in favor of the inhabitants of the territories ceded by Mexico. Its understanding that all of that agreement is contained in the IIId article of the Treaty of Louisiana. In consequence, all the privileges and guarantees, civil, political and religious, which would have been possessed by the inhabitants of the ceded territories, if the IXth article of the Treaty had been retained, will be enjoyed by them without any difference under the article which has been substituted.

Second

The American Government, by suppressing the Xth article of the Treaty of Guadalupe did not in any way intend to annul the grants of lands made by Mexico in the ceded territories. These grants, notwithstanding the suppression of the article of the Treaty, preserve the legal value which they may possess; and the grantees may cause their legitimate titles to be acknowledged before the American tribunals.

Conformably to the law of the United States, legitimate titles to every description of property personal and real, existing in the ceded territories, are those which were legitimate titles under the American law in California and New

Mexico up to the 13th of May 1846, and in Texas up to the 2d March 1836.

Third

The Government of the United States by suppressing the concluding paragraph of article XIIth of the Treaty, did not intend to deprive the Mexican Republic of the free and unrestrained faculty of ceding, conveying or transferring at any time (as it may judge best) the sum of the twelfe [sic] millions of dollars which the same Government of the United States is to deliver in the places designated by the amended article.

And these explanations having been accepted by the Minister of Foreign Affairs of the Mexican Republic, he declared in name of his Government that with the understanding conveyed by them, the same Government would proceed to ratify the Treaty of Guadalupe as modified by the Senate and Government of the United States. In testimony of which their Excellencies the aforesaid Commissioners and the Minister have signed and sealed in quintuplicate the present protocol.

[Seal] A.H. Sevier
[Seal] Nathan Clifford
[Seal] Luis de la Rosa

SOURCES:

Griswold del Castillo, Richard, *The Treaty of Guadalupe Hidalgo: A Legacy of Conflict*. University of Oklahoma Press, Norman, 1990.

Grolier's *New Electronic Encyclopedia*, 1991.

Appendix C

California Declaration of Rights (1849)

Preamble

WE, the People of California, grateful to Almighty God for our freedom: in order to secure its blessings, do establish this Constitution.

Article I. Declaration of Rights.

Sec. 1

All men are by nature free and independent, and have certain unalienable rights, among which are those of enjoying and defending life and liberty; acquiring, possessing and protecting property; and pursuing and obtaining safety and happiness.

Sec. 2.

All political power in inherent in the people. Government is instituted for the protection, security and benefit of the people; and they have the right to alter or reform the same, whenever the public good may require it.

Sec. 3.

The right of trial by jury shall be secured to all, and remain inviolate for ever; but a jury trial may be waived by the parties, in all civil cases, in the manner to be prescribed by law.

Sec. 4.

The free exercise and enjoyment of religious profession and worship, without discrimination or preference, shall forever be allowed in this State; and no person shall be rendered incompetent to be a witness on account of his opinions on matters of religious belief; but the liberty of conscience, hereby secured, shall not be so construed as to acts of licentiousness, or justify practices inconsistent with the peace or safety of this State.

Sec. 5.

The privilege of Habeas Corpus shall not be suspended, unless when, in cases of rebellion or invasion, the public safety may require its suspension.

Sec. 6.

Excessive bail shall not be required, nor excessive fines imposed, nor shall cruel or unusual punishments be inflicted, nor shall witnesses be unreasonably detained.

Sec. 7.

All persons shall be bailable by sufficient sureties; unless for capital offenses, when the proof is evident or the presumption great.

Sec. 8.

No person shall be held to answer for a capital or otherwise infamous crime (except in cases of impeachment, and in cases of militia when in actual service, and the land and naval forces in time of war, or which this State may keep with the consent of Congress in time of peace, and in cases of petit larceny under the regulation of the Legislature), unless on presentment or indictment of a grand jury; and in any trial in any court whatever, the party accused shall be allowed to appear and defend in person and with counsel, as in civil actions. No person shall be subject to be twice put in jeopardy for the same offence; nor shall he be compelled, in any criminal case, to be a witness against himself, nor be deprived of life, liberty, or property, without due process of law; nor shall private property be taken without just compensation.

Sec. 9.

Every citizen may freely speak, write, and publish his sentiments on all subjects, being responsible for the abuse of that right; and no law shall be passed to restrain or abridge the liberty of speech or of the press. In all criminal prosecutions on indictments for libels, the truth may be given in evidence to the jury; and if it shall appear to the jury that the matter charged as libelous is true, and was published with good motives and for justifiable ends, the party shall be acquitted; and the jury shall have the right to determine the law and the fact.

Sec. 10.

The people shall have the right freely to assemble together, to consult for the common good, to instruct their representatives, and to petition the Legislature for redress of grievances.

Sec. 11.

All laws of a general nature shall have a uniform operation.

Sec. 12.

The military shall be subordinate to the civil power. No standing army shall be kept up by this State in time of peace; and in time of war no appropriation for a standing army shall be for a longer time than two years.

Sec. 13.

No soldier shall, in time of peace, be quartered in any house, without the consent of the owner; nor in time of war, except in the manner to be prescribed by law.

Sec. 14.

Representation shall be according to population.

Sec. 15.

No person shall be imprisoned for debt, in any civil action on mesne or final process, unless in cases of fraud; and no person shall be imprisoned for a militia fine in time of peace.

Sec. 16.

No bill of attainder, ex post facto law, or law impairing the obligation of contracts, shall ever be passed.

Sec. 17.

Foreigners who are, or may hereafter become bona fide residents of this State, shall enjoy the same rights in respect to the possession, enjoyment, and inheritance of property, as native born citizens.

Sec. 18.

Neither slavery, nor involuntary servitude, unless for the punishment of crimes, shall ever be tolerated in this State.

Sec. 19.

The right of the people to be secure in their persons, houses, papers, and effects, against unreasonable seizures and searches, shall not be violated; and no warrant shall issue but on probable cause, supported by oath or affirmation, particularly describing the place to be searched, and the persons and things to be seized.

Sec. 20.

Treason against the State shall consist only in levying war against it, adhering to it enemies, or giving them aid and comfort. No person shall be convicted of treason, unless on the evidence of two witnesses to the same overt act, or confession in open court.

Sec. 21.

This enumeration of rights shall not be construed to impair or deny others retained by the people.

Signers of the Original California Constitution

The signers of the original California Constitution were the 48 delegates to the constitutional convention. The convention met from September to November 1849 at Colton Hall in Monterey, California. The Constitution was written in both English and Spanish and provided that all major legislation was to be written in both languages. This requirement was dropped when a new constitution was formulated in 1878–1879.

Name	Nativity	Residence	Age
John A. Sutter	Switzerland		47
H.W. Halleck	New York	Monterey	32
William M. Gwin	Tennessee	San Francisco	44
William M. Steuart	Maryland	San Francisco	49
Joseph Hoborn	Maryland	San Francisco	39
Thomas L. Vermeule	New Jersey		35
O.M. Wozencraft	Ohio	San Joaquin	34
B.F. Moore	Florida	San Joaquin	29
William E. Shannon	New York	Sacramento	27
Winfield S. Sherwood	New York	Sacramento	32
Elam Brown	New York	San Jose	52
Joseph Aram	New York	San Jose	39
J.D. Hoppe	Maryland	San Jose	35
John McDougal	Ohio	Sutter	32
Elisha O. Crosby	New York	Vernon	34
H.K. Dimmick	New York	San Jose	34
Julian Hanks	Connecticut	San Jose	39
M.M. McCarver	Kentucky	Sacramento	42
Francis J. Lippitt	Rhode Island	San Francisco	37
Rodman M. Price	Massachusetts	Monterey	47
Thomas O. Larkin	New York	San Francisco	36
Louis Dent	Missouri	Monterey	26
Henry Hill	Virginia	Monterey	33
Charles T. Betts	Virginia	Monterey	40
Myron Norton	Vermont	San Francisco	27
James M. Jones	Kentucky	San Joaquin	25
Pedro Sainsevain	Bordeaux	San Jose	26

Name	Nativity	Residence	Age
José M. Covarrubias	France	Santa Barbara	41
Antonio M. Pico	California	San Jose	40
Jacinto Rodriguez	California	Monterey	36
Stephen G. Foster	Maine	Los Angeles	28
Henry A. Tefft	New York	San Luis Obispo	26
J.M.H. Hollingsworth	Maryland	San Joaquin	25
Abel Stearns	Massachusetts	Los Angeles	51
Hugh Reid	Scotland	San Gabriel	38
Benjamin S. Lippincott	New York	San Joaquin	34
Joel P. Walker	Virginia	Sonoma	52
Jacob R. Snyder	Pennsylvania	Sacramento	34
Lansford W. Hastings	Ohio	Sacramento	30
Pablo de la Guerra	California	Santa Barbara	30
M.G. Vallejo	California	Sonoma	42
José Antonio Carrillo	California	Los Angeles	53
Manuel Dominguez	California	Los Angeles	46
Robert Semple	Kentucky	Benicia	42
Pacificus Ord	Maryland	Monterey	33
Edward Gilbert	New York	San Francisco	27
A.J. Ellis	New York	San Francisco	33
Miguel de Pedrorena	Spain	San Diego	41

SOURCES:

Bancroft, Hubert Howe, *History of California.* San Francisco, A. L. Bancroft, 1884-90. Volume VI. p. 288.

Hart, James D. *A Companion to California.* Berkeley, University of California Press, 1987. p. 108

Appendix D

Federal Fugitive Slave Act (1850)

The Fugitive Slave Act was part of the group of laws referred to as the "Compromise of 1850." In this compromise, the antislavery advocates gained the admission of California as a free state, and the prohibition of slave-trading in the District of Columbia. The slavery party received concessions with regard to slaveholding in Texas and the passage of this law. Passage of this law was so hated by abolitionists, however, that its existence played a role in the end of slavery a little more than a dozen years later. This law also spurred the continued operation of the fabled Undergound Railroad, a network of over 3,000 homes and other "stations" that helped escaping slaves travel from the southern slave-holding states to the northern states and Canada.

SEC. 1.

BE ITenacted by the Senate and House of Representatives of the United States of America in Congress assembled, That the persons who have been, or may hereafter be, appointed commissioners, in virtue of any act of Congress, by the Circuit Courts of the United States, and Who, in consequence of such appointment, are authorized to exercise the powers that any justice of the peace, or other magistrate of any of the United States, may exercise in respect to offenders for any crime or offense against the United States, by arresting, imprisoning, or bailing the same under and by the virtue of the thirty-third section of the act of the twenty-fourth of September seventeen hundred and eighty-nine, entitled "An Act to establish the judicial courts of the United States" shall be, and are hereby, authorized and required to exercise and discharge all the powers and duties conferred by this act.

SEC. 2.

And be it further enacted, That the Superior Court of each organized Territory of the United States shall have the same power to appoint commissioners to take acknowledgments of bail and affidavits, and to take depositions of witnesses in civil causes, which is now possessed by the Circuit Court of the United States; and all commissioners who shall hereafter be appointed for such purposes by the Superior Court of any organized Territory of the United States, shall possess all the powers, and exercise all the duties, conferred by law upon the commissioners appointed by the Circuit Courts of the

United States for similar purposes, and shall moreover exercise and discharge all the powers and duties conferred by this act.

SEC. 3

And be it further enacted, That the Circuit Courts of the United States shall from time to time enlarge the number of the commissioners, with a view to afford reasonable facilities to reclaim fugitives from labor, and to the prompt discharge of the duties imposed by this act.

SEC. 4.

And be it further enacted, That the commissioners above named shall have concurrent jurisdiction with the judges of the Circuit and District Courts of the United States, in their respective circuits and districts within the several States, and the judges of the Superior Courts of the Territories, severally and collectively, in term-time and vacation; shall grant certificates to such claimants, upon satisfactory proof being made, with authority to ake and remove such fugitives from service or labor, under the restrictions herein contained, to the State or Territory from which such persons may have escaped or fled.

SEC. 5.

And be it further enacted, That it shall be the duty of all marshals and deputy marshals to obey and execute all warrants and precepts issued under the provisions of this act, when to them directed; and should any marshal or deputy marshal refuse to receive such warrant, or other process, when tendered, or to use all proper means diligently to execute the same, he shall, on conviction thereof, be fined in the sum of one thousand dollars, to the use of such claimant, on the motion of such claimant, by the Circuit or District Court for the district of such marshal; and after arrest of such fugitive, by such marshal or his deputy, or whilst at any time in his custody under the provisions of this act, should such fugitive escape, whether with or without the assent of such marshal or his deputy, such marshal shall be liable, on his official bond, to be prosecuted for the benefit of such claimant, for the full value of the service or labor of said fugitive in the State, Territory, or District whence he escaped: and the better to enable the said commissioners, when thus appointed, to execute their duties faithfully and efficiently, in conformity with the requirements of the Constitution of the United States and of this act, they are hereby authorized and empowered, within their counties respectively, to appoint, in writing under their hands, any one or more suitable persons, from time to time, to execute all such warrants and other process as may be issued by them in the lawful performance of their respective duties; with authority to such commissioners, or the persons to be appointed by them, to execute process as aforesaid, to summon and call to their aid the bystanders, or posse comitatus of the proper county, when necessary to ensure a faithful observance of the clause of the Constitution referred to, in conformity with the provisions of this act; and all good citizens are hereby commanded to aid and assist in the prompt and efficient execution of this law, whenever their services may be required, as aforesaid, for that purpose; and said warrants shall run, and be executed by said officers, any where in the State within which they are issued.

SEC. 6.

And be it further enacted, That when a person held to service or labor in any State or Territory of the United States, has heretofore or shall hereafter escape into another State or Territory of the United States, the person or persons to whom such service or labor may be due, or his, her, or their agent or attorney, duly authorized, by power of attorney, in writing, acknowledged and certified under the seal of some legal officer or court of the State or Territory in which the same may be executed, may pursue and reclaim such fugitive person, either by procuring a warrant from some one of the courts, judges, or commissioners aforesaid, of the proper circuit, district, or county, for the apprehension of such fugitive from service or labor, or by seizing and arresting such fugitive, where the same can be done without process, and by taking, or causing such person to be taken, forthwith before such court, judge, or commissioner, whose duty it shall be to hear and determine the case of such claimant in a summary manner; and upon satisfactory proof being made, by deposition or affidavit, in writing, to be taken and certified by such court, judge, or commissioner, or by other satisfactory testimony, duly taken and certified by some court, magistrate, justice of the peace, or other legal officer authorized to administer an oath and take depositions under the laws of the State or Territory from which such person owing service or labor may have escaped, with a certificate of such magistracy or other authority, as aforesaid, with the seal of the proper court or officer thereto attached, which seal shall be sufficient to establish the competency of the proof, and with proof, also by affidavit, of the identity of the person whose service or labor is claimed to be due as aforesaid, that the person so arrested does in fact owe service or labor to the person or persons claiming him or her, in the State or Territory from which such fugitive may have escaped as aforesaid, and that said person escaped, to make out and deliver to such claimant, his or her agent or attorney, a certificate setting forth the substantial facts as to the service or labor due from such fugitive to the claimant, and of his or her escape from the State or Territory in which he or she was arrested, with authority to such claimant, or his or her agent or attorney, to use such reasonable force and restraint as may be necessary, under the circumstances of the case, to take and remove such fugitive person back to the State or Territory whence he or she may have escaped as aforesaid. In no trial or hearing under this act shall the testimony of such alleged fugitive be admitted in evidence; and the certificates in this and the first [fourth] section mentioned, shall be conclusive of the right of the person or persons in whose favor granted, to remove such fugitive to the State or Territory from which he escaped, and shall prevent all molestation of such person or persons by any process issued by any court, judge, magistrate, or other person whomsoever.

SEC. 7.

And be it further enacted, That any person who shall knowingly and willingly obstruct, hinder, or prevent such claimant, his agent or attorney, or any person or persons lawfully assisting him, her, or them, from arresting such a fugitive from service or labor, either with or without process as aforesaid, or shall rescue, or attempt to rescue, such fugitive from service or labor, from the custody of such claimant, his or her agent or attorney, or other person or persons lawfully assisting as aforesaid, when so arrested, pursuant to the authority herein given and declared; or shall aid, abet, or assist such person so owing service or labor as aforesaid, directly or indirectly, to escape from such claimant, his agent or attorney, or other person or persons legally authorized as aforesaid; or shall harbor or conceal such fugitive, so as to prevent the discovery and arrest of such person, after notice or knowledge of the fact that such person was a fugitive from service or labor as aforesaid, shall, for either of said offences, be subject to a fine not exceeding one thousand dollars, and imprisonment not exceeding six months, by indictment and conviction before the District Court of the United States for the district in which such offence may have been committed, or before the proper court of criminal jurisdiction, if committed within any one of the organized Territories of the United States; and shall moreover forfeit and pay, by way of civil damages to the party injured by such illegal conduct, the sum of one thousand dollars for each fugitive so lost as aforesaid, to be recovered by action of debt, in any of the District or Territorial Courts aforesaid, within whose jurisdiction the said offence may have been committed.

SEC. 8.

And be it further enacted, That the marshals, their deputies, and the clerks of the said District and Territorial Courts, shall be paid, for their services, the like fees as may be allowed for similar services in other cases; and where such services are rendered exclusively in the arrest, custody, and delivery of the fugitive to the claimant, his or her agent or attorney, or where such supposed fugitive may be discharged out of custody for the want of sufficient proof as aforesaid, then such fees are to be paid in whole by such claimant, his or her agent or attorney; and in all cases where the proceedings are before a commissioner, he shall be entitled to a fee of ten dollars in full for his services in each case, upon the delivery of the said certificate to the claimant, his agent or attorney; or a fee of five dollars in cases where the proof shall not, in the opinion of such commissioner, warrant such certificate and delivery, inclusive of all services incident to such arrest and examination, to be paid, in either case, by the claimant, his or her agent or attorney. The person or persons authorized to execute the process to be issued by such commissioner for the arrest and detention of fugitives from service or labor as aforesaid, shall also be entitled to a fee of five dollars each for each person he or they may arrest, and take before any commissioner as aforesaid, at the instance and request of such claimant, with such other fees as may be deemed reasonable by such commissioner for such other additional services as may be necessarily performed by him or them; such as attending at the examination, keeping the fugitive in custody, and providing him with food and lodging during his detention, and until the final determination of such commissioners; and, in general, for performing such other duties as may be required by such claimant, his or her attorney or agent, or commissioner in the premises, such fees to be made up in conformity with the fees usually charged by the officers of the courts of justice within the proper district or county, as near as may be practicable, and paid by such claimants, their agents or attorneys, whether such supposed fugitives from service or labor be ordered to be delivered to such claimant by the final determination of such commissioner or not.

SEC. 9.

And be it further enacted, That, upon affidavit made by the claimant of such fugitive, his agent or attorney, after such certificate has been issued, that he has reason to apprehend that such fugitive will be rescued by force from his or their possession before he can be taken beyond the limits of the State in which the arrest is made, it shall be the duty of the officer making the arrest to retain such fugitive in his custody, and to remove him to the State whence he fled, and there to deliver him to said claimant, his agent, or attorney. And to this end, the officer aforesaid is hereby authorized and required to employ so many persons as he may deem necessary to overcome such force, and to retain them in his service so long as cir-

cumstances may require. The said officer and his assistants, while so employed, to receive the same compensation, and to be allowed the same expenses, as are now allowed by law for transportation of criminals, to be certified by the judge of the district within which the arrest is made, and paid out of the treasury of the United States.

SEC. 10.

And be it further enacted, That when any person held to service or labor in any State or Territory, or in the District of Columbia, shall escape therefrom, the party to whom such service or labor shall be due, his, her, or their agent or attorney, may apply to any court of record therein, or judge thereof in vacation, and make satisfactory proof to such court, or judge in vacation, of the escape aforesaid, and that the person escaping owed service or labor to such party. Whereupon the court shall cause a record to be made of the matters so proved, and also a general description of the person so escaping, with such convenient certainty as may be; and a transcript of such record, authenticated by the attestation of the clerk and of the seal of the said court, being produced in any other State, Territory, or district in which the person so escaping may be found, and being exhibited to any judge, commissioner, or other officer authorized by the law of the United States to cause persons escaping from service or labor to be delivered up, shall be held and taken to be full and conclusive evidence of the fact of escape, and that the service or labor of the person escaping is due to the party in such record mentioned. And upon the production by the said party of other and further evidence if necessary, either oral or by affidavit, in addition to what is contained in the said record of the identity of the person escaping, he or she shall be delivered up to the claimant. And the said court, commissioner, judge, or other person authorized by this act to grant certificates to claimants or fugitives, shall, upon the production of the record and other evidences aforesaid, grant to such claimant a certificate of his right to take any such person identified and proved to be owing service or labor as aforesaid, which certificate shall authorize such claimant to seize or arrest and transport such person to the State or Territory from which he escaped: Provided, That nothing herein contained shall be construed as requiring the production of a transcript of such record as evidence as aforesaid. But in its absence the claim shall be heard and determined upon other satisfactory proofs, competent in law.

Approved, September 18, 1850

SOURCE:

United States Statutes at Large

Appendix E

Railroad Land Grants in California

from a People's Independent Party map of 1875

Appendix F

Chinese Exclusion Act

Forty-Seventh Congress. Session I. 1882

An act to execute certain treaty stipulations relating to Chinese.

Preamble.

Whereas, in the opinion of the Government of the United States the coming of Chinese laborers to this country endangers the good order of certain localities within the territory thereof:

Therefore,

Be it enacted by the Senate and House of Representatives of the United States of America in Congress assembled, That from and after the expiration of ninety days next after the passage of this act, and until the expiration of ten years next after the passage of this act, the coming of Chinese laborers to the United States be, and the same is hereby, suspended; and during such suspension it shall not be lawful for any Chinese laborer to come, or, having so come after the expiration of said ninety days, to remain within the United States.

SEC. 2.

That the master of any vessel who shall knowingly bring within the United States on such vessel, and land or permit to be landed, and Chinese laborer, from any foreign port of place, shall be deemed guilty of a misdemeanor, and on conviction thereof shall be punished by a fine of not more than five hundred dollars for each and every such Chinese laborer so brought, and may be also imprisoned for a term not exceeding one year.

SEC. 3.

That the two foregoing sections shall not apply to Chinese laborers who were in the United States on the seventeenth day of November, eighteen hundred and eighty, or who shall have come into the same before the expiration of ninety days next after the passage of this act, and who shall produce to such master before going on board such vessel, and shall produce to the collector of the port in the United States at which such vessel shall arrive, the evidence hereinafter in this act required of his being one of the laborers in this section mentioned; nor shall the two foregoing sections apply to the case of any master whose vessel, being bound to a port not within the United States by reason of being in distress or in stress of weather, or touching at any port of the United States on its voyage to any foreign port of place: Provided, That all Chinese laborers brought on such vessel shall depart with the vessel on leaving port.

SEC. 4.

That for the purpose of properly indentifying Chinese laborers who were in the United States on the seventeenth day of November, eighteen hundred and eighty, or who shall have come into the same before the expiration of ninety days next after the passage of this act, and in order to furnish them with the proper evidence of their right to go from and come to the United States of their free will and accord, as provided by the treaty between the United States and China dated November seventeenth, eighteen hundred and eighty, the collector of customs of the district from which any such Chinese laborer shall depart from the United States shall, in person or by deputy, go on board each vessel having on board any such Chinese laborer and cleared or about to sail from his district for a foreign port, and on such vessel make a list of all such Chinese laborers, which shall be entered in registry-books to be kept for that purpose, in which shall be stated the name, age, occupation, last place of residence, physical marks or peculiarities, and all facts necessary for the identification of each of such Chinese laborers, which books shall be safely kept in the custom-house; and every such Chinese laborer so departing from the United States shall be entitled to, and shall receive, free of any charge or cost upon application therefor, from the collector or his deputy, at the time such list is taken, a certificate, signed by the collector or his deputy and attested by his seal of office, in such form as the Secretary of the Treasury shall prescribe, which certificate shall contain a statement of the name, age, occupation, last place of residence, personal description, and fact of identification of the Chinese laborer to whom the certificate is issued, corresponding with the said list and registry in all particulars. In case any Chinese laborer after having received such certificate shall leave such vessel before her departure he shall deliver his certificate to the master of the vessel, and if such Chinese laborer shall fail to return to such vessel before her departure from port the certificate shall be delivered by the master to the collector of customs for cancellation. The certificate herein provided for shall entitle the Chinese laborer to whom the same is issued to return to and re-enter the United States upon producing and delivering the same to the collector of customs of the district at which such Chinese laborer shall seek to re-enter; and upon delivery of such certificate by such Chinese laborer to the collector of customs at the time of re-entry in the United States, said collector shall cause the same to be filed in the custom house and duly canceled.

SEC. 5.

That any Chinese laborer mentioned in section four of this act being in the United States, and desiring to depart from the United States by land, shall have the right to demand and receive, free of charge or cost, a certificate of identification similar to that provided for in section four of this act to be issued to such Chinese laborers as may desire to leave the United States by water; and it is hereby made the duty of the collector of customs of the district next adjoining the foreign country to which said Chinese laborer desires to go to issue such certificate, free of charge or cost, upon application by such Chinese laborer, and to enter the same upon registry-books to be kept by him for the purpose, as provided for in section four of this act.

SEC. 6.

That in order to the faithful execution of articles one and two of the treaty in this act before mentioned, every Chinese person other than a laborer who may be entitled by said treaty and this act to come within the United States, and who shall be about to come to the United States, shall be identified as so entitled by the Chinese Government in each case, such identity to be evidenced by a certificate issued under the authority of said government, which certificate shall be in the English language or (if not in the English language) accompanied by a translation into English, stating such right to come, and which certificate shall state the name, title, or official rank, if any, the age, height, and all physical peculiarities, former and present occupation or profession, and place of residence in China of the person to whom the certificate is issued and that such person is entitled conformably to the treaty in this act mentioned to come within the United States. Such certificate shall be prima-facie evidence of the fact set forth therein, and shall be produced to the collector of customs, or his deputy, of the port in the district in the United States at which the person named therein shall arrive.

SEC. 7.

That any person who shall knowingly and falsely alter or substitute any name for the name written in such certificate or forge any such certificate, or knowingly utter any forged or fraudulent certificate, or falsely personate any person named in any such certificate, shall be deemed guilty of a misdemeanor; and upon conviction thereof shall be fined in a sum not exceeding one thousand dollars, an imprisoned in a penitentiary for a term of not more than five years.

SEC. 8.

That the master of any vessel arriving in the United States from any foreign port or place shall, at the same time he delivers a manifest of the cargo, and if there be no cargo, then at the time of making a report of the entry of vessel pursuant to the law, in addition to the other matter required to be reported, and before landing, or permitting to land, any Chinese passengers, deliver and report to the collector of customs of the district in which such vessels shall have arrived a separate list of all Chinese passengers taken on board his vessel at any foreign port or place, and all such passengers on board the vessel at that time. Such list shall show the names of such passengers (and if accredited officers of the Chinese Government traveling on the business of that government, or their servants, with a note of such facts), and the name and other particulars, as shown by their respective certificates; and such list shall be sworn to by the master in the manner required by law in relation to the manifest of the cargo. Any willful refusal or neglect of any such master to comply with the provisions of this section shall incur the same penalties and forfeiture as are provided for a refusal or neglect to report and deliver a manifest of cargo.

SEC. 9.

That before any Chinese passengers are landed from any such vessel, the collector, or his deputy, shall proceed to examine such passengers, comparing the certificates with the list and with the passengers; and no passenger shall be allowed to land in the United States from such vessel in violation of law.

SEC. 10.

That every vessel whose master shall knowingly violate any of the provisions of this act shall be deemed forfeited to the United States, and shall be liable to seizure and condemnation on any district of the United States into which such vessel may enter or in which she may be found.

SEC. 11.

That any person who shall knowingly bring into or cause to be brought into the United States by land, or who shall knowingly aid or abet the same, or aid or abet the landing in the United States from any vessel of any Chinese person not lawfully entitled to enter the United States, shall be deemed guilty of a misdemeanor, and shall, on conviction thereof, be fined in a sum not exceeding one thousand dollars, and imprisoned for a term not exceeding one year.

SEC. 12.

That no Chinese person shall be permitted to enter the United States by land without producing to the proper officer of customs the certificate in this act required

of Chinese persons seeking to land from a vessel. And any Chinese person found unlawfully within the United States shall be caused to be removed therefrom to the country from whence he came, by direction of the United States, after being brought before some justice, judge, or commissioner of a court of the United States and found to be one not lawfully entitled to be or remain in the United States.

SEC. 13.

That this act shall not apply to diplomatic and other officers of the Chinese Government traveling upon the business of that government, whose credentials shall be taken as equivalent to the certificate in this act mentioned, and shall exempt them and their body and household servants from the provisions of this act as to other Chinese persons.

SEC. 14.

That hereafter no State court or court of the United States shall admit Chinese to citizenship; and all laws in conflict with this act are hereby repealed.

SEC. 15.

That the words "Chinese laborers," whenever used in this act, shall be construed to mean both skilled and unskilled laborers and Chinese employed in mining.

Approved, May 6, 1882

SOURCE:

United States Statutes at Large

Appendix G

Executive Order No. 9066 Japanese Relocation Order (1942)

AUTHORIZING THE SECRETARY OF WAR TO PRESCRIBE MILITARY AREAS

Executive Order No. 9066

WHEREAS the successful prosecution of the war requires every possible protection against espionage and against sabotage to national-defense material, national-defense premises, and national-defense utilities as defined in section 4, Act of April 20, 1918, 40 Stat. 533, as amended by the act of November 30, 1940, 54 Stat. 1220, and the Act of August 21, 1941, 55 Stat. 655 (U. S. C., Title 50, Sec. 104):

NOW, THEREFORE, by virtue of the authority vested in me as President of the United States, and Commander in Chief of the Army and Navy, I hereby authorize and direct the Secretary of War, and the Military Commanders whom he may from time to time designate, whenever he or any designated Commander deems such actions necessary or desirable, to prescribe military areas in such places and of such extent as he or the appropriate Military Commanders may determine, from which any or all persons may be excluded, and with such respect to which, the right of any person to enter, remain in, or leave shall be subject to whatever restrictions the Sectary of War or the appropriate Military Commander may impose in his discretion. The Secretary of War is hereby authorized to provide for residents of any such area who are excluded therefrom, such transportation, food, shelter, and other accommodations as may be necessary, in the judgement of the Secretary of War or the said Military Commander, and until other arrangements are made, to accomplish the purpose of this order. The designation of military areas in any region or locality shall supersede designations of prohibited and restricted areas by the Attorney General under the Proclamations of December 7 and 8, 1941, and shall supersede the responsibility and authority of the Attorney General under the said Proclamations in respect of such prohibited and restricted areas.

I hereby further authorize and direct the Secretary of War and the said Military Commanders to take such other steps as he or the appropriate Military Commander may deem advisable to enforce compliance with the restrictions applicable to each Military area herein-above authorized to be designated, including the use of Federal troops and other Federal Agencies, with authority to accept assistance of state and local agencies.

I hereby further authorize and direct all Executive Departments, independent establishments and other Federal Agencies, to assist the Secretary of War or the said Military Commanders in carrying out this Executive Order, including the furnishing of medical aid, hospitalization, food, clothing, transportation, use of land, shelter, and other supplies, equipment, utilities, facilities and services.

This order shall not be construed as modifying or limiting in any way the authority heretofore granted under Executive Order No. 8972, dated December 12, 1941, nor shall it be construed as limiting or modifying the duty and responsibility of the Federal Bureau of Investigation, with respect to the investigation of alleged acts of sabotage or the duty and responsibility of the Attorney General and the Department of Justice under the Proclamations of December 7 and 8, 1941, prescribing regulations for the conduct and control of alien enemies, except as such duty and responsibility is superseded by the designation of military areas hereunder.

FRANKLIN D. ROOSEVELT
February 19, 1942

Appendix H

WESTERN DEFENSE COMMAND AND FOURTH ARMY
WARTIME CIVIL CONTROL ADMINISTRATION

Presidio of San Francisco, California
May 3, 1942

INSTRUCTIONS

TO ALL PERSONS OF

JAPANESE

ANCESTRY

Living in the Following Area:

All of that portion of the City of Los Angeles, State of California, within that boundary beginning at the point at which North Figueroa Street meets a line following the middle of the Los Angeles River; thence southerly and following the said line to East First Street ; thence westerly on East First Street to Alameda Street ; thence southerly on Alameda Street to East Third Street; thence northwesterly on East Third Street to Main Street; thence northerly on Main Street to First Street; thence north-westerly on First Street to Figueroa Street; thence northeasterly on Figueroa Street to the point of beginning.

Pursuant to the provisions of Civilian Exclusion Order No. 33, this Headquarters, dated May 3, 1942, all persons of Japanese ancestry, both alien and non-alien, will be evacuated from the above area by 12 o'clock noon, P. W . T., Saturday, May 9, 1942.

No Japanese person living in the above area will be permitted to change residence after 12 o'clock noon, P.W.T., Sunday, May 3, 1942, without obtaining special permission from the representative of the Commanding General, Southern California Sector, at the Civil Control Station located at:

Japanese Union Church,
120 North San Pedro Street,
Los Angeles, California.

321

Such permits will only be granted for the purpose of uniting members of a family, or in cases of grave emergency.

The Civil Control Station is equipped to assist the Japanese Population affected by this evacuation in the following ways:

1. Give advice and instructions on the evacuation.

2. Provide services with respect to the management, leasing, sale, storage or other disposition of most kinds of property, such as real estate, business and professional equipment, household goods, boats, automobiles and livestock.

3. Provide temporary residence elsewhere for all Japanese in family groups.

4. Transport persons and a limited amount of clothing and equipment to their new residence.

The Following Instructions Must Be Observed:

1. A responsible member of each family, preferably the head of the family, or the person in whose name most of the property is held, and each individual living alone, will report to the Civil Control Station to receive further instructions. This must be done between 8:00 A. M. and 5:00 P. M. on Monday, May 4, 1942, or between 8:00 A. M. and 5:00 P. M. on Tuesday, May 5, 1942.

2. Evacuees must carry with them on departure for the Assembly Center, the following property:

(a) Bedding and linens (no mattress) for each member of the family;

(b) Toilet articles for each member of the family;

(c) Extra clothing for each member of the family;

(d) Sufficient knives, forks, spoons, plates, bowls and cups for each member of the family;

(e) Essential personal effects for each member of the family.

All items carried will be securely packaged, tied and plainly marked with the name of the owner and numbered in accordance with instructions obtained at the Civil Control Station. The size and number of the packages is limited to that which can be carried by the individual or family group.

3. No pets of any kind will be permitted.

4. No personal items and no household goods will be shipped to the Assembly Center.

5. The United States Government through its agencies will provide for the storage, at the sole risk of the owner, of the more substantial household items, such as iceboxes, washing machines, pianos and other heavy furniture. Cooking utensils and other small items will be accepted for storage if crated, packed and plainly marked with the name and address of the owner. Only one name and address will be used by a given family.

6. Each family, and individual living alone, will be furnished transportation to the Assembly Center or will be authorized to travel by private automobile in a supervised group. All instructions pertaining to the movement will be obtained at the Civil Control Station.

Go to the Civil Control Station between the hours of 8:00 A. M. and 5:00 P. M.,
Monday, May 4, 1942, or between the hours of 8:00 A. M. and 5:00 P. M.,
Tuesday, May 5, 1942, to receive further instructions.

J.L DeWITT
Lieutenant General, U. S. Army
Commanding

Appendix I

Joel Franks

Progressives and the California Alien Land Laws

As California's population has evolved and changed so too has the state's body of law. People of color have had very different experiences with the United States law than have most Whites. Native Americans had to recover from the impact of treaties and later reservation laws. Africans on the way to becoming African Americans experienced slave codes and Jim Crow laws. Chicanos too have lost vast amounts of land, including California itself as a result of a treaty and now endure the selective enforcement policies of immigration officials. California's Muslim population is coming to be very weary of airport travel in the post-September 11, 2001, atmosphere since they too now so often "fit the profile."

The mere presence of various Asian Americans has activated harsh responses including legal restrictions from California's once majority Whites. In the article that follows, Joel Franks describes the significance of anti-Japanese laws during what was supposed to be a "progressive" era. It is a description that provides insight about why California's politicians would later lead efforts to "intern" Japanese Americans during World War II. Difficult it may be, but reading the language of law is often necessary. Only if carefully read can these illegitimate legal strictures be successfully challenged. (SMM)

Topical Information

During the first two decades of the 1900s, California was a hotbed of anti-Asian, especially anti-Japanese, sentiments. Organized Labor played a significant role in making this so as did the widespread fear of the "Yellow Peril"—the Japanese military threat to U.S. interests in Asia and the Pacific. Plain old racism, with a long pedigree in the Golden State, also stirred up anti-Asian sentiments. But we should also pay some attention to the impact the Progressive Movement had on inspiring Anti-Asian Californians toward achieving key political successes such as the passage of Alien Land Laws.

Historian Alan Dawley states:

Progressivism was an attempt to reconcile state and society that drew in varying degrees upon each of America's leading political traditions—liberal, republican, populist, and socialist. Its ranks ranged from leaders in the American Federation of Labor and reformers in the National Consumers League to social engineers such as Herbert Croly and patricians such as Theodore Roosevelt. (Dawley: 1991, 128)

Thus the Progressive Movement in the United States possessed highly varied elements that would by the Great Depression come into conflict with one another. However, in the 1900s and 1910s they could be held together by a contempt for laissez-faire government and a corresponding respect for the capitalist economy. Government, progressives generally agreed, was needed to give capitalism something of a human face; make it kinder and gentler—to coin a phrase. At the same time, many, but not all, progressives believed that more active government would curb socialism by removing social injustices caused by greed, ignorance, and corruption, not by capitalism itself.

Progressives might differ on how much social reform was necessary, but they generally were profoundly disturbed by social implications of unrestricted immigration to the United States. Some progressives, like Jane Adams, professed a belief that immigrants, at least those from Europe, were capable of being good Americans if freed from social injustice. Some, like Theodore Roosevelt and Woodrow Wilson, believed in the superiority of people of Western and Northern European Protestant ancestry, but were capable of removing themselves from blanket condemnations of non-Western and Northern Euroamericans. Others, like pioneering social scientist, E. A. Ross, believed in Teutonic racial superiority and restrictive immigration legislation.

Significantly, Roosevelt, Wilson, and Ross were not Klan-like hoodlums. They could claim a sincere respect for America's republican institutions. However, they tended to believe that the people of Nordic or Anglo-Saxon background were best suited to support such institutions. Immigrants from Southern and Eastern Europe, they argued, presented a real threat to destroy America's fragile balance of limited democracy and equality, on the one hand, and social order, on the other. Such people, many progressives explained, were prone to blind obedience, irrational anarchism, or violent criminality.

If progressives suspected the intelligence and morality of Eastern and Southern Europeans, in California they willingly supported and led the anti-Asian movement. In part, anti-Asian progressives wanted to win organized labor support for progressive politicians such as Hiram Johnson. In part, they wisely appreciated the fact that anti-Asian politics generated votes in the Golden State. In part, they saw Japan as an obstacle to U.S. expansion in Asia and the Pacific and feared that overseas Japanese patriotically supported Japan's own imperialism. Yet they also doubted whether Asian immigrants and American political and economic institutions were a good mix; that Asians could ever fully embrace the duties and obligations of being good Americans. Thus they were quite willing to see economic advances by Japanese and other Asian immigrants as evidence of a growing threat rather than a desire on the part of Asian immigrants to make the United States their permanent home.

Sparked by Hiram Johnson, who became governor of California in 1910, U.S. Senator James Phelan, and Sacramento newspaperman V. S. McClatchey, a stirring reform movement emerged in California, "vitiated by an unprincipled demagogic manipulation of feelings against Orientals" (McWilliams: 1979, 180). While on the one hand seemingly determined to bend government to the will of the people, these progressives possessed a very limited view of who were the people. Thus, these progressives would not have regarded their concern for the security of representative government as hypocritical. In their minds, Asian immigrants, like corrupt political bosses and greedy corporations, menaced republican institutions in the United States. And even though some of their enemies regarded progressives as dangerous radicals, the progressive movement, as Dawley maintains, was deeply embedded within American political traditions—conservative, as well as radical.

The enactment of Alien Land Laws became an important feature of the progressive agenda in California. As early as 1907, an Alien Land Law was introduced in the California state legislature. The Asiatic Exclusion League, hoping to stem the economic advances of people of Japanese descent and curb whatever gains were made by other Asian Californians, proposed an Alien Land Law in 1912. In 1913, both houses of the California state legislature enacted an Alien Land act, signed into law by Governor Hiram Johnson. The first document below is the proposal made by the Asiatic Exclusion League. The second is the actual act passed and signed in 1913, which, if anything, is harsher than the AEL proposal. Note though in both documents that no reference is made to the national or racial origins of any people. Rather the buying and leasing of land will be denied aliens who can't become citizens—Asian immigrants.

Among the political reforms successfully attained by California progressives was the initiative. The initiative was ideally a way for Californians to enact laws directly without going through their state representatives. Accordingly, the state ballot proposition joined California's political merry-go-round. The third document was

Proposition One passed by California voters in November, 1920. Its purpose was to close the loopholes discovered in the 1913 act. Issei farmers, for example, could sign over landownership to their citizen children or they could purchase land through corporations in which they owned more than fifty percent. Moreover, the onset of World War I generated such a fervent desire for food production that authorities generally left Asian immigrant farmers alone. However, the 1920 proposition eliminated the right to lease land, forbade the signing over of land to minors, and the formation of Asian majority-owned corporations to buy land.

In 1923, the California State legislature passed an amendment to the 1920 law. By this time, the Progressive political influence had waned, but it, nevertheless, fed into a vibrant nativist, racist post-World War I movement that swept up much of the Euroamerican population against people of color and immigrants from Southern and Eastern Europe, as well as Asia. This amendment banned "cropping" agreements between landowners and alien farmers. These "cropping" agreements called upon alien farmers to plant and harvest crops for wages. So, technically, Asian farmers possessed no legal ownership, but, in reality, they might claim a good share of the profits. This act is, then, the fourth document printed below.

Appendix B

The Alien Land Law of 1913 as Proposed by the Asiatic Exclusion League on December 19, 1912, Cf. A. E. L., Proceedings, pp. 278–279

An Act

To Regulate the Ownership and Possession of Real Property in the State of California by Certain Classes of Aliens.

The People of the State of California, represented in Senate and Assembly, do enact as follows:

Section 1. No alien who is not eligible to citizenship under the Constitution and laws of the United States of America shall acquire title to or own land or real property in the State of California, except as hereinafter provided, but he shall have and enjoy in the State of California such rights as to personal property as are or shall be accorded a citizen of the United States, under the law of the Nation to which such alien belongs, or by the treaties of such Nation with the United States, except as the same may be affected by the provisions of this Act, or the Constitution of this State.

Sec. 2. This Act shall not apply to lands or real property now owned in this State by such aliens so long as they are held by the present owners.

Sec. 3. All such aliens who may hereafter acquire real property in California by devise, descent or by purchase where such purchase is made under any legal proceedings enforcing a debt or lien in favor of such a lien, may hold the same for the period of five years and no longer from the date of so acquiring such title.

Sec. 4. Any such alien who shall hereafter hold real property in the State of California in contravention of the provisions of this Act may nevertheless convey the fee simple title thereof to any person who is legally entitled to own real property in California and to no other person at any time before the institution of escheat proceedings, as hereinafter provided; provided, however, that if any such conveyance shall be made in trust or for the purpose and with the intention of evading the provisions of this Act, such conveyance shall be null and void and the rights of all persons therein shall immediately cease and determine and any such real property so conveyed shall be forfeited and escheated to the State of California, absolutely for the benefit and use of the public-school funds.

Sec. 5. It shall be the duty of the District Attorney of the county wherein the real property is situate, or the Attorney-General of the State of California, should the District Attorney fail or neglect to act, when he shall be informed or have reason to believe that any real property in the State is being held contrary to the provision of this Act, to institute suit in behalf of the State of California in the Superior Court of the county in which said lands are situate, praying for the escheat of the same in behalf of the State, and he shall proceed therein as in cases provided by law for escheats of lands or property where such property has no known owner; provided, that due service of process shall be made

and service upon the holder of title be had as provided by law, and the court having jurisdiction shall then proceed to final judgment and the sale of the property as sales are conducted under foreclosure. It shall be a good defense to any such proceeding that the title to such lands had been prior to the commencement of such proceedings conveyed in good faith by such alien to a citizen of the United States or to an alien authorized to own real property in this State. Said court shall tax as costs such fees as shall be reasonable, not exceeding twenty per centum of the amount, which shall be bid for such lands at any such sale thereof, and shall allow to the officer making such sale the same fees as are allowed for the sale of lands under decree of foreclosure of mortgages, and all fees and costs shall be paid out of the proceeds by sale of such real estate. If any District Attorney shall neglect or refuse to proceed by information as herein provided within thirty days after it shall be brought to his notice that any such alien is holding title to lands in this State contrary to the provisions of this Act, then any citizen may proceed by information in the name of the People of the State in the same manner as such District Attorney might have proceeded under the provisions of this section, and he and his attorney may be allowed such reasonable fees for their services, to be taxed as costs, as the court may direct, not exceeding in the aggregate twenty per centum of the amount which shall be paid for such lands at the sale thereof.

Sec. 6. In case the lands at the time escheat proceedings are about to be commenced are owned by a minor or minors or by a person or persons of unsound mind the process herein provided shall be served as provided by law upon the guardian of the minor or minors or person or persons of unsound mind, and if there is no such guardian the District Attorney or the Attorney-General of the State shall make application in the name of the People of the State to the court having jurisdiction and procure the appointment of a guardian ad litem, to represent such minor or minors or person or persons of unsound mind in such proceedings, and such guardian or guardians ad litem shall appear and defend the action.

Sec. 7. If it shall be determined upon the trial of any such proceedings that lands are held contrary to the provisions of this Act, the court trying such cause shall render judgment condemning such lands and ordering the same to be sold under an order of the court as in cases of sale under foreclosure proceedings; the proceeds of such sale after deducting the costs of the proceeding shall be paid to the clerk of the court rendering the judgment, where the same shall remain for one year from the date of such payment, subject to the order of the alien owner of such lands, his heirs and legal representatives, and if not claimed within the period of one year such clerk shall pay the same into the treasury of the State for the benefit of the available school funds of the State; provided, that when any money shall have been paid to the State Treasurer as herein provided the alien or his heirs may procure the same to be returned by applying for and procuring an order from the court condemning the property showing that such judgment escheating such property was procured by fraud or mistake, or that there was material irregularity in the pro-

ceedings; this application, however, must be made within two years from the date such moneys were turned over to the State Treasury; provided, further, that in no event shall the State be liable or called upon to refund any further sum than the actual cash transmitted and delivered to such treasury.

Sec. 8. Every contract agreement or lease of any land made with or to any alien not eligible to citizenship under the laws of the United States shall be null and void.

Appendix C

Alien Land Law of 1913, Statutes of California, 1913, Chapter 113, pp. 206–208

Section 1. All aliens eligible to citizenship under the laws of the United States may acquire, possess, enjoy, transmit and inherit real property, or any interest therein, in this state, in the same manner and to the same extent as citizens of the United States, except as otherwise provided by the laws of this state.

Sec. 2. All aliens other than those mentioned in section one of this act may acquire, possess, enjoy and transfer real property, or any interest therein, in this state, in the manner and to the extent and for the purposes prescribed by any treaty now existing between the government of the United States and the nation or country of which such alien is a citizen or subject, and not otherwise, and may in addition thereto lease lands in this state for agricultural purposes for a term not exceeding three years.

Sec. 3. Any company, association or corporation organized under the laws of this or any other state or nation, of which a majority of the members are aliens other than those specified in section one of this act, or in which a majority of the issued capital stock is owned by such aliens, may acquire, possess, enjoy and convey real property, or any interest therein, in this state, in the manner and to the extent and for the purposes prescribed by any treaty now existing between the government of the United States and the nation or country of which such members or stockholders are citizens or subjects, and not otherwise, and may in addition thereto lease lands in this state for agricultural purposes for a term not exceeding three years.

Sec. 4. Whenever it appears to the court in any probate proceeding that by reason of the provisions of this act any heir or devisee cannot take real property in this state which, but for said provisions, said heir or devisee would take as such, the court, instead of ordering a distribution of such real property to such heir or devisee, shall order a sale of said real property to be made in the manner provided by law for probate sales of real property, and the proceeds of such sale shall be distributed to such heir or devisee in lieu of such real property.

Sec. 5. Any real property hereafter acquired in fee in violation of the provisions of this act by any alien mentioned in section two of this act, or by any company, association or corporation mentioned in section three of this act, shall escheat to, and become and remain the property of the State of California. The attorney general shall institute proceedings to have the escheat of such real property adjudged and enforced in the manner provided by section 474 of the Political Code and title eight, part three of the Code of Civil Procedure. Upon the entry of final judgment in such proceedings, the title to such real property shall pass to the State of California. The provisions of this section and of sections two and three of this act shall not apply to any real property hereafter acquired in the enforcement or in satisfaction of any lien now existing upon, or interest in such property, so long as such real property so acquired shall remain the property of the alien, company, association or corporation acquiring the same in such manner.

Sec. 6. Any leasehold or other interest in real property less than the fee, hereafter acquired in violation of the provisions of this act by any alien mentioned in section two of this act, or by any company, association or corporation mentioned in section three of this act, shall escheat to the State of California. The attorney general shall institute proceedings to have such escheat adjudged and enforced as provided in section five of this act. In such proceedings the court shall determine and adjudge the value of such leasehold, or other interest in such real property, and enter judgment for the state for the amount thereof together with costs. Thereupon the court shall order a sale of the real property covered by such leasehold, or other interest, in the manner provided by section 1271 of the Code of Civil Procedure. Out of the proceeds arising from such sale, the amount of the judgment rendered for the state shall be paid into the state treasury and the balance shall be deposited with and distributed by the court in accordance with the interest of the parties therein.

Sec. 7. Nothing in this act shall be construed as a limitation upon the power of the state to enact laws with respect to the acquisition, holding or disposal by aliens of real property in this state.

Sec. 8. All acts and parts of acts inconsistent, or in conflict with the provisions of this act, are hereby repealed.

Appendix D

Proposition Number One, Adopted November 2, 1920, Statutes of California, 1923, pp. lxxxiii–lxxxvi

The people of the State of California do enact as follows:

Section 1. All aliens eligible to citizenship under the laws of the United States may acquire, possess, enjoy, transmit and inherit real property, or any interest therein, in this state, in the same manner and to the same extent as citizens of the United States, except as otherwise provided by the laws of this state.

Sec. 2. All aliens other than those mentioned in section one of this act may acquire, possess, enjoy and transfer real property, or any interest therein, in this state, in the manner and to the extent and for the purpose prescribed by any treaty now existing between the government of the United States and the nation or country of which such alien is a citizen or subject, and not otherwise.

Sec. 3. Any company, association or corporation organized under the laws of this or any other state or nation, of which a majority of the members are aliens other than those specified in section one of this act, or in which a majority of the issued capital stock is owned by such aliens, may acquire, possess, enjoy and convey real property, or any interest therein, in this state, in the manner and to the extent and for the purposes prescribed by any treaty now existing between the government of the United States and the nation or country of which such members or stockholders are citizens or subjects, and not otherwise. Hereafter all aliens other than those specified in section one hereof may become members of or acquire shares of stock in any company, association or corporation that is or may be authorized to acquire, possess, enjoy or convey agricultural land, in the manner and to the extent and for the purposes prescribed by any treaty now existing between the government of the United States and the nation or country of which such alien is a citizen or subject, and not otherwise.

Sec. 4. Hereafter no alien mentioned in section two hereof and no company, association or corporation mentioned in section three hereof, may be appointed guardian of that portion of the estate of a miner which consists of property which such alien or such company, association or corporation is inhibited from acquiring, possessing, enjoying or transferring by reason of the provisions of this act. The public administrator of the proper county, or any other competent person or corporation, may be appointed guardian of the estate of a minor citizen whose parents are ineligible to appointment under the provisions of this section.

On such notice to the guardian as the court may require, the superior court may remove the guardian of such an estate whenever it appears to the satisfaction of the court:

(a) That the guardian has failed to file the report required by the provisions of section five hereof; or

(b) That the property of the ward has not been or is not being administered with due regard to the primary interest of the ward; or

(c) That facts exist which would make the guardian ineligible to appointment in the first instance; or

(d) That facts establishing any other legal ground for removal exist.

Sec. 5. (a) The term "trustee" as used in this section means any person, company, association or corporation that as guardian, trustee, attorney-in-fact, or agent, or in any other capacity has the title, custody or control of property, or some interest therein, belonging to an alien mentioned in section two hereof, or to the minor child of such an alien, if the property is of such a character that such alien is inhibited from acquiring, possessing, enjoying or transferring it.

(b) Annually on or before the thirty-first day of January every such trustee must file in the office of the Secretary of State of California and in the office of the county clerk of each county in which any of the property is situated, a verified written report showing:

(1) The property, real or personal, held by him for or on behalf of such alien or minor;

(2) A statement showing the date when each item of such property came into his possession or control;

(3) An itemized account of all expenditures, investments, rents, issues and profits in respect to the administration and control of such property with particular references to holdings of corporate stock and leases, cropping contracts and other agreements in respect to land and the handling or sale of products thereof.

(c) Any person, company, association or corporation that violates any provision of this section is guilty of a misdemeanor and shall be punished by a fine not exceeding one thousand dollars or by imprisonment in the county jail not exceeding one year, or by both such fine and imprisonment.

(d) The provisions of this section are cumulative and are not intended to change the jurisdiction or the rules of practice of courts of justice.

Sec. 6. Whenever it appears to the court in any probate proceeding that by reason of the provisions of this act any heir or devisee cannot take real property in this state or membership or shares of stock in a company, association or corporation which, but for said provisions, said heir or devisee would take as such, the court, instead of ordering a distribution of such property to such heir or devisee, shall order a sale of said property to be made in the manner provided by law for probate sales of property and the proceeds of such sale shall be distributed to such heir or devisee in lieu of such property.

Sec. 7. Any real property hereafter acquired in fee in violation of the provisions of this act by any alien mentioned in section two of this act, or by any company, association or corporation mentioned in section three of this act, shall escheat to, and become and remain the property of the State of California. The Attorney General or district attorney of the proper county shall institute proceedings to have the escheat of such real property adjudged and enforced in the manner provided by section four hundred seventy-four of the Political Code and title eight, part three of the Code of Civil Procedure. Upon the entry of final judgment in such proceedings, the title to such real property shall pass to the State of California. The provisions of this section and of sections two and three of this act shall not apply to any real property hereafter acquired in the enforcement or in satisfaction of any lien now existing upon, or interest in such property, so long as such real property so acquired shall remain the property of the alien, company, association or corporation acquiring the same in such manner. No alien, company, association or corporation mentioned in section two or section three hereof shall hold for a longer period than two years the possession of any agricultural land acquired in the enforcement of or in satisfaction of a mortgage or other lien hereafter made or acquired in good faith to secure a debt.

Sec. 8. Any leasehold or other interest in real property less than the fee, hereafter acquired in violation of the provisions of this act by any alien mentioned in section two of this act, or by any company, association or corporation mentioned in section three of this act, shall escheat to the State of California. The Attorney General or district attorney of the proper county shall institute proceedings to have such escheat adjudged and enforced as provid-

ed in section seven of this act. In such proceedings this court shall determine and adjudge the value of such leasehold or other interest in such real property, and enter judgment for the state for the amount thereof together with costs. Thereupon the court shall order a sale of the real property covered by such leasehold, or other interests, in the manner provided by section twelve hundred seventy-one of the Code of Civil Procedure. Out of the proceeds arising from such sale, the amount of the judgment rendered for the state shall be paid into the state treasury and the balance shall be deposited with and distributed by the court in accordance with interest of the parties therein. Any share of stock or the interest of any member in a company, association or corporation hereafter acquired in violation of the provisions of section three of this act shall escheat to the State of California. Such escheat shall be adjudged and enforced in the same manner as provided in this section for the escheat of a leasehold or other interest in real property less than the fee.

Sec. 9. Every transfer of real property, or of an interest therein, though colorable in form, shall be void as to the state and the interest thereby conveyed or sought to be conveyed shall escheat to the state if the property interest involved is of such a character that an alien mentioned in section two hereof is inhibited from acquiring, possessing, enjoying or transferring it, and if the conveyance is made with intent to prevent, evade or avoid escheat as provided for herein.

A prima facie presumption that the conveyance is made with such intent shall arise upon proof of any of the following groups of facts:

(a) The taking of the property in the name of a person other than the persons mentioned in section two hereof if the consideration is paid or agreed or understood to be paid by an alien mentioned in section two hereof;

(b) The taking of the property in the name of a company, association or corporation, if the memberships or shares of stock therein held by aliens mentioned in section two hereof, together with the memberships or shares of stock held by others but paid for or agreed or understood to be paid for by such aliens, would amount to a majority of the membership or the issued capital stock of such company, association or corporation;

(c) The execution of a mortgage in favor of an alien mentioned in section two hereof if said mortgage is given possession, control or management of the property.

The enumeration in this section of certain presumptions shall not be so construed as to preclude other presumptions or inferences that reasonably may be made as to the existence of intent to prevent, evade or avoid escheat as provided for herein.

Sec. 10. If two or more persons conspire to effect a transfer of real property, or of an interest therein, in violation of the provisions hereof, they are punishable by imprisonment in the county jail or state penitentiary not exceeding two years, or by a fine not exceeding five thousand dollars, or both.

Sec. 11. Nothing in this act shall be construed as a limitation upon the power of the state to enact laws with respect to the acquisition, holding or disposal by aliens of real property in this state.

Sec. 12. All acts and parts of acts inconsistent or in conflict with the visions hereof are hereby repealed; *provided,* that—

(a) This act shall not affect pending actions or proceedings, but the same may be prosecuted and defended with the same effect as if this act had not been adopted;

(b) No cause of action arising under any law of this state shall be affected by reason of the adoption of this act whether an action or proceeding has been instituted thereon at the time of the taking effect of this act or not and actions may be brought upon such causes in the same manner, under the same terms and conditions, and with the same effect as if this act had not been adopted;

(c) This act in so far as it does not add to, take from or alter an existing law, shall be construed as a continuation thereof.

Sec. 13. The legislature may amend this act in furtherance of its purposes to facilitate its operation.

Sec. 14. If any section, subsection, sentence, clause or phrase of this act is for any reason held to be unconstitutional, such decision shall not affect the validity of the remaining portions of this act. The people hereby declare that they would have passed this act, and each section, subsection, sentence, clause and phrase thereof, irrespective of the fact that any one or more other sections, subsections, sentences, clauses or phrases be declared unconstitutional.

Appendix E

Alien Land Law of 1923, Statutes of California, 1923, Chapter 441, pp. 1,020–1,025

Section 1. Section one of an act entitled "An act relating to the rights, powers and disabilities of aliens and of certain companies, associations and corporations with respect to property in this state, providing for escheats in certain cases, prescribing the procedure therein, requiring reports of certain property holdings to facilitate the enforcement of this act, prescribing penalties for violation of the provisions hereof, and repealing all acts or parts of acts inconsistent or in conflict herewith," adopted and approved by the electors of the State of California, November 2, 1920, is hereby amended to read as follows:

Section 1. All aliens eligible to citizenship under the laws of the United States may acquire, possess, enjoy, use, cultivate, occupy, transfer, transmit and inherit real property, or any interest therein, in this state, and have in whole or in part the beneficial use thereof, in the same manner and to the same extent as citizens of the United States, except as otherwise provided by the laws of this state.

Sec. 2. Section two of said act is hereby amended to read as follows:

Sec. 2. All aliens other than those mentioned in section one of this act may acquire, possess, enjoy, use, cultivate, occupy and transfer real property, or any interest therein, in this state, and have in whole or in part the beneficial use thereof, in the manner and to the extent, and for the purposes prescribed by any treaty now existing between the government of the United States and the nation or country of which such alien is a citizen or subject, and not otherwise.

Sec. 3. Section three of said act is hereby amended to read as follows:

Sec. 3. Any company, association or corporation organized under the laws of this or any other state or nation, of which a majority of the members are aliens other than those specified in section one of this act, or in which a majority of the issued capital stock is owned by such aliens, may acquire, possess, enjoy, use, cultivate, occupy and transfer real property, or any interest therein, in this state, and have in whole or in part the beneficial use thereof, in the manner and to the extent and for the purposes prescribed by any treaty now existing between the government of the United States and the nation or country of which such members or stockholders are citizens or subjects, and not otherwise. Hereafter all aliens other than those specified in section one hereof may become members of or acquire shares of stock in any company, association or corporation that is or may be authorized to acquire, possess, enjoy, use, cultivate, occupy and transfer real property, or any interest therein, in this state, in the manner and to the extent and for the purposes prescribed by any treaty now existing between the government of the United States and the nation or country of which such alien is a citizen or subject, and not otherwise.

Sec. 4. Section four of said act is hereby amended to read as follows:

Sec. 4. Hereafter no alien mentioned in section two hereof and no company, association or corporation mentioned in section three, hereof, may be appointed guardian of that portion of the estate of a minor which consists of property which such alien is inhibited from acquiring, possessing, enjoying, using, cultivating, occupying, transferring, transmitting or inheriting, or which such company, association or corporation is inhibited from acquiring, possessing, enjoying, using, cultivating, occupying or transferring, by reason of the provisions of this act. The public administrator of the proper county, or any other competent person or corporation, may be appointed guardian of the estate of a minor citizen whose parents are ineligible to appointment under the provisions of this section.

On such notice to the guardian as the court may require, the superior court may remove the guardian of such an estate whenever it appears to the satisfaction of the court:

(a) That the guardian has failed to file the report required by the provisions of section five hereof; or

(b) That the property of the ward has not been or is not being administered with due regard to the primary interest of the ward; or

(c) That facts exist which would make the guardian ineligible to appointment in the first instance; or

(d) That facts establishing any other legal ground for removal exist.

Sec. 5. Section five of said act is hereby amended to read as follows:

Sec. 5. (a) The term "trustee" as used in this section means any person, company, association or corporation that as guardian, trustee, attorney in fact or agent, or in any other capacity has the title, custody or control of property, or some interest therein, belonging to an alien mentioned in section two hereof, or to the minor child of such an alien, if the property is of such a character that such alien is inhibited from acquiring, possessing, enjoying, using, cultivating, occupying, transferring, transmitting or inheriting it.

(b) Annually on or before the thirty-first day of January every such trustee must file in the office of the secretary of state of California and in the office of the county clerk of each county in which any of the property is situated, a verified written report showing:

(1) The property, real or personal, held by him for or on behalf of such alien or minor;

(2) A statement showing the date when each item of such property came into his possession or control;

(3) An itemized account of all such expenditures, investments, rents, issues and profits in respect to the administration and control of such property with particular reference to holdings of corporate stock and leases, cropping contracts and other agreements in respect to land and the handling or sale of products thereof.

(c) Any person, company, association or corporation that violates any provision of this section is guilty of a misdemeanor and shall be punished by a fine not exceeding one thousand dollars or by imprisonment in the county jail not exceeding one year, or by both such fine and imprisonment.

(d) The provisions of this section are cumulative and are not intended to change the jurisdiction or the rules of practice of courts of justice.

Sec. 6. Section seven of said act is hereby amended to read as follows:

Sec. 7. Any real property hereafter acquired in fee in violation of the provisions of this act by any alien mentioned in section two of this act, or by any company, association or corporation mentioned in section three of this act, shall escheat as of the date of such acquiring to, and become and remain the property of the State of California. The attorney general or district attorney of the proper county shall institute proceedings to have the escheat of such real property adjudged and enforced in the manner provided by section four hundred seventy-four of the Political Code and title eight, part three of the Code of Civil Procedure. Upon the entry of final judgment in such proceedings, the title to such real property shall pass to the State of California, as of the date of such acquisition in violation of the provisions of this act. The provisions of this section and of sections two and three of this act shall not apply to any real property hereafter acquired in the enforcement or in satisfaction of any lien now existing upon or interest in such property so long as such real property so acquired shall remain the property of the alien, company, association or corporation acquiring the same in such manner. No alien, company, association or corporation mentioned in section two or section three hereof shall hold for a longer period than two years the possession of any agricultural land acquired in the enforcement of or in satisfaction of a mortgage or other lien hereafter made or acquired in good faith to secure a debt.

Sec. 7. Section eight of said act is hereby amended to read as follows:

Sec. 8. Any leasehold or other interest in real property less than the fee, including cropping contracts which are hereby declared to constitute an interest in real property less than the fee, hereafter acquired in violation of the provisions of this act by any alien mentioned in section two of this act, or by any company, association or corporation mentioned in section three of this act, shall escheat to the State of California, as of the date of such acquiring in violation of the provisions of this act. The attorney general or district attorney of the proper county shall institute proceedings to have such escheat adjudged and enforced in the same manner as is provided in section seven of this act. In such proceedings the court shall determine and adjudge the value of such leasehold or other interest in such real property, as of the date of such acquisition in violation of the provisions of this act, and enter judgment for the state for the amount thereof together with costs. The said judgment so entered shall be considered a lien against the real property in which such leasehold or other interest less than the fee is so acquired in violation of the provisions of this act, which lien shall exist as of the date of such unlawful acquisition. Thereupon the court shall order a sale of the real property covered by such leasehold, or other interest, in the manner provided by section one thousand two hundred seventy-one of the Code of Civil Procedure. Out of the proceeds arising from such sale, the amount of the judgment rendered for the state shall be paid into the state treasury and the balance shall be deposited with and distributed by the court in accordance with the interest of the parties therein. Any share of stock or the interest of any member in a company, association or corporation hereafter acquired in violation of the provisions of section three of this act shall escheat to the State of California as of the date of such acquiring in violation of the provisions of said section three of this act, and it is hereby declared that any such share of stock or the interest of any member in such a company, association or corporation so acquired in violation of the provisions of section three of this act is an interest in real property. Such escheat shall be adjudged and enforced in the same manner as is provided in this section for the escheat of a leasehold or other interest in real property less than the fee.

Sec. 8. Section nine of said act is hereby amended to read as follows:

Sec. 9. Every transfer of real property, or of an interest therein, though colorable in form, shall be void as to the state and the interest thereby conveyed or sought to be conveyed shall escheat to the state as of the date of such transfer, if the property interest involved is of such a character that an alien mentioned in section two hereof is inhibited from acquiring, possessing, enjoying, using, conveyance is made with intent to prevent, evade or avoid escheat as provided for herein.

A prima facie presumption that the conveyance is made with such intent shall arise upon proof of any of the following groups of facts:

(a) The taking of the property in the name of a person other than the persons mentioned in section two hereof if the consideration is paid or agreed or understood to be paid by an alien mentioned in section two hereof,

(b) The taking of the property in the name of a company, association or corporation if the memberships or shares of stock therein held by aliens mentioned in section two hereof, together with the memberships or shares of stock held by others but paid for or agreed or understood to be paid for by such aliens, would amount to a majority of the membership or issued capital stock of such company, association or corporation;

(c) The execution of a mortgage in favor of an alien mentioned in section two hereof if such mortgagee is given possession, control or management of the property.

The enumeration in this section of certain presumptions shall not be so construed as to preclude other presumptions or inferences that reasonably may be made as to the existence of intent to prevent, evade or avoid escheat as provided for herein.

Sec. 9. Section ten of said act is hereby amended to read as follows:

Sec. 10. If two or more persons conspire to violate any of the provisions of this act they are punishable by imprisonment in the county jail or state penitentiary not exceeding two years or by a fine not exceeding five thousand dollars, or both.

Sec. 10. Section eleven of said act is hereby amended to read as follows:

Sec. 11. Nothing in this act shall be construed as a limitation upon the power of the state to enact laws with respect to the acquisition, possession, enjoyment, use, cultivation, occupation, transferring, transmitting or inheriting by aliens of real property in this state.

Notes

1. "Laissez-faire" was a French term that meant hands-off. After the Civil War, this term reflected a belief that government should limit its interest in interfering in the affairs of business and society; in particular the way a person manages his or her own property.

References

Dawley, Alan. 1991. Struggles for Justice: *Social Responsibility and the Liberal State*. Cambridge, MA: The Belknap Press of Harvard University Press.

McWilliams, Carey. 1979. *California: The Great Exception*. Santa Barbara: Peregrine Smith Publishers.

Appendix J

Constitution of the United Farm Workers' Union

Preamble to the Constitution of the UFW, 1973

We, the United Farm Workers of America, have cultivated the ground, we have sown the seeds and we have harvested the crops. We have supplied abundant food to the town in the cities, the nation and the world, but we have not had sufficient food for our own children.

While the industrial workers, living and working in one place, have been united and grown strong, we have been isolated, scattered and crippled from uniting our forces. While other workers have defeated economic injustice, we have inherited the exploitation, the suffering and the poverty of our parents and of their parents. But, in spite of our segregation, suffering, imprisonment, beatings and murders, we persist bravely and determined to build our Union as a wall against future exploitation.

The right of being associated with a union is recognized universally, but it is a right that the bosses of the fields have denied us without mercy. And as Pope Leo XIII said, "To exert pressure to take advantage of the poor and defenseless, and to profit from the need of others is condemned by every law, human and divine."

Devoutly we believe in the dignity of cultivating the ground and harvesting the crops, and we reject the idea that a farm job is no more than a stop on the way to a job in the factories and to a life in the city. And, as farm work is arduous, so also is the task of building a Union. We promise to fight as much as necessary to reach our goals. Above all, we believe that all the men should behave toward one another in the spirit of brotherhood, and that our Union should guarantee that all are treated with equal dignity and rights.

The United Farm Workers' Union

Constitution of the United Farm Workers, 1973.

SECOND PART–OBJECTIVES AND THE DEDICATION TO NON VIOLENCE

ARTICLE VI –OBJECTIVES AND PROPOSITIONS OF THE UNION

SUMMARY: The Union was created and exists for these reasons: to unite all farm workers under the black eagle, to negotiate contracts to improve the salaries and living conditions of farm workers, to safeguard the rights of farm workers to strike and boycott, to participate in political activities that will improve the welfare of farm workers, and to guarantee each farm worker the dignity and liberty that are the rights of every human being.

The objectives of the Union will be:

(a) To unite under its flag every individual employed as a farm worker, without consideration to his or her race, creed, sex or nationality;

(b) To negotiate and to enter into collective bargaining, to sign contracts, or otherwise to work with the employers of the agriculture industry concerning payment, hours, conditions of labor, grievances, job disputes and other related matters;

(c) To assure recognition by the employers and the public of the rights of farm workers to organize for our mutual benefit and to enter collective negotiations;

(d) To protect the moral and legal rights of the farm workers to exert pressure on recalcitrant employers, including the right, without restriction, to conduct strikes, boycotts and other non violent activities that will have the objective of obtaining recognition for the Union and collective bargaining with such employers;

(e) To promote the development and maintenance of health, welfare and security in the job and such educational programs of training among its members that serve to give them a better knowledge of their rights, responsibilities, welfare and interests;

(f) To promote, to sponsor, to develop and to improve the ability, efficiency and knowledge of the job necessary for those workers;

(g) To promote peace in the industry and to develop a harmonious relationship between the employees and the employers;

(h) To work and cooperate with other unions for the mutual benefit of their respective members, and to build solidarity within the labor movement, and to provide aid to unions and other organizations in this country and everywhere in the world that have the same or similar purposes and objectives as this Union;

(i) To develop effective programs to improve, advance and increase opportunities for employment.

(j) To promote a better understanding by the government and the public of the propositions and objectives of this Union and the Labor Movement in general;

(k) To participate in legislative activities to promote, to protect and to improve the physical, economic, and social welfare of the workers;

(l) To promote participation in the census, voting and other civil activities, involving the membership and their families and communities, to assure the election of candidates and passage of better legislation in the interest of all workers, and the defeat or revocation of those laws that are unjust to the labor movement and prejudicial to its membership;

(m) To put forth such investigative activities as are appropriate and necessary;

(n) To promote legal and appropriate activities for the defense and advancement of the interests of the Union and of its members;

(o) To promote and to protect the jurisdiction of this Union;

(p) To distribute, economic, social, political and other information that affect its welfare;

(q) To protect the civil rights and liberties of its members and of all other persons and to guarantee them a powerful voice in the institutions and decisions that govern and affect their lives;

(r) To aid charitable organizations and institutions;

(s) To take any other actions that conserve and promote the welfare and interests of this Union and of its members;

(t) To promote the complete and equal participation of women in all the matters and activities and positions of leadership in the Union.

ARTICLE VII, DEDICATION TO NON VIOLENCE

SUMMARY: These objectives and purposes to be gained by non-violent methods only. Each member totally rejects the use of violence.

The purposes and objectives established above are to be carried out only by totally non-violent methods because each member of this Union swears to reject the use of violence in any form, for any activity of the Union.